More praise for
A CONTEST FOR
SUPREMACY

"A considered and compelling examination of the Sino-American relationship from various angles . . . that propels Aaron L. Friedberg to the high table of American politics scientists. . . . This is a book that will be read broadly and discussed widely. . . . [*A Contest for Supremacy*] is a nuanced warning about the risks in bilateral great power relations and the ways to avoid sleepwalking into decline."　　　—Asle Toje, *International Affairs*

"Like tossing a dead skunk into a garden party, *A Contest for Supremacy* aims to shake things up among the foreign-policy elite inside the United States. Friedberg presents all of the arguments employed in favor of optimism and complacency regarding the trends facing the United States in East Asia then systemically shoots them down. His book is the most thorough wake-up call yet regarding the security challenges presented by China's rise. It is also a plea to have an honest conversation about the difficult questions facing the United States in Asia."　　　—Robert Haddick, *Foreign Policy*

"*A Contest for Supremacy* should be on the 'must read' list of all who think about—or think they understand—China's recent history and potential impact on world affairs."　　　　　　　　　　　—Thomas Fingar,
Survival: Global Politics and Strategies

"Anyone seriously interested in China's global role and its relationship with the US should definitely read Aaron Friedberg's *A Contest for Supremacy*. This book has several things to commend it. It is a compact reflection on the full scope of the rise of China; it is a work of genuine and profound scholarship; and it specifically addresses the complex history and the various possible futures of Sino-American relations. Few other books on the subject have this combination of qualities. . . . Read this book and understand."　　　　　　　　　　　　　—Paul Monk, *Australian*

"Friedberg delivers a definitive assessment of the changing balance of power in Asia and its implications for war and peace in the great continent.... Yet, there is no credible and easily accessible work on the unfolding changes in the Sino-American relationship. Friedberg's *A Contest for Supremacy* fills that gap."
—C. Raja Mohan, *Indian Express*

"Friedberg's modus operandi is to methodically analyse the 'known knowns' about China and offer prudent responses to the 'known unknowns'. In this, he succeeds in doing so more calmly, cogently and incisively than other authors—meaning that *A Contest for Supremacy* is likely to be read, remain relevant, and to the delight of the publisher, still be selling well for years to come."
—John Lee, *American Review*

"A stern, carefully worded warning about why the United States should be more wary of China's meteoric rise. Friedberg . . . is a forward thinker versed in the 'fast-changing politics of post-Cold War Asia' . . . [and] lays out the various ongoing arguments for containment or alignment.... An important cry to heed."
—*Kirkus Reviews*

"In this fine, superbly documented and blessedly well-organized analysis of the state of play between the United States and China, Aaron L. Friedberg weaves a multitude of highly detailed scenarios and possibilities around a gently made central point.... [Friedberg] is a very good writer indeed, with an enviable talent for appealing to both the general reader and the specialist."
—Rosemary Michaud, *Post and Courier*

"[*A Contest for Supremacy*] is a really fine read about China, their very long view of the world, and our need to really pay attention to what's going on in that part of the world."
—Rick Perry

"An energetically written, well-argued book." —*Times Higher Education*

"Aaron Friedberg has written a definitive book on the strategic challenge posed by China. It is clear, concise, and balanced." —Robert D. Kaplan, author of *Monsoon: The Indian Ocean and the Future of American Power*

A CONTEST FOR SUPREMACY

ALSO BY AARON L. FRIEDBERG

The Weary Titan:
Britain and the Experience of Relative Decline, 1895–1905

In the Shadow of the Garrison State:
America's Anti-Statism and Its Cold War Grand Strategy

A CONTEST FOR SUPREMACY

China, America, and the
Struggle for Mastery in Asia

AARON L. FRIEDBERG

W. W. NORTON & COMPANY
NEW YORK · LONDON

First published as a Norton paperback 2012

For information about permission to reproduce selections from this book,
write to Permissions, W. W. Norton & Company, Inc.,
500 Fifth Avenue, New York, NY 10110

For information about special discounts for bulk purchases, please contact
W. W. Norton Special Sales at specialsales@wwnorton.com or 800-233-4830

Book design by Kristen Bearse
Production manager: Devon Zahn

Library of Congress Cataloging-in-Publication Data
Friedberg, Aaron L., 1956–
A contest for supremacy : China, America, and the struggle for
mastery in Asia / Aaron L. Friedberg. — 1st ed.
p. cm.
Includes bibliographical references and index.
ISBN 978-0-393-06828-3 (hardcover)
1. United States—Foreign relations—China. 2. China—Foreign relations—United States.
3. United States—Foreign relations—Asia. 4. Asia—Foreign relations—United States.
5. China—Foreign relations—Asia. 6. Asia—Foreign relations—China. 7. Asia—Strategic
aspects. 8. Asia—Foreign relations—21st century. 9. Geopolitics—Asia. I. Title.
JZ1480.A57C6 2011
327.5105—dc23

2011017661

ISBN 978-0-393-34389-2 pbk.

W. W. Norton & Company, Inc.
500 Fifth Avenue, New York, N.Y. 10110
www.wwnorton.com

W. W. Norton & Company Ltd.
Castle House, 75/76 Wells Street, London W1T 3QT

TO ANDREW W. MARSHALL AND
TO THE MEMORY OF SAMUEL P. HUNTINGTON (1927–2008).
TEACHERS, MENTORS, EXEMPLARS.

Contents

Acknowledgments

I began work on this book in the fall of 2001 while serving as the first occupant of the Henry Alfred Kissinger Chair in Foreign Policy and International Relations at the Library of Congress. I am extremely grateful to James Billington, the Librarian of Congress, and to Peg Christoff of the John W. Kluge Center for their hospitality and assistance. During the summer of 2002 I had the chance to gain some fresh perspective on Asian security issues by spending six weeks as a visitor at the Australian Strategic Policy Institute. I wish to thank Hugh White and Alan Dupont for their help in making this possible.

Generous grants from the Smith Richardson Foundation and the Harry and Lynde Bradley Foundation enabled me to finish the writing of this book in a timely fashion. I wish to express my sincere appreciation to Marin Strmecki and Allan Song at Smith Richardson and Diane Sehler at Bradley for their continuing support of my work. I am also grateful to Anne-Marie Slaughter, former dean of the Woodrow Wilson School of Public and International Affairs, who encouraged me to return to Princeton in 2005 after a two-year stint in government.

I have been fortunate to have the help of several extremely able research assistants. Daniel Nikbakht, Owen Fletcher, and Rex Douglass all assisted greatly in the early stages of the project. Rushabh Doshi went above and beyond the call of duty in tracking down sources and footnotes and in locating and translating material from dozens of Chinese-language sources.

I wish to thank my agent, Eric Lupfer of the William Morris Agency, and my editor, Maria Guarnaschelli, and her assistant, Melanie Tortoroli, at W. W. Norton for their enthusiasm and encouragement. Mary Babcock did an outstanding job in copyediting the manuscript.

As always, I benefited greatly from the comments of many friends and colleagues. Steven David, Kurt Guthe, Andrew Marshall, Jacqueline Newmyer, Stephen Rosen, and Shivaji Sondhi all read the manuscript in whole or in part and offered numerous useful suggestions. Gabriel Schoenfeld read everything from the first proposal to the final draft and played a crucial role in helping me to find a publisher.

My wife, Adrienne Sirken, and my sons, Eli and Gideon, tolerated my work on this project with as much good grace as could reasonably be expected under the circumstances. I humbly beg their forgiveness for my prolonged absences and perpetual preoccupation.

I wish that I could have had the chance to give copies of this book to my father, Simeon Friedberg, and to my father-in-law, Irving Sirken.

This book is dedicated to two men who have had a profound impact on my intellectual and professional development: Andrew W. Marshall, director of the Office of Net Assessment in the Office of the Secretary of Defense, and the late Samuel P. Huntington of Harvard University.

No one else bears the blame for any errors of fact or interpretation that this book may contain. Only I am responsible for its contents.

Preface

This book took the better part of five years to research and write, but it has been gestating for a good deal longer than that. Although not by training a regional expert, a linguist, or a country specialist, in the early 1990s I began to spend much of my time thinking and writing about the fast-changing politics of post–Cold War Asia. In contrast to most of Europe, where nationalist passions, territorial disputes, and arms races were fast dwindling into historical memory, Asia seemed ripe for the reemergence of traditional great power rivalries. Among its other effects, the collapse of the Soviet Union had removed almost overnight the rationale for twenty years of close cooperation between the United States and China. The 1989 Tiananmen Square massacre also served as an inescapable reminder that, despite its undeniable economic progress, China was still ruled by a brutal authoritarian regime. By the mid-1990s, a trans-Pacific contest for power and influence between a still-dominant America and a fast-growing China began to seem an increasingly likely prospect. Over the years, I took part in a number of academic conferences and government-sponsored studies on "alternative futures" for Asia in general, and China in particular. Finally, in the closing months of the Clinton administration, I was asked to participate in a review of the intelligence community's assessments of China's economic performance, political stability, strategic intentions, and military power.

These experiences left me deeply troubled about where China was headed and about the future direction of relations between that country and my own. I also found myself puzzled and frustrated by what struck me as a willful, blinkered optimism on these matters prevalent at the time in the academic and business communities and across significant portions of the U.S. government. Most of the China experts whom I encountered seemed to believe that a Sino-American rivalry was either highly unlikely, too terrifying to contemplate, or (presumably because talking about it might increase the odds that it would occur) too dangerous to discuss. Whatever the reason, it was not something that serious people spoke about in polite company.

Not being a card-carrying member of the China-watching fraternity freed me from most of these inhibitions. In November 2000 the journal *Commentary* published an essay in which I speculated about what a future strategic competition between the United States and China might look like and how it could unfold. Aiming to grab potential readers by the lapels, I titled the piece "The Struggle for Mastery in Asia" (a play on British historian A. J. P. Taylor's study of eighteenth- and nineteenth-century European diplomatic history) and began it with the following words:

> Over the course of the next several decades there is a good chance that the United States will find itself engaged in an open and intense geopolitical rivalry with the People's Republic of China. Such an outcome is not inevitable; few things in international politics are. But there are strong reasons to believe that it is at the very least plausible, and even quite likely. Indeed, there are reasons to believe that it is already under way.

This was by no means a view unique to me, but it was still, at the time, a distinctly minority position. While the article received some favorable attention, it was generally dismissed by specialists as, at best, unduly pessimistic and, at worst, prone to stoke unfounded fears about China's future capabilities and intentions. Ten years later, as this book goes to print, things have begun to change. The suggestion that the United States and China are destined to compete vigorously with one another, if not necessarily to clash, no longer seems far-fetched; and the notion that we are already, in certain respects, engaged in an intensifying strategic rivalry is, if not universally shared, certainly more widespread today than it was a decade ago.

These shifting opinions are a product of both tangible developments and changes in mood and perception. At the turn of the century, America's unmatched power and the likely longevity of its "unipolar moment" were the prevailing themes among scholars and pundits. After a decade marked by terrorist attacks, two draining and divisive wars, and the worst economic crisis since the Great Depression, the talk is more often of America's inevitable decline. Like yesterday's excessive exuberance, today's pessimism will no doubt prove to have been exaggerated. Still, the idea that the United States may face a serious challenge to its preeminent position, and perhaps sooner rather than later, has become commonplace.

While the United States has recently been buffeted by shocks and setbacks, China has thus far shown a remarkable ability to stay on a steep upward trajectory. With annual growth rates at close to 10 percent, in the past decade the Chinese economy has surpassed the output of all the other advanced industrial nations and is rapidly closing the gap with the United States. Thanks to sustained double-digit increases in the size of its military budget, China's armed forces have also advanced markedly in sophistication, capability, and reach. And as the wealth and power at its command have grown, Beijing has begun to exert increasing influence, both in Asia and around the world.

None of this should have come as any surprise to American analysts, planners, and political leaders. For much of the past decade, however, their collective attention has largely been directed elsewhere. Since 9/11 the focus of the U.S. national security establishment has been on the Middle East and Southern, rather than Eastern, Asia, and on combating terrorism and blocking the further spread of nuclear weapons rather than preparing for a possible long-term strategic rivalry with what the Pentagon likes to call a major "peer competitor." After 9/11 American policy makers also made a deliberate decision to try to play down differences and avoid friction with Beijing, in part because they hoped to gain its cooperation against terrorists and "rogue states." As the urgency of these problems has receded somewhat, as questions have begun to arise about the extent to which China has truly been helpful in dealing with them, and as evidence of China's expanding capabilities and ambitions has continued to accumulate, focus has naturally started to shift back in its direction. Part of the recent change in mood regarding China is due to the fact that more people in high places are paying attention, and are more inclined to be skeptical, than was previously the case.

More than anything else, it is Beijing's behavior in the last several years that has made the reality of the emerging Sino-American rivalry more difficult to ignore. For most of the last two decades, China's leaders have generally been quite cautious about doing anything that would arouse anxiety in other Asian countries or, even more importantly, in the United States. Since the onset of the global financial crisis in 2008–9, however, they have been far more assertive in word and deed than ever before. Beijing has been more forceful in resisting external pressure for change in its economic and human rights policies, more open in displaying its rapidly evolving military capabilities, blunter in warning its neighbors against opposing its wishes, more willing to use its growing economic clout in an attempt to exert diplomatic leverage, and more open in questioning the likely longevity of America's leading role in Asia and the world.

Whether or not these developments prove transient or turn out to be a sign of things to come remains to be seen. For the time being, at least, they have helped to raise questions and stir doubts about the future direction of Sino-American relations and about the wisdom and sustainability of current U.S. policies for dealing with an increasingly powerful and ambitious China. Although I cannot claim to have anticipated it when I began to write this book, the moment for a searching debate on these questions seems finally to have arrived.

A CONTEST FOR SUPREMACY

A CONTEST FOR SUPREMACY

If we could first know *where* we are, and *whither* we are tending,
we could then better judge *what* to do, and *how* to do it.
—ABRAHAM LINCOLN, June 16, 1858

The United States and the People's Republic of China are today locked in a quiet but increasingly intense struggle for power and influence, not only in Asia but around the world. This competition first began to take shape in the early 1990s, following the collapse of the Soviet Union, and it has accelerated markedly since the turn of the century.

Despite what many earnest and well-intentioned commentators seem to believe, the emerging Sino-American rivalry is not the result of easily erased misperceptions or readily correctible policy errors; it is driven instead by forces that are deeply rooted in the shifting structure of the international system and in the very different domestic political regimes of the two Pacific powers. Throughout history, relations between dominant states and rising ones have been uneasy and often violent. Established powers tend to regard themselves as the defenders of an international order that they helped to create and from which they continue to benefit; rising powers feel constrained, even cheated, by the status quo and struggle against it to take what they think is rightfully theirs. These age-old patterns are clearly visible today in the behavior of the United States and China.

Ideological differences add a crucial extra measure of mistrust and volatility to this mix. Though Washington and Beijing are generally careful not to state them openly, each has strategic objectives that threaten the fundamental interests of the other side. For its part, the United States aims to promote "regime change" in China, nudging it away from authoritarianism and toward liberal democracy, albeit by peaceful, gradual means. China's current rulers, meanwhile, have every intention of preserving the one-party system over which they presently preside. It is largely because they see the United States as the most serious external threat to their continued rule that they feel the need to constrict its military presence and diplomatic influence in the Western Pacific, pushing it back and ultimately displacing it as the preponderant power in East Asia.

In addition to the powerful ideological and geopolitical forces impelling the United States and China toward rivalry, there are clearly other, countervailing factors at work. Because of the enormous potential costs and dangers, neither party seeks direct conflict, and indeed both are eager to avoid it if at all possible. This is not always the case in relations between great powers, and it serves as a strong source of caution and mutual restraint. Washington and Beijing may mistrust one another, but they remain willing to seek cooperation in areas of overlapping strategic interest. Despite recent frictions over trade issues, both sides also continue to see benefit in their deep economic entanglement. Perhaps most important, at least for the moment, Washington and Beijing both appear to believe that time is on their side. American policy makers remain confident that in the long-run China's economic growth will pave the way for political liberalization and lasting peace. While they are clearly nervous about navigating the near term, China's current rulers also seem certain that the tides of history are running in their country's favor.

Both of these views cannot be correct, and the opening decades of this century will reveal which is closer to the truth. If China stays on its current path, if it grows richer and stronger without also becoming a liberal democracy, the present, muted rivalry with the United States is likely to blossom into something more open and dangerous. On the other hand, while there will doubtless be difficult moments, if China liberalizes, the prospects for a true trans-Pacific entente seem certain to improve.

As the twenty-first century unfolds, our country faces no task more important than managing its mixed, complex, uncertain, and potentially unstable relationship with China. For a variety of reasons, however, this is not a test for which we are especially well prepared. Since 9/11 our government has been heavily preoccupied with responding to the urgent dangers of terrorism and proliferation, dismantling jihadist networks, confronting "rogue states" like North Korea and Iran, and trying simultaneously to stabilize, transform, and pull back from Afghanistan and Iraq. While Washington has not ignored China or Asia more generally, as critics have sometimes claimed, neither has it been able to devote as much time or energy to the region as it deserves. Our resources are enormous but not infinite. If not for 9/11, much of the money, manpower, and brainpower that has been directed to analyzing and responding to more immediate threats would doubtless have been directed toward Asia and the long-term challenge of a rising China.

Although they will eventually recede in prominence, today's pressing problems will continue to receive priority for some years to come. The national security "pie" is thus going to have to be divided among several very different missions; it is also going to be smaller than might have been expected only a few years ago. Thanks to the lingering aftereffects of the 2008–9 financial crisis, budgets will be especially tight and money scarce for at least the next decade, if not beyond. Just as the U.S.-China rivalry begins to heat up, our government will be facing unusually stringent fiscal restraints.

Even without the distraction and costs of dealing with other dangers, responding to China's rise would not be easy. Our country has dealt with other powerful nations in the course of its own rise to primacy, but for well over a century we have not had to face a strategic competitor of the sort that China now seems set to become. Nazi Germany and imperial Japan did not have the people, the resources, or the industrial base to compete on an equal footing with us. The Soviet Union might have been able to do so, but fortunately for the democratic world, its leaders were committed to disastrously inefficient policies of economic autarky and centralized planning.

China has vast human and natural resources, and over the last thirty years it has adopted a market-oriented approach to development that has produced extraordinarily rapid rates of economic growth and technological progress. While its huge population ensures that it will remain comparatively poor in terms of per capita income, the sheer size of China's economic output may soon begin to approach that of the United States. Such an outcome is not preordained; China will have to avoid numerous obstacles and pitfalls if it is to keep its economy on track. If and when this transition occurs, however, it will mark something truly new under the sun. Not since the 1880s, when it displaced Britain as the "workshop of the world," has America faced a potential strategic rival with an economy bigger than its own.

Rapid growth makes it easier for Beijing to afford a sustained, fast-paced, and wide-ranging military buildup. In marked contrast to the Soviet Union, China's engagement in the global economy also guarantees it ready access to many of the cutting-edge technologies it needs to become a world-class industrial and military power. Finally, although participation in commerce creates vulnerabilities, it also gives China powerful new instruments for exerting diplomatic influence. This too is an advantage that the Soviet Union denied itself. Both in its own neighborhood and beyond, Beijing has already proved adept at using its growing economic clout to shape the perceptions and policies of its trading partners, including the United States.

During much of the twentieth century, Americans were generally able to divide the world's major powers into two camps. On one side were friends and allies, who, for the most part, also happened to be liberal democracies and America's top trading partners. On the other were its enemies: fascist or communist regimes with which the United States did little business and had limited, strained diplomatic relations. This division of the world had the virtue of simplicity, and it permitted at least the appearance of moral clarity. The United States was willing at times to trade or align itself strategically with those with whom it had ideological differences, but its leaders, and the American people as a whole, have always been far more comfortable dealing closely with those they regard as "good," while remaining aloof from those they consider "evil." China does not fit cleanly into either camp or, indeed, into any existing category of American strategic thought; it is a major trading partner but not a democracy, and at this point it is neither a trusted friend nor a sworn enemy. Moreover, barring some sudden shift, it is likely to remain in this ambiguous gray zone for some time to come. In addition to its more obvious, material aspects, the rise of China therefore poses a major intellectual challenge to both American strategists and the nation as a whole.

Meeting this test will be difficult, in part, because it has become virtually impossible to discuss China in a measured and dispassionate way. Those who worry about its rise often mischaracterize the nature of the challenge China poses, overstate its current capabilities, and exaggerate its propensity for overt aggression. Contrary to what some have claimed, China's economic development does not, in itself, pose a threat to America's prosperity, it is not about to gobble up all the world's manufacturing jobs, its military is not ten feet tall, and its current leaders do not (as the title of one recent book proclaims) "want war with the United States."[1]

Despite such warnings, and despite recent tensions in Sino-American relations, the balance of opinion among China-watchers in academia, commerce, and government remains heavily weighted toward a far more optimistic view of what the future holds. For a mix of theoretical, political, emotional, and moral reasons (mingled, in the case of those doing business there, with a healthy dose of self-interest), most experts remain strongly committed to the belief that Chinese and American interests are steadily converging, while trade and economic development are moving China rapidly down the road to real democratic reforms and hence to stable, peaceful relations with the United States. Americans need to have patience, to not rock the boat, and, above all, to avoid doing anything that might antagonize Beijing and reverse the basically favorable flow of events. "Treat China as an enemy," goes one piece of well-worn conventional wisdom, "and it will become one."

What follows from this view, unfortunately, is a discomfort with debate, a lack of tolerance for dissent, and a reluctance to face unpleasant facts. Those who raise questions about the strategic implications of China's rise, or the adequacy of current policies for responding to it, risk being characterized as ill-informed alarmists. Worse yet, they are likely to find themselves accused of creating problems where none need otherwise exist.

This is not a healthy state of affairs, and it could prove to be profoundly dangerous. Downplaying or denying the competitive aspects of Chinese behavior will not make them disappear, but it could make it much harder to respond to them in a measured and timely way. Fear of creating self-fulfilling prophecies may cause our nation and our friends and allies to refrain from doing things that might actually help to deter threats, reduce risk, and keep the peace. And failure to acknowledge potential future dangers could leave us ill-prepared to deal with them should they eventually emerge. A serious discussion of how best to meet the challenges posed by a rising China cannot wait until we have dealt with other urgent problems; debate on this issue is not only necessary, it is long overdue.

For the fact is that if current trends continue, we are on track to lose our geopolitical contest with China. Defeat is more likely to come with a whimper than a bang. China's leaders do not seek confrontation. To the contrary, since the end of the Cold War they have been pursuing a cautious strategy of expanding their own power and influence while workng to undermine and constrict the power and influence of the United States. If Beijing's military buildup continues apace and if, due to a mix of fiscal constraints, domestic political pressures, and misplaced strategic inhibitions, we do not respond more vigorously than we have to date, the military balance in the Western Pacific is going to start to tilt sharply in China's favor. Such a change would weaken the security guarantees that we extend to our allies and on which our entire posture in the region rests. Doubts about our continuing commitment, combined with economic inducements and diplomatic pressures emanating from Beijing, could compel some of our longtime friends to reappraise their own national security policies, including their alignments with us. Our position in Asia already depends on a relatively small number of alliances and quasi-alliance partnerships. If these are dissolved or reduced to insignificance, we could find ourselves pushed to the margins of Asia if not out of the region altogether. In time our military presence could be reduced to a few bases on a handful of small islands that remain under our sovereign control, like Guam, Saipan, and Tinian. Long before matters reached this point, our government too would likely feel compelled to seek an accommodation with China and to acknowledge it as the preponderant regional power.

What difference would any of this make? Why should Americans care if their country is no longer recognized as the most powerful and influential player in a region that is, after all, half a world away? Since the early part of the twentieth century an axiomatic goal of U.S. foreign policy under both Republican and Democratic administrations has been to prevent the domination of either end of the Eurasian landmass by one or more potentially hostile powers. The reasons for this have always involved a combination of economic, strategic, and ideological considerations. If Western Europe or East Asia were to fall under the sway of by unfriendly forces, the United States could find itself denied access to markets, technology, and vital resources. A hostile power or coalition might be able to draw on the wealth and military capabilities of the region under its control, using it as a secure base from which to challenge American interests and perhaps even to attack the United States itself. Last but by no means least, American statesmen have long been concerned about the implications for their vision of a freer world if Europe or Asia were to be "lost" to antidemocratic forces.

These concerns are as valid today as they were one hundred years ago. If through inadvertence, error, or deliberate decision we permit China as presently constituted to dominate Asia, our prosperity, security, and hopes of promoting the further spread of freedom will be seriously impaired. Our businesses could find their access to the markets, high-technology products, and natural resources of some of the world's most dynamic economies constricted by trade arrangements designed to favor their Chinese counterparts. While it is unlikely to engage in outright military conquest, an unchecked China would be well situated to enforce claims over resources and territory that are currently disputed by its weaker neighbors. Control over the vast oil and gas reserves believed to lie beneath the South and East China Seas, plus assured access on favorable terms to energy imports from Central Asia and Russia, could greatly reduce Beijing's dependence on seaborne imports from the Persian Gulf and hence its vulnerability to a possible American (or Indian) naval blockade.

With the United States gone from East Asia, China would be able to bring Taiwan to terms, and it would most likely be able to block, neutralize, or preempt the emergence of serious military challenges from Japan or South Korea. Freed of the necessity of defending against possible threats from its maritime periphery, Beijing would be able to devote more resources to setting terms with its continental neighbors and it would be able to more easily project military power to defend or advance its interests in other parts of the world, including the Middle East, Africa, and Latin America. Before it can hope to compete with the United States on a global scale, China must first establish itself as the foremost power in its own region.

If Asia comes to be dominated by an authoritarian China, the prospects for liberal reform in any of its non-democratic neighbors will be greatly diminished. Even the region's established democracies could find themselves inhibited from pursuing policies, foreign and perhaps domestic as well, that might incur Beijing's wrath. With its enhanced global reach and influence, China would also be able to more effectively support non-democratic regimes in other parts of the world and to present some variant of its own internal arrangements as a viable alternative to the liberal democratic capitalism of the West.

Former prime minister of Singapore Lee Kuan Yew has observed that "the 21st century will be a contest for supremacy in the Pacific because that's where the growth will be. . . . If you do not hold your ground in the Pacific you cannot be a world leader."[2] Lee is right: if we permit an illiberal China to displace us as the preponderant player in this most vital region, we will face grave dangers to our interests and our values throughout the world. My purpose in writing this book is to warn of a serious and fast-growing challenge, to explain its sources, describe its manifestations, and outline the policies by which it can best be met.

One

MEANS OF ASCENT

THE "VASCO DA GAMA EPOCH"

L et us begin at the beginning: if not for the fact that over the last three decades China's economy has grown at an average annual rate of between 9 and 10 percent, talk of an emerging Sino-American rivalry would appear laughable on its face. It follows that if we are to understand the forces currently shaping relations between the two nations, we need to start by examining the sources of China's rapidly growing wealth and power. In order to do that, in turn, we need to pause for a moment, disentangle ourselves from the latest headlines and the details of recent events, and look back at a wider span of history. For, as consequential as it may turn out to be, China's rise is only part of a much bigger story. During most of the past two hundred years, global wealth and power have been heavily concentrated in the "West," or Euro-Atlantic region. Now, and with increasing rapidity, the balance is shifting toward the "East," or the Asia-Pacific. China's rise is one aspect of this momentous transformation, albeit, for now, the driving force behind it.[1]

As it happens, the start of the process by which the West came eventually to overshadow the East can be dated with some precision. In 1498, after a year spent feeling his way down Africa's western shores and around the Cape of Good Hope, Portuguese explorer Vasco da Gama succeeded in reaching India. Fifteen years later, in 1513, one of his countrymen completed a voyage to China. It was the first recorded visit by a European since Marco Polo made the trip over land almost two hundred years before.[2]

At the start of what historian K. M. Panikkar has labeled the "Vasco da Gama epoch,"[3] West and East were on more or less equal footing. One thousand years after the fall of Rome, Europe's kingdoms, principalities, and proto-states were no more highly developed than their Asian counterparts and in some respects were markedly less so. Retrospective estimates suggest that at this point per capita incomes at either end of the Eurasian landmass were roughly equal. With the critically important exceptions of shipbuilding, navigation, and lightweight cannon, however, European technology generally lagged behind Asia's, and especially China's.[4] Europe's eventual dominance could hardly have been predicted. If anything, "in 1500 an observer might more logically have looked forward to the 'Asianization' of Europe" than to the opposite.[5] Certainly the first arrivals did not make a very favorable or imposing impression. Contemporary accounts make clear that their wary Asian hosts regarded the Europeans with disdain, seeing them, not without justification, as "desperadoes . . . barbarous, truculent and dirty."[6]

For the next 250 years, from 1500 to roughly 1750, the Europeans contented themselves with nibbling around the edges of eastern Eurasia. Explorers and entrepreneurs from Portugal and Spain were soon followed by others from Holland, England, and France. These seafaring adventurers did business and established occasional outposts, but they did not attempt to assert political dominion over those they encountered nor, for the most part, did they venture very far inland. While trade was no doubt profitable for those directly involved, it was limited in volume and value. Shifting local circumstances and naval warfare among the major European powers also helped to render East-West commercial ties "weak, tenuous, and liable to interruption."[7] Whether for good or ill, economic exchange between Europe and Asia during the preindustrial era did not have a major impact on the pace of development in either region. As Panikkar puts it, "If by an Act of God the relations of Europe with Asia had ceased all of a sudden in 1748, little would have been left to show for two and a half centuries of furious activity."[8]

During this period, European societies began to accumulate advantages in wealth and technology, but these remained minor. In the eighteenth and early nineteenth centuries, thanks to improvements in agricultural productivity, China's overall growth rate may actually have been higher than Europe's, but because its population also grew rapidly, per capita incomes remained steady. Despite their more modest economic performance, Europe's less fecund peoples were therefore able to enjoy a somewhat better standard of living than their Asian counterparts.[9] On the eve of the Industrial Revolution, the gap in per capita incomes was still relatively small, but it was beginning to widen.[10]

While historians agree on *what* happened next, they disagree vehemently about exactly *why*. By the closing decades of the eighteenth century, Europeans had begun to achieve notable success in substituting machines and inanimate sources of energy for the labor of humans and animals. The cumulative effect of these innovations eventually permitted a rapid, self-sustaining rise in worker productivity, aggregate output, and per capita incomes.[11] The first breakthroughs came in Britain, but the process of mechanization and industrialization quickly spread, via imitation and competition, to other parts of Western Europe.

Why did the Industrial Revolution happen first in the West rather than the East? The voluminous scholarly literature on this question can be divided into two broad categories.[12] On the one hand are those who argue that Europe was simply lucky. Prior to the late eighteenth century, the agrarian economies of both Europe and Asia labored under similar constraints imposed by scarcities of land and energy. According to economic historian Kenneth Pomeranz, it was only the discovery of readily accessible sources of coal (especially in England) and the opening of vast tracts of land in the New World that allowed Europe to become a "fortunate freak," capable of shattering "the fundamental constraints of energy use and resource availability that had previously limited *everyone's* horizons."[13]

The other, more traditional view is that Europe had some special, intrinsic characteristics that enabled it, in effect, to make its own luck. After all, the discovery of the Americas and the development of technologies for mining coal and using it to generate steam power were not mere windfalls. They were manifestations of an inclination toward innovation and enterprise that appears to have been especially powerful in Europe at this time. Well before the onset of the Industrial Revolution, Europeans had distinguished themselves as explorers, inventors, risk-takers, and merchants. But where did those characteristics come from?

The German sociologist Max Weber famously argued that the Protestant Reformation gave rise to modern capitalism by encouraging the forms of individual behavior on which it depended, including, in the words of historian David Landes, "hard work, honesty, seriousness, the thrifty use of money and time."[14] When he examined China, by contrast, Weber concluded that Confucianism promoted passivity, lack of curiosity, irrationality, dishonesty, and economic stagnation.[15] While modern scholars reject Weber's thoroughgoing critique of Confucian culture, some continue to emphasize the role of religious developments in preparing the West for industrial "take off." "The proximate roots of the epoch of modern economic growth lie in the growth of science and diffusion of modern education," writes Richard Easterlin. These, in turn, were the products of "the secular, rationalistic, materialistic trend of intellectual thought that evolved from the Renaissance and Reformation."[16] In this view, the church's loss of authority over all of Western Christendom cleared the way for a scientific revolution, which enabled the Industrial Revolution.

Even if we accept this notion, it is still possible to discern deeper forces at work. Doctrinal schisms both reflected and, through decades of religious warfare, reinforced Europe's long-standing fragmentation into many separate political actors. After the fall of Rome, no single power was ever again able to bring all of western Eurasia under its control. By 1500 Europe was broken up into over five hundred kingdoms and principalities of varying shapes, sizes, and degrees of autonomy. This pattern of division gave rise to chronic insecurity and near-constant warfare, but it was also a critical source of Europe's dynamism. Surrounded by enemies, eager for resources and superior weaponry, kings and princes became enthusiastic benefactors of exploration, experimentation, and innovation. Many were also compelled to strike deals with lesser nobles and merchants, granting them property rights and legal protections in return for contributing men and money to the defense of the realm. These bargains laid the ground for expanding market economies and, ultimately, for the diffusion of political power and the birth of democracy.[17]

By contrast, as early as 221 BC, large swaths of continental eastern Eurasia had been incorporated into a single empire. Despite periods of upheaval, imperial China remained unified and, over time, expanded its domain. Most of the kingdoms along China's periphery that remained outside the empire were comparatively small and weak. Economic historian E. L. Jones argues that these circumstances contributed to an eventual divergence in the paths followed by Europe and Asia. He notes that "a large empire which monopolized the means of coercion and was not threatened by more advanced neighbors had little incentive to adopt new methods." All-powerful emperors could also make "wrong-headed and incontrovertible systems-wide decisions" that closed off potentially promising avenues of advance. The most striking example is the decision of the Ming emperors to shut down long-range maritime exploration early in the fifteenth century, despite the fact that initial expeditions had succeeded in reaching the shores of South Asia and Africa. Instead of pushing outward, and perhaps establishing its own distant dominions, China drew back to passively await the arrival of European intruders. This portentous choice, possible in a highly centralized empire, "could not happen, or be enforced in a decentralized system of states." Europe's division, Jones concludes, "was an insurance against economic and technological stagnation."[18]

These speculations lead to one final question: what accounts for the differences in the political maps of Europe and Asia? Jones and others have suggested that the answer may lie in their differing natural environments. Until the end of the preindustrial era, Europe was a "scatter of regions of high arable potential set in a continent of wastes and forests." High mountains, wide rivers and marshes, and stretches of ocean divided western Eurasia, making conquest and consolidation more difficult and enabling many, smaller units to survive.[19]

Where Europe had many natural core areas, around which states eventually grew, the eastern Eurasian mainland had only one. Seeking to explain what he describes as China's "chronic unity," anthropologist Jared Diamond observes that its "heartland is bound together from east to west by two long navigable river systems in rich alluvial valleys . . . and it is joined from north to south by relatively easy connections between these two river systems." As a result, China very early developed two highly productive regions "only weakly separated from each other and eventually fused into a single core." China's unity and vast size gave it some initial advantages but eventually held it back.[20] As the unified East stagnated, the West, divided, quarrelsome, and inventive, surged ahead.

Perhaps Europe was lucky after all.

EXPANSION AND DOMINATION

The causes of the Industrial Revolution will no doubt provide fodder for endless academic debates; fortunately there is somewhat greater agreement about its consequences. For our purposes, the most important of these was a marked improvement in the ability of European states to project and sustain military power far from their own frontiers. Steamships could travel great distances at higher speeds than their sail-driven counterparts, carrying arms and men quickly wherever they were needed. Thus, by the 1850s, the time for a voyage from England to India had been cut from eight months or even longer, to only two or three months. Smaller steam-powered vessels could also navigate more reliably up rivers, permitting the Europeans to bring superior force to bear well away from the coasts of Asia and Africa. This ability to penetrate inland was further enhanced later in the nineteenth century by the construction of railway lines.[21]

Industrialization also brought stunning advances in firepower. At the close of the eighteenth century, European and Asian armies carried virtually identical muzzle-loading flintlock muskets and smoothbore cannon.[22] By the middle of the nineteenth century, improvements in metallurgy, machine tools, and chemical propellants had begun to enable the mass production of breech-loading rifles, mobile artillery pieces, and explosive shells, to be followed soon by rapid-fire machine guns. These weapons had greater range, accuracy, and killing power than the ones they replaced, and were generally far better than those available to non-European forces. The "firearms revolution" gave the Europeans a "crushing superiority" over those they encountered on the battlefield and allowed them reliably to defeat even far-larger enemy forces.[23]

Over the course of the nineteenth century, the Western powers used their growing advantages in wealth and technology to extend their influence across all of Asia and to establish direct political control over much of it. In 1800 the only places under Western rule were the Philippines (a Spanish colony) and a few islands in the Indonesian archipelago governed by Holland. One hundred years later the situation was inverted; only Japan and Siam (Thailand) remained truly independent, and China, though not a colony, had surrendered key aspects of its sovereignty, as well as substantial chunks of its territory to foreign intruders.[24]

The West enveloped Asia as if in a great pincer movement, advancing on it from all directions. To the south, by the middle of the nineteenth century the British had conquered most of India and, motivated in part by a desire to secure its frontiers, drove east into Burma, Malaya, and northern Borneo. Eager to ensure their own access to markets and materials, the French proceeded to bring most of Indochina under their control, moving northward in a series of campaigns, across Annam (Vietnam), Cambodia, and finally Laos. Meanwhile, in maritime Southeast Asia, the Dutch expanded outward from their previously limited footholds to annex ever-larger portions of the Indonesian archipelago.[25]

While these developments were unfolding to the south and southeast, from the west and north, czarist Russia was moving into Central Asia and consolidating its position in the Far East. Beginning in the 1840s, the Russians used superior organization, tactics, and weaponry to subdue Kazakh, Turkmen, Kirghiz, and Tadzhik tribesmen armed with "lances, ancient flintlocks, and crude cannon." By 1895 Russia's Central Asian frontiers had shifted hundreds of miles to the south and were contiguous with those of Persia, Afghanistan, India, and China.[26] These moves were matched in the Far East by expeditions that pushed Russia's borders south and east from Siberia and put it in control of a large swath of land along the shores of the northern Pacific. After the turn of the century, as China grew weaker, the Russians also gained spheres of influence in Outer Mongolia and Northern Manchuria.[27]

The final axis of advance was from the east, across the Pacific. Starting in the 1850s and culminating with its war against Spain in 1898, the United States took control of a series of island stepping stones that eventually extended from Hawaii to Guam, Midway, and the Philippines, only a few hundred miles off China's coasts. The arrival of American ships in Japan in 1853–54 also helped force that country out of its self-imposed isolation and set it on the path to becoming a major regional player and an imperial power in its own right.

Starting with the Opium Wars of the 1840s, first Britain, then France and the United States, and finally Japan and Germany all brought pressure to bear on China from along its eastern seaboard. In part because they were wary of one another and feared triggering a territorial scramble, the powers for the most part did not seize land or establish direct colonial rule. But they did demand and, thanks to their superior coercive power, were able to extract extraordinary concessions. Through a series of "unequal treaties," foreigners claimed "rights, privileges, dignities, and prerogatives, which . . . backed by force, developed . . . into a special corpus of international law controlling practically every aspect of Chinese life."[28] In addition to so-called treaty ports, where they controlled trade and were beyond the reach of local law, foreign powers used gunboats to protect businessmen and missionaries upriver and, in general, to extend their influence deep into the interior.

By the turn of the twentieth century, the situation in Asia was characterized by a degree of Western dominance that seemed beyond any possibility of challenge.[29] Not only did the Western powers exert either direct or indirect control over much of eastern Eurasia, but also they had opened a wide, fast-growing, and apparently self-sustaining economic and technological lead over most of its inhabitants. Asian workers found it impossible to keep pace with their now far more efficient Western competitors, and local manufacturers using outmoded techniques were crushed by a mass of inexpensive imports. As Europe and America became more heavily industrialized, China and India moved in the opposite direction. By the end of the nineteenth century, per capita levels of industrialization were actually lower in these countries than they had been at the beginning.[30] Meanwhile, across Southeast Asia, the imperial powers did little to develop local economies, focusing instead on the extraction of agricultural products, minerals, and other raw materials necessary to feed and fuel their own economies.[31] While the nations of Western Europe and North America leapt ahead, Asia fell further and further behind.

Japan is the exception that proves the rule. Because they preserved their sovereignty, the Japanese were able to organize an effective response to the Western powers, following them quickly down the path to industrialization, the creation of modern armed forces, and the acquisition of imperial possessions and "spheres of influence" of their own, first in Korea and Taiwan, later in Manchuria. Following Europe's example, they proceeded to exploit for their own purposes the human and natural resources of these regions.[32]

The aggregate statistics trace the story of Asia's relative decline. From the start of the Industrial Revolution to the end of the Second World War, the major Asian economies (again, excluding Japan) advanced slowly in absolute terms and at only a fraction of the rate of the Western industrial powers. With populations continuing to grow rapidly, per capita incomes stagnated and, in the case of China, probably declined. As incredible as it may seem today, in the early 1950s most people in Asia were little better off than their ancestors had been over a century before, and many were less so. Not surprisingly, Asia's weight in the world economy fell precipitously over this interval. In the preindustrial age, the people of China, Japan, and the Indian subcontinent together had been responsible for roughly half of global production, with China alone accounting for as much as a third. Europe's share, by contrast, was only about a quarter of the total.[33] Between 1820 and 1890, Asia's portion of worldwide production fell from 50 percent to 25 percent; by 1952 that figure had been halved again and stood at only 12 percent.[34] The West's superiority over the East seemed complete and irreversible.

ASIAN RENAISSANCE

As even some economists will admit, in the real world, economics is subordinate to politics. Without a framework of rules and laws, and an appropriate balance between market forces and political decisions, sustained economic progress would be impossible. Even if they achieve some initial success, states that seek to control the allocation of all scarce resources will end up choking growth. On the other hand, governments that fail to protect property rights, ensure domestic tranquility, and provide security against foreign depredations cannot hope to achieve continuing improvements in the well-being of their citizens.

States can thus be too strong, but they are also at times too weak. Asia's reemergence can best be understood as the result of a two-stage process in which the region's societies eventually arrived at a workable balance point between these extremes. In the first phase, which began even before the Second World War ended and had largely run its course by 1960, most of Asia's people shook off foreign rule, created (or reestablished) sovereign nation-states, and assumed responsibility for their own governance. Independence was generally followed, however, by the adoption of some form of heavily state-directed economic strategy. While these strategies may have helped to jump-start development, they also produced distortions and quickly outlived their usefulness. Starting in the 1960s, Asian governments found their way, via differing paths, to policies that gave much wider play to market forces. These shifts enabled rapid, sustained growth and, in time, the beginnings of an historic realignment in the global balance of wealth and power.

Albeit unintentionally, the Western imperial powers helped clear the way for the eventual formation of modern Asian nation-states. As early as the second half of the nineteenth century, advocates of reform and "self-strengthening" in Japan and China had begun to argue that if they were to resist the intruders and control their own destinies, Asian societies would have to adopt Western methods. What was needed were European-style states capable of mobilizing mass sentiment, collecting taxes, conscripting manpower, building modern armies and navies, and guiding the construction of industrialized economies.[35]

In addition to serving as a model, the West also helped to create some of the preconditions for successful nation-building. As they sought to extend and consolidate their control during the nineteenth century, the imperialists in many places redrew the map, forcing disparate groups into single administrative units, thereby creating at least the beginnings of a shared identity. The common experience of subjugation by, and eventual resistance to, foreign rulers helped forge national consciousness where none had previously existed. On a more positive note, the imperial powers also generally provided education and training that prepared local elites for self-governance, often inspiring them to seek it sooner rather than later.

Finally, and perhaps most important, Western philosophers and statesmen developed and spread ideas that eventually contributed to the collapse of their own empires. The notion that "national self-determination" was the only legitimate basis for political organization gained worldwide attention in 1919, when Woodrow Wilson argued that it should provide the template for a postwar settlement in Europe. Although Wilson himself did not intend for it to be applied to non-Western peoples, the principle he advanced so forcefully had obvious, and ultimately revolutionary, implications for the entire international system.[36] Wilson's words served as an inspiration for the nationalist movements that were beginning to take shape across Asia.[37]

The First World War eroded the foundations of Western dominance by intensifying the desire of Asian peoples for autonomy, but it also began to weaken the European powers' resolve to maintain their grip in the East. The hypocrisy of applying supposedly universal principles only to certain races and regions was increasingly hard to hide. Moreover, in the aftermath of the war's unprecedented bloodletting, it became more difficult to accept that Europe truly represented the pinnacle of global civilization with an inherent right, even an obligation, to rule over others. The "glad, confident imperial morning" of the nineteenth century was over, and some sensitive observers had begun to detect inklings of twilight.[38] As the French poet Paul Valéry mused in 1919, "We now see that the abyss of history is large enough for everyone. . . . Will Europe keep its preeminence in all things? Will Europe become what in fact it is, that is to say a small corner of the Asian continent?"[39]

What the First World War began, the Second finished, and with astonishing speed. In a single year, the Japanese defeated American forces in the Philippines and drove the Dutch out of Indonesia, the French out of Indochina, and the British out of Burma and Malaya. These territories were added to Japan's existing northern empire, which now extended from Taiwan, across a swath of eastern China, through Manchuria, and down the Korean peninsula. India and Australia were the only remaining outposts of Western power in Asia, and by the end of 1942, these too appeared to be in imminent danger.

Japan's quick victories destroyed any remaining vestige of belief in European superiority, moral or material. Despite the fact that their rule was often even more brutal than the rule of those they replaced, the Japanese portrayed themselves as liberators, encouraged anticolonial sentiments, and, in many places, including Burma, Indochina, and Indonesia, put nationalist leaders in charge of local governments. Watching as the tides of battle shifted back in favor of the Allies, nationalists in Southeast Asia, notes historian John Fairbank, "accepted the forms of 'independence' proffered by the Japanese and at the same time prepared to turn against them in defeat."[40]

By 1945 the political situation had been transformed and the way cleared for an entirely new order. In Northeast Asia, even before the war's outbreak, Japan itself had been the dominant imperial power. Its defeat and withdrawal made possible within a few years the creation of a new central state with authority over all of mainland China, an independent government on Taiwan (which also proclaimed its right to rule the mainland), and the establishment of two Korean states, one in the north, the other in the south, each of which declared itself the rightful ruler of the entire peninsula. As a consequence of its aggression, Japan was finally forced to submit to foreign occupation, but by 1952 it had regained its sovereignty and was once again an autonomous national actor, albeit now under American tutelage and protection.

To the south, Japan's short-lived expansion had swept away the Western imperial powers. When the war ended, the question was whether these countries would have the will and the capacity to return and reestablish their empires. The answer in every case proved eventually to be no. The French and Dutch governments did not lack the desire to reclaim their Asian colonies; indeed, they regarded this as essential to the prospects for recovery from the terrible damage inflicted on their homelands. After the humiliation and loss of war, regaining control of Indochina seemed to many Frenchmen to promise "a new power, prosperity, and prestige."[41] For their part, Dutch statesmen believed that to avoid becoming "another Denmark," they had no choice but to retake their eastern empire.[42]

Despite these convictions, neither France nor Holland had sufficient economic resources, military power, or political will to do the job. Exhausted by a war fought on their own soil, and facing well-armed and organized nationalist movements that had sprung up in their absence, both were ultimately forced to relinquish their claims and retreat from Asia. By 1949, following three years of war, the Dutch were compelled to accept the establishment of an independent Indonesian state. Five years later, after long and bitter fighting, the French abandoned their attempts to hold on to Vietnam.

In sharp contrast to the European powers, the United States had more than enough power to reclaim its former Pacific possessions, had it wanted to do so. By 1945 its economic and military might were greater than ever before. By this point, however, America's brief, turn-of-the-century flirtation with formal empire-building had long since passed, and Washington saw itself as competing with Moscow for the role of the world's foremost scourge of imperialism and leading advocate of "national liberation." In the 1930s, the U.S. government had made a commitment to grant formal independence to the Philippines, and within months of the war's end, it fulfilled its promise. The United States retained military bases in its former colony and throughout the region (including in Japan, South Korea, and Taiwan), but with the exception of a handful of small islands, and the Japanese prefecture of Okinawa, which it controlled until 1972, Washington no longer claimed the right to fly its flag over any part of the Western Pacific.

In terms of both attitudes and capabilities, the British fell somewhere in between the other European empires and their American allies. Like France and Holland, Britain viewed continued close commercial ties with its colonies as essential to postwar economic recovery, but it hoped to be able to achieve much of what it needed within the confines of a loose commonwealth. The British were also increasingly divided over the propriety of continuing to rule over subject peoples. While some still supported the imperial project with enthusiasm, others had come to regard it as an anachronism, if not an embarrassment. There had always been a significant strand of liberal anti-imperialism in British political thought, and the fact that the recent world war had been fought in the name of freedom and in opposition to doctrines of racial superiority caused these sentiments to grow stronger.

Aside from considerations of principle, there were the hard facts of Britain's weakened postwar condition. The severe strains that had been imposed on its economy, the price tag for expanded social welfare programs promised during the war, and the likelihood of active resistance from local nationalist movements all contributed to the belief that the costs of trying to hold on to at least the Asian portions of the empire now exceeded the benefits. In 1947 the British granted independence to India and oversaw the creation of the new Muslim nation of Pakistan. One year later, Burma followed suit. In 1957, after lingering to help put down a protracted Communist insurgency, Britain withdrew from Malaya.[43]

With the exception of Soviet Russia's Central Asian possessions, the end of the Second World War marked the end of Western imperial rule in Asia. Where it had once depicted divisions into colonies and spheres of influence, the map of the region was now delineated into nation-states of varying sizes, populations, regime types, and degrees of cohesion. The people of Asia had shaken off their colonial overseers. The question now was what they would do with their newfound independence.

ACHIEVING GROWTH

Historian Niall Ferguson has written that, in retrospect, the "true narrative arc" of the twentieth century is revealed to be "not 'the triumph of the West,' but rather the crisis of the European empires, the ultimate result of which was the inexorable revival of Asian power and the descent of the West." Having by 1900 achieved a seemingly insurmountable superiority, the West (meaning, in this context, primarily Europe) proceeded to exhaust itself in a "Fifty Year War" of unprecedented violence and destruction. In Ferguson's telling, the Second World War was "the decisive turning point" in the rise of the East and the decline of the West.[44]

This account has much to commend it, but it elides one critically important fact: even after war had cleared the way, a revival of Asian power was far from inevitable. The collapse of the European and Japanese empires and the establishment of nation-states were necessary conditions for renewal, but they were not, in themselves, sufficient to produce it. As long as their people stayed poor, Asia's newly independent nations would remain weak in relation to their former masters. A true renaissance would depend on achieving and sustaining rapid economic growth.

At war's end, even the most optimistic observers had difficulty imagining such a possibility. As one survey summarized the situation in 1951, "Not until independence came could the full magnitude of the obstacles to Asia's modernization be appreciated. The production of goods, and sometimes even of food was inadequate; there were marked shortages of trained personnel and capital; the peoples of Asia were predominantly illiterate; and old social practices and attitudes stood in the way of change." Large swaths of Asia remained essentially untouched by the effects of the Industrial Revolution. In India and China the great mass of men and women still lived in conditions of crushing rural poverty, much as they had always done. Across the region, existing industrial facilities and transportation infrastructure had been damaged or destroyed during the war or in the postcolonial conflicts that followed. Some areas (including Japan, Korea, and Taiwan) lacked significant natural resources; others (including most of Southeast Asia) had little else, and therefore seemed destined to fall back into their economically marginal role of providing raw materials to the more advanced industrial West. In short, "the creation of national states was only a beginning—an opportunity" rather than a guarantee of progress.[45]

We now know that despite all of the obstacles, and with lags, reversals, and a few notable gaps, the second half of the twentieth century was marked by a dramatic improvement in material conditions across virtually all of Asia. For the first time in almost two hundred years, local economies grew faster than those of other regions and faster than their own populations. The nations of Asia were thus able both to improve the lives of their citizens and to increase their collective weight in world affairs.

This historic breakthrough was in part due to international factors, most notably the achievement by the 1970s, after an initial thirty-year interval of widespread turmoil and violence, of overall regional peace and stability, and the creation of an increasingly open global economy into which Asia could be integrated. But Asia's progress was, first and foremost, the result of developments within the societies that made it up. Spurred on by the desire to keep pace with their neighbors, and the need to produce results for their people, governments in one country after another implemented packages of policies conducive to rapid economic growth. The details varied across countries and over time. Seen in its entirety, however, the broad trend was toward an expanding role for markets and a diminished, though still important, role for states.

The move to market-driven growth, and Asia's transformation from backwater to economic dynamo, came in a series of five overlapping waves, starting with Japan's postwar recovery and extending, most recently, to the liberalization of India's economy in the early 1990s. The opening three stages in this process were marked by experimentation and policy adjustments in what were already capitalist countries. The fourth and fifth stages saw the effective (though not always openly acknowledged) abandonment of communism and socialism in favor of a form of capitalism.[46]

With help and direction from Washington, Japan's government drove the postwar reconstruction of the country's economy. Bureaucrats in Tokyo laid out detailed plans for rebuilding productive capacity and infrastructure, and provided loans and subsidies to the private firms chosen to do the work. One study of East Asia's economic "miracle" notes that "in the immediate postwar period, Japan's industrial policy was akin to socialist economic planning." By the mid-1950s, with initial reconstruction complete, the government eased back its role and gave greater play to market forces, but it continued to guide development by offering tax breaks and tariff protection to industries deemed essential for further growth, including steel, shipbuilding, fertilizer, and power generation.[47] Once a basic industrial foundation had been built, government planners began to focus incentives on industries thought to be capable of competing in international markets, such as computers, petrochemicals, and automobiles.[48]

The effectiveness of targeted industrial policies remains a subject of controversy. More certain are the benefits from Tokyo's persistent efforts to ensure favorable underlying conditions for continued growth by keeping taxes and inflation low, funding basic education, and preserving political stability.[49] By the end of the 1950s these policies had started to bear fruit. Over the next two decades Japan emerged as a major economic powerhouse, sustaining annual growth rates as high as three times those of the Western advanced industrial countries, expanding its exports at a rapid pace, and increasing its share of total world trade.

Japan's early successes were noted and soon copied by the four "Little Tigers": Taiwan, South Korea, Singapore, and Hong Kong. Like Japan, the Tigers lacked natural resources but were able to mobilize skilled, literate, and comparatively low-wage workforces.[50] In the 1950s, South Korea and Taiwan, in particular, sought to promote growth by insulating themselves from world markets and attempting to nurture a wide array of domestic "import-substituting industries." Starting in the early 1960s, with encouragement from the United States and Japan, the Tigers shifted away from this intrusive, protectionist, and ultimately inefficient approach, lowering many tariff barriers and using tax breaks to encourage private investment in industries with export potential.[51] Once again, an export-oriented model proved to be highly successful. During the 1960s the Tigers were able to match Japanese growth rates and to maintain the pace into the 1970s, even as Japan began to slow down.

The third Asian growth wave had its epicenter in Southeast Asia, most notably in Malaysia, Thailand, and Indonesia. Especially during the early stages of the Cold War, these nations experienced periods of political instability as well as gyrations in economic policy.[52] All three began the postwar period heavily dependent on exports of raw materials. Each subsequently passed through a phase in which its government sought to promote industrialization by erecting high tariff barriers to imported goods and encouraging the manufacture of inferior homegrown alternatives. Following the lead of their northern neighbors, and with substantial assistance, including investments by Japanese, Taiwanese, and South Korean firms, in the 1980s Thailand, Malaysia, and Indonesia all eventually shifted away from import-substituting industrialization and toward a more open, market-oriented approach. Aspiring Southeast Asian governments began to focus on creating a favorable environment for foreign direct investment in manufacturing facilities where local workers would produce goods for export as well for domestic consumption.[53]

The fourth and fifth stages of Asia's renaissance involved the most dramatic departures from previously existing policies. Thanks to the sheer size and productive potential of the economies involved, these developments will also prove in the long run to have been the most important. As I discuss more fully later, in the late 1970s, China started to move away from state-controlled central planning and toward a form of capitalism, albeit within a rigid authoritarian political framework and with a continuing, substantial government role in the economy. China's apostasy was followed in the mid-1980s by the beginnings of similar developments in Vietnam.

India is the last major country to join Asia's economic revival. Stephen Cohen has speculated that one reason for this delay may be that for much of the postwar period, this "giant, inward-gazing" nation regarded the economic success of others as largely irrelevant to its own future. Powerful groups in Indian society also favored the continuation of existing policies. Despite the progress being made in other parts of Asia, India clung through most of the Cold War to its "quasi-command, bureaucratized economy."[54]

Major liberalizing reforms did not come until the 1990s. The proximate causes of this development were a debt crisis and the election in 1991 of a new ruling coalition no longer committed to socialist principles. By this point it was also obvious that deep changes were afoot. The impending collapse of India's longtime Soviet ally, and China's continuing growth, signaled potentially unfavorable shifts in the balance of power. The dissolution of the Soviet empire also meant that virtually all of the rest of the world was now being integrated into a truly global economy. If India failed to join in this process, warned one of the architects of the new policy, it ran the risk of "increasing marginalization."[55]

In a sharp break with the past, India's new rulers abandoned the long-standing policy of promoting virtual autarky and began to lower tariffs and to lift many restrictions on foreign investment. The government also took steps to restrict its previously over-weaning presence in the domestic economy, cutting back on regulations, selling off some state-owned assets, and permitting competition in sectors long dominated by the state, including electric power and telecommunications. These changes had a powerful psychological, as well as an economic, impact. As one observer put it, "We felt as though our second independence had arrived: we were going to be free from a rapacious and domineering state."[56]

The reforms of the 1990s helped move India onto a much steeper growth path. Economists had previously speculated, only half-jokingly, that 3.5 percent per year might be the "Hindu rate of growth," the upper limit of what the country could achieve given all of its burdens and traditions. Now some began to argue that this comparatively low figure was, in fact, only the "Hindu-*socialist*" growth rate, a self-imposed limit produced by decades of misguided policies rooted in a wrong-headed economic philosophy. This view was borne out by the results. By the close of the twentieth century, a reforming India had become one of the fastest expanding economies in the world, achieving an average annual growth rate of over 6 percent.[57]

The combined, cumulative effects of the shift to market-driven growth across Asia have become unmistakable in recent decades. Once again, aggregate statistics reveal the broad outlines of the story. From the early 1950s to the late 1970s, the share of total world output of India, Japan, and

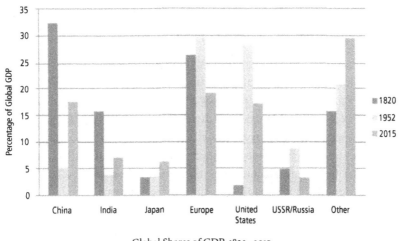

Global Shares of GDP, 1820–2015.
Data from Angus Maddison, *Chinese Economic Performance in the Long Run*
(Paris: Organisation for Economic Co-operation and Development, 1998).

China together grew by about a third, from 12 percent in 1952 to 16 percent
in 1978. Most of the increase during this period was due to Japan's exceptional performance. From 1978 to 1995, with China now the growth leader,
the combined share of Asia's three economic giants increased by about
half, to nearly 25 percent of total world gross domestic product (GDP).
With the remainder of the region included, Asia's 1995 share stood at 34
percent, versus 45 percent for the United States and the other capitalist
countries. By 2015, according to one set of estimates, these fractions could
be reversed: 43 percent for Asia, 36 percent for the United States and the
rest of the advanced industrial nations.[58]

CHINA'S RISE

China's part in the story of Asia's postwar renaissance is delineated by
two dates. On October 1, 1949, Mao Zedong, chairman of the Chinese
Communist Party, proclaimed the establishment of a "People's Republic."
Mao's speech marked the end of China's civil war and the final victory of
Communist forces over their Nationalist foes. Fighting between the two

groups had dragged on for over twenty years, finally reaching a decisive phase only after Japan's surrender and the withdrawal of its forces from Chinese soil.

The founding of a new regime signaled the restoration of Chinese sovereignty. For nearly a century, China had been what would today be called a "failed state." The central government was usually weak and incapable of exerting unchallenged authority within its borders; indeed, for extended periods, it effectively ceased to exist. From the mid-nineteenth century onward, Beijing faced mutually reinforcing external and internal challenges. Foreign intrusion triggered rebellions and popular uprisings, which provided the pretext for yet more encroachments. The inability of the Qing emperors to mount effective resistance to pressure from foreigners further diminished their prestige and authority at home and paved the way for the dynasty's eventual collapse. After a brief period in which it seemed that the leaders of the newly proclaimed republic might be able to build a strong, modern state, China was thrust into another downward spiral of warlordism, civil war, and Japanese intervention.

With Japan finally gone and the Nationalists defeated, the new Communist regime quickly consolidated its hold on mainland China, incorporating all of the territories previously claimed at the high watermark of Qing rule. As elsewhere in Asia, the establishment of order and the creation (or, in this case, the *re*-creation) of a sovereign state opened new possibilities for achieving material progress. Unfortunately for China's people, their new masters were in the grips of an ideology that demanded total government control of the economy and justified the virtually unlimited use of coercion and violence by the state in order to achieve its objectives. To make matters worse, ultimate authority in China was soon revealed to lie in the hands of one man, with his own extreme and highly idiosyncratic views on how best to promote development and retain political power.

The Communists started by collectivizing farms, nationalizing industry, and expropriating the assets of foreigners, landlords, and China's own, comparatively small, entrepreneurial class. Instead of relying on market forces, government bureaucrats took on the responsibility for setting wages and prices, controlling the allocation of labor, and making all of the decisions about investment. Beijing's central planners set about to engineer a wholesale redirection of national resources, sharply constricting consumption, squeezing agriculture, and boosting investment in heavy industry. The state also established a monopoly on foreign trade, restricting imports, eliminating foreign direct investment, and aiming for the highest possible degree of self-sufficiency.[59]

These policies were similar to those that had been adopted in the Soviet Union and reflected the prevailing Marxist-Leninist formula for "building Communism." Not content merely to read from the Soviet playbook, however, Chairman Mao soon ordered several disastrous experiments of his own devising. During the so-called Great Leap Forward of 1958–61, he sought to accelerate the pace of industrialization by extracting even more resources from the agricultural sector. (Among other expedients, farmers were ordered to abandon their crops in order to build primitive backyard steel furnaces.) The results were catastrophic. As many as thirty-eight million people are thought to have died in the subsequent famine, making it the worst in recorded history. Five years later, Mao launched the Cultural Revolution, purging critics of his Great Leap, real and imagined, and sending scientists and engineers, among others, to toil in the countryside to rekindle their revolutionary spirit. Three million people were killed over the next decade, and by the Communist Party's own subsequent admission, one hundred million had their lives upended. Higher education and scientific research were especially hard hit. By the time the Cultural Revolution ended, China's economy was in shambles.[60]

Despite inefficient policies and periodic upheavals, China under Mao did manage to make headway. As bad as they were, conditions in the country were still on the whole more stable, and hence more conducive to growth, than they had been during the preceding decades of civil war and foreign occupation. Through the use of wasteful and often brutal techniques, the Communists succeeded in forcing the pace of industrialization. Improvements in basic health care and literacy also meant that workers lived longer and were better prepared for factory labor than their predecessors.

After having stagnated for over a century, China was able to achieve an average annual growth rate of over 4 percent between 1952 and 1978. This was fast enough to permit an increase in the per capita incomes of China's growing population, but it was not enough to allow it to keep pace with other nations. While Chairman Mao ruled, China's share of world GDP

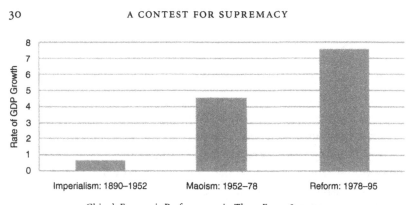

China's Economic Performance in Three Eras, 1820–1995.
Data from Angus Maddison, *Chinese Economic Performance in the Long Run*
(Paris: Organisation for Economic Co-operation and Development, 1998).

actually declined. The nation was finally moving forward, but others, and especially many of those in its immediate neighborhood, were progressing far more rapidly.[61]

The second crucial date in China's reemergence as a great power is December 18, 1978, the opening day of the Third Plenum of the Eleventh Communist Party Central Committee. Coming just two years after Mao's death, this meeting marked "the decisive break with the past and the beginning of China's reform era."[62] Cautiously at first, and then with increasingly bold and confident strokes, Mao's successors began to unwind the policies he had put in place. Huge, inefficient collective farms were broken up and turned over to families who were now free to enjoy the fruits of their labors. The resulting increases in productivity boosted agricultural output, unleashing a flood of now redundant farm laborers from the countryside into the cities.

Shifts in agriculture were accompanied by changes in industrial policy. Subsidies to many state-owned enterprises were cut back or eliminated and some were broken up and sold outright.[63] Instead of continuing to direct virtually all national resources toward heavy industry, the government stood back and permitted the manufacture of consumer goods for export and for the domestic market. Private entrepreneurship and private ownership were permitted and, up to a point, actively encouraged. Albeit gradually, the span of control of the government's massive planning system began to shrink. Where bureaucrats once set prices across every sector of the economy, the state increasingly gave way to the forces of supply and demand.

From the start, engagement with the outside world was crucial to the process of reform. Long-standing barriers to foreign direct investment were removed, and foreign companies were encouraged to build plants and factories that could take advantage of China's fast-growing pool of low-wage workers. Abandoning the Maoist principles of isolation and self-reliance, China plunged into global markets and was soon importing machinery and raw materials and exporting a prodigious volume and variety of manufactured goods.[64]

China's move toward market-driven economics, like those of its Asian neighbors, was the product of both internal and external factors. Mao's death had been followed by a brief and lopsided power struggle between his wife and a handful of radical supporters, and a group of more moderate pragmatists led by Deng Xiaoping. Twice purged by Mao, who accused him of wanting to follow the "capitalist road," Deng was hardly a principled advocate of economic liberalism. His approach was more practical than theoretical; he wanted results and was willing to try new methods to get them. Unlike Mao, who fancied himself a solitary creative genius, Deng was open to learning from the experience of others, including the smaller but more prosperous nations of East Asia. While he does not appear at the outset to have had a fully developed plan for liberalizing China's economy and opening it up to the world, he was willing to follow the logic of the process wherever it led. When initial reforms proved successful, he pressed ahead with more far-reaching measures.

Deng and his advisors doubtless believed that raising the living standards of China's long-suffering citizens was desirable for its own sake. After thirty years of Maoism, basic necessities remained in short supply and millions of peasants still lived in fear of starvation.[65] The Soviet Union's collapse after decades of stagnation, and the Chinese Communist Party's own near-death experience when mass protests swept the country in 1989, added an extra dose of urgency to their calculations. Continued material progress now seemed essential to preserving the party's grip on power. After a brief period of retrenchment, in which hard-liners sought unsuccessfully to restore the state to its central role, Deng renewed his push for reform. By the early 1990s, writes Barry Naughton, it was evident that "there was no alternative to a market economy."[66]

From the beginning of the reform process, China's leaders were also motivated by a desire to enhance their nation's international power and prestige. Mao had secured a place at the superpower table through bluff, shrewd diplomacy, and acquisition of a rudimentary nuclear arsenal, but his successors knew that in virtually every meaningful measure of national strength, they lagged far behind the United States and even the Soviet Union. Closing the gap, and establishing China as a power to be reckoned with, would require a concerted, decades-long program of economic and technological "catch-up." Mao's policies had left China dangerously far behind; a change in direction was clearly necessary.

Deng's reforms initiated a period of "supergrowth" that continued unabated into the first decade of the twenty-first century.[67] Annual GDP growth rates increased to an average of just under 9 percent. Thanks to a simultaneous slowdown in birth rates, per capital incomes grew almost as fast, averaging around 7 percent per year.[68] China's exceptional performance permitted its economy to double in size roughly every eight years. Because it was expanding so much faster than the rest of the world's, China was able to increase its share of total world output from 5 percent at the start of reforms to 10 percent by the mid-1990s, to 13 percent by 2004.[69]

China's growth has propelled it upward through the ranks of the world's largest national economies. At the start of the twenty-first century, its GDP stood at number six, trailing Italy, France, Germany, Japan, and the United States. By 2005 it had surpassed Italy and France and was closing in on Germany.[70] By 2008, depending on the method of comparison used, China either was number three or had already overtaken Japan to move into the number two position.[71]

As for overtaking the United States, Western economists have recently been engaged in a kind of bidding war, with each prediction more jaw-dropping than the last. An oft-quoted 2003 study by Goldman Sachs identified 2041 as the year when China would overtake the United States. Five years later, economist Albert Keidel of the Carnegie Endowment set 2035 as the crossover point, and in the wake of the global financial crisis, Goldman wound its own clock back to 2027. In 2010 Nobel laureate Robert

Fogel raised the stakes even higher. By 2040 China not only will have long since surpassed the United States, but also its economy will be nearly three times as large and will account for fully 40 percent of total world output. "This," writes Fogel, "is what economic hegemony will look like."[72]

WILL CHINA CONTINUE TO RISE?

As these comments suggest, much recent commentary on China is guilty of what might be called "straightline-itis," the natural human tendency to assume that prevailing trends will continue indefinitely; some is characterized by "collapse-ism," the somewhat less common belief that what goes up must inevitably come down. While the second possibility cannot be ruled out, the first certainly can be. No country can sustain high growth rates forever. As development proceeds, previously underutilized resources are put to work, incomes and consumption rise, investment's share of national income falls, and growth slows. China too is subject to the laws of economic gravity; its upward trajectory will not always be as steep as it has been for the past thirty years.

In addition to the normal challenges of development, the list of special obstacles that China must surmount if it is to maintain its forward momentum is unusually long and daunting. In the relatively near term, Beijing will have to deal with the unintended consequences of a long-standing development strategy that has stimulated growth through huge fixed capital investments. Thanks in part to the government's attempts to sustain growth in the wake of the 2008–9 financial crisis and global recession, the magnitude of these investments in relation to GDP has now risen to levels that are without historical precedent. In Japan and South Korea, for example, investment topped out at less than 40 percent of GDP before those countries made the transition to slower, consumption-based growth. In China, by some estimates fixed investment now stands at 50 percent of GDP and may still be climbing. This is despite ample evidence that there is already massive excess capacity in many heavy-industry sectors, as well as in construction and commercial real estate. As suggested by Japan's experience in the 1990s, if not managed properly, bubbles of the sort that seem now to be inflating rapidly in China can burst and lead to bank failures, stubbornly low growth rates, and sustained high levels of unemployment.[73]

Even if Beijing dodges this particular bullet, there could well be others headed its way a few years further down the line. The small size of most Chinese families (in part due to the "one-child" population control policy of the 1980s and 1990s) means that the seemingly endless torrent of young people entering the workforce each year will soon begin to dwindle. As labor grows scarcer, wages will rise, exports will become more expensive, and China will begin to lose one of the advantages that have thus far fueled its exceptionally rapid growth. China's unusual demographic profile also means that a relatively small group of younger workers will soon have to bear the burden of supporting a much larger cohort of retirees. Increased spending on pensions and medical care will be necessary to maintain a decent society, but it will also divert some resources from investment in more productive activities.[74]

China's demographic patterns are only one of the potential obstacles to its continued progress. Years of unchecked growth have despoiled the country's natural environment, damaging the health of its people and running up a massive, unpaid bill for mitigation and cleanup. Thanks to an unwholesome mingling of business and politics, China's banks are weighed down with bad loans, leaving the nation's financial system fragile and badly in need of reform. The economy's continuing high levels of dependence on access to export markets and imported resources means that it is vulnerable to potential external shocks, whether a rise in protectionism due to a renewed global recession, or a jump in energy prices resulting from war in the Middle East. Fearful of turning millions out of work, the central government still wastes vast sums on unproductive state-owned enterprises. Indeed, in part as a result of its response to the recent global crisis, the weight of such enterprises in the economy has actually begun to increase. A lasting expansion in the state sector at the expense of privately owned enterprises could hurt long-term prospects for growth.[75] Chinese society is marked by deepening divisions between urban "haves" and rural "have-nots," and between a small number of ostentatiously wealthy, well-connected plutocrats and the modestly well-to-do middle class. And this is to say nothing of a pervasive culture of official corruption and a system of governance that commands neither wide respect nor deep loyalty.[76]

Whether as a result of the normal process of maturation, an accumulation of costly domestic problems, or some combination of the two, China's growth *will* slow down; the only questions are when and how quickly. The preferred path for China, and for the rest of the world, would obviously be a gradual, graceful reversion to the type of performance that is more typical of advanced industrial countries. But there are other possibilities. After decades of good fortune and nearly uninterrupted growth, China may yet experience a sharp economic crisis from which it will have great difficulty recovering. If that happens, the remarkable progress of recent decades could give way to social unrest and political upheaval, and the "Chinese century" that so many have predicted could be over before it really has a chance to get started.

Such pessimistic scenarios are not outside the realm of possibility, and they certainly warrant more serious consideration than they have generally received. For the moment, however, continued rise, albeit at a somewhat slower and perhaps less steady pace, seems a better bet than catastrophic decline. Indeed, barring some major setback, China will probably continue to grow for several more decades at rates well above those of the advanced industrial countries. If it does, then by the middle of this century, at the latest, its economy will indeed be the largest in the world. After a run of over 150 years, the United States will no longer be "number one."

Two

ROOTS OF RIVALRY

"PREDICTION IS DIFFICULT, ESPECIALLY ABOUT THE FUTURE"[1]

Suppose that China *does* continue to rise, further narrowing the gap in wealth, power, and influence that currently separates it from the United States. Over the course of the next several decades, what is likely to be the character of relations between the two Pacific powers? Will they be marked by rising levels of cooperation, trust, and stability? Or, to the contrary, by deepening mutual suspicions, increasingly open geopolitical competition, and a rising risk of war?

The answers to these questions are obviously of enormous importance. If Sino-American tensions continue to mount, all of Asia, and perhaps other regions as well, could be divided in a new cold war. Should this happen, the prospects of confrontation and conflict would certainly grow. On the other hand, a deepening U.S.-China entente would bring with it increased possibilities for stable, sustained worldwide economic growth, the peaceful resolution of outstanding regional disputes, and the successful management of pressing global problems including terrorism, climate change, and the proliferation of nuclear weapons.

As important as it will undoubtedly be, the future temper and tone of America's relationship with China is not merely unknown; it is also, at this point, unknowable. Despite the authority and assurance with which they typically make their pronouncements, no scholar, politician, pundit, intelligence analyst, or business guru has a computer model or theory or crystal ball capable of peering accurately even one year ahead, to say nothing of ten or twenty. Politics is simply too complex and contingent a business to permit precise predictions of this kind.

One thing is certain, however: whatever its character, tomorrow's relationship between the United States and China will be the product of many contending factors and forces. Some, such as the high levels of trade and investment that currently link the two economies, may continue, on balance, to promote cooperation and peace. Others, such as the mistrust and miscalculations that almost always accompany rapid shifts in the balance of world power, will probably push the two states toward greater competition and a heightened risk of open conflict. Those who make confident predictions about the future generally assume that one or the other of these factors will be so strong as to outweigh all the rest. Thus, so-called realists believe that the competitive dynamics of great-power politics will overwhelm the cooperative impulses associated with international trade, while "liberals" typically believe the opposite.

Reality is rarely that simple, and it is certainly not in this case. In fact, a variety of contending forces are at work simultaneously. Trying to anticipate the future shape of Sino-American relations requires first identifying the most important of these forces, then assessing their relative weights, and finally making judgments about how they are likely to combine with one another to determine the overall direction of events. This kind of analysis is an inexact science, to say the least, and because it focuses attention on things that are observable and measurable (like trade flows and arms budgets), it tends to underestimate the impact of personalities, unforeseeable errors, and random occurences. Still, an attempt to take account of at least some of the many influences at play is far preferable to the usual single-factor, straight-line projections.[2]

In the rest of this chapter I provide my own assessment of seven distinct factors that various observers have identified as important in shaping the evolution of Sino-American relations. Of these, two (the narrowing gap in national power and the continuing deep differences in their ideologies and domestic political structures) will tend to push the United States and China toward intensified competition, while the other five (economic interdependence, the possible evolution of China toward liberal democracy, its ongoing integration into a web of international institutions, the presence of common threats, and the existence of nuclear weapons) are generally seen as favoring cooperation and peace.

In my judgment, the first two factors are stronger and more deeply rooted than is widely assumed, and they also tend to reinforce one another in important and potentially dangerous ways. Of the five peace-inducing factors, by contrast, two (the benefits of continued trade and the risk of nuclear war) can help to damp down the escalating Sino-American rivalry, but are not going to be sufficient, in themselves, to reverse it. (Contrary to widespread expectations, economic issues may also turn out to be an increasingly important source of bilateral friction.) Neither China's participation in international institutions nor the presumed existence of common dangers such as terrorism or climate change shows any signs of promoting deep and lasting cooperation with the United States. In the long run, I believe that only one factor (the possible political liberalization of China) has the potential to push the relationship decisively toward a stable and lasting peace.

All of which points to the following clear, if conditional prediction: if China's power continues to grow, and if it continues to be ruled by a one-party authoritarian regime, its relations with the United States are going to become increasingly tense and competitive. That is the path along which events are presently proceeding, and like it or not, it is the future for which America and its allies have no choice but to prepare.

THE NARROWING POWER GAP

The history of relations among great powers is a story of persistent rivalry and recurrent warfare, punctuated by occasional, usually brief, periods of peace. Every conflict has its particular causes, of course, but the deeper reason for this pattern is the fact that in contrast to what generally goes on *within* countries (at least those that are not caught up in civil war), in international affairs no one is really in charge. There is no "sovereign," no world government or global dictator stronger than any state or combination of states, and therefore capable of resolving disputes, imposing order, and keeping peace among them.

In the absence of a higher power, states are always, in some measure, insecure. Those that have the resources to do so will generally try to increase their military capabilities so as to reduce their vulnerability to coercion and attack (or, if they have expansive aims, to better enable them to defeat and subdue their rivals). Both strong and weak states may also enter into alliances intended to fend off potential enemies, or to overwhelm opposing powers or coalitions. The mistrust, military buildups, and diplomatic maneuvering that have long characterized politics among nations can sometimes result in periods of dynamic balance and tenuous stability. As recently as the middle of the last century, however, these intervals have always broken down eventually, giving way to major wars.[3]

As we shall see in a moment, there may be features of today's world (such as the destructiveness of modern weapons, the deepening of international economic interdependence, and the existence of international institutions) that increase the long-term prospects for peace. To judge from their behavior, however, none of the contemporary great powers (including China, the United States, Japan, India, and Russia) is yet prepared to place its faith entirely in such expedients. All continue to look to their own defenses and to pursue diplomatic strategies that would be familiar to the statesmen of earlier eras, from Bismarck to Castlereagh to Pericles. Insecurity continues to be the defining feature of international life. Even if great-power war is a thing of the past, great-power rivalry certainly is not.

The fact that there are competitive elements to the relationship between China and the United States therefore comes as no surprise. But these countries are not just any two great powers; their relative positions in the international system make them especially prone to regard one another as rivals. Since the end of the Cold War, the United States has been by any measure the richest and most powerful country in the world. China is, by contrast, the nation whose capabilities have been growing most rapidly. World history is replete with examples of the troubled, often violent, relations between fast-rising states and their once-dominant rivals. Indeed, this storyline, with its Shakespearean overtones of youth and age, vigor and decline, is among the oldest in recorded history. As far back as the fifth century BCE the great Greek historian Thucydides began his study of the Peloponnesian War with the deceptively simple observation that the war's deepest, truest cause was "the growth of Athenian power and the fear which this caused in Sparta."[4]

At least insofar as their more established counterparts are concerned, rising powers tend to be troublemakers. As a state's capabilities grow, its leaders generally define their interests more expansively and seek a greater degree of influence over what is going on around them. Rising powers typically attempt not only to secure their borders but also to reach out beyond them, taking steps to ensure access to markets, materials, and transportation routes; to protect their citizens far from home and defend their foreign friends and allies; to promulgate their religious or ideological beliefs; and, in general, to have what they consider to be their rightful say in the affairs of their region and of the wider world.[5]

As they begin to assert themselves, rising powers usually feel impelled to challenge territorial boundaries, international institutions, and hierarchies of prestige that were put in place when they were still relatively weak. Their leaders and people typically feel that they were left out unfairly when the pie was divided up, and may even believe that because of prior weakness, they were robbed of what ought to be theirs. Like Japan starting in the late nineteenth century, or Germany at the turn of the twentieth century, rising powers tend to want their "place in the sun." This is what typically brings them into conflict with the established great powers, which are the architects, principal beneficiaries, and main defenders of any existing international system.

The clash of interests between rising and status quo powers can be dealt with in a number of ways, but the resulting disputes have seldom been resolved peacefully. Recognizing the growing threat to their position, dominant powers (or a coalition of status quo powers) have occasionally tried to attack and destroy a rising state before it can grow strong enough to become a threat. On the other hand, some great powers have taken the opposite approach: trying to appease potential challengers, looking for ways to satisfy their demands and ambitions without conflict and seeking to incorporate them peacefully into an existing international order.[6]

However sincere, these efforts have almost always failed. Sometimes the reason is clearly the character of the demands of the rising state. As was true of Adolf Hitler's Germany, for example, a rising power may have ambitions that are so extensive as to be impossible for the status quo powers to satisfy without effectively consigning themselves to servitude or committing national suicide. Even when the demands being made of them are less onerous, the status quo powers are often either reluctant to make concessions, thereby fueling the frustrations and resentments of the rising power, or too eager to do so, feeding its ambitions and triggering a spiral of escalating demands. Successful policies of appeasement are conceivable in theory, but in practice they have proved devilishly difficult to implement. This is why periods of transition, when a new, rising power begins to overtake the previously dominant state, have so often been marked by war.[7]

Samuel Huntington points out that since the start of the nineteenth century, all emergent great powers have behaved in a similarly assertive, and often disruptive, fashion. As he notes, "The external expansion of the UK and France, Germany and Japan, the Soviet Union and the United States coincided with phases of intense industrialization and economic development." As for China, Huntington anticipated in the early 1990s that it too would "undoubtedly be moving into such a phase in the coming decades."[8] In a similar vein, political scientist John Mearsheimer has predicted that so long as its power continues to grow, China will seek to dominate its neighbors, its region, and, if it can, the world. As he puts it, "China, like all previous potential hegemons, [will] be strongly inclined to become a real hegemon."[9]

I will return to the question of China's long-term objectives in a later chapter. For now it is sufficient to note that they are unknown, and perhaps at this point only partially formed. If the behavior of other countries in similar situations is any guide, however, there is good reason to expect that China's ambitions will grow as its power expands. For their part, as they watch China become richer and stronger, American strategists cannot help but worry that at some point, it will begin to use its capabilities in ways that threaten U.S. interests. This concern introduces an irreducible element of wariness into American policy toward China. On the other hand, whatever actions Washington takes to shore up its position will tend to heighten Beijing's belief that the Americans are out to block its rise, deny its rightful claims, and prevent it from acquiring its place in the sun.

As we shall see, there is already ample evidence that this self-reinforcing dynamic of mutual suspicion is at work in the relationship between the two Pacific powers.

THE ENDURING IDEOLOGICAL DIVIDE

Deep-seated patterns of power politics are driving the United States and China toward mistrust and competition, if not yet toward open conflict. The fact that one is a liberal democracy while the other remains under authoritarian rule is a significant additional impetus to rivalry. The yawning ideological chasm that separates the two nations is both an obstacle to measures that might reduce uncertainty and dampen competition, and a source of mutual hostility and mistrust. Relations between democracies and non-democracies are always conducted in what political theorist Michael Doyle describes as an "atmosphere of suspicion," in part because of "the perception by liberal states that non-liberal states are in a permanent state of aggression against their own people."[10] Democracies, in short, regard non-democracies as less than legitimate because the latter do not enjoy the freely given consent of their own people. In their heart of hearts, most self-governing citizens simply do not believe that all states are created equal or that they are entitled to equal respect regardless of how they are ruled.

Seen in this light, disputes between the United States and China over such issues as censorship and religious freedom are not just superficial irritants that can be dissolved or wished away. They are instead symptomatic of much deeper difficulties. To most Americans, China's human rights violations are not only intrinsically wrong but also a powerful indicator of the true, morally distasteful (some would say "evil") nature of the Beijing regime. While the United States may be able to do business with such a government on at least some issues, the possibility of a warm, trusting, and stable relationship is remote, to say the least.

Moral judgments about domestic behavior aside, democracies also tend to regard non-democracies as inherently untrustworthy and dangerously prone to external aggression. Because of the secrecy in which their operations are cloaked, the intentions and often the full extent of the capabilities of non-democratic states are difficult to discern. In recent years U.S. officials have pressed their Chinese counterparts to be more "transparent" about defense spending, but there is little expectation that these pleas will yield meaningful results. Even if Beijing were suddenly to unleash a flood of information, American analysts would regard it with profound skepticism, scrutinizing it carefully for signs of deception and disinformation. And they would be right to do so; the centralized, tightly controlled Chinese government is far better able to carry off such schemes than its open, divided, and leaky American counterpart.

Their capacity for secrecy also makes it easier for non-democracies to use force without warning. Since 1949, China's rulers have shown a particular penchant for deception and surprise attack.[11] This tendency may reflect deep strains in Chinese strategic culture extending back to the great philosopher of war Sun Tzu, but it is also entirely consistent with the character of its current domestic regime. Indeed, for most American analysts the authoritarian nature of China's government is a far greater concern than its culture. If China were a democracy, the deep social and cultural foundations of its strategic and political behavior might be little changed, but American military planners would be much less worried that it might someday attempt a lightning strike on U.S. forces and bases in the Western Pacific.

Anxiety over their own lack of legitimacy at home can cause non-democratic governments to try to deflect popular frustration and discontent toward external enemies, real or imagined. Some Western observers fear, for example, that if China's economy falters, its rulers will try to blame foreigners and even to manufacture crises with Taiwan, Japan, or the United States in order to rally their people and redirect their anger. Whatever Beijing's intent, such confrontations could easily spiral out of control. Democratic leaders are not immune from the temptation of foreign adventures. However, because the stakes for them are so much lower (being voted out of office rather than being overthrown and imprisoned, or worse), they are probably less likely to take extreme risks to retain their hold on power.[12]

Ideology inclines the United States to be more suspicious and hostile toward China than it would be for strategic reasons alone. It also tends to reinforce Washington's willingness to help other democracies that feel threatened by Chinese power, even if this is not what a pure power political calculation of its interests might seem to demand. Thus the persistence, indeed the deepening of American support for Taiwan during the 1990s cannot be explained without reference to the fact that the island was evolving during that time from an authoritarian bastion of anticommunism, to a true liberal democracy. Severing the last U.S. ties to Taiwan would remove a major source of friction with China, and a potential cause of war. Such a move might even be conceivable if Taiwan still appeared to many Americans as it did in the 1970s, as an oppressive, corrupt dictatorship. But the fact that Taiwan is now seen as a genuine (if flawed) democracy will make it extremely difficult for the U.S. government to ever willingly cut it adrift.[13]

For Americans the success of a mainland regime that blends authoritarian rule with market-driven economics is a puzzle and an affront. Such a combination is not supposed to be possible, at least in the long run. Growth requires freedom of choice in the economic realm, which is supposed to lead ineluctably to the expansion of political freedoms. Aside from whatever philosophical discomfort it causes, China's continued growth under authoritarian rule could complicate and slow America's long-standing efforts to promote the spread of liberal political institutions around the world. The existence of an alternative model gives hope to antidemocratic holdouts that seemed, after the collapse of the Soviet Union, to be headed for the garbage heap of history. Washington's efforts to isolate, coerce, and possibly undermine dictatorial "rogue" states (such as Iran and North Korea) have already been complicated, if not defeated, by Beijing's willingness to engage with them. As China emerges onto the world stage, it is becoming a source of inspiration and material support for embattled authoritarians in the Middle East, Africa, and Latin America, as well as Asia.[14]

China's current rulers do not see themselves as they once did, as the leaders of a global revolutionary movement. But they do believe that they are engaged in an ideological struggle of sorts, albeit one in which, until very recently, they have been almost entirely on the defensive. While they regard Washington's professions of concern for human rights and individual liberties as cynical and opportunistic, China's leaders do not doubt that the United States is motivated by genuine ideological fervor. As seen from Beijing, the United States is a dangerous, crusading liberal quasi-imperialist power that will not rest until it imposes its views and its way of life on the entire planet. Anyone who does not grasp this need only read the speeches of top American officials, with their promises to "enlarge the sphere of democracy" and "rid the world of tyranny."[15]

Having watched it topple the Soviet Union through a combination of confrontation and subversion, China's strategists now fear that Washington aims to do the same to them. This belief colors Beijing's perceptions of virtually every aspect of U.S. policy, from its enthusiasm for economic engagement to its efforts to encourage the development of China's legal system. It also shapes leadership assessments of U.S. activities across Asia and informs China's own policies toward the region.

Fear of isolation may also play an increasing role in shaping China's policies toward countries in other parts of the world. If the United States can pressure and perhaps depose the current leaders of Venezuela, Zimbabwe, and Iran it may be emboldened in its efforts to do something similar to China. By helping those regimes survive, Beijing wins friends and allies for future struggles, weakens the perception that democracy is on the march, and deflects some of America's prodigious energies away from itself. At the same time, it also heightens concern in Washington about China's own ideological motivations and intentions, thereby adding more fuel to the competitive fire.

"CHIMERICA"?

If ideology and power politics were the only factors driving the United States and China, they would be much farther along toward an open, intense, and unchecked rivalry than they are at present. There are clearly other, constraining forces at play here. To date, however, these peace-inducing impulses have not proved to be nearly as potent, nor as consistent in their effects, as optimistic observers have hoped and predicted. While they may have prevented, or at least slowed, a sharp downward spiral in relations, they have thus far been insufficient to push the two nations irresistibly toward ever-greater cooperation and an ever-deepening peace.

Take trade, for example. Since Immanuel Kant's 1795 treatise on "Perpetual Peace," liberal theorists of international relations have argued that commerce among nations is a powerful force for peace. Cross-border exchange creates shared interests in stability. The greater the volume of trade and investment flowing between two countries, the more people on both sides should have a strong desire to avoid conflict.[16]

The United States and China are now putting these propositions to the test. The two countries are tied together as never before by flows of goods, services, capital, people, and ideas. Indeed, the connections between their respective economies have grown so numerous and so deep in recent years that some analysts have suggested that the two have effectively fused into a single organism known as "Chimerica."[17]

Is Chimerica a mythical beast or a real phenomenon? It is clearly true that since the end of the Cold War the gains from trade, and the prospect of still more to be had in the future, have been the strongest forces binding China and America together. If not for trade, many Americans would see little but danger in China's rise, and some in China would feel even more threatened by America's preponderance. Instead, in both countries, a wide swath of the political and business elite believes that keeping commercial channels open is crucial to national prosperity and, in many cases, to their own personal well-being. For this reason, if for no other, a stable, cooperative diplomatic climate is vital. At least for the moment, leading figures in both countries do not appear to need much convincing on these points.

Trade may continue to dampen any tendencies toward conflict and perhaps in time could help to draw the United States and China closer than they are today. But there are grounds for skepticism. Unfortunately, there is little reason in theory or historical experience to believe that economic links alone are sufficient to create lasting stability, still less perpetual peace.[18] Even if interdependence helps suppress mutual hostility, it will not necessarily constrain nations from engaging in various forms of competitive behavior, including arms races and the construction of opposing alliances. Such geopolitical maneuvering can lead to escalatory spirals of mistrust, a breakdown in political and economic relations, and even open conflict.

It is also sadly the case that governments are not always deterred by the prospect of economic loss. Leaders often underestimate the costs of their decisions, whether because they do not recognize that a certain course of action will lead to conflict or because they assume, mistakenly, that whatever trouble results will be short and minimally disruptive. Even if it means knowingly damaging the livelihood of powerful interest groups, or of an entire nation, rulers sometimes choose to put reasons of state above concerns for material well-being. One does not have to go very far afield to find potential illustrations of this point. China is bound even more tightly by economic ties to Taiwan than it is to the United States. Yet few observers doubt that Beijing would use force to prevent moves toward independence, despite the enormous direct costs of doing so, to say nothing of the possibility of economic sanctions, limited conventional conflict, and perhaps even a nuclear exchange with the United States.

History suggests that when the chips are down, politics trumps trade. Before the start of the First World War, Britain and Germany were major commercial partners.[19] But this did not stop Britain's leaders from seeing Germany's growing power as a threat to their colonial empire and, eventually, to the stability of Europe. Nor did it prevent the Kaiser and his advisors from concluding that Britain was intent on retaining its preponderant position and blocking Germany's rise. Strong economic ties could not slow the deterioration in Anglo-German relations that led eventually to war. To the contrary, by the turn of the twentieth century the growth in volume and quality of imported German manufactured goods was yet another factor fueling British fears of unfavorable long-term shifts in the balance of power.[20]

As this example suggests, economic interdependence is not always a cause of friendship and can, at times, become a major source of insecurity and friction.[21] Over the course of the past decade, this has clearly been the case in Sino-American relations. As China has grown, and as the extent of its entanglement with the United States has deepened, economic issues have become a cause of increasingly serious disputes between them. This was true even before the 2008–9 financial crisis and the worldwide recession that followed, and it has become even more so since.[22] In the 1990s expressions of anxiety about trade were mostly limited to the labor unions and older manufacturing industries that were the first to feel the pressure of inexpensive Chinese imports. As the volume of trade has exploded, however, and the gap between imports and exports has generally widened, these concerns have become more widespread.

The unprecedented magnitude of America's trade deficit with China has led to accusations that Beijing is gaining an unfair advantage by artificially suppressing the value of its currency. Since the turn of the century, exchange rate policy has been a regular and contentious topic in high-level meetings between U.S. and Chinese officials, with the Americans trying to persuade their counterparts to make adjustments through "jawboning," a diplomatic term for nagging. These efforts have met with only limited success. If the American economy is slow to recover from the aftereffects of the financial meltdown, and Beijing's exchange rate policies are seen to be at least partly to blame, the prospect of protectionism, retaliation, and a major U.S.-China diplomatic confrontation will grow.

The financial crisis has also drawn anxious attention to China's vast hoard of dollar-denominated assets. Beijing's willingness to buy endless quantities of American debt enabled the U.S. government to finance its budget deficits while keeping interest rates low and growth rates high. In the process it also helped pump up the real estate bubble whose bursting set off the global financial meltdown. These facts, and the unwholesome effects of some parts of the U.S.-China economic relationship, are clearer in retrospect than they were while the crisis was taking shape. Some observers now fear that China's financial holdings could give it leverage over U.S. foreign policy by allowing China to threaten to plunge the American economy into turmoil by dumping dollars, driving down their value and forcing interest rates to rise. For their part, Chinese experts worry that no matter what they do, the parlous state of America's finances could lead to a sudden drop in the value of the dollar, a shift that would erase a large part of the value of their assets virtually overnight.[23]

Some of the potential solutions to the present imbalances could cause yet more political problems. China could reduce its dollar holdings by investing some of them directly in the U.S. economy, but efforts by Chinese enterprises to purchase American oil and computer companies have already aroused controversy in the United States on national security grounds, and this, in turn, has fueled resentment in China. Even as Washington encourages Beijing to "recycle" some of its dollars, it will remain wary of Chinese investment. This ambivalence, with all that it implies about American attitudes toward China, could itself become a major source of irritation.[24]

This kind of situation is not without precedent. Relations between the United States and Japan were severely strained during the 1980s by disputes that bear some resemblance to those now emerging between the United States and China. By the end of the Cold War some writers were even suggesting that differences over economic issues might lead to a breakdown in the U.S.-Japan alliance and perhaps even to another Pacific war.[25] Despite these dire warnings, the damage was eventually contained, and the alliance emerged even stronger than it had been before. Part of the reason was economic: Japan's prolonged slump during the 1990s helped reduce trade frictions and ease U.S. fears of decline. But political and strategic factors were ultimately decisive. Whatever their differences over trade issues, American and Japanese policy makers continued to believe that they were bound together by common security concerns (first over the Soviet Union, then North Korea, and ultimately China), as well as a sense of shared democratic values. If the political foundations of the U.S.-Japan relationship had been weaker, trade disputes might well have caused it to collapse.

For the past twenty years, trade has helped hold the United States and China together, giving them time to build a stronger political basis for trust and cooperation. But the era of relative commercial harmony may now be coming to an end. If disputes over trade imbalances, exchange rates, investment flows, access to and control over scarce commodities become increasingly vituperative, even as other sources of mistrust and animosity are growing, the entire relationship could unravel with surprising speed.[26]

A DEMOCRATIC PEACE?

One of the most frequently cited reasons for optimism about Sino-American relations has been the widely held belief that, thanks largely to its rapid economic growth, China was on a fast track toward liberal democracy. If it is really true, as many political scientists believe, that democracies do not fight one another, then this transformation would greatly improve the prospects for peace. Although the process may take time, open conflict between America and a stable democratic China should eventually become as unthinkable as war among the members of the European Union appears to be today.[27]

Since the start of the economic reform process in the late 1970s, many observers have claimed that China was being carried inexorably toward democracy. There seemed to be ample historical justification for this view. Economic growth leads to rising per capita incomes and an expanding middle class. In Europe and North America in the eighteenth and nineteenth centuries, and more recently in places like South Korea and Taiwan, it is the middle classes who have been in the vanguard of the fight for political rights. These are people who are generally well educated, who have had a taste of economic freedom, and whose incomes allow them to do more than merely attend to the daily struggle for existence. China now has a sizable, fast-growing middle class. At some point, perhaps its members too will begin to play their historic role and demand political rights.

Some scholars have even been bold enough to predict precisely how long this transformation will take. In the mid-1990s economist Henry Rowen measured the level of GDP per capita at which other Asian countries had made the transition from authoritarianism. Drawing on their experience, and estimates of Chinese growth rates, Rowen calculated that the People's Republic of China would become a democracy by 2015.[28] Others have used different methods to reach somewhat less precise, but broadly similar judgments. Based on an analysis of the social and political forces at work, political scientist Bruce Gilley concludes that the Chinese Communist Party may "limp along through the first and perhaps even second decades of this century." However, by 2019 the CCP will have been in power for seventy years and will be approaching the "upper limit" of its life span.[29]

Such projections may yet be borne out by events. As I discuss more fully in chapter 8, the road to democracy is turning out to be longer and rockier than many had once hoped. Despite nearly three decades of exceptional economic growth, there is as yet no evidence of movement toward meaningful political reform. Although the government now permits ordinary citizens greater freedom to travel, choose their jobs, own property, and engage in at least certain forms of personal expression, it retains a stranglehold on political power and shows no sign of loosening up. Fundamental criticism of the party or the state (as opposed to complaints about particular policies or lower-ranking officials) is still forbidden, as is the formation of independent opposition parties. For now, at least, the ideological divide between China and the United States remains as wide as ever.

Even if China begins to narrow the gap by moving toward greater openness and expanded political competition, the very process of change could itself increase the risk of confrontation and conflict. Political scientists Edward Mansfield and Jack Snyder suggest that it is precisely when nations are in the midst of a transition from authoritarianism to democracy that they are most likely to pick fights with their neighbors. In such societies, pressure for political participation generally runs far ahead of the creation of democratic mechanisms for choosing leaders and sharing power. Faced with rising demands from those previously excluded, and eager to retain their own privileges, traditional elites often seek unity in appeals to "the nation" or "the people." Nationalism helps rulers to deflect popular frustrations, mobilize and channel mass support, forge coalitions among disparate groups, and win the backing of those who might otherwise seek their ouster. Strident patriotism is usually accompanied by the glorification of military power and by "the scapegoating of enemies of the nation, at home and abroad." These tendencies, in turn, can lead to heightened international tensions, and often to war.[30] If historical patterns are any guide, the early stages of democratization in China could be a time of heightened risk for the rest of the world. In short, as regards U.S.-China relations, things may get worse before they get better.

By the same token, if China ultimately succeeds in making the transition to stable, fully institutionalized liberal democracy, there is no reason to believe that its behavior will differ dramatically from the behavior of other states that have followed a similar path. Though it may be assertive, even obstreperous, a liberal democratic China will have little cause to fear its democratic counterparts, still less to use force against them. Because others are less likely to see it as a threat, a transformed China should find it easier to get along with Japan, India, and South Korea, among others, as well as with the United States. The relatively high levels of trust and mutual respect that eventually grow between democracies should increase the odds of attaining negotiated settlements of outstanding disputes over borders, offshore islands, and resources. A democratic government in Beijing would also stand a better chance of achieving a mutually acceptable resolution to its sixty-year standoff with Taiwan.[31]

All of these positive developments may lie ahead. For now, and probably for some time to come, the character of China's domestic political regime will continue to act as a stimulant to rivalry with the United States and its democratic partners rather than as a constraint.

A "RESPONSIBLE STAKEHOLDER"?

Prior to the end of the Cold War there were few multilateral institutions in East Asia, and China took a wary, standoffish attitude toward those that did exist. Since the early 1990s, however, everything has changed. Regional institutions of all descriptions have proliferated, and China has become an eager participant in many of them.[32] In addition to formal organizations like the Asia-Pacific Economic Cooperation (APEC) group and the Association of Southeast Asian Nations (ASEAN) Regional Forum, China now partakes in an expanding network of bilateral military-to-military talks and an even wider array of quasi-official security dialogues. Over the course of the 1990s, the PRC sought entry into several important global institutions, including the World Trade Organization and the nuclear nonproliferation regime and it also began to play a more active and prominent role in the United Nations.

The United States and China are being drawn into a thickening web of ties that go well beyond traditional, bilateral diplomatic channels. Optimists claim that this will facilitate communication, cooperation, and even trust, or at the very least, that it will reduce the likelihood of gross misperception. In recent years American policy makers have expressed the hope that China's increasing participation in international institutions will cause it to become a "responsible stakeholder," with a growing commitment to the stability and continuity of the existing global order.[33] This, in turn, should reduce the probability that it will act in ways that run counter to American interests.

The most enthusiastic advocates of multilateral institutions believe that in time, Chinese bureaucrats, diplomats, and political leaders who rub elbows regularly with their counterparts in such settings will be transformed by the experience. They will become "socialized," accepting and internalizing the prevailing norms and practices of the contemporary international system regarding the use of force, and the value of transparency, confidence-building measures, and arms control treaties.[34]

Institutions clearly have their uses. Established venues and habits of communication can help states to avoid unwanted confrontations or to manage crises when they arise. But the mere existence of multilateral mechanisms affords no guarantee that conflict can be avoided, provided the stakes are high enough. The fact that both the United States and China are members of the UN, or the ASEAN Regional Forum, or APEC will not keep the peace between them if, for example, Washington were to back a Taiwanese declaration of independence.

Nor is there any reason to believe that participation in institutions will, by itself, serve to dampen interstate rivalries. To the contrary, if the underlying geopolitical and ideological motives for competition are sufficiently strong, institutions themselves are likely to become just another venue for struggle. This was certainly the way in which the United States and the Soviet Union came to regard the United Nations during the Cold War. While the United States and China are nowhere close to this level of open rivalry at present, there are clearly competitive elements in their approach to the various organizations and groupings that have sprung up across Asia in recent years.

One reason for Beijing's recent enthusiasm for regional institutions is its evident desire to ensure that they cannot be used as platforms to criticize China or to contain its rise. Playing the role of good institutional citizen is also a low-cost way for Beijing to reduce regional anxieties about its long-term objectives and, where possible, to draw a distinction between its own commitment to multilateral cooperation and Washington's alleged unilateralism, or its preference for old-fashioned, Cold War–style bilateral military alliances. Whatever else can be said of it, as I explain in chapter 7, China's embrace of institutions is clearly part of its larger strategy for dealing with the United States.

As long as China remains relatively weak, an accommodating approach makes a great deal of sense. Whether, as it becomes stronger, Beijing will be as solicitous of its smaller neighbors, or as concerned about their opinions, remains to be seen. A more powerful China may well decide to shake off the constraints imposed by its membership in existing institutions or to abandon them altogether. Like other rising great powers, it will ultimately seek to alter the existing institutional architecture in ways that are more conducive to its interests.

The notion that China's participation in international institutions is helping to "socialize" its elites and to bring them around to what are essentially Western liberal internationalist modes of thinking about world politics smacks of self-congratulation, if not self-delusion.[35] China's leaders are the inheritors of a tradition of statecraft that has been in the making for thousands of years. To believe that they will simply abandon old concepts and categories and adopt new ones of foreign origin seems fanciful. Even if some of the "new thinking" diplomats and academics with whom Westerners most often interact have, in fact, made this leap, others in the Chinese system, especially those in the military, domestic security, and intelligence services, likely lag behind. Perhaps it is only a matter of time before these less visible and less accessible "old thinkers" catch up. In the meantime, their more traditional views will continue to exert a substantial, perhaps decisive, impact on policy. Indeed, it may be that the "new thinkers" represent only a thin outer crust, beneath which lies the deep accumulated bedrock of conservative Chinese realism. Eroding that with a steady drip of dialogue could take a very long time indeed.

COMMON THREATS?

What brought the United States and China together initially in the late 1960s was not economic interdependence, or institutions, or common values, but rather a convergence of interest caused by the existence of a common enemy. With the demise of the Soviet Union, pundits and policy makers on both sides have cast about for some new threat that could take its place as a force that would bind the two powers together. Among the most prominent possibilities are the proliferation of weapons of mass destruction, Islamist terrorism, global warming, energy security, and deadly emerging diseases. Perhaps one of these, or several of them in combination, will someday prove sufficiently threatening to force the United

States and China into closer cooperation, regardless of their mutual suspicions and animosities, and no matter what goes on between them in the
economic domain.

At least to date, this has not happened. While Washington and Beijing
see each of these challenges as a potential danger to their interests, they
have yet to achieve a consensus on the precise nature and magnitude of the
threat, differ on the priority they attach to dealing with it, and disagree
about the best strategies for doing so. Indeed, albeit to varying degrees,
these new problems have themselves become issues of contention rather
than simply sources of deeper cooperation.

The real problem in U.S.-China relations is not the absence of cooperation on specific issues, but rather the underlying divergence of interests
and the tensions and mutual mistrust that make cooperation so difficult
in the first place. Even if collaboration proves possible on climate change,
or piracy, or any of the other "nontraditional" security challenges, it does
not follow that traditional geopolitical concerns, or long-standing ideological differences, will dissolve as a result. What seems more likely is that
instances of cooperation will remain limited, isolated elements in a larger
relationship that continues to be heavily colored by competition.

NUCLEAR WEAPONS?

One final factor that could help to keep a U.S.-China rivalry within
bounds is their mutual possession of nuclear weapons. Because an armed
conflict between them could lead to unimaginable destruction, both will
presumably act with an abundance of caution and restraint. Fear of where
a direct military showdown might lead will make both Washington and
Beijing extremely wary about getting into one in the first place, and even
about making the kinds of threats or aggressive moves that could lead to
unintended escalation.[36] According to Avery Goldstein, nuclear weapons
provide "the strongest reasons to expect that the dangers associated with
China's arrival as a full-fledged great power will be limited." As regards
the relationship between the United States and the PRC, in particular,
Goldstein argues that the two powers have already entered into a relationship of mutual deterrence that "provide[s] not only a robust buffer against

general war, but also a strong constraint on both limited war and crisis behavior."[37]

The history of the Cold War is not entirely reassuring on these points. While it is true that the United States and the Soviet Union managed to avoid a nuclear conflagration, there were times when they came terrifyingly close. That their forty-year face-off ended peacefully owes at least as much to luck as it does to the rationality and good judgment of leaders on both sides. The threat of mutual annihilation did not prevent the superpowers from engaging in some extremely dangerous behavior, including operational procedures for handling nuclear weapons that might have led to unauthorized launches or accidents, alerts and exercises that could have been misconstrued as preparations for war, deliberately provocative flights by reconnaissance aircraft meant to test the capabilities of enemy warning systems, and support for allies who could have dragged the superpowers into war on their behalf.[38]

Nor did the nuclear stalemate that eventually developed between them prevent the United States and the Soviet Union from engaging in a protracted and expensive competition across a wide range of fronts. Even when it appeared that they had reached the point of diminishing returns, the superpowers continued to pour huge sums into their nuclear rivalry, procuring ever-more sophisticated ballistic missiles, bombers, submarines, and missile defenses. The fact that the two had reached a state of rough nuclear parity became, in itself, a justification for spending even more money on conventional weapons, on the grounds that if nuclear weapons canceled each other out, nonnuclear conflict might actually be more likely. And this is to say nothing of the resources both sides devoted to propaganda, espionage, insurgencies, counterinsurgencies, and the support of friends and allies around the world.

The specter of nuclear devastation may make war between the United States and China less likely, even if it does not render it unthinkable. But the existence of nuclear weapons can do little to quell a military competition between the two Pacific powers and could even encourage it in certain respects.

A FRAGILE BALANCE

Today's Sino-American rivalry is rooted in deep ideological differences and in the stubborn realities of power politics. At least for the moment, however, these forces are counterbalanced and, to a degree, offset by others that tend to promote cooperation and a measure of stability. Of these the presumed benefits of economic interdependence and the likely costs of conflict are the most powerful. The supposed cooperation-inducing effects of institutions and common threats appear, by contrast, to have been greatly overstated.

For as long as they remain as strong as they are today, the fear of war and the hope of continued gains from trade may be enough to make both the United States and China extremely cautious about using force directly against one another, taking steps that could lead to the use of force, or initiating policies that would greatly increase the risk of a breakdown in relations. Whether by themselves or in combination with others, however, these factors will not be sufficient to fundamentally transform the U.S.-China relationship. For that, a change in China's domestic regime will be necessary. While they might induce some initial instability, liberalizing reforms would eventually ease or eliminate ideology as a driver of competition, enhance the prospects for cooperation in dealing with a variety of issues, from trade to proliferation, and reduce the risk that future disputes might escalate to war.

The balance that exists at present between the forces favoring competition and those tending toward cooperation is fragile. While it is possible to imagine circumstances in which relations between China and America could move suddenly in a more positive direction (e.g., the emergence of a Gorbachev-style reformer in Beijing), sharp shifts toward more open rivalry (due to a clash over Taiwan, or Korea, or events in South Asia or off the coasts of Japan) are also conceivable. Barring such dramatic events, if China's power continues to grow while its regime remains essentially unchanged, the competitive aspects of the Sino-American relationship will increase in importance and intensity. Cooperation may persist, but it is likely to become more limited and more difficult, while the relationship as a whole becomes increasingly brittle.

Three

FROM CONTAINMENT
TO ALIGNMENT

POWER AND PRINCIPLE

To this point I have been speaking mainly of the big, material forces that are usually seen as the engines of history. In the end, however, the rise and fall of great powers and the ebb and flow of relations among nations are not solely the predictable end product of such impersonal forces. The course of events is determined as well by the perceptions (and misperceptions) of leaders, the struggles of domestic interest groups, and the strategies (however imperfectly conceived and implemented) of governments. Karl Marx, a theorist not usually noted for his belief in free will, put it best: "Men make their own history, but they do not make it just as they please."[1]

I want to change analytic altitude now and drop down from a "35,000 foot level" survey of broad trends and abstract theories to a much closer examination of actual deliberations, decisions, and strategies. This chapter and the next four are devoted to analyzing the origins, evolution, and current status of America's China policy (this chapter and chapter 4) and of China's strategy for dealing with the United States (chapters 5, 6, and 7). In the first instance I look all the way back to the founding of the People's Republic; in the second I focus somewhat more narrowly on the period since the end of the Cold War.

The United States' China policy has now passed through three distinct twenty-year phases. In the first phase, extending from shortly after the creation of the People's Republic to the inauguration of Richard Nixon, the United States sought to isolate and contain China from without, while undermining and weakening it from within. This was a policy of nearly pure competition with virtually no elements of cooperation.

In 1969 Washington began to reverse course, and over the next twenty years, the policy pendulum swung far in the opposite direction. During this period the United States entered into an increasingly close and collaborative strategic alignment with the same country it had once feared and reviled. While they did not go so far as to form a true alliance with China against the Soviet Union, as some might have preferred, American policy makers did greatly expand the scope of cooperation while easing back on some of the more aggressive aspects of the previous strategy of containment.

For the past two decades, from 1989 to the present, successive U.S. administrations have sought to blend elements of both cooperation and competition into a single strategy. On the one hand, the United States has continued to engage China through trade and diplomacy. On the other, it has taken steps aimed, not at containing Beijing as it did during the Cold War, but rather at maintaining a balance of power in Asia that continues to favor the interests of the United States and its regional allies, even as China grows richer, stronger, and more influential. This mixture, which I discuss in the next chapter, has sometimes been referred to as a policy of "congagement." The question now confronting American strategists is whether, in light of China's remarkable rise, such an approach can be sustained for much longer.

Shifts in U.S. strategy have been driven by dramatic events: China's entry into the war in Korea in 1950, sharp Sino-Soviet border clashes in 1969, and the mass killing of students at Tiananmen Square and the nearly contemporaneous collapse of the Berlin Wall twenty years later. This is not to say that U.S. policy has been entirely reactive. Especially in the case of the move from containment to alignment, top decision makers seized on events to promote changes that they had already come to see as desirable. Still, in this area, as in most other domains of both foreign and domestic policy, the American system of government is remarkable more for its inertial qualities than for its flexibility. If history is any guide, the next big change in U.S.-China strategy will be preceded by some substantial, unanticipated event.

Despite how it has often been described, America's approach to China has never been a matter of pure power political calculation, nor of unyielding ideological obsession; rather it has always contained a mix of these two elements. If the United States was a traditional great power (or, at least, the sort of bloodless "rational actor" that contemporary theorists of international relations imagine such powers to be), it would have tried harder to split China from the Soviet Union in the early years of the Cold War, and it would almost certainly have gone further and faster in forming an outright anti-Soviet alliance with China in the 1970s and 1980s. A traditional great power, focused only on material capabilities, and indifferent to the current and possible future domestic political orientation of other nations, would no doubt be hard at work today trying to block China's rise. By the same token, leaders whose every decision was determined by considerations of ideological purity would never have moved to establish contact with Beijing in the first place.

CONTAINMENT: 1949–69

Twenty years before Richard Nixon and Henry Kissinger made their first overtures to Beijing, the United States briefly considered, but then quickly abandoned, a pure *realpolitik* policy of playing China off against the Soviet Union. Instead, following the PRC's entry into the Korean War, Washington shifted toward a strategy of attempting to contain both halves of what was assumed to be a unified Sino-Soviet alliance.

With Japan's surrender in August 1945, the twenty-year civil war between Communist and Nationalist Chinese forces entered its terminal phase. After suffering a series of devastating defeats, the battered remnants of the Nationalist (Kuomintang or KMT) armies fled to Taiwan, together with their leader Generalissimo Chiang Kai-shek. Meanwhile, on the mainland, Communist Party Chairman Mao Zedong entered Beijing as a conquering hero, declared the founding of the People's Republic, and proceeded to consolidate control over his war-ravaged country.

American strategists watched these developments with a mix of dismay and fatalistic detachment. While they would certainly have preferred that China not fall under Communist control, most had long since lost faith in Chiang's abilities as a military commander and political leader. The

Nationalists continued to have powerful friends in Congress, but Chiang's arrogance and authoritarianism, the corruption of his associates, and the poor performance of his forces in the field combined to make him deeply unpopular with U.S. officials who had to work with him on a day-to-day basis.[2]

As the civil war neared its inevitable climax, the State Department concluded that events in China were being shaped by "tremendous, deep-flowing indigenous forces which are beyond our power to control." While some military planners hoped that Chiang's position could be shored up with additional increments of aid, civilian experts warned that this was wishful thinking. It was now "abundantly clear" that the Nationalists lacked "the political dynamism to win out." Clinging to Chiang meant throwing good money after bad, but it would also limit Washington's freedom of maneuver. "The tide is against us," concluded the authors of an October 1948 planning paper. The time had come to stand back, let the revolution run its course, and formulate a fresh approach to dealing with China and securing America's interests in Asia.[3]

The essential features of this new policy were laid out at the end of 1949 in a paper entitled "The Position of the United States with Respect to Asia." According to the authors, the fundamental aim of American strategy must remain what it had been since the turn of the twentieth century and the days of the "Open Door" policy: to prevent "the domination of Asia by a nation or coalition of nations capable of exploiting the region for purpose of self-aggrandizement."[4] Despite its volatility and backwardness, Asia was home to vast human and natural resources. If a substantial portion of these could be mobilized and controlled by a hostile power, the security of the rest of the region, and indeed of the United States, would be at risk.

In Asia, as in Europe, it was the Soviet Union that threatened to become the regional hegemon. Here too the war had weakened Moscow's traditional enemies, leaving it free to expand its influence and extend its strategic frontiers. With the defeat of Japan, the establishment of a friendly regime in China, and the movement of Soviet forces into northern Korea, Sakhalin, and the Kurile Islands, the USSR had become "an Asiatic power of the first magnitude with expanding influence and interests extending throughout continental Asia and into the Pacific."[5]

In order to block further Soviet expansion, the United States would have to establish an off-shore defensive perimeter running from Japan in the north, down through the Ryukyu island chain (of which Okinawa was the largest, farthest west, and of greatest strategic significance) to the Philippines. This would keep Japan's economy, "the key to the development of a self-sufficient war-making complex in the Far East," out of hostile hands, while also creating a series of island strong points that the United States could defend at reasonable cost with its unsurpassed air and naval capabilities.[6]

Moving inland from the shores of the Pacific, however, America's ability to project superior military power dwindled rapidly and then disappeared. On the Asian mainland it would therefore be necessary to rely on economic and diplomatic instruments to combat the Soviet Union's efforts to extend and consolidate its sphere. Notwithstanding the disturbing course of recent events in China, the planners back in Washington believed that they might have a hidden, and potentially decisive, long-term advantage. There was a chance that the most powerful ideological force in postwar Asia would turn out not to be communism but rather nationalism, as expressed in the desire of people throughout the region to throw off colonial rule and rid themselves of foreign domination in all its forms. If the United States could somehow get on the right side of this world-historical trend, distancing itself from its imperialist European allies, and identifying "its own cause with that of the Asian peoples," it could help shape a region that was congenial to American interests and resistant to Soviet expansionism.[7]

As the self-proclaimed headquarters of international communism, Moscow was supportive of revolutionary, anticolonial movements, but it demanded fealty, subordination, and ideological conformity in return. It was therefore reasonable to expect that frictions would arise eventually between "Asiatic nationalisms and USSR imperialism."[8] If the Kremlin tried to control China in the same way as it had already established quasi-imperial rule over its new European satellites, the reaction would redound to Washington's benefit. Just as Tito had done in Yugoslavia, Mao or his successors would seek to shake off Moscow's influence, thereby weakening its overall position in Asia.

To hasten this development the United States needed to disentangle itself, once and for all, from China's civil war. Sending troops to save Taiwan would cast America in the role of the imperialist villain, and give the Beijing regime a cause with which to "rally almost unanimous public sentiment behind them." It was better to stand aside and leave Chiang Kai-shek to his fate. Once the Nationalists were out of the picture, the United States could establish formal diplomatic relations with Beijing and move ahead with its plans to woo China away from the Soviet Union.[9]

Any possibility of an early opening to China was swept aside within months of the start of the Korean War. Despite the fact that South Korea clearly lay outside the defensive perimeter identified by U.S. officials, President Harry Truman decided immediately that he could not stand by and allow it to be conquered by the invading armies of the Communist North. American forces, led by General Douglas MacArthur, intervened and drove the attackers back across the dividing line that had been drawn through the middle of the Korean peninsula at the end of the Second World War. Eager to deal a devastating defeat to international communism, Mac-Arthur proceeded to push north toward the Chinese border. But Chairman Mao had plans for a stunning blow of his own. As the Americans drew close to the Yalu River, Mao marshaled his forces in secret on the other side, then sent them south in a massive surprise attack. By the end of the year American and Chinese troops were locked in bloody combat across the breadth of the Korean peninsula. Back in Washington, attitudes toward China hardened overnight, those who had earlier advocated an attempt at diplomatic outreach were denounced as naive at best, if not secretly sympathetic to communism, and U.S. strategy congealed into the form it would retain for the better part of the next two decades.[10]

From 1950 onward, the United States practiced a form of containment toward China that was in many respects even tougher and more unyielding than its approach to the Soviet Union. Instead of potential antagonists, the two Communist giants were now seen as partners in what would be referred to henceforth as the "Sino-Soviet bloc"; they were presumed to be allies, joined at the hip by a shared revolutionary ideology and committed to using force and subversion to spread Marxist-Leninist dogma. The strategy of containment thus needed to be applied equally at either end of the Eurasian landmass. In the case of China, however, the United States refused even to acknowledge the legal existence of the Communist government in Beijing. This policy of "non-recognition" was sometimes carried to the point of seeming absurdity, as when Secretary of State John Foster Dulles ostentatiously refused to shake the hand of his counterpart, Zhou Enlai, and instructed all American participants in the 1954 Geneva Conference to "ignore at all times the presence and existence of the Chinese delegation."[11]

While it may appear gratuitous, even childish, such behavior did have a serious strategic purpose and some real diplomatic consequences. If other countries followed suit (as, for a time, many did), the People's Republic could be denied the status and legitimacy of a sovereign state, barred from membership in the United Nations, and prevented from acquiring what U.S. planners referred to as an aura of "prestige and permanence."[12] China was to be treated as a pariah, or what in later American parlance would be called a "rogue state." Walled off and forced to live on the fringes of international society, the Beijing regime would eventually either collapse from within or abandon its revolutionary challenge to the existing international order. In the meantime, the refusal of the United States to recognize "Red China" meant that official contacts between the two were few and furtive, and direct, high-level communication between their governments virtually nonexistent. For the better part of the next two decades, mid-ranking American and Chinese officials met one another only sporadically in Geneva, then in Warsaw, and their exchanges were limited to technical matters involving the repatriation of prisoners and seized assets.[13]

There is no question but that the Eisenhower administration's attitude toward China was rooted in ideological animus. To conclude, however, that American policy during the 1950s and early 1960s was characterized primarily by "strident moralism," and "an intensely emotional reaction" to Chinese Communism, or to describe it as "a runaway locomotive," is to overlook its underlying geopolitical logic.[14] While its ultimate goal proved unattainable, Washington's refusal to engage with Beijing was part of a coherent, integrated strategy that aimed to slow the growth of China's power, to compel it to expend more resources on maintaining domestic order, and, albeit indirectly, to provoke tensions with its Soviet ally.

At the same time as it sought to isolate China diplomatically, the United States also worked to build a physical cordon around it by establishing a network of alliances and bases to the east and south. By the mid-1950s

Washington had signed mutual defense pacts with Australia and New Zealand (1951), the Philippines (1951), South Korea (1953), and its newly rediscovered friends on Taiwan (1954), as well as with its former Japanese enemies (1951). Seeking to replicate its success in establishing the North Atlantic Treaty Organization (NATO) in Western Europe, in 1954 the United States also launched the Southeast Asia Treaty Organization (SEATO), whose members included local allies (Australia, New Zealand, the Philippines, Thailand, Pakistand, and Taiwan) and European partners with Asian interests (Great Britain and France). Together with the Central Treaty Organization (CENTO), composed of Turkey, Iran, Iraq, Pakistan, and Great Britain, SEATO was intended to form the eastern flank of an unbroken chain of alliances extending around the perimeter of Eurasia.

While SEATO and CENTO boasted impressively long lists of members, divergences of interest and the lack of a shared strategic vision quickly rendered them ineffectual and then irrelevant. In Asia, as compared to Europe, the work of containment would have to be done on a bilateral basis, with Washington cooperating with a series of separate local partners. Because most of these countries were either underdeveloped or recovering from the effects of war, or both, their most significant contribution during the early years of the Cold War was to permit the American military to maintain naval and air bases, ground force garrisons, and intelligence collection facilities on their soil. Prior to World War II the Philippines had marked the westernmost extension of American power in the Pacific, linked by a thin tail of tiny American-owned islands (Guam, Wake, and Midway) to Hawaii and back to the mainland. Now the United States occupied positions running north to south all along China's coast, including massive air and naval bases in the Philippines, Okinawa, South Korea, and the Japanese home islands. By the early 1950s America's military predominance in the Western Pacific was unquestioned. Indeed, at least insofar as air and naval capabilities were concerned, it was, for all intents and purposes, unchallenged.

Despite the chastening experience of Korea, there were still some in Washington who longed for a second chance to confront and defeat Beijing. Largely to appease the more aggressive elements in his own party, during his 1952 presidential campaign Dwight Eisenhower had flirted with the notion that if elected, he would seek to "roll back" Communist

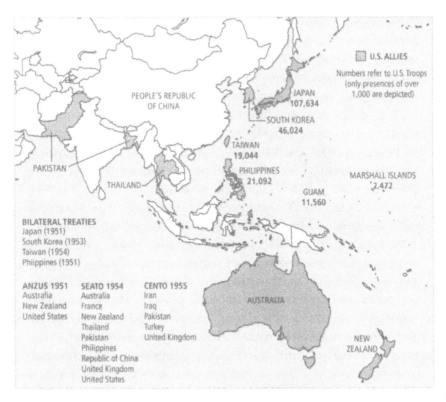

U.S. Alliances and Troop Deployments in Asia, 1958.
Deployment statistics from Department of Defense and Heritage Foundation.

advances in Europe and Asia rather than being content merely to contain them. Once in office, however, Eisenhower made very clear to his subordinates that he was unwilling to run the risks that such an aggressive policy would have entailed. This caution is reflected in NSC 166/1, the new administration's definitive statement of its policy toward China, circulated in November 1953. In a notable departure from the usual format and "can-do" tone of such documents, this one opened with a list of options that were regarded as "currently unacceptable." Above all, the United States would not commit its own armed forces to the "overthrow or replacement of the Chinese government regime," nor would it provide support to "the Chinese government on Formosa [Taiwan]" to achieve this goal. Either course of action would likely lead to a dangerous transfer of American forces from Europe to Asia, the possible use of "a significant proportion of the U.S. atomic stockpile," and the "very high risk" of Soviet intervention and rapid escalation to "global war."[15]

What the United States *would* do, in addition to augmenting its own capabilities and building up China's non-Communist neighbors, was take steps aimed at "weakening or at least retarding the growth of Chinese Communist power *in China*" (emphasis added). Some of these measures, such as support for irregular military operations inside the PRC, would have to be "unconventional and covert." There was already a precedent for such action. During the Korean War the CIA had helped Nationalist commandos conduct raids against targets along China's coast and on off-shore islands under the mainland's control. The purpose of these pinprick attacks was to do some limited economic damage, force Beijing to devote resources to coastal defense and internal security, and, above all, make the Communist regime look weak and ineffectual, thereby encouraging further resistance from within. Shortly after the Korean armistice, Eisenhower authorized continued support for Taiwanese raids on the mainland and against "seaborne commerce with Communist China."[16]

By the mid-1950s the CIA was also providing arms, training, and logistical support to indigenous guerrillas seeking to expel Chinese forces from Tibet. This covert campaign would continue into the early 1970s. Once again, American decision makers had few illusions about the prospects for victory, but they wanted to find ways of harassing Beijing, forcing it to pay a price to maintain domestic stability and retaliating in kind for its support of Communist guerrilla movements throughout Southeast Asia.[17]

In addition to possible internal fissures, postrevolutionary China's economic backwardness presented another vulnerability that appeared ripe for exploitation. Despite some early signs of the Communist government's success in restoring agricultural production and beginning to invest in industry, American analysts were skeptical that China could ever succeed in becoming a major economic power. In addition to the counterproductive policies being pursued by its rulers, the sheer size of China's population and its relative lack of natural resources seemed certain to hold it back, perhaps indefinitely. The new regime's prospects were assumed, in any event, to heavily depend on its ability to acquire foreign capital and technology. China was in desperate need of machine tools, precision instruments, metals, chemicals, and engineering know-how with which to jump-start its own belated industrial revolution. If the United States and the other Western nations worked together to deny these things, they could impose "difficulty and some delay on Chinese Communist attempts at large scale industrialization." At a minimum, an effective economic embargo would slow and complicate Beijing's ability to expand its military capabilities.[18]

While some government officials feared that an embargo would simply force the Soviet Union and China even closer together, the prevailing assessment was more optimistic. Because the USSR and its East European satellites had their own postwar reconstruction problems to deal with, they were unlikely to be able to meet China's needs by themselves. To the extent that the Chinese saw the Soviet Union as a disappointment, and the Soviets came to regard China as a burden, tensions between the two were likely to rise. It might still be possible to drive a wedge between Moscow and Beijing, albeit now by further isolating and pressuring China, rather than by reaching out to it with warm words and olive branches.

Starting in 1950, Washington imposed what amounted to a total embargo on trade with China and urged its allies to follow suit. In addition to barring exports of petroleum and any machinery or materials that could be used in arms production, the United States sought to deny China access to international financial and shipping services. The importation of Chinese products was also banned on the theory that this would deprive the Beijing regime of foreign exchange earnings that it could use to do business with other countries.

Although some of its allies began to ease restrictions after the Korean armistice, Washington refused to budge, continuing to wage economic war on China throughout the 1950s and into the 1960s. Toward the end of the Eisenhower administration, a review of existing policy concluded that regardless of what other nations did, the United States should continue its policy of refusing to trade with China. Given the size and technical sophistication of the American economy, even a unilateral embargo had a "retarding effect on the Communist Chinese military/industrial buildup . . . denies them foreign exchange, limits their sources of goods in short supply and denies them items in which the U.S. has a total monopoly of production, production know-how, or technology."[19] Economic warfare would remain an important element in the overall policy of containment for almost a quarter of a century, and trade between the United States and China would not resume until 1972.

During the formative opening stage of their strategic interaction, Americans tended to see "Red China" as a uniquely dangerous and frightening foe.[20] Compared to the Soviet Union, China might lack industrial prowess and scientific sophistication, but it more than made up for these shortcomings in sheer size, cunning, brutality, and ideological fanaticism. The mass, "human wave" attacks carried out by the People's Liberation Army in Korea reinforced the image of China as a "slave state" whose leaders were indifferent to human life and willing to sacrifice their own people in vast numbers to achieve their goals. The harsh treatment of American POWs by their Chinese captors, including the alleged use of "brainwashing" tactics to extract information and elicit confessions, reinforced stereotypes of cruel Asiatics expert in the dark arts of torture. As the Communists consolidated their power at home and, later, when Mao tried to accelerate the process of industrialization with his disastrous Great Leap Forward, reports reached the West of mass executions and widespread starvation. Even as the Soviet regime showed some signs of mellowing after Stalin's demise in 1953, China appeared to be moving in the opposite direction. Mao's "cult of personality" elevated him to a near-godlike status, and as part of his bid for leadership of the world Communist movement, in the late 1950s he began to criticize the Soviets for being overly cautious in spreading revolution and standing up to the West.[21]

For all of these reasons, the prospect of a nuclear-armed China was especially troubling to American and, increasingly, to Soviet strategic planners. Despite the fact that they had assisted Mao in his nuclear program, the Soviets now began to fear that if he got the bomb, he might actually use it, regardless of the risk of triggering a worldwide conflagration.[22] Even if his behavior proved more prudent than his rhetoric, Mao would almost certainly feel emboldened to engage in lesser forms of aggression, including stepped-up support for regional insurgencies and perhaps the direct use of conventional military power to attack or intimidate his neighbors. The acquisition of nuclear weapons by China therefore threatened to weaken, if not to destroy, the foundations of America's containment strategy in Asia. In the words of a 1962 assessment of the likely impact of a Chinese nuclear test, there could be "little doubt but that over the long run a Chicom nuclear program could have a degrading effect on the U.S. political and military positions" in the region.[23]

In order to forestall this danger, the United States gave serious consideration to going beyond merely containing China to actually waging preventive war against it by destroying its known nuclear facilities. As evidence grew of an impending Chinese atomic bomb test, Presidents John Kennedy and Lyndon Johnson canvassed a variety of options, from using U.S. special operations forces, or conventionally armed bombers, to destroy key targets, to assisting the Taiwanese in achieving similar objectives using their own forces.[24]

It is interesting, though ultimately fruitless, to speculate on how the course of history might have been altered if the United States had, in fact, acted to prevent China from acquiring nuclear weapons. Certainly the impending Sino-American rapprochement would have been deferred, perhaps for many decades. A weakened and humiliated China might have been forced back into the arms of the Soviet Union. And, without a strong, hostile neighbor to worry about, the Soviets would have been in a better position to prosecute a prolonged Cold War competition with the United States.

In the end, the Johnson administration chose to do nothing. The probable diplomatic costs of striking first without obvious provocation, the possibility that an attack might fail, fear that Beijing would retaliate by stepping up its involvement in the widening war in Vietnam, and a lack of certainty over whether a nuclear-armed China would, in fact, be unmanageable, combined to make passivity seem preferable to action. Free of outside harassment, on October 16, 1964, China successfully tested an atomic bomb and became the world's fifth nuclear-armed nation.

ALIGNMENT: PHASE I (1969–79)

In the span of only a few years, the United States reversed course on virtually every aspect of its strategy for dealing with China. Instead of isolating the Beijing regime and refusing to acknowledge its existence, Washington began to move, albeit slowly and with pangs of discomfort, to "de-recognize" the Nationalist government on Taiwan so that it could establish formal diplomatic ties to the PRC. Discreet, low-level meetings in remote capitals were replaced by triumphal presidential trips to Beijing and, somewhat later, return visits by Chinese leaders to the United States. The long-standing trade embargo was lifted; various forms of cultural, educational, and scientific exchange were encouraged; and many, though not all, of the Korean War–era controls on high-tech exports were loosened or removed. Instead of plotting preemptive strikes on Chinese nuclear installations, American military planners began to contemplate the possibility of a war in which the United States would join forces with its former archenemy to defeat the Soviet Union.[25]

The motivating force behind all of these changes was a perceived shift in the global balance of power in favor of Moscow. By the end of the 1960s it was clear that America's adventure in Vietnam was destined to end in failure, and that a painful, and likely protracted, process of withdrawal would have to begin. The newly elected president, Richard Nixon, and his principal foreign policy advisor, Henry Kissinger, feared that the war would do lingering damage not only to their country's reputation for resolve, but also to its future willingness and ability to play a leading world role. Disillusioned by fruitless sacrifice and demoralized by the unfamiliar experience of defeat, the American people might once again succumb to the temptations of isolationism. They certainly could not be expected to continue to support with enthusiasm the kind of expensive, risky, forward-leaning foreign policy that their leaders had been urging on them since the end of the Second World War. The nation was due for an interval of retrenchment, at the very least, and perhaps for a permanent diminution in its global role. In their not-infrequent moments of existential gloom, Nixon and Kissinger believed that they had been fated by history to manage America's decline.[26]

With the United States seemingly on the downswing, the Soviet Union appeared to be on the rising side of the power equation. This was certainly true as regards the distribution of military capabilities, where the Soviets seemed to be surging ahead on all fronts. As recently as 1962, Nikita Khrushchev had made a desperate attempt to offset what was then a growing U.S. advantage in long-range nuclear missile forces by sneaking shorter-range rockets into Cuba. Following the humiliating outcome of the ensuing crisis, and the subsequent ouster of its author on charges of "hare-brained scheming," the new Kremlin ruling group launched a massive, across-the-board buildup in Soviet military power.

Now, after nearly a decade, this unrelenting effort had begun to bear fruit. By the early 1970s, the size of the USSR's strategic nuclear arsenal had drawn equal to that of the United States. Instead of stopping at "parity," as most Western experts expected they would, the Soviets pressed ahead, deploying still more long-range bombers and ballistic missiles. Many American strategists had convinced themselves that nuclear superiority was meaningless or, in any event, unachievable, but Moscow seemed to have reached disturbingly different conclusions. Alongside the nuclear buildup, the Soviets and their Warsaw Pact allies launched a major expansion in conventional forces, increasing their margin of numerical advantage in tanks, planes, and artillery and beginning to erase the gap in quality and technological sophistication that had long separated them from U.S. and NATO forces.[27]

In Asia too, Moscow was hard at work. The personality clashes, strategic debates, and ideological disagreements that had roiled Sino-Soviet relations since the death of Stalin had blossomed by the 1960s into an open, undisguised animosity bordering on mutual hatred. With his country not yet fully recovered from the manmade disasters of the Great Leap Forward, in 1966 Chairman Mao unleashed another cycle of destruction and upheaval. The ostensible goal of the so-called Cultural Revolution was to rekindle the fervor of the masses, spurring them on to even greater accomplishments. Its real purpose, however, was to unleash popular forces that Mao could then use to silence critics and crush potential rivals, especially those who had dared to call attention to the abject failure and catastrophic cost of his economic policies.[28]

In response to the mounting chaos inside China, and the increasingly belligerent anti-Soviet rhetoric emanating from Beijing, Moscow began in the mid-1960s to deploy large numbers of tanks, mechanized infantry, aircraft, and tactical nuclear weapons along their Far Eastern frontiers. With the PRC seemingly on the brink of civil war, the Soviets appeared to be preparing to do what the Americans had declined to do only a few years before: destroying China's small nuclear stockpile before it could be used by the country's increasingly unpredictable rulers. The clashes between

Soviet and Chinese border guards that took place in the Far East in early 1969 came against a backdrop of mounting tension and were widely interpreted as the prelude to a much larger conflict.[29]

For Nixon and Kissinger the intensifying crisis provided an opportunity to move forward with a diplomatic opening to China. This gambit was intended initially to strengthen their hand in dealing with the USSR and, in particular, to give them some badly needed leverage in the Strategic Arms Limitation Talks just then getting under way. Even if they could not prevent the superpower balance from tilting further toward Moscow, Nixon and Kissinger hoped that the unspoken threat of a possible U.S.-China entente would help persuade the Soviets to accept some limits on their military buildup. Kissinger's frequent denials that he sought to "collude against the Soviet Union" were, in one sense, disingenuous. He meant to do precisely that. But he also planned to play the USSR off against China or, as he put it more decorously in his memoirs, "to give each Communist power a stake in better relations with us."[30]

The elegant triangle that Kissinger originally envisioned soon collapsed into a much simpler, two-sided form. As the Soviets continued their military buildup and sought to expand their influence in the Third World, relations with the United States deteriorated, and the United States and China were drawn closer together. During the final phase of the Cold War, from the unraveling of the brief superpower detente that began in the mid-1970s, to the Soviet Union's terminal crisis in the late 1980s, Washington and Beijing entered into what can perhaps best be described as a strategic alignment. This relationship had many of the attributes of a full-fledged alliance, but in the end it fell well short of deserving that label. The United States and China shared a common interest in countering the rise of Soviet power, but for the most part they pursued it through independent, parallel policies rather than direct, deliberate coordination.

The reasons for this failure to achieve an even higher level of cooperation are many and varied, reflecting the complex motives of both parties. On balance, however, it was American hesitation that proved decisive. Despite what appeared to be compelling geopolitical arguments in favor of working even more closely with Beijing, and despite the enthusiasm for doing so expressed by top officials at various times, the U.S. government (including parts of both the executive branch and Congress) and the

American people as a whole never entirely overcame their ambivalence about entering into a genuine alliance with the People's Republic of China. This ambivalence, in turn, was rooted in judgments about the character of the Beijing regime. Power politics may have attracted the United States to China, in short, but it was ideology that continued to hold them apart.

American discomfort manifested itself above all in a reluctance simply to abandon Taiwan. Although it would later undergo a striking transformation, the KMT government was at this point far from democratic. It was, however, strongly anti-Communist and had been, since the early 1950s, a loyal ally of the United States. Whatever its failings, few Americans believed the regime in Taipei was as bad as the one in Beijing. In any event, there could be little doubt of the fate that would befall Taiwan's leaders, and many of its people, if they were finally brought under the mainland's control.

As card-carrying "realists," Nixon and Kissinger were less troubled by the moral implications of abandoning Taipei than by the damage that such a shift might do to America's reputation for reliability and resolve. Still, on balance, they believed the strategic benefits of an alignment with China to be worth the costs of casting aside a longtime ally. Despite their penchant for secret diplomacy, however, the president and his national security advisor still had to answer to Congress and, ultimately, to the American people. Neither they nor their successors could simply accede to Beijing's demands that the United States cut all ties to Taiwan and deliver it on a platter to the mainland. The resulting delays and disagreements prevented the full flowering of a Sino-American strategic partnership during the years when the two parties were most anxious about Soviet power and when, absent the Taiwan issue, they would almost certainly have gone even further in their attempts to counter it.

By the early 1970s the goal of U.S. strategy was no longer to weaken China but to strengthen it. The most obvious and direct way of doing so would have been to provide the poorly equipped People's Liberation Army with the modern weapons it needed if it were to have any chance of standing up to Soviet aggression. But arming China turned out to be more difficult in practice than it appeared to be in theory. Despite what Nixon and Kissinger's grand strategic machinations seemed to require, the American system could not simply be turned on a dime. Much of the national security bureaucracy, Congress, and, to the extent that it was engaged on the issue, the public remained leery of selling military hardware to China. Even if Chairman Mao could be trusted not to turn U.S.-made weapons against America's East Asian allies, there was no telling what his successors might do. Given the recent twists and turns in Chinese politics, and the lack of any predictable mechanisms for transferring domestic power in an authoritarian regime, there was a strong case to be made against treating the PRC as if it were just another strategic partner, let alone a true ally.

Pending the resolution of differences over Taiwan, and the establishment of formal diplomatic relations in 1979, the question of how far to go in cooperating with China remained largely academic. Until these issues could be addressed, neither Washington nor Beijing was willing to take the next steps toward establishing a direct military supply relationship. In order to maintain some semblance of momentum, and to provide China with at least a measure of strategically meaningful assistance, Nixon and his successor, Gerald Ford, therefore decided to authorize the sale of a number of so-called dual-use systems. Included among these were a ground station for picking up and rebroadcasting satellite television signals, ten Boeing 707s, and two high-speed computers. In addition, in 1975, at Kissinger's urging, Washington agreed not to invoke Cold War export restrictions that could have been used to block the sale of British-made Rolls-Royce jet engines to China. These engines were suitable for installation on civilian aircraft, but they were clearly intended to improve the performance of underpowered Chinese fighter planes.[31]

Aside from selling it arms and military equipment, another way to bolster China in the face of possible Soviet aggression would have been to offer it some kind of security guarantee. Such a move would have had obvious risks, including the possibility that it might embolden Beijing, provoke Moscow, and drag the United States into an unwanted war. Absent a formal pledge of assistance, the United States could still have engaged with China in joint planning, training, and other preparations for coalition warfare against a common foe. If a conflict were to occur, these steps would have at least given the two sides the option of joining forces. Even at its moments of greatest warmth, however, the Sino-American relationship never achieved these levels of intimacy, trust, and mutual commitment. Despite the desirability in purely strategic terms of doing so, many of the same obstacles that slowed the development of a military supply relationship also prevented the formulation of serious plans for working with China if a war had actually broken out.

From an American perspective, China fulfilled a useful strategic function simply by remaining independent and continuing to resist Soviet domination. In peacetime, the presence on the USSR's thinly populated Far Eastern frontiers of a large, apparently implacable foe forced Moscow to increase overall defense spending and to divert resources that might otherwise have been directed against Europe or the United States. Given the long distances and harsh climate, maintaining forces in Siberia was also disproportionately expensive. In a crisis in which the Soviets were contemplating the use of force on either flank, the prospect of a two-front war might serve to deter aggression. But suppose that deterrence failed and the Soviet Union attacked China. What should the United States do then to help its new strategic partner? What *could* it do? And what kinds of actions would Congress and the American people actually be willing to support?

These questions bedeviled American planners from the very start of their alignment with China, and they arose with special urgency on the several occasions when it appeared that conflict might actually be imminent. In the summer of 1969, following renewed border clashes, Soviet officials approached American diplomats to ask how their government would respond to a surgical strike on China's small nuclear force. Over a leisurely August lunch at the Beef and Bird restaurant in downtown Washington, a mid-level official from the Soviet embassy told a State Department counterpart that his government was "completely serious" about this possibility. From Moscow's perspective, a successful preemptive attack would have the advantage not only of destroying China's nuclear capability but also of discrediting the "Mao clique" and possibly clearing the way for "dissident senior [military] officers and Party cadres" to "gain the ascendancy in Peking."[32] Several weeks later at a diplomatic reception in Tehran, a Soviet Air attaché informed an American officer that his country would "not hesitate to use nuclear weapons against the Chinese" if they attacked in strength across the border.[33]

Nixon and Kissinger had already concluded that a major Sino-Soviet conflict would tip the global balance of power dangerously in favor of the USSR. As Nixon put it, American interests would suffer if China were "smashed" in a war with the Soviets.[34] Given how recently the U.S. government had itself been contemplating similar preemptive action, and the fear and suspicion with which China was still widely regarded in Washington, this was, as Kissinger would later note, a "revolutionary thesis."[35] What followed from it was, above all, the necessity of conveying American disapproval of a possible Soviet strike in no uncertain terms and through all available channels. Beyond this, however, U.S. options were severely limited. If Moscow ignored its warnings, there was little Washington could do beyond breaking off bilateral negotiations and issuing condemnatory statements. As matters stood, it would have no choice but to live with the consequences of a Sino-Soviet war, whatever they might turn out to be.

Kissinger was dissatisfied with this situation, but he recognized the inherent difficulty of the problem. If the United States tried to remain neutral, it would, in effect, be siding with the Soviets. On the other hand, supporting China might mean backing a losing cause, and it could lead to World War III. Influencing the outcome of a conflict between the two Communist giants would require "massive activity" by the United States on Beijing's behalf. But indications that Washington intended to undertake anything of the kind could well provoke the Soviets into taking preemptive action. As Kissinger told his colleagues, "While he understood the question, he did not know the answer." The issue clearly required further study.[36]

Strategic complexities aside, the idea of helping China resist Soviet aggression raised serious domestic political issues. Popular backing for such a policy was, at this point, nonexistent. The prevailing view, as expressed by one State Department official, was that "massive support for China, with the implication of military support, was unthinkable as U.S. policy."[37] As a result, Kissinger realized that "if the cataclysm occurred, Nixon and I would have to confront it with little support in the rest of the government—and perhaps the country—for what we saw as the strategic necessity of supporting China."[38]

Fortunately for all concerned, the 1969 crisis eventually cooled. Two years later, during the 1971 Indo-Pakistan war, it appeared for a time as if China and Russia might intervene to help their respective allies. Kissinger and Nixon feared that if China moved against India, the Soviets would respond by attacking China. The United States would again have to face the decision of whether to stand by or "assist a country that until a year earlier had been considered our most implacable enemy." The president and his national security advisor were clear in their own minds that at least in this situation, the United States would have no choice but to provide China with "some significant assistance" to prevent it from suffering a humiliating defeat. Given the absence of any advance planning or political support, however, the details would have to "be worked out when the circumstances arose."[39]

To prepare for the possibility of intervention, and to send a signal of resolve to both the Soviets and the Indians, Nixon decided to dispatch a carrier task force to the Bay of Bengal. No doubt in part to preclude any possibility of leaks or opposition from inside the government, this move was made without the secretaries of state and defense having been informed in advance. Despite the improvised nature of the U.S. response, in the aftermath of the crisis Kissinger assured the Chinese that he and Nixon had been fully prepared "if you came under military attack . . . [to] take whatever measures were necessary to prevent it."[40] Whether Nixon would actually have ordered U.S. forces into battle, what impact naval airpower could have had on a major ground war in South Asia, to say nothing of the massive Sino-Soviet engagements that might be taking place thousands of miles to the north, and what escalatory steps the president might have been forced to consider if a few air strikes failed to end the conflict quickly are all questions that cannot be answered. What is clear, however, is that while its top political leaders were prepared to act, at this point the U.S. government as a whole still lacked the plans and dedicated capabilities it would need to offer China meaningful assistance in the event of Soviet aggression. Whether or not Congress and the American public would have been willing to support such action is also open to question.

In 1973, the Russians once again raised the possibility of a disarming attack on China's growing nuclear capabilities. Kissinger (now secretary of state) informed the Chinese of these approaches and of his impression that they were deadly serious. For the first time he also began to discuss in detail how the United States would respond, eventually making a series of proposals and promises that have been described as amounting to an offer of "a secret military alliance with China."[41]

But what Kissinger had to offer was something well shy of an alliance. Seeking to allay Beijing's lingering fears of a possible double-cross, the secretary of state assured the Chinese ambassador that the United States would not, under any circumstances, provide "military or other supplies to the Soviets if they attacked the PRC." Instead, Washington would cut off all credits and, indeed, would suspend "all economic ties" with the Soviet Union. Acknowledging that "we don't know whether that would be enough," Kissinger confided that he had set up a "very secret group . . . to see what the U.S. could do if such an event occurred." Because of the risks of provoking the Soviets and perhaps, although Kissinger did not say so, the danger that its existence would arouse domestic opposition, this group "will never be publicly known." Nevertheless, the United States was prepared to "exchange views on this subject if it can be done in secret."[42]

When he visited Beijing again toward the end of the year, Kissinger had two suggestions. In the event of a protracted war, he told Zhou Enlai, "we could be helpful by supplying equipment and other services." Kissinger offered no details of what he had in mind, nor did he propose further discussions by the two countries' military staffs to flesh out what was, at this point, something less than a serious proposal. Instead, he focused on a less visible plan to help reduce China's vulnerability by offering it early warning of a possible Soviet first strike. This would require the establishment of a hotline "between our satellites and Beijing by which we could transmit information to you in a matter of minutes" and the creation of a reliable, rapid domestic communications network to spread the word to other military districts and commands. Recognizing that the latter might be beyond the PRC's current level of technical sophistication, Kissinger noted that "we could probably help you with that in some guise."[43]

Zhou expressed interest in a hotline, provided it could be set up in "a manner so that no one feels we are allies." For as long as the Americans refused to cut all ties to Taiwan, Beijing would not agree to anything that smacked of a formal alignment or implied an indefinite willingness on its part to accept the status quo. Journalist Patrick Tyler concludes that while Kissinger remained hopeful that the Chinese would eventually "pick up his offer for a hot line, for satellite links, for communication networks, and for war planning coordination . . . [they] quietly demurred each time these proposals were mentioned."[44] But for the restraints imposed on them by domestic political opposition, much of it rooted in ideology and centered in the congressional wing of the Republican Party, Kissinger and Nixon, and later Gerald Ford, would have pushed ahead sooner with normalization. Had they done so, the United States and China would likely have taken some significant additional steps toward a genuine strategic alliance against the Soviet Union.[45]

By the mid-1970s, U.S. fear of an imminent Soviet attack had begun to wane. With it, at least for a time, went the perceived urgency of finding ways to bolster China's strength. At the start of the Carter administration, officials expressed confidence in their ability to check Soviet ambitions in Asia without explicit coordination with China and, somewhat surprisingly, at the same time as they were reducing America's presence in the region. Presidential Review Memorandum 10, the administration's initial examination of national strategy and military force posture, concluded that the "primary U.S. objective in [East Asia] has become a stabilization of the current relatively favorable balance among the great powers as opposed to containment of a Sino-Soviet threat." Given that China no longer seemed to pose a challenge to American interests, the United States could afford to pull back substantially from East Asia. Indeed, doing otherwise might appear threatening to Beijing and could also provoke the Soviets into expanding their own regional presence. The most important thing the United States could do to preserve the existing coincidence of interest with China was "paradoxically" to strengthen its position in Europe while continuing the post-Vietnam drawdown of its forces in Asia.[46]

That process was already well under way. In addition to pulling out of Vietnam, the United States had withdrawn one division from South Korea and planned to remove all remaining ground forces there. It had taken some units off Okinawa, cut the number of carrier task groups operating in the Western Pacific from three to two, removed forces from Thailand, and "significantly reduced" those based in Japan and on Taiwan. The United States was "moving toward an offshore posture" that would greatly lower its profile in East Asia, while preserving at least a residual capacity to conduct military operations there should the need ever again arise. The skeletal outlines of the Cold War, containment-era structure of alliances and bases would be retained, even as most of the meat and muscle were cut away.[47]

At the same time that it assessed the broad outlines of the American posture in Asia, the Carter administration also ordered an evaluation of U.S.-China policy, including "a broad review of our policies toward sale of defense-related technology and equipment."[48] The study's conclusions reflected the consensus view in the bureaucracy: in addition to being unnecessary, military sales were simply too risky. Along with the more familiar dangers, there was the possibility that they might antagonize the Soviets on the eve of a planned push for a new strategic arms limitation agreement. For the next several years, as relations with Moscow worsened and Cold War tensions deepened, the question of how best to strengthen China lay unresolved.

ALIGNMENT: PHASE II (1979–89)

To a certain extent the establishment of formal diplomatic relations between Washington and Beijing did clear the way for renewed movement toward a deeper strategic alignment. But the final acts of the normalization drama at the end of 1978 and the beginning of 1979 also set the stage for future controversy. In an expression of its unease at abandoning an anti-Communist friend, within a matter of a few months Congress passed legislation requiring that the executive branch continue to provide Taiwan with the hardware it needed to defend itself against attack or coercion by the PRC. At the same time as it aligned more closely with China in order to balance the Soviet Union, the United States, at the insistence of Congress, and despite the misgivings of President Carter and his advisors, thus retained a critical link to its longtime ally. Reflecting the intensity of the sentiment on this issue, the so-called Taiwan Relations Act passed both the House and the Senate by overwhelming, veto-proof majorities.[49] This legislation was more than mere symbolism. Instead it directly "contradicted the thrust" of the normalization communiqué that the leaders of the United States and China had just signed, and made clear that, at least as far as Congress was concerned, "the United States expected Taiwan to remain separate from the mainland and under U.S. protection for the foreseeable future."[50]

Despite the fact that normalization was now complete, and its assessment of Soviet intentions and capabilities was growing darker, the Carter administration remained cautious about providing Beijing with arms. Still wary of possible Soviet reactions and of potential congressional opposition, the administration preferred instead to further loosen restrictions on the sale of dual-use technologies such as airborne infrared geological survey equipment.[51]

It would take the Soviet invasion of Afghanistan in December 1979 to push the strategic relationship further along. Following the invasion, the United States took some tentative steps toward synchronizing its plans and policies more closely with China's. During a January 1980 trip to Beijing, Secretary of Defense Harold Brown proposed an ongoing series of exchanges between high-level defense officials. The goal, as Brown explained it, was a relationship that would still fall well short of an outright alliance but would involve much closer contact and communication between the two defense establishments than had ever existed before. The American and Chinese militaries would not be "planning together," Brown explained, but rather telling each other "what our programs and plans are."[52]

As the implications of Soviet action began to sink in, President Carter announced that he would approve export licenses for a lengthening list of dual-use technologies and also authorized for the first time the sale of so-called nonlethal military systems, including over-the-horizon radar, transport aircraft, helicopters, and communications hardware.[53] Despite clear expressions of interest from China, however, Carter still refused to take the final step of selling weapons that could actually kill Soviet soldiers.[54]

Ronald Reagan had no such inhibitions, but he was also more viscerally anti-Communist than his predecessor and, as a result, more sympathetic to arguments in favor of continuing to help Taiwan. The new administration's efforts to square this circle would further delay the development of a close strategic partnership with Beijing. Reagan's first secretary of state, former Kissinger deputy Alexander Haig, longed to follow in the footsteps of his mentor. Haig aimed to make a bold move that would leave his own imprint on U.S.-China relations while elevating them to what he considered to be the next logical level in their development. Toward this end, he proposed to forge what he called a "strategic association" between the two nations that would be an alliance in all but name. A central element in this new partnership would be large-scale sales of lethal weapons to China.[55]

Haig's broad strategic goal of balancing the Soviet Union's growing power was shared by others in the administration, including the military. In a 1981 study of the evolving security relationship, the Joint Chiefs of Staff concluded that China was already contributing to "the global balance, primarily by occupying Soviet forces along its border." The goal of U.S. policy going forward should be to "increase Soviet concern about the USSR's Asian flank" by devising a strategy that "improves current and projected Chinese military capabilities [and] attempts to focus those capabilities toward mutually advantageous goals."[56]

In contrast to Haig, however, both the military and the civilian leadership of the Defense Department remained leery about simply opening the floodgates and showering China with the latest in high-tech weaponry. Given the risks and uncertainties, it was still important to "proceed cautiously and discreetly." The United States should sell China what it needed to defend itself from a Soviet invasion, but it should avoid transfers of technology that might contribute to "the development of Chinese strategic [nuclear] weapons and power projection capabilities."[57]

Haig was frustrated by what he regarded as the shortsighted objections of narrow-minded bureaucrats. He believed that he could forge ahead with his strategic association with China while at the same time fulfilling America's moral and now its legal obligations to Taiwan, as well as mollifying potential critics in Congress. In fact, Haig was convinced that the prospect of gaining access to U.S. weaponry would dampen Beijing's opposition to a planned, simultaneous sale of arms to Taipei.

It did not take long to become apparent that Haig's brilliant stratagem was based on a fundamental miscalculation. Once it learned of his intentions, the Chinese government denounced the United States for meddling in its "internal affairs," refused to proceed with discussions of its own possible arms purchases, and, in general, brought further progress toward enhanced cooperation to a grinding halt. As had happened before, the stubborn attachment of many Americans to Taiwan, and their continuing mistrust of the Chinese Communist regime, stood in the way of a closer strategic alignment.

Another two years would pass before Washington and Beijing papered over their differences with an ambiguously worded communiqué in which the United States pledged eventually to taper off its support for Taiwan. With this out of the way, in 1983 Secretary of Defense Caspar Weinberger announced that along with several other steps intended to increase military-to-military contact and cooperation, the United States was now willing to sell "defensive" weapons systems to China. This was a more restrained offer than Haig's, but it at least represented a statement of policy on which the rest of the government had agreed and was ready to act. Weinberger's announcement was followed by a formal determination that the PRC was eligible to make direct government-to-government purchases of military equipment and by a parallel decision that for purposes of granting export licenses to firms wishing to sell dual-use technologies, the Commerce Department would now treat China in the same way as it did other "friendly but non-allied" countries.[58]

During the second half of the 1980s the U.S. government agreed to sell torpedoes, tactical radars, equipment for manufacturing artillery shells, and an avionics package for installation in a Chinese-made fighter interceptor. American officials also expressed willingness to discuss purchases of sophisticated antitank missiles, modern antisubmarine warfare sonar devices, gas turbine engines for naval vessels, and an antiaircraft missile system.[59] Washington was now prepared to sell selected items of lethal and nonlethal military hardware in large quantities, but only the first and more modest of these proposed transactions was ever completed. By the mid-1980s, the Soviet Union's deepening domestic difficulties, the emergence of Mikhail Gorbachev, and the dawning of the new era of *glasnost* had combined to convince China's leaders that the risk of great-power war was declining. The prospect of improving relations with the Soviets, and the opportunity to divert some resources from defense to civilian economic development, caused Beijing to pull back from major new arms purchases. With the U.S. arsenal finally open for business, Beijing preferred instead to "window shop," buying a few selected items and learning as much as possible about American weaponry in the process. China would rely on commercial transactions and a newly expanded access to Western dual-use technologies to accelerate growth and lay the ground for the long-term development of national military power.[60] As Patrick Tyler explains, by the end of the decade, little remained of "Washington's grand plans to refurbish the Chinese armed forces." The few, small military programs put in place were "really only a sideline to what was occurring in the civilian economy."[61]

In addition to arms sales, if not for the near breakdown in relations over Alexander Haig's plan to sell weapons to Taiwan, Washington and Beijing might have moved in the early 1980s toward some form of joint planning for war against the Soviets. Despite deep residual mistrust of China, Reagan Defense Department officials were at least willing to consider a variety of possible options for enhanced interaction, ranging from the symbolic (ship visits) to the substantive (combined bilateral training of individual units) to the truly serious (combined military planning and large-scale exercises).[62]

In any event, it was not until 1983 that the Reagan administration took what proved to be the last significant steps toward closer strategic cooperation with China. Secretary of Defense Weinberger's visit to Beijing was followed by a series of exchanges between civilian officials and military officers at all levels. As with arms sales, it was the Americans who now took the lead in proposing new forms of integration while the Chinese were more circumspect. Harry Harding reports, for example, that although the United States sought actual joint naval exercises, in the end the Chinese were willing to accept only "a U.S. proposal for ships of the two navies to pass each other in review on the high seas."[63] American officials also reportedly floated ideas about deploying tactical aircraft to bases near Vladivostok, developing "joint early warning and air defense systems," and gaining permission to refuel U.S. transport planes carrying supplies for the anti-Soviet Afghan resistance. With Beijing now looking to improve its relations with Moscow, however, none of these proposals was ever seriously considered.[64]

CONVERGENCE?

Ideological factors, disapproval of China's domestic political institutions, distrust of its totalitarian leaders, and sympathy for anti-Communist

Taiwan helped prevent the formation of a true Sino-American strategic alliance during the closing decades of the Cold War. It is also the case, however, that popular perceptions changed over time, generally becoming more favorable about conditions in China and more optimistic about its future during the second decade of the period of alignment than they were during the first.

In contrast to their leaders, who seemed to fall easily under the spell of China's culture and history (to say nothing of the calculating flattery of their counterparts), the American people for a time retained a healthy skepticism about China. When U.S. officials first visited Beijing, the Cultural Revolution was still under way, and their host was the man who had summoned the whirlwind and steered it on its destructive path. There was, if anything, even more reason to regard Mao and his colleagues as ruthless ideologues in the early 1970s than there had been only a few years before. Yet Kissinger and Nixon appeared to view China's leaders much as they saw themselves: tough-minded, to be sure, but also rational, pragmatic, worldly, even charming.

Treatment of China by journalists and opinion makers became markedly more favorable after the initial American opening, and the volume of information available to Western readers and viewers grew exponentially. What had once appeared impenetrable and foreboding now seemed alluring and accessible. Old images of China as rigidly totalitarian, colorless, and conformist gradually gave way to a more realistic awareness of the country's vast human diversity and its capacity for change.

Still, it was not until the 1980s, following the establishment of formal diplomatic relations and the full flowering of Deng's economic reform policies, that public attitudes toward China began to shift. Throughout the 1970s, following the first rush of curiosity and enthusiasm, only about a quarter of those questioned in opinion polls expressed a favorable attitude toward China, while two-thirds or more generally had an unfavorable view. In the 1980s these figures were inverted so that by February 1989, the ratio of favorable to unfavorable opinion was 72 percent to only 13 percent.[65]

What fueled this increasing warmth was the belief that, even if it had not yet entirely done so, China was about to experience profound political change. Greater openness had clearly quickened the pace of economic development. Goods and services, people and money, ideas and information were now flowing more freely in and out of China, and within its borders, than had been the case since the Communists took power. Surely liberalizing reforms, and a movement toward genuine democratic rule, could not be far behind.

Four

"CONGAGEMENT"

THE END OF ALIGNMENT

O n the evening of June 3 and the early morning hours of June 4, 1989, troops of the People's Liberation Army and the People's Armed Police entered Tiananmen Square in the center of Beijing. Acting on orders agreed to by Deng Xiaoping and his most senior and trusted associates (the so-called Party Elders), the soldiers proceeded to clear the square of the throngs of pro-democracy protestors who had gathered there over the preceding weeks. While the death toll remains in dispute, it is widely believed that over one thousand people, most of them young, were killed in the process. These events marked the beginning of a nationwide crackdown that would eventually see thousands more imprisoned and others executed or driven into exile.[1]

If it had happened a decade earlier, the Tiananmen Square "incident" might have produced some hand wringing back in Washington, but it would probably not have been sufficient to force a change in the fundamentals of American strategy. After all, the original decision to pursue an alignment with China had not been premised on any judgment about that country's domestic institutions. To the contrary, Nixon and Kissinger made plain from the outset that, in the president's words, what mattered was "not a nation's internal philosophy" but rather "its policy toward the rest of the world and toward us."[2] Nixon's comments, it should be noted, were made in private. His successors, more in harmony with their country's ideological traditions, were also more cautious in disclaiming any interest in China's "internal philosophy" and, in fact, periodically expressed hope that China would someday move toward liberal democracy; but they had never made this a precondition of their policies.

As long as the Soviet Union was seen as the greatest danger to American security, Washington would stay committed to an alignment with China. By the end of the 1980s, however, the threat appeared to be waning, and it was no longer certain that the Cold War would remain forever as a defining feature of the international landscape. The fall of the Berlin Wall in November 1989 signaled the end of the Soviet empire and set in motion a chain of events that would lead, in two years' time, to the collapse and fragmentation of the Soviet Union itself. It was this sudden and unexpected shift in the global balance of power, combined with the bloody events in the heart of Beijing, that called the strategy of alignment into question. With the USSR gone, it was not at all clear why the United States should continue to cooperate with the Chinese government, assisting it in enhancing its military power and looking the other way while it oppressed its citizens.

The year 1989 marked the beginning of a third major change in U.S.-China strategy. Twenty years earlier Washington had moved quickly from a harsh and unyielding form of containment to a serious diplomatic and military alignment against a common foe. With that enemy now suddenly gone, and renewed attention focused on the character and intentions of the Beijing regime, American policy began to shift once again, this time away from the more cooperative end of the strategic spectrum and back toward its center. The eventual result of this process of equilibration is what has sometimes been referred to, rather awkwardly, as a strategy of "congagement."[3] While continuing to "engage" China through trade and diplomacy, successive administrations have also taken steps to revitalize at least some of the elements of the earlier strategy of containment: bolstering U.S. capabilities in East Asia, strengthening ties with regional friends and allies, and, to the extent feasible, slowing the growth of China's military power.

Like the two earlier shifts in policy, this one too followed in the wake of dramatic, disruptive events. As was true of both containment and alignment, congagement was also the product of a mix of ideologically rooted beliefs and power political calculations. Unlike its predecessors, however, the new strategy did not result from a deliberate, self-conscious process of assessment, deliberation, and decision, nor was it ever memorialized in carefully reasoned policy papers. Congagement grew and evolved in the 1990s and early 2000s, and in certain respects it continues to do so. Albeit with some comparatively minor shifts in emphasis, this mixed policy has now survived three presidential transitions: from George H. W. Bush to Bill Clinton, from Clinton to George W. Bush, and most recently, as I describe in the concluding section of this chapter, from Bush to Barack Obama. The longevity of congagement is in part due to its organic, protean qualities; a more rigid, formalized approach might not have been able to survive the twists and turns of the past twenty years. Whether the strategy has now outlived its usefulness is a question to which we will have reason to return.

THE CASE FOR CONTINUED ENGAGEMENT

In the immediate aftermath of Tiananmen, the relationship with China was carried forward by momentum, force of habit, and an inchoate conviction on the part of President George H. W. Bush and his top advisors that whatever else might be going on in the world, staying on good terms with Beijing remained vital to America's national interests. In a democracy, however, inertia is seldom sufficient in itself to sustain policy. Faced with the need to convince a wary public and a skeptical Congress, Bush and later Bill Clinton advanced three distinct but overlapping arguments for continuing to engage China.[4]

The first and most straightforward of these was based on the cold logic of national interest. Having emerged from its self-imposed isolation, China was now a major player in world affairs, and provided it did not lapse again into disorder, its power seemed certain to grow with time. Even if there was no longer a clear common danger against which they could unite, and despite the recent reminder of the regime's true nature, Washington and Beijing had an interest in remaining on good terms, avoiding conflict and, where possible, working together to achieve shared objectives.

This argument appealed to the "realist" leanings of Bush and his advisors (most notably national security advisor and former Kissinger protégé General Brent Scowcroft), and it soon emerged as the first Bush administration's primary justification for moving quickly to restore a close partnership with China. Within a few months after Tiananmen, Deputy Secretary of State Lawrence Eagleburger presented Congress with a list of areas in which continued Sino-American cooperation would be vital. Eagleburger acknowledged that tensions with the Soviet Union were dwindling, but he insisted that the "strategic value" of the relationship with China was not. To the contrary, Washington and Beijing shared an array of new concerns that could be adequately addressed only through continuing, close cooperation. Among these were the spread of ballistic missiles, the proliferation of nuclear and chemical weapons, and the growing problem of environmental pollution.[5] Over the next twenty years, American officials would add terrorism, energy security, global warming, emerging diseases, and management of the global economy to Eagleburger's original list.[6] Still, the basic argument that he laid out in 1990 remained unchanged: whatever their differences, and even in the absence of a single, unifying threat of the traditional sort, Washington needed to engage with Beijing in order to seek out areas where their interests overlapped and where they might be able to work together.

A second rationale for diplomatic engagement placed it in a somewhat broader and more ambitious strategic context. Through dialogue and negotiation with China, Washington could hope not only to solve (or avoid) specific problems but also to actually change the way in which Chinese decision makers assessed their own interests and thought about their country's place in the world. Intense, continuous interaction in an assortment of diplomatic venues and across a range of issues would draw China into a new post–Cold War international order that would still be designed and largely dominated by the United States. As it became tangled in a thickening web of institutions and agreements, the Beijing regime would come to see itself as having a substantial stake in supporting the prevailing order and a strong need to avoid actions that might lead to its disruption. In time, even if China's domestic political institutions remained unchanged, its leaders would absorb and internalize the accepted rules and norms of an open, liberal international order. While U.S. government officials did not put it quite so bluntly, engagement was thus intended to "tame" China, inducing it to adjust its external policies so that it could become a member in good standing of the existing global system.

This justification first emerged at the start of the Clinton administration. Instead of following through on a plan to coerce Beijing into improving its treatment of political dissidents by threatening to withhold "most favored nation" (MFN), low-tariff trading privileges, in 1994 the administration announced that it would henceforth pursue a policy of "comprehensive engagement." As the president put it, "We will have more contacts. We will have more trade. We will have more international cooperation."[7] Out of all this would come a number of benefits, including, as one administration official explained, an "increase in China's stake in cooperating . . . and complying with a wide range of international norms."[8] Ultimately, as China's power grew and it became more fully integrated into the existing system, it would cease to be simply a passive follower and, in the words of U.S. Ambassador James Sasser (1996–99), would begin to "help make the global rules."[9] In this way, China would acquire an even deeper commitment to upholding and defending a status quo that happened also to reflect America's values and to serve its interests.

The George W. Bush administration embellished this concept and ultimately made it a central feature of its China policy. In a much-quoted 2005 speech, Under Secretary of State Robert Zoellick argued, in effect, that the initial aims of "comprehensive engagement" had been achieved. China had, in fact, been successfully drawn into the international system and had benefited greatly from partaking in its rules and institutions. Now the time had come to move to the next level of engagement by pressing Beijing to become a "responsible stakeholder," a nation ready to "work with us to sustain the international system that has enabled its success."[10] The underlying assumption here was, again, that giving China a greater role would constrain its behavior and cause it to modify its objectives in ways that made them converge ever-more closely with those of the United States. By this logic, even if it continued to be ruled for some time by a one-party dictatorship, there was no reason why China could not be a good international citizen.

The third and final argument for engagement was the most potent politically but also, for obvious diplomatic reasons, the most delicate. Tiananmen made it impossible for Americans to ignore the repressive nature of China's domestic regime, or merely to express the fond hope that it might someday evolve into a liberal democracy. To achieve and maintain the necessary level of public support for continued engagement, a new post-alignment strategy would have to address in some way Beijing's evident disregard for human rights and political liberties.

Bill Clinton had tried at first to do this by tackling the problem head-on with his threat to link China's eligibility for MFN status directly to its performance on human rights. By the spring of 1994, however, this approach had been defeated by a combination of Chinese intransigence, fear of provoking a full-blown crisis with Beijing, and the lobbying efforts of American businesses eager to profit from the fast-growing China trade. In an adroit reversal, the Clinton administration began to assert that it could best promote change, not by *withholding* the benefits of trade and investment, but rather by enveloping China in a close economic embrace.[11]

This was not an entirely new claim, to be sure. In seeking to defend itself against charges from then candidate Bill Clinton that it was kowtowing to the "butchers of Beijing," the first Bush administration had made occasional, passing references to the possibility that economic engagement, as well as other forms of societal exchange, would lead eventually to political reform.[12] But the logic underlying the connection that was assumed to exist between commerce and democracy had never been developed openly and in detail, nor had economic engagement been placed squarely at the center of the nation's long-term strategy for dealing with China.

With the MFN problem resolved, attention turned in the second half of the 1990s to the question of whether to bring China fully into the global trading system by supporting its entry into the World Trade Organization. In the course of debating this issue, advocates made a wide variety of claims about the beneficial effects on China's domestic political development of its deepening participation in the international economic system. In characteristically loquacious fashion, President Clinton laid out virtually the entire panoply of these arguments in a single speech, given on the eve of a 1997 visit to the United States by Chinese leader Jiang Zemin. According to the president, trade would accelerate China's growth, leading to higher incomes, greater freedom of choice in employment, housing, and travel, and an accompanying increase in demands for political rights. In addition to this pressure from below, China's leaders would also eventually be confronted by the realization that in a modern, information-age society, restrictions on speech and communication are incompatible with continued, rapid growth. Once introduced, technology in the form of "the Internet, fax machines and photo-copiers, modems and satellites" would help to tear down the last remaining obstacles to freedom. As Clinton explained, "The more ideas and information spread, the more people will expect to think for themselves, express their own opinions and participate [and] the harder it will be for their government to stand in their way."[13]

During his 2000 campaign for the presidency, George W. Bush criticized the Clinton administration for referring to China as a "strategic partner" and vowed to treat it more as a "strategic competitor." But there was never the slightest indication that Bush or his advisors gave serious consideration to abandoning the economic element of his predecessor's policy. To the contrary, perhaps with an eye toward reassuring potential business supporters, candidate Bush went out of his way to embrace what, in the space of less than a decade, had become the reigning orthodoxy in both political parties. As he put it in a 1999 address that laid out the fundamental principles of his approach to foreign policy, "Economic freedom creates habits of liberty. And habits of liberty create expectations of democracy. . . . Trade freely with China, and time is on our side."[14]

Engagement would do more than merely "tame" China; in the long run trade would help to transform it. This claim reflected deeply rooted liberal beliefs in the inevitability of progress and the links between free markets and democratic politics. It also happened to coincide nicely with the interests and ambitions of a broadening swath of the U.S. business community. In China, as so often in other parts of the world, Americans preferred to believe that they could do good while also doing well.

Once in office the George W. Bush administration tended to downplay the presumed linkage between economic engagement and political liberalization. No one had ever said the process would be rapid, and in any event, with bilateral trade exploding after Beijing's admission into the WTO, there seemed every reason to believe that it was well under way. China's growing importance as a trading partner, and after September 11, 2001, the administration's urgent desire to enlist it as an ally against terrorism and proliferation, also caused Washington to put a premium on maintaining the best possible relationship with Beijing. With so much else at stake, and with no pressing need to persuade the public or Congress of the virtues of engagement, there seemed little to be gained by reminding the Chinese leader that the ultimate aim of American policy was to someday put them out of a job.

Thus, even as it trumpeted its desire to spread the blessings of liberty to the Middle East, the Bush administration grew increasingly circumspect in describing its hopes for China. The claim that engagement would lead eventually to transformation did not disappear entirely from public rhetoric; indeed, by this point, it had become so familiar that it hardly bore repeating. But official discussions of the topic tended to be understated in tone and cautious in declaring any direct American role in bringing about liberalization. As the president put it in one of his final statements on the subject, "Change in China will arrive on its own terms and in keeping with its own history. . . . Yet change will arrive." After all, "young people who grow up with the freedom to trade goods will ultimately demand the right to trade ideas."[15] It was all just a matter of time.

RECOGNIZING THE CHALLENGE: THE TAIWAN CRISIS AND THE RETURN OF "CONTAINMENT"

Engagement was, in a sense, a continuation, amplification, and elaboration of some elements of the previous policy of alignment. The United States had been trading, talking, and partaking in scientific, cultural, and other forms of exchange with China since the early 1970s. These activities, and especially those in the commercial arena, now assumed even greater centrality and importance. Meanwhile, in the wake of Tiananmen, contacts between the military establishments, intelligence organizations, and defense industries of the two sides were suspended and, for the most part, never renewed.

The really big change in U.S. policy was the revival of at least some elements of the old strategy of containment. Before this could happen, however, it was necessary to acknowledge that China was no longer a strategic partner of the United States, but rather a potential threat to its interests and those of its allies. This recognition was slow in coming. Prior to 1996,

Pentagon planners paid little attention to the prospect that China might someday pose a significant challenge, and possibly even a serious threat, to American military preponderance in East Asia. In the aftermath of the Soviet collapse and with memories of the first Gulf War still fresh, Defense Department officials shifted their focus from a global war with another superpower to so-called major regional contingencies involving lesser opponents like North Korea or a reconstituted Iraq. The only real question was how many of these "MRCs" the United States should be prepared to fight at once. Neither the first Bush administration's analysis of the requirements for a post–Cold War "Base Force," nor the incoming Clinton administration's subsequent "Bottom-Up Review" of defense requirements made more than a passing reference to China; neither hinted at the possibility that it might become a strategic rival, still less an enemy.[16]

In the waning days of the first Bush presidency a leaked draft of an internal long-range planning study stirred controversy, largely because it identified preventing the "emergence of a rival superpower" as a top priority in America's post–Cold War strategy. In retrospect it seems obvious that there was only one plausible candidate for that position, but even in its early, classified form the document made only brief mention of China. When a later "sanitized" version was finally released, all reference to precluding possible rivals had been removed, North Korea was identified as "our most active regional security concern in Asia," and China was referred to, albeit warily, in a few short sentences.[17]

The reluctance to name China openly as a potential future rival cannot be explained simply as the result of diplomatic *politesse*. Despite a presumed proclivity for sniffing out new threats, to say nothing of the fact that they had recently lost the enemy that had for so long justified their existence, America's intelligence agencies were surprisingly slow to fix their attention on China. Throughout the first half of the 1990s, the annual "threat assessments" of the Central Intelligence Agency and Defense Intelligence Agency dealt sparingly with that country, if at all. At this point, the main threats emanating from China were seen to be the result of its stubborn insistence on selling ballistic missiles and other "extremely potent weapons technologies" (including some relevant to the production of nuclear weapons) to autocratic regimes in the Middle East and South Asia.[18]

All of this began to change in 1996 following Taiwan's first democratic presidential election. In the run-up to the vote, China twice lobbed dummy missile warheads into the Taiwan Strait in a vain attempt to frighten voters away from an avowedly pro-independence candidate.[19] The intensity and belligerence of Beijing's response and its imaginative, albeit reckless use of ballistic missiles were troubling enough in themselves. The missile firings also highlighted an area of increasing Chinese competence and demonstrated a capability against which neither Taiwan nor the United States, for that matter, had an effective defense. In the course of dispatching two carrier battle groups to the region to signal resolve, and secretly preparing to send ammunition, spare parts, and advisors to the island if it were attacked, American military planners were forced to grapple for the first time in over thirty years with what it would mean to actually fight a war against China.[20] Adding further gravity to the situation were reports of thinly veiled warnings from Chinese officials that they were prepared to risk a nuclear exchange with the United States, and to endure millions of casualties, if that was what it took to stop Taiwan from achieving independence. According to one story in wide circulation at the time, the chief of intelligence of the People's Liberation Army suggested to a visiting American that if it came to war, the United States would have to decide if it was really ready to "sacrifice Los Angeles to protect Taiwan."[21]

The aftershocks of the missile crisis reverberated throughout the U.S. national security establishment. In its aftermath, the intelligence community began to devote more resources to tracking China's evolving military capabilities and trying to understand its intentions. The conclusions were worrisome, if not immediately alarming. Even allowing for questionable data and incomplete information, the persistent year-on-year increases in Beijing's publicly announced defense budgets made plain that it was engaged in a major military buildup. Russia's willingness to export sophisticated arms to keep its own arsenals in business meant that the People's Liberation Army was able to expand its capabilities more rapidly than would otherwise have been possible. Thanks to the growing size and sophistication of its own industrial base, China's indigenous capacity for the development and manufacture of arms was steadily improving.

In 2000, at the urging of a concerned Congress, the Defense Department began to issue an annual report on the "military power of the People's Republic" that provided a detailed catalogue of its rapidly advancing strength. Over the course of the next several years careful readers of these documents could track not only the rising curve of China's power but also successive, upward revisions in the Defense Department's assessments of its current and likely future capabilities. In a number of areas (such as conventional ballistic missiles and submarines) the People's Liberation Army deployed more weapons, more quickly than Western observers had initially expected; in others (including computer network attack, anti-satellite warfare, and the possible use of land-based ballistic missiles to strike surface vessels hundreds of miles from shore) it was surprisingly forward-leaning in developing and demonstrating weapons that were new or at least previously untested.[22]

The Taiwan crisis also caused the U.S. government to sharpen its assessment of China's intentions. Prior to 1995–96, the intelligence community had said little publicly about Beijing's goals; afterward, its spokesmen began to describe them in stark and troubling terms. In his February 1996 annual threat assessment briefing, CIA Director John Deutch observed simply that "we still know very little about Beijing's future leadership and intentions."[23] One year later, however, following the standoff over Taiwan, Deutch's successor, George Tenet, claimed that China's "actions and statements show it is determined to assert itself as the paramount East Asian power."[24] By 1998, Tenet felt confident in reporting that China's leaders had "a clear goal: the transformation of their country into East Asia's major power and a leading world economy on a par with the United States by the middle of the 21st Century."[25] While later assessments used somewhat more cautious language, their message remained essentially the same: China was a fast-rising power, determined to increase its influence, and likely some day to challenge America's preponderance in Asia and perhaps beyond.

The evident growth in China's capabilities and the apparent expansiveness of its intentions raised the question of whether it might one day emerge as what defense planners referred to as a "peer competitor" of the United States. This label meant different things to different people, but it was generally used to describe a rival on par with the Soviet Union at the peak of its power. Such a country would be able to develop forces similar in sophistication and performance to those of the United States, and it would be capable of deploying them effectively anywhere in the world.

This standard set a very high bar, and at least initially, it may have encouraged a degree of complacency about the Chinese buildup. Thus, in 1997 in its first "quadrennial defense review" (QDR) the Defense Department identified China as a potential "global peer competitor," but not before the study's 2015 time horizon.[26] Four years later the second QDR struck a more cautious tone. While the United States might not have to face a true peer in "the near future," lesser powers could still develop capabilities that would threaten American forces, and interests, closer to their own territory. Especially in Asia, there was a strong possibility that "a military competitor with a formidable resource base" would eventually emerge. When this happened, "maintaining a stable balance" would become "a complex task." The problem was in part due to geography. For the United States the East Asian littoral, the region "from the Bay of Bengal to the Sea of Japan," was a "particularly challenging area." The distances involved were "vast," and the entire area was a very long way from the centers of American military power. The United States had fewer of its own bases there, and less assured access to the facilities of friendly local states than it did in other important regions like Europe and the Middle East.[27]

For these reasons an Asian rival could pose a serious strategic challenge to U.S. interests without actually becoming a peer. Taking advantage of its proximity to the theater of operations, and its "formidable" resources, this unnamed nation could buy large numbers of weapons (such as ballistic missiles, air, sea, and ground-launched cruise missiles, and diesel submarines) capable of striking targets at comparatively modest distances from its own shores. Even if these were not as sophisticated in every respect as their American counterparts, they could still be used with great effectiveness to sink ships at sea and to damage or destroy the relatively small numbers of ports, airfields, storage depots, and communications facilities on which the United States depended to sustain its forces in East Asia. The goal would be to develop what planners came to refer to as an asymmetric, "anti-access" (or "area-denial") capability, a combination of weapons and operational concepts built with the purpose not to match, but to neutralize America's overwhelming advantages in global power projection.[28]

The implications for defense planning were not difficult to discern, and the 2001 QDR spelled them out in some detail. To ensure that it could not be locked out of Asia either by military action or by diplomatic pressure on its friends, the United States needed to diversify its limited port-folio of bases, securing "additional access and infrastructure agreements" in the region. In addition, in the somewhat longer run, it would have to develop "systems capable of sustained operations at great distances with minimal theater-based support" and less vulnerable to enemy bombard-ment. While the QDR avoided recommendations regarding the cancel-lation or development of specific weapons systems, some in the military hoped (and others feared) that this would mean less investment in Cold War–era weapons like aircraft carriers and short-range fighters, and more in new ones like low-observable "arsenal ships" loaded with hundreds of long-range conventional missiles, armed unmanned aerial vehicles that could loiter unseen for days over enemy territory, and a new generation of stealthy, high-speed, intercontinental-range bombers.[29]

The second QDR was all but finished before the September 11, 2001, terrorist attacks. Following some hasty revisions it was published shortly thereafter. But for the attacks, and the events that followed, the QDR's analysis of the shifting strategic balance in Asia would have had a more immediate and obvious impact on U.S. defense planning and procurement policy. Indeed, in more tranquil circumstances the report would likely have served as the blueprint for Secretary of Defense Donald Rumsfeld's planned "transformation" of the American military and its reorientation toward the Pacific. After 9/11, however, the "global war on terror" got first call on resources, and the attention of defense planners shifted from a hypothetical future high-intensity conflict in Asia to two very real, ongo-ing counterinsurgencies in Afghanistan and Iraq.

Recognition of the need to respond to China's growing capabilities did not disappear altogether from discussions of defense requirements, but the problem was sometimes cast in terms that made it seem rather more abstract and remote. By the time the third quadrennial review was pub-lished in 2006, China had receded into the background and, at first glance, was barely visible amid a thicket of generic, notional challenges. The task facing the United States was now described, not as preparing to deter or defeat an advanced opponent armed with sophisticated anti-access capa-bilities, but rather as "shaping the choices of countries at strategic cross-roads." Included in this category were unnamed states in the Middle East,

Latin America, and Central Asia, as well as Russia and India and, as if as an afterthought, China.[30]

American policy makers would seek to "shape" the policies of these countries not only by ensuring that they were "integrated as constructive actors and stakeholders into the international system" but also by creating "prudent hedges against the possibility that cooperative approaches by themselves may fail to preclude future conflict." Despite being cast as only one of a set of similar challenges, China was obviously uppermost in the minds of the Pentagon's long-range planners. It had "the greatest potential to compete militarily with the United States" and "could over time offset traditional U.S. military advantages absent . . . counter strategies." Indeed, the "pace and scope" of its buildup were "already [putting] regional military balances at risk." Moreover, Beijing was seen as "likely to continue making large investments in high-end, asymmetric military capabilities" designed to take down America's computer networks, disable its satellites, sink its surface ships, engage its aircraft, and bombard its regional bases. The combination of China's growing capabilities, "the vast distances of the Asian theater, China's continental depth, and the challenge of en route and in-theater U.S. basing" placed "a premium on forces capable of sustained operations at great distances into denied areas." Acquiring these forces would require "the pursuit of investments . . . in key strategic and operational areas, such as persistent surveillance and long-range strike, stealth . . . air dominance and undersea warfare."[31]

PRESERVING THE BALANCE

Even before the nature and extent of the challenge to American military preponderance had come fully into focus, U.S. policy makers began to take a number of steps intended, not to "contain" China's rise, but to preserve a favorable balance of power in East Asia in spite of its growing capabilities. These were essentially of three types: actions designed to preserve or strengthen U.S. military capabilities in the region; efforts to bolster existing alliance relationships or to build new and generally less formal strategic partnerships with other powers; and attempts to slow the growth of China's high-end military capabilities by restricting its access to at least some advanced technologies.

Bolstering U.S. military power in the Pacific

The Clinton administration's principal contribution to this first aspect of the balancing process was its decision not to cut U.S. forces in East Asia beneath a certain size and level of capability. This move was not explicitly directed at China, and indeed, in the first instance it had more to do with deterring possible North Korean aggression and offering general reassurance to America's regional friends and allies. As intended, the administration's public declaration that it would not allow forward deployed forces to be reduced to fewer than 100,000 soldiers, sailors, and airmen helped to stave off domestic demands for deeper cuts and an even bigger post–Cold War "peace dividend."[32]

While it would certainly have done more if not for 9/11, during its two terms in office the Bush administration did begin a process of redistributing American military power around the globe and allocating an increasing fraction of it to Asia. The operative word here is "redistribution." Most of what was done involved moving existing forces rather than developing or building new ones for the specific purpose of conducting a military competition with China. In the short run, however, the end result was the same: the United States reinforced its position and achieved at least a temporary slowdown in the erosion of the regional balance of power.

As a result of a "global posture review" undertaken by the Rumsfeld Pentagon, U.S. forces in both Japan and Korea were consolidated into a smaller number of more efficient bases, some ground units were withdrawn and redeployed, and greater reliance was placed on facilities located on American soil, including Hawaii, Alaska, and, above all, the small island of Guam.[33] Here the air force and navy expanded existing ports and airfields, and made preparations for the permanent basing of long-range strike and reconnaissance aircraft, attack submarines, and the possible forward deployment of an entire carrier battle group. Operating from the westernmost piece of sovereign U.S. territory, these forces were safe from eviction by an anxious host government and, at least for the time being, less vulnerable to attack with conventional ballistic missiles. Most important, they were also within relatively easy range of possible conflict zones from the South China Sea, to the Taiwan Strait, to the Korean peninsula.[34] As one admiral explained, "We are putting forces in places where we think we might be able to use them . . . without any request from any party for permission to do that."[35]

By the close of the Bush administration, both the navy and the air force had begun to deploy increasing numbers of their most capable units to the Pacific. In 2007, for the first time since the end of the Cold War, more than half of the navy's ships were assigned to the Pacific Fleet. Among these were six of a total of eleven aircraft carriers, almost all of the eighteen advanced Aegis-class cruisers and destroyers capable of providing a mobile theater missile defense shield, and twenty-six of a total of fifty-seven attack submarines. Within a few years a total of thirty-four, or 60 percent of the navy's fleet of attack submarines, were to be deployed at bases throughout the region, including Guam.[36] For its part, the air force made preparations for the forward deployment of several squadrons of its newest F-22 air superiority fighters, B-2 bombers, and Global Hawk, long-range unmanned aerial vehicles.[37]

Despite the usual vague talk about "flexibility," occasional references to everything from counterterrorism to humanitarian relief (or somewhat more persuasively, possible future contingencies involving North Korea), the true target of these steps was unmistakable. When called on to explain what they were doing, U.S. military officers found ways to get the point across, albeit with varying degrees of subtlety. "We must maintain the . . . powerful overmatch we currently enjoy," declared U.S. Pacific Command commander Admiral Timothy Keating in 2007, using the purposefully vague locutions of an experienced soldier-diplomat. "[We] must retain the ability to dominate in any scenario, in all environments, without exception."[38] A newly arrived commander of all U.S. Air Force units in the Pacific put the matter more bluntly and perhaps also a bit plaintively: "The question is, how do we deal with China?"[39]

Strengthening alliances and quasi-alliances

In addition to taking steps to bolster America's own capabilities in the region, both the Clinton and Bush administrations devoted considerable effort to strengthening its Asian alliances and to creating a number of new, quasi-alliance partnerships. At the start of the 1990s some observers had predicted the imminent demise of the Cold War alliance system. With the Soviet Union gone, there seemed little need to maintain a large and costly regional presence. Trade tensions with Japan, and the desire for defense cutbacks and a domestic "peace dividend," made retrenchment seem all the more likely. Yet, in the years that followed, Washington managed to preserve all of its existing bilateral relationships and to strengthen several of them in substantial ways.

It was the U.S.-Japan alliance, the most important in the region, that saw the most notable initial gains. In 1997 and again in 2005, American and Japanese officials negotiated significant alterations in the rules governing cooperation between their defense forces. The main thrust of these changes was to lower the barriers to coordination, especially in responding to challenges that did not involve a direct attack on Japan. While there were still questions about how far Japan's "peace constitution" would permit it to go in taking part in such contingencies (whether through actual combat, the provision of rear-area support to U.S. forces, or merely the passive granting of permission to use bases on Japanese soil), the likelihood that it would become actively involved was clearly increased by successive revisions to the so-called defense guidelines.[40]

The range of conflicts in which Tokyo might choose to take part was also broadened. The 1997 guidelines referred rather vaguely to "situations in areas surrounding Japan," a phrase that could have been interpreted to include disaster relief and other noncombat scenarios as well as an actual shooting war.[41] To the extent that it was meant as a warning to potential opponents, this language could just as easily have been aimed at North Korea as at China. In 2005 the allies clarified the point when, for the first time, they expressed their shared desire to see the Taiwan issue resolved by peaceful means. Despite the mild wording, this was less an expression of lofty sentiment than a thinly veiled warning to Beijing: if China used force against Taiwan, it now risked provoking a response from Japan as well as the United States.[42]

Alongside changes in language were a number of more concrete initiatives intended to improve the ability of the allies to fight together side by side. Following the Taiwan crisis (and a series of North Korean missile tests) the Defense Department began to press for, and ultimately won, closer Japanese cooperation in developing a workable theater missile defense network. Using an array of closely interconnected American and Japanese sensors, command centers, and land- and sea-based interceptors, such a system would initially provide protection against a handful of North Korean rockets headed for Japan's home islands. But it could also serve as the foundation on which to build a much bigger system, one capable of handling large numbers of Chinese missiles and perhaps extending to cover Taiwan.[43]

In the final analysis, the greatest obstacles to closer alliance coordination, and a weightier Japanese role in maintaining a military balance with China, were legal and political rather than technical. So long as the prevailing interpretation of Japan's postwar constitution was that it forbade participation even in "collective self-defense," U.S. and Japanese forces could not plan and train together in the way that allies typically do. While taking care to avoid the appearance of meddling in sensitive domestic issues, the Bush administration thus gave quiet encouragement to those who favored constitutional reform. Because of strong domestic political opposition, rapid movement in this direction was impossible. Still, with strong support from Washington, and in the face of vocal objections from Beijing, after September 11, 2001, Tokyo demonstrated a new willingness to send its armed forces far from home and to use them in support of joint military operations. The deployment of resupply vessels to the Indian Ocean, and assignment of a small contingent of ground troops to Iraq, were widely seen as major milestones in Japan's reemergence as a "normal" nation, ready to play a more active part in the game of power politics.[44]

The 9/11 attacks also provided the occasion for a significant expansion of defense cooperation with three of the remaining four U.S. allies in Asia. As early as 1996, the United States and Australia had reaffirmed the importance of their long-standing alliance for dealing with new, post–Cold War security challenges, including those that might be posed by China. After 9/11, American and Australian forces fought side by side in Afghanistan and Iraq; defense consultation and intelligence cooperation, already close, became closer; and the two parties signed a treaty streamlining defense trade and discussed the possible use of Australian facilities for joint training and to assist in the deployment and resupply of U.S. forces.[45]

Following the end of the Cold War, Washington's relations with the Philippines and Thailand had grown more distant, in the first case, due to disputes over basing rights and, in the second, due to resentments over what was widely seen as an inadequate American response to the 1997 Asian financial crisis. With the rise of China's economy and its growing influence in Southeast Asia, the countries of the region had also begun to see potential disadvantages in becoming too closely aligned with the United States. After 9/11 the Bush administration sought to revitalize defense cooperation, and in 2003, it declared Thailand and the Philippines to be "non-NATO major allies," thereby easing the way for the provision of sizable increases in security assistance.[46] As with Australia, these moves were motivated, in the first instance, by the need to combat Islamist terrorism. From the American perspective, at least, they were also part of a continuing, quiet effort to counterbalance China's rising power.

Washington's initial attempts to retool its alliances for a possible competition with China did not always meet with equal success. In contrast to Japan, during the Bush years South Korea refused to join in developing a full-scale theater missile defense system and resisted any steps that might draw it into a future confrontation between the United States and China. As part of the Bush administration's plan to redistribute forces and bases around the globe, the Defense Department sought to reduce ground and air force units in South Korea while concentrating those that remained in new facilities farther south, away from the border with North Korea. This redeployment was intended to make U.S. forces less vulnerable in the event of another war on the peninsula, but it also had the effect of better positioning them for use in conflicts elsewhere in Northeast Asia. A quick glance at the map made plain that the most likely site for such a conflict was Taiwan.

The South Korean government eventually agreed to a "realignment" of U.S. forces and acknowledged the American desire for greater flexibility. But during the presidency of domestic reformer and alliance skeptic Roh Moo-hyun, it insisted on a public declaration that "in the implementation of flexibility, the U.S. respects the ROK position that it shall not be involved in a regional conflict in Northeast Asia against the will of the Korean people."[47] While it did not give Seoul a veto, this pledge committed the United States to consult before using its Korean-based forces in an extra-peninsular contingency, thereby presumably limiting its ability to employ them in a confrontation with China.

As it strengthened its formal bilateral partnerships, the United States also began in the mid-1990s to bolster and broaden its portfolio of quasi-alliance relationships in Asia. Of these, the oldest and most delicate was the link to Taiwan. To Beijing's great irritation, even after it broke formal diplomatic relations with Taipei in 1979, the United States continued to sell "defensive arms" to its former ally. As U.S.-China relations improved during the 1980s, concern over a possible attack by the mainland dwindled, and these periodic sales came to be seen in Washington more as symbolic gestures of commitment than as part of a serious program to improve Taiwan's capacity for self-defense.

Following its 1996 confrontation with China, the Clinton administration quietly began a series of regular conversations with Taiwanese defense officials. The United States was in the rather unusual position of preparing to help Taiwan defend itself without having done any kind of joint planning or training. The talks that began in 1997 were not a substitute, but they did permit the two sides to exchange views on the nature of the threat and how each proposed to meet it. With the assistance of unofficial visits by American observers, Taiwan was able to identify a range of weaknesses in its defenses and to formulate a wish list of items that would help to correct them. This process culminated at the start of the Bush administration in a request for a large arms package that included submarines, antisubmarine warfare aircraft, and ballistic missile defense batteries.[48]

Washington was not always the one pushing for closer defense cooperation. As the Cold War wound down, the leaders of the tiny, wealthy, and strategically located island nation of Singapore feared that they might be left to the tender mercies of their larger Muslim neighbors on the one hand, and China on the other. In the early 1990s, when the U.S. Navy and Air Force were in the process of being evicted from their longtime bases in the Philippines, Singapore offered them the use of its own ports and airfield. American interest in these facilities grew alongside its concerns about China. In 1998, the Singaporean government agreed to pay the costs of building a new harbor big enough to accommodate U.S. aircraft carriers.[49] The port opened in 2001. In 2003 the two countries agreed to further enhance their defense cooperation. While both sides emphasized terrorism as the most important near-term threat, both also saw their continued, close cooperation as essential to prevent a rising China from eventually dominating Southeast Asia.[50] Although the results were less visible and less dramatic, a similar mix of concerns lay behind the Bush administration's decision to renew defense cooperation with Indonesia and to pursue closer strategic as well as economic ties with Vietnam.[51]

Of all the diplomatic balancing moves made during the late 1990s and early 2000s, the establishment of a quasi-alliance with India had the greatest long-term potential. Throughout the Cold War, despite the fact that they shared a common language and a commitment to democracy, the United States and India had seldom been close. American policy makers were annoyed by India's stubborn adherence to the principle of "nonalignment" and troubled by its strategic ties to the Soviet Union. Indians, for their part, resented America's hectoring and its support for their archenemy Pakistan. While the end of the Cold War seemed to open new possibilities, relations took a sharp turn for the worse in 1998, when India conducted a string of nuclear weapons tests, Pakistan responded in kind, and the United States imposed sanctions on both parties.

Despite these unfavorable developments, in the last months of the Clinton presidency, and especially following the election of George W. Bush, the United States reversed direction and began to move toward an increasingly close relationship with India.[52] As always, this shift had a number of causes, but the deepest and most important was a newly shared concern over the rise of China. In the months before the 9/11 attacks, the Bush administration had already made clear its intention to seek better relations with Delhi. In the wake of the attacks, it moved quickly to lift sanctions and to expand intelligence and defense contacts, including everything from high-level dialogues to arms sales and joint exercises. In order to clear away remaining diplomatic and legal obstacles to even closer cooperation, the Bush administration also began the arduous process of "grandfathering" India into the nuclear nonproliferation regime. The aim of all this activity, as administration spokesmen explained with surprising candor, was to "make India a global power."[53] What remained unspoken was precisely why it should be in the interest of one established power to promote the emergence of another. The answer, of course, was the rise of yet a third great power whose interests and ambitions were potentially at odds with those of the other two.

Slowing the growth of Chinese military power

During the eras of containment and alignment, the military and economic aspects of American strategy coincided easily with one another. In the 1950s and 1960s the United States sought to deny China access to technology (or anything else, for that matter) that might have contributed to the development of its economy or the growth of its military power. Once the decision had been made to build up China as a counterweight to the Soviet Union, trade and investment were encouraged, restrictions on technology flows were eased, and the United States even began to sell some military equipment directly to the People's Liberation Army.

After 1989 there was an irreducible measure of tension between American efforts to engage China economically while at the same time countering the growth of its military power. By continuing to open its markets and invest its capital, the United States was contributing substantially to the rapid expansion of China's GDP. This fueled Beijing's sustained military buildup, which in turn stimulated Washington to strengthen its Asian alliances and bolster its own forces in the region. Continued engagement thus helped to create the need for more balancing.

The area where the contradictions between engagement and balancing continued regularly to reemerge was the one in which the connections between trade and military power were most obvious and direct. Investing in factories, buying Chinese-made consumer goods, and thereby contributing to the overall growth of China's economy was one thing; transferring technology that might find its way directly into advanced weapons, or speed the day when China could develop them on its own, was much harder to justify. Yet it was precisely in the high-technology sectors that U.S. industry had the greatest advantages and Chinese firms were most eager to do business.

How could the U.S. government promote American exports without undermining national security? Policy makers struggled with this conundrum over the twenty years following Tiananmen without finding a fully satisfactory or stable solution. Part of the reason for their difficulty was the very rapid evolution and spread of technology during this period and the increasingly blurry line separating "military" from "civilian" technologies. In contrast to the 1950s or 1960s, American-based companies were no longer the only possible source of many of the relevant products, and it was by no means clear that even the most rigorous system of domestic export controls could prevent China from acquiring what it wanted on the global market.

The effort to slow the growth of China's military power by restricting its access to critical technologies was also buffeted by contradictory domestic impulses. Commercial considerations, as expressed by influential executives and powerful industry lobbying groups, generally weighed heavily in favor of loosening controls and easing access. These pressures for greater openness were offset, albeit only partially and temporarily, by growing concerns over China's capabilities and intentions. The result was a pattern in which periods of relaxation alternated with intervals of anxiety, but in which the overall trend was toward fewer and more narrowly focused controls.

Dealing with actual armaments proved to be the easiest part of the problem. After Tiananmen, the first President Bush imposed a total ban on the sale of lethal weapons and munitions to China and urged U.S. allies around the world to do likewise. While Bush and his advisors clearly intended for the arms embargo to be temporary, the evaporation of the old rationale for defense cooperation following the Soviet collapse, and the accompanying emergence of concern over China's rising power, transformed it into a permanent fixture. From the early 1990s onward the possibility of renewing arms sales was never seriously considered.

So-called dual-use technologies were another matter. Here the general direction of policy during the 1990s was toward a further loosening of existing, Cold War–era constraints. In 1991 and again in 1993, Presidents Bush and Clinton had blocked the export of satellites intended for launch from China. But these were sanctions imposed in response to Beijing's own sale of missiles to its Third World clients, rather than part of a concerted effort to slow its military development. Moreover, as James Mann notes, newly elected President Clinton's decision to prohibit satellite exports "harmed precisely those elements of the American business community that had most strongly supported" his recent campaign. This issue "roused the American business community from its slumber" and stirred a lobbying effort that led eventually to a relaxation of controls on high-speed supercomputers as well as satellites, and helped to create an atmosphere in which the burden of proof was on those who advocated retaining tough restrictions on technology exports.[54] Not surprisingly, U.S. companies generally favored looser requirements that enabled them to compete more effectively with their European and Japanese counterparts for a share of the growing Chinese market. For the most part, the Clinton administration was happy to oblige.

Over the course of the 1990s, despite emerging concerns over China's military buildup, the U.S. Commerce Department approved hundreds of requests for licenses to sell sensitive dual-use items such as equipment for making and testing semiconductors, precision machine tools, and specialized testing devices. At least some of these products were later found to have gone directly to companies and laboratories involved in the development and manufacture of military radars, cruise missiles, and nuclear weapons. Others were shipped to civilian enterprises, but their ultimate destinations, and the uses to which they were eventually put, could not be determined with certainty.[55]

In 1998–99 a series of loosely related scandals caused the Clinton administration's relaxed approach to the problem of technology transfer to be called into question. The resulting allegations culminated in criminal charges, a highly publicized congressional investigation, and, despite differences over the extent to which China had, in fact, succeeded in stealing secrets, new legislation intended to increase congressional oversight of the enforcement of existing espionage laws and export regulations.[56]

After 9/11, slowing China's buildup took a backseat to the urgent necessity of organizing a global campaign to stop terrorists from acquiring nuclear, chemical, and biological weapons of mass destruction. The former problem receded into the background for a time, but it never entirely disappeared. What caused the issue to reemerge was a debate that began in Brussels in 2004 over whether to finally lift the European Union's 1989 embargo on military sales to China. The embargo had been imposed originally for diplomatic rather than strategic reasons; its purpose was to signal Western disapproval of the role of the People's Liberation Army in crushing domestic opposition, rather than to slow the further development of its capabilities. In the view of many EU political and business leaders, the fifteen-year-old restrictions had long since outlived their usefulness. Eliminating them would open up new opportunities for European aerospace and electronics firms. Moreover, with the Bush administration now downplaying tensions and singing Beijing's praises for its help in combating terrorism and proliferation, there seemed little reason to fear a harsh American reaction.

European governments were thus taken aback when, at the eleventh hour, the Bush administration expressed its displeasure and organized an intense and ultimately successful campaign to stop the proposed changes. In making the case for a continued embargo, the administration was forced to restate some of its concerns, not about China's past behavior on human rights, but about its future military capabilities and strategic intentions.[57] At the same time, discussion within the U.S. government over how to deal with the European challenge led to a reexamination of American export controls and yet another attempt to refine and, in certain respects, to tighten them, primarily by trying to determine the ultimate "end use" of high-tech products purchased by Chinese firms.[58] These adjustments, announced in 2007, were one more in a series of attempts to find the right balance between engagement and containment or, as a Commerce Department official put it, to take account of the "duality inherent in America's relationship with China. We seek actively to encourage legitimate civilian trade . . . even as we prudently hedge against the rapid growth in China's military capabilities."[59]

THE OBAMA ADMINISTRATION
EMBRACES CONGAGEMENT

Bill Clinton and George W. Bush came to power seemingly prepared to take a firmer stance toward China than their predecessors, but both quickly changed course and became enthusiastic, outspoken advocates of engagement. During his first year in office Barack Obama appeared to move in the opposite direction, initially stressing engagement above all else before seeming to rediscover the importance of balancing.

Following on the heels of an administration that it regarded as excessively ideological and confrontational, the Obama team began by declaring its desire to "reset" strained relations with nations like Russia and Iran. In the case of China, where the diplomatic climate was generally acknowledged already to be favorable, the president and his top advisors looked for ways to make it even better, raising the relationship to an entirely new level of closeness and cooperation. Thus, within weeks of taking office, Secretary of State Hillary Clinton announced the U.S. desire to resume mid-level military discussions, which Secretary of Defense Rumsfeld had suspended, to broaden the scope of engagement "to reach beyond ministerial buildings and official meeting halls . . . to engage civil society," and to pursue "collaboration on clean energy and greater efficiency" that offered "a real opportunity to deepen the overall U.S.-Chinese relationship."[60] Dealing with climate change, emerging diseases, and the aftereffects of the global financial crisis of late 2008 was assumed to demand the closest possible coordination between Washington and Beijing. Although the idea never gained official endorsement, immediately after the election some leading foreign policy pundits with ties to the new president floated proposals for creating a "G-2" mechanism that would elevate China to the position of America's most important diplomatic partner.[61]

As it looked for ways to broaden and deepen engagement, the new administration also signaled its desire to avoid friction over perennially contentious issues like human rights. During her first official visit to Beijing, Secretary Clinton suggested that the United States would not permit disagreements on this sensitive subject to "interfere with the global economic crisis, the global climate change crisis, and the security crisis."[62] As if to underline the point, President Obama declined to meet with the Dalai Lama prior to his own inaugural trip to China in November 2009. This was the first time since 1991 that a president had refused a request for a meeting with the exiled Tibetan religious leader and it was widely seen as "an attempt to gain favor with China."[63]

Seeking to codify the administration's new approach, Deputy Secretary of State James Steinberg asserted that Beijing and Washington should henceforth pursue a policy of "strategic reassurance" toward one another, avoiding deeds as well as words that might heighten mutual insecurity and mistrust.[64] For his part, Secretary of Defense Robert Gates made clear his view that the United States should focus on fighting and preparing for so-called irregular wars against insurgents and terrorists, while cutting back on procurement of expensive, high-end systems like the F-22 fighter or a possible replacement for the B-2 "stealth" bomber that would be of use primarily in high-intensity conventional warfare against a "near-peer competitor."[65] Whether or not they were intended in precisely this way, the administration's initial decisions on defense matters were interpreted in some quarters as sending "an unmistakable (indeed, arguably historic) signal to Beijing: the U.S. strategy of hedging its bets over potential wars is being scaled back. Maybe we don't think you guys are a threat after all."[66]

Despite all of these signs and portents, within a year of taking office, the Obama administration began to tack back toward a tougher, or at least a more balanced, approach. Instead of sidestepping confrontations over delicate issues, in January 2010 Secretary of State Clinton went out of her way to criticize Beijing for censoring the Internet and conducting cyber-surveillance on the e-mail accounts of human rights advocates.[67] Later the same month, despite vociferous protests from Beijing, the administration announced that it would adhere to the policy of five previous presidents by selling "defensive" arms to Taiwan.[68] Safely back from China, the president met (albeit somewhat furtively, in the White House basement) with the Dalai Lama.[69]

During the spring and summer of 2010 Washington and Beijing were at odds over a series of issues involving use of the waters of the Western Pacific. When Chinese officials made statements seemingly amplifying their claims to virtually all of the South China Sea, the United States offered to help mediate outstanding disputes between the countries of the region. Couched in the polite language of diplomacy, this move was clearly intended to prevent Beijing from imposing its will on its smaller, weaker neighbors.[70] Similarly, Washington's efforts to ease tensions following the arrest and detention of a Chinese fishing boat captain by Japanese forces off the disputed Senkaku Islands were obviously meant to signal support for its traditional ally.[71] When Beijing objected to exercises off its coasts involving American and South Korean naval vessels, U.S. officials acknowledged Chinese concerns while pointedly reasserting their right to conduct operations as they saw fit in international waters.[72]

In addition to stiffening its diplomatic posture, the Obama administration took other steps to reinforce the balancing portion of U.S. strategy. When a newly elected Japanese government threatened to block the relocation of a U.S. airbase on Okinawa, Washington chose to push back, even at the risk of straining relations with Tokyo, because it regarded the facilities as critical to maintaining a favorable balance of power with China.[73] While it was more circumspect in certain respects in discussing the problem, the QDR released in February 2010 did not differ fundamentally from its predecessor in its diagnosis of the "anti-access" challenge, and at least on paper, its recommendations for how to respond were essentially the same.[74] Finally, in the spring of 2010 the Obama administration announced that it would try its hand at reforming the export control system, streamlining the process while tightening controls on what were referred to as "the crown jewels" of American technology.[75]

To a certain extent, the apparent shift in strategic emphasis from engagement to balancing was an optical illusion, or rather a matter of timing. The decision on arms sales to Taiwan and the content of the QDR would not have been much different if they had been announced in mid-2009, when relations appeared to be on an upward trajectory, rather than in early 2010, when they seemed to be on the decline. At least initially, the stiffening in the Obama administration's posture toward China also had to do with frustrations on the engagement side of the agenda, regarding trade and climate change negotiations.[76] Still, within a year of taking office, the new president was forced to confront troubling evidence that his initial attempts at "reassurance" had not only failed to cause Beijing to moderate its behavior, but may actually have encouraged it to act more assertively than it might otherwise have done. Having tried briefly to push policy toward the engagement end of the spectrum, the Obama administration was being forced back toward the congagement mean.

THE RESILIENCE OF CONGAGEMENT ... AND ITS RISKS

This is nothing new. To the contrary, the past twenty years have been marked not only by a process of virtually continuous equilibration and adjustment, but also by a high level of overall stability and continuity. Despite rhetorical gyrations and marginal shifts in policy, America's mixed strategy has remained unchanged in its essentials since the mid-1990s.

The resilience of congagement is due to both the essential soundness of its strategic logic and the sturdiness of its domestic political foundations. Given all the uncertainties, it has made eminently good sense for the United States to continue to engage economically and diplomatically with China while seeking simultaneously to balance against its rising power. In any event, there is no alternative approach that is clearly superior on its merits. Congagement also contains elements that appeal to a variety of different segments of American society. The attractions of engagement are obvious and manifold; it means trade, talk, and the hope of democratic reforms and perpetual peace. In a nation as deeply imbued with liberal beliefs as the United States it is difficult to find anyone who opposes these things in principle, and easy to find many who embrace them almost as a matter of faith. More concretely, engagement is strongly favored by a sizable slice of American business, most academics, many influential former government officials, and a large group of congressmen and senators whose constituents do business with China. Within the executive branch it is backed by most members of the permanent State Department bureaucracy and, albeit with caution and some caveats, by many in the intelligence community and the uniformed military.

The containment or balancing side of congagement also has its supporters, though they tend to be, by comparison, a weaker and less cohesive group. Among the more active and vocal are those driven by nonstrategic considerations. Human rights and religious organizations that object to the way the Beijing regime treats its own people are usually sympathetic to the idea that its external actions must also be closely watched and, if necessary, opposed. Representatives of unions and domestic industries hurt by cheap labor and inexpensive imports sometimes favor a tougher stance on defense as well as trade issues.[77] Although the "Taiwan lobby" is not what it was in the 1950s and 1960s, since the democratic reforms of the 1990s Taipei actually has a broader base of sympathy and support, both in Congress and among the general public.

Hollywood stereotypes of fire-breathing militarists notwithstanding, there is in fact no enthusiasm within the armed forces for a new Cold War with China. Because of the geography of Asia and the size of the opponent, the U.S. Army and Marine Corps ground forces would have virtually no role in such a rivalry. The U.S. Air Force and Navy, meanwhile, are deeply ambivalent about giving top priority to a challenge that, if taken seriously, might consume all available resources, crowd out preparations for other missions, and require disruptive changes in existing procurement programs and service priorities. As China's anti-access capabilities mature, the navy may have to abandon its decades-long love affair with the aircraft carrier and turn to less glamorous but more survivable undersea and low-observable surface vessels. Similarly, as Chinese air defenses grow more capable, and U.S. bases in East Asia become more vulnerable, the air force may find itself pressed to spend less on relatively short-range air superiority fighters that have long been its top priority and more on stealthy long-range bombers and unmanned aerial vehicles.

The defense industry is similarly divided. Many of the firms that might stand to gain from an arms race with China are now happily engaged in selling it products like civilian airliners, commercial satellites, and air traffic control systems. Other companies see greater potential in supplying the Pentagon with the sensors, vehicles, and light weaponry it needs to wage "irregular warfare" than in trying to persuade its leaders to prepare for the high-intensity conflicts that they clearly believe to be improbable. Finally, like some of their military customers, the manufacturers of big-ticket items such as fighters and carriers are doubtless reluctant to play up threats that could make their products obsolete. In sum, while it may be a force in favor of more vigorous balancing, the industrial side of the "military-industrial complex" is not as strong nor as unified a factor in shaping strategy as is often assumed.

Can congagement be sustained? Critics of a mixed strategy have generally focused on the danger that attempts at balancing could undermine engagement. They warn that as the United States deploys more forces in East Asia, tightens its alliances, arms Taiwan, and frets openly about technology transfer, it signals its mistrust of Chinese intentions, stirs deep-seated fears of encirclement, and lends credence to those who argue that Beijing must pursue a tougher policy of its own. China's responses to American actions will then be taken as further evidence of its aggressive inclinations and of the need for yet more balancing. Regardless of which side actually made the first move, action will provoke counteraction, which will compel counter-counteraction, and so on, until the two powers are at swords' points. As security concerns rise, engagement will be constricted. Diplomatic cooperation will dwindle due to mutual mistrust and a sense that any gain for the other side is a loss for one's own. In the commercial sphere, each party will seek to reduce its dependence on the other in order to minimize its vulnerability to coercion or economic warfare. Regardless of what either initially intended, the United States and China will end up in a new Cold War, if not an actual shooting war.

There is certainly a possibility that this could happen, but the strength of the domestic interests arrayed in favor of continued engagement and against "excessive" balancing make it a far less likely scenario than it might otherwise be. Any attempt to move away from the current mix of policies and toward one that places heavier emphasis on military preparedness and overt alliance building is certain to provoke resistance from a variety of influential quarters. The coalition of individuals and groups with a stake in maintaining good relations with China is broader, stronger, and more influential today than it was in the early 1990s. The idea that trade will eventually promote democracy and peace is also more widely accepted, both in and out of government, as is the belief that diplomacy and military-to-military dialogue will produce an increasing convergence of interests. On the other hand, the assertion that "if we treat China like an enemy it will become one" has become a piece of elite conventional wisdom that few pause to examine.[78] "Respectable opinion" in academic, political, and policy-making circles is still solidly behind engagement and wary of balancing.

Building up American military strength to keep pace with China will also be costly and hence unpopular with advocates of smaller federal budgets and lower taxes, as well as those who favor increased spending on health care and other social welfare programs. Especially in the wake of two protracted wars and a major financial crisis, the public appetite for new defense expenditures will be limited at best. Some elements in a program of intensified balancing might also arouse anxiety from America's Asian allies, to say nothing of sharp protests from Beijing, and these voices too would be heard in the context of an open debate over policy.

In sum, the obstacles to a substantial increase in balancing are many and weighty. They are likely to be broken down by a protracted process of erosion, a sudden crisis or, perhaps most likely, the former followed by the latter. On the other hand, despite the Obama administration's recent disappointments, a gradual move in the opposite direction, toward even more engagement and less investment in balancing, appears to be much more plausible. Putting aside for the moment the question of what the optimal mix of elements would be from a strategic perspective, the political playing field is clearly tilted in a way that favors such a development.

Uncertainty over China's trajectory could also help to make such a shift in the overall mix of U.S. strategy more likely. There will always be debates, as there are now, over the scope, pace, and significance of China's military buildup and the meaning and sincerity of its diplomatic initiatives. For as long as the country is ruled by a closed and secretive regime, there will be doubts among outsiders about the true nature of its intentions. If it takes care to conceal its motives and avoid premature confrontations, if it ensures that its interlocutors and trading partners continue to enjoy the benefits of engagement, if it can delay the responses of potential rivals and discourage them from cooperating effectively with one another, China may eventually be able to develop its strength to the point where balancing appears hopeless and accommodation to its wishes seems the only sensible option. For a rising power facing a still-strong rival, this would be a prudent path to follow. In fact, as I argue in the next three chapters, it is just such a strategy that has guided China's actions since the end of the Cold War.

Five

"THE PROPENSITY OF THINGS"

"SEEK TRUTH FROM FACTS"

Speculating on the likely future course of Soviet Russia's foreign policy on the eve of the Second World War, Winston Churchill famously described that country as "a riddle, wrapped in a mystery, inside an enigma."[1] China today is far more open than the Soviet Union ever was, yet the shape of its goals and the content of its long-term strategy remain subjects of intense speculation and debate among outside observers. In part the reasons for this are the same as in the 1930s. Beijing is not Moscow, and Hu Jintao is certainly no Stalin, but the state over which he presides is just as deeply committed to secrecy and equally practiced in the arts of deception. A one-party authoritarian regime is under little pressure to reveal its plans or justify its choices to its own people, let alone to foreigners. Beijing's ability to conceal its deliberations, control information, and shape perceptions of its plans and ambitions, while less than perfect, is still substantial. The difficulty that foreigners encounter in trying to pierce this veil is hardly accidental.

There are other, deeper reasons for the prevailing uncertainty about China's intentions. Especially as regards the definition of long-range objectives, its current leaders may be divided, or even undecided. The consensus that evidently exists today on the general direction of policy rests to some degree on the deferral of decisions that will eventually have to be faced. Thus, even if foreign intelligence services could penetrate the innermost recesses of the leadership compound at Zhongnanhai, they might find that the answers to key questions simply do not exist, at least not yet.

Outsiders may not be able to figure out precisely where China is headed because the country's rulers do not yet know themselves.

Complicating matters still further is the prospect of regime change. For as long as the Communist Party remains in power, there is reason to expect a high degree of continuity in China's external goals and strategies. Just as America's foreign policy is shaped, although not entirely determined, by its democratic institutions and liberal beliefs, so too China's stance toward the world is in part a reflection of its authoritarian political structure and the ideological foundations on which that system rests. At some point in the next several decades, however, the PRC may undergo a fundamental political transformation, perhaps evolving into anything from a multiparty liberal democracy to a corporatist, hyper-nationalist, quasi-fascist dictatorship. In twenty or thirty years' time, China could well be a profoundly different place, with altered institutions, new elites, and a new ideology. The rulers of a post-Communist state will doubtless have a distinctive view of their nation's interests, and of the best means for achieving them. Better insight into today's planning therefore does not guarantee an accurate forecast of future behavior. Still, we have to begin somewhere, and trying to understand what the current regime is up to is the most logical and appropriate place to start.

Analysts of contemporary Chinese strategy are confronted at once by a confusing blend of cacophony and silence. As compared to the Maoist era, China's top leaders, and the entire apparatus of the party-state, are veritable fonts of information and opinion. Public discussion of almost any issue used to consist of little more than Delphic statements from the Great Helmsman, echoed ad nauseum by the organs of a vast propaganda machine. Today an assortment of Chinese officials and government agencies makes meaningful policy statements and prepares comparatively professional reports on a wide variety of topics. There is, of course, no shortage of sloganeering and blather, but there is also a good deal of wheat amid the chaff.

On some topics, however, the regime remains tight-lipped. To the extent that they deal at all with future plans, defense budget statements and "white papers" are opaque and incomplete. Speeches and reports on foreign policy still repeat key phrases with mind-numbing regularity and China's aims are discussed in only the most cursory and anodyne ways.

Even seemingly innocuous bureaucratic details of the strategy-making process, such as the composition of the various ad hoc cross-departmental "leading small groups" in which issues are discussed and options formulated, are typically treated as state secrets.

While the system remains tightly closed at the top, there has been some significant loosening at the lower levels. The thirty years since the beginning of the period of "reform and opening up" have seen a profusion of think tanks, journals, and academic research institutes devoted to the study of international relations, foreign policy, and national defense. Many of these organizations and individuals are directly linked to and funded by government departments, including the Ministry of Foreign Affairs, the Ministry of State Security, and the People's Liberation Army. Scholars and government analysts now participate in wide-ranging public discussions of national strategy, as well as in debates that are restricted and, in some cases, highly classified.[2]

The open source literature that is readily available outside China contains a wealth of useful material. Intriguing as they are, however, these writings must be approached with caution. At least some of what is available in the public domain may be intended to deceive or confuse foreign readers. While the range of opinions expressed is far greater than ever before, certain positions are still clearly out of bounds. Even if they are sincere, the views of some authors may not be widely shared or have any bearing on actual policy. Finally, despite its apparent variety, the sample of sources that is either published in English or finds its way easily into translation appears to be biased toward civilian academics, institutes, and agencies and away from the military and, to a lesser degree, the security services. As we shall see, the arguments most easily overheard by Westerners are hardly bland and reassuring; but there is reason to believe that even tougher, more aggressive (and possibly more influential) opinions are being expressed within the confines of the Chinese system. (Readers interested in learning more about the various Chinese journals and authors cited in chapters 5 through 7 should consult the brief appendix titled "Sources and Methods," which begins on p. 285.)

In the end, any attempt to construct a coherent, plausible account of China's strategy and intentions, whether from classified information, published writings, interviews, an analysis of observed behavior, or some combination of sources, will contain gaps and inferential leaps. All such interpretations involve acts of imagination, but that does not mean they should be permitted to become works of pure fiction. Analysts have an obligation not only to heed Deng Xiaoping's admonition to "seek truth from facts," but also to be clear about where the facts inevitably leave off and speculation necessarily begins.

With this injunction in mind I have divided what follows into three parts. In the remainder of this chapter I summarize the main points of an assessment of China's strategic situation that is widely, if not universally, shared by the nation's analysts and policy makers. Next, in chapter 6, I lay out three basic principles or axioms that, while not codified in any official form, appear to set the general direction of Beijing's approach to dealing with the United States and the wider world. Finally, in chapter 7, I offer a frankly speculative interpretation of China's broad strategic objectives and of the policies that it is now pursuing to achieve them.

CHINESE STRATEGISTS ASSESS "THE PROPENSITY OF THINGS"

Based on a close reading of ancient texts, French philosopher François Jullien concludes that there are profound differences in the way Eastern and Western thinkers have approached the problems of military and political strategy. Since the Greeks, the "Western way" has been to work backward from a desired end state. Westerners begin by defining a goal, then devise a plan for achieving it, mobilize the necessary resources, and drive forward to reach their objective. Victory goes to the leader who has the strength, both moral and physical, to overcome all obstacles and to impose his will on the environment, and the opponent.

By contrast, Jullien writes, Eastern strategic thought is more organic and improvisational and less mechanical and deterministic. Outcomes are the product of many converging factors and forces, most of which are not under the direct control of even the bravest, most resolute commander. The successful strategist is the one who best grasps the essence of the situation, "the propensity of things," or the direction in which events are tending, and exploits this understanding to his advantage.

For these reasons, concludes Jullien, "a Chinese general does not elaborate a plan that he projects upon the future and that leads to a predetermined goal and then define how to link together the means best suited to realize that plan. Instead, he begins by making a minute evaluation of the relation of the forces in play so that he can make the most of the favorable factors implied in the situation, exploiting them constantly, whatever the circumstances he encounters."[3]

This way of thinking has a number of important practical implications. If the Chinese philosophers are right, the essential virtue of the successful strategist is not so much strength and decisiveness as wisdom or insight. The commander who understands how the world really works will spend less time on planning and more on assessment. Above all, he will start by making "a painstaking study of the forces present" in order to assess "which are favorable to each of the two camps."[4] He will realize that it is fruitless to try to specify a precise objective and misleading to imagine that he can lay out in advance a series of specific steps that will lead him to it. The wise commander will define his goal as achieving a more favorable configuration of forces, albeit one that he recognizes to be transitory and continually evolving, rather than reaching an imaginary end point.

While it may be for reasons other than (or in addition to) deeply rooted features of their history and culture, the writings of today's Chinese strategists conform with Jullien's interpretation in at least two critical respects. Any reader familiar with comparable Western analyses cannot help but be struck by the extent to which Chinese strategic thinkers devote their energies to assessing the situation their country confronts, as compared to offering prescriptions for the policies it should follow. And, at least insofar as their public writings are concerned, these analysts are also remarkably reticent about discussing China's strategic goals in anything but the most general terms. This silence may be the product of a deliberate effort at concealment, but it could also reflect a more flexible and open-ended approach to strategic thinking and planning.

Contemporary Chinese assessments of the propensity of things center on providing answers to three questions, each of which I examine here: What are the dominant trends in today's world? What is the distribution of power within the contemporary international system? And what are the sources of the most important challenges or threats confronting China?

"PEACE AND DEVELOPMENT"

While Chairman Mao was alive, the prevailing tendencies in the world were seen to be toward "war and revolution." This judgment, rendered by Mao himself, was beyond challenge and it persisted, with some modifications, into the mid-1980s. Until the late 1970s, the official Chinese Communist Party line was that as long as the forces of "imperialism" (led by the United States) and "social imperialism" (led by the Soviet Union) continued to exist, a new world war was inevitable. The essential features of China's domestic and foreign policies, emphasizing national defense and aligning with the United States against the greater danger of the Soviet Union, followed from this expectation.

The late 1970s saw the consolidation of Deng Xiaoping's rule and the start of the era of "reform and opening up." This was followed, a few years later, by Mikhail Gorbachev's rise and his ultimately fatal experiments with *glasnost* and *perestroika*. Deng's decision to give priority to economic development rested on and, in a sense, required a softening in official assessments of the strategic environment. This shift became much easier to justify as the Soviet Union grew less menacing and then collapsed. With the closest and most immediate threat to China's security suddenly gone, and the Cold War standoff at an end, the wisdom of Deng's choices seemed self-evident.

In 1985 top Chinese officials declared that "peace and development" were the "great issues" or most important trends in the world.[5] Another global conflagration was no longer inevitable, nor even especially likely. As we have seen, during the second half of the Reagan administration, this assessment led to a cooling in Beijing's enthusiasm for a closer strategic alignment with the United States. It also set the tone for the subsequent evolution of Chinese diplomacy and for redoubled efforts to promote economic growth.

Deng's dictum was challenged on at least two occasions. Following the 1989 Tiananmen incident, more conservative Communist Party leaders criticized his economic reform policies as a betrayal of socialist principles and warned against continuing to pursue more open and cordial relations with the West. In their view China's embrace of peace and development had opened the door to corruption, subversion, and unrest. By the early 1990s Deng had succeeded in beating back these attacks and winning a reaffirmation of his basic assessment of the strategic environment.[6]

Ten years later, after Deng's death, the question of the prevailing tendency in world affairs was once again a subject of fierce disagreement. This time the precipitating event was an external crisis, and the focus of discussion was squarely on foreign policy and national defense. In the spring of 1999 the United States and several NATO allies used air power to compel Serbia to withdraw troops from its ethnic minority province of Kosovo. While attacking targets in the capital city of Belgrade, American planes accidentally struck the Chinese embassy, killing a number of its occupants.

The Belgrade bombing triggered angry anti-American demonstrations, a debate within China's top leadership, and, for the first time, an outpouring of commentary expressing a variety of viewpoints on national strategy in the government-controlled media. At issue was the question of whether the world was now moving in new and more dangerous directions. If so, China might have to respond by adjusting its own course, increasing defense spending, slowing domestic reforms, and perhaps reconsidering its push to enter the World Trade Organization.[7]

After several months, public discussion of these questions was brought to a close by the promulgation of a new party line. In what amounted to a split decision, the regime settled on an assessment characterized by the phrase "Three No Changes and Three New Changes." Deng's successor, Jiang Zemin, reiterated that despite recent setbacks, peace and development were still the trend of the times. Thanks in part to the increasing openness and interconnectedness of the world's economies, the probability of major war would remain low, and the overall relaxation of international tensions that followed the end of the Cold War would continue. "Globalization" was now seen as a major factor supporting continued peace and development. At the same time, however, there were some troubling signs on the horizon. In a veiled reference to the United States, party strategists noted that "hegemonism and power politics" were on the rise while the trend toward "military interventionism" was increasing. A careful assessment gave grounds not only for continued long-term optimism but also for heightened vigilance, especially in the near to medium term. This basic reading of the strategic environment would persist through the first decade of the twenty-first century.[8]

WAITING FOR MULTIPOLARITY

In addition to trying to grasp the underlying dynamics of global politics, Chinese analysts devote great energy to assessing the "world configuration of power," or what Western scholars generally refer to as the structure of the international system.[9] Most observers in Chinese think tanks, universities, and government ministries believe that the conduct of international relations is heavily shaped, if not entirely determined, by the current and likely future distribution of what they refer to as "comprehensive national power." In contrast to their essentially fixed view of the prevailing trend toward peace and development, the Chinese strategic community's consensus judgment on this issue has already passed through two phases and appears to be at the start of a third.

Deng Xiaoping's announcement in the mid-1980s of the end of the era of war and revolution was premised in part on his judgment that both the United States and the Soviet Union were entering into a period of decline, while the developing countries (including China) were on the rise. The narrowing gap between the capabilities of the superpowers and those of the rest of the world would act as a check on their hegemonistic impulses. The impending demise of Cold War bipolarity thus heralded the arrival of a new, more equitable, and more stable international system in which many centers of roughly equal power would tend to check and counterbalance one another.[10]

Although Deng clearly anticipated something more gradual and less traumatic, the collapse of the Soviet Union seemed, for a time, to vindicate his prediction. In the early 1990s the age of multipolarity appeared finally to be at hand. From the start, however, there were troubling signs. The first Gulf War provided an opportunity for the United States to show off its now unrivaled ability to project air, naval, and ground power and to defeat even large, heavily armed opponents far from home without suffering significant casualties of its own. Washington also displayed a newfound ability to mobilize international support for its interventionist schemes, including winning the backing of the UN Security Council, something that the prospect of a Soviet veto had rendered virtually impossible during the Cold War.

America's subsequent actions in Bosnia (1995), the Taiwan Strait (1996), and Kosovo (1999) further highlighted how the end of the Cold War had left Washington emboldened and essentially unconstrained. By the close of the decade the United States had shown that it could win wars with airpower alone and without even the fig leaf of UN approval. The ouster of Iraqi forces from Kuwait in 1991 could at least be justified as a defense of the traditional principle of national sovereignty. Eight years later, the Americans used force in Kosovo to defend a separatist movement and assist in the partition of an existing nation-state. The United States now seemed to have both the capacity and the desire to single-handedly rewrite the rules of the international game.

In the early 1990s, Chinese analysts anticipated that the collapse of the Soviet Union would be followed in short order by the dissolution of America's alliances, the accelerated growth and increasing independence of its former allies, and a sustained deterioration in its own national economic performance. These predictions echoed those of prominent Western "declinists." The end result, in the view of Chinese strategists, would be a world with five or possibly six major players, including Japan, a reunited Germany (or perhaps a united Europe), a recovering Russia, a diminished America, possibly India, and, although they seldom referred directly to their own country, a rising China.[11]

For those eagerly awaiting the new era of multipolarity, the nineties proved to be a disappointing decade. Instead of continuing to slump economically, as it had done in the late 1980s, the United States rebounded smartly and began a prolonged period of increasing productivity and above-average GDP growth. Meanwhile Japan, once widely touted as the next "number one" nation in the global economy, fell on hard times and saw its growth rates dwindle to near zero. In Europe a unified, capitalist Germany struggled to absorb its impoverished former Communist cousins, while the other advanced industrial economies labored under the burden of high taxes, regulation, generous social welfare programs, and aging populations. Russia entered into a period of economic stagnation and social decay. Both India and China enjoyed rapid economic growth, but neither yet had the full range of capabilities necessary to be considered a truly great power, still less a match for the United States.

By the end of the first post–Cold War decade, Chinese strategists were coming to the painful realization that bipolarity would be followed, not by an immediate transition to a multipolar world, but by an extended period of American predominance. Because multipolarity was still expected to arrive eventually, Deng's prognostication did not have to be directly challenged or formally overturned. But a realistic appraisal now had to begin by acknowledging that fundamental structural change might be many years in the offing. For the time being, the international system could most generously be described as having "one superpower, many great powers." According to one participant in these discussions, however, by the turn of the century he and his colleagues had come to accept that the superpower was "more super, and the many great powers . . . less great" than they had anticipated only a few years before.[12]

In addition to reiterating Deng's assessment of the dominant trend in world affairs, the "great peace and development debate" of 1999 also reaffirmed his views about the eventual structure of the international system. It was still the case that, as an official news item put it, "no force can block the tide of development of multipolarization."[13] At the same time, it was now widely acknowledged that "the trend of multipolarism is obviously slowing down," while at least for the foreseeable future, "the U.S. pole will be further strengthened."[14] Though there was no formal statement to this effect, by the turn of the century analyst David Finkelstein writes that China's leaders had concluded that the "much-hoped-for multipolar world order was *not* around the corner" and that the United States would retain its status as the sole superpower for "15 to 20 years if not longer."[15]

This basic finding remained intact during the first term of the George W. Bush administration. Indeed, in the immediate aftermath of the 9/11 attacks, Chinese analysts tended to upgrade still further their assessments of American power and resolve. In Afghanistan and, at least during the opening, conventional stages of the war in Iraq, the United States demonstrated yet again the full measure of its military superiority. No other nation could combine precision air strikes with comparatively small, light ground forces to win swift victories in mountains and deserts half a world away. In going to war in Iraq, the Americans also showed that they were willing to defy the United Nations, shrug off the entreaties of even some of their closest allies, and attack another country without any visible provocation. This was behavior characteristic of a nation that was not merely first among equals, but a true hegemon like those from China's distant past, a ruthless and cunning foe determined to preserve its place and willing to crush any who dared stand in its way.[16]

In retrospect it appears that the conclusion of what were officially referred to as "major combat operations" in Iraq in May 2003 marked an inflection point in Beijing's assessments of U.S. power. The failure to find stockpiles of weapons of mass destruction, lingering ill will over Washington's prewar diplomacy, and, above all, the growing chaos and violence in Iraq combined to raise questions about America's capabilities and competence. Cautiously at first, and then with increasing certainty (and a measure of ill-disguised glee), Chinese observers began to recalibrate their assessments.

Shortly before George W. Bush's second inaugural in January 2005, Wang Jisi, dean of China's America-watchers, observed that although the decline of U.S. hegemony was "inevitable," he could not yet see "any sign of a sustained decline in U.S. comprehensive power." Still, while the United States remained strong, the Iraq war had put it in a situation of "unprecedented international isolation," causing a "serious depletion of [its] 'soft [power]'" and leading to intensified "contradictions" between it and the EU, Japan, and Russia, among others. Iraq was clearly hurting the United States, though to what extent remained to be seen.[17]

Other analysts were more optimistic in their judgments. The United States might still be the leading *global* power, but its standing in key regions, including Asia, had been weakened by the course of the Iraq war. According to an October 2005 article in an official weekly, the Bush administration's "selfish and overbearing behavior" in going to war and subsequent revelations about the mistreatment of captured Iraqi soldiers at Abu Ghraib prison were "trashing U.S. prestige" and contributing to an erosion in the foundation of American hegemony in Asia.[18]

Despite some improvement in the situation on the ground in Iraq resulting from the "surge" in U.S. forces and the shift to a counterinsurgency strategy that began in early 2007, Chinese analysts continued to believe that the war would have harmful long-term consequences for the American position in Asia. In a May 2007 paper (commissioned by a think tank associated with the Ministry of State Security), Professor Shi Yinhong of Renmin University argued that the United States had "fallen into a fearful predicament" that had left it confused and demoralized. More concretely, the "task of pacifying Iraq" had created "a major long-lasting constraint on U.S. resources, energy, and attention." As a result, the Americans now found themselves unable to block ongoing shifts in the balance of power, most notably the rise of China.[19] Having exhausted itself at home and abroad, the Bush administration had, in the words of a People's Liberation Army–sponsored journal, "no energy left to formulate a new strategy to deal with China's rise . . . Simply put, the United States has begun to enter a period of relative decline."[20] While the United States wallowed, other potential power centers would continue to grow and "of course, China first of all."[21]

The global financial meltdown that began in late 2008 and the severe recession that followed in its wake reinforced this basic judgment. The crisis and its lingering aftereffects were widely seen as having had a significant "across-the-board impact on America's hegemony," undermining its "political and economic status," erasing the "power and prestige of neo-liberal theory," altering "the trend of an ideologically strong West and an ideologically weak East," shattering the West's claim to "truth hegemony," and generally accelerating the "democratization" of the international system.[22] According to a February 2009 article in the official CCP newspaper, "U.S. strength is declining at a speed so fantastic that it is far beyond anticipation."[23] As a result, the "process of multipolarization has been accelerated."[24]

While a few observers went so far as to declare that "the great crash of 2008" marked the end of the unipolar system, the consensus view was more cautious.[25] Despite the blows to its prestige and relative power, "the United States is still the strongest country,"[26] and "no turning point has appeared in the 'one superpower and several powers' pattern."[27] After assessing the various aspects of its comprehensive national power, most Chinese analysts now appear to have concluded that the United States will retain its edge in military capabilities, technology, soft power, and overall economic capacity for years, possibly decades into the future.

As to what will come next, the most commonly expressed opinion is that in the long sweep of history, the era of American dominance will mark a relatively brief detour on the road from Cold War bipolarity to a truly multipolar world. In other words, on this, as on so many other issues, Deng Xiaoping will ultimately be proved to have been correct. Albeit tentatively, some Chinese analysts have begun to raise another possibility: if the United States is declining, and China is rising faster than any of the other potential power centers, perhaps what lies in store is not multipolarity at all but a new form of bipolarity. As was true during the Cold War, the two leading powers may not be equal in all dimensions, but they will be roughly equivalent, and in any event, they will be more similar in their capabilities to one another than they are to any other member of the international system. A world of "extensive unilateral US supremacy" may be replaced by one in which China and the United States are each dominant in different domains.[28]

Members of China's strategic community no doubt recognize that predicting bipolarity carries with it certain risks, both at home and abroad. On the one hand, it means going against what is still the party line. At the same time, loudly proclaiming that China will someday be one of two superpowers, instead of only one among many great powers, could appear overly ambitious, and even threatening, to foreign governments, not least to the United States. Despite these dangers, Chinese commentators have recently become more forthright in stating that at a minimum, their country is well on its way to becoming "Mr. Second," in relation to America's "Mr. Big."[29] At a conference held in late 2009, one leading analyst declared his willingness to "go out on a limb and predict that China may become the second largest power after the United States."[30] While resisting the suggestion that their country is ready to form a "G-2" grouping with the United States and assume shared responsibilities for global management, many observers are now prepared to acknowledge that "China and the United States are the most influential countries in the world."[31] Some have suggested that in a few decades, "chances are that China will evolve into another superpower."[32]

Perhaps someday China may even become "Mr. Big" itself. And why not? Noting that Britain launched the Industrial Revolution and built a global empire with a comparatively small population, and the United

States "created the myth of the sole superpower" with on the order of 100 million people, Professor Jin Canrong of China People's University asks rhetorically, "What will the industrialization of China, with its 1.3 billion people, mean for the world?"[33] The answer seems clear enough though, for now, neither Professor Jin nor the vast majority of his colleagues are willing to put it into words.

THE AMERICAN THREAT

A review of their internal personnel files concludes that China's fourth-generation leaders see the United States as "the main obstacle to global stability and international law," "the source of hegemonism and power politics" in the world, and a "looming threat" to the sovereignty of their country and the survival of their regime. While they face a variety of dangers closer to home, none exceeds in urgency or magnitude that posed by the United States. In remarks to his Communist Party colleagues, Hu Jintao described the management of relations with a dominant and potentially aggressive America as "the central thread in China's foreign policy strategy."[34]

Hu, his colleagues, and his likely successors believe that the American threat derives from deep sources; it is not merely the product of a particular administration's misguided policies or the ideological excesses of one political party. To the contrary, as they seek to analyze and explain how the United States has dealt with them since the end of the Cold War, Chinese observers see far more continuity than change. This is in part due to the fact that, to a considerable extent, they see Washington's behavior as the product of impersonal, material forces rather than the quirks and obsessions of individual leaders. Foremost among these "objective factors" is America's still-preponderant place in today's international order. Its vastly superior power has cast the United States in the role of a hegemon. By jealously guarding its privileged position against potential challengers, it is merely doing what any similarly advantaged state would do in its place.

The Soviet collapse eliminated the only country capable of matching American power and holding it in check. A Chinese general writes that freed from constraint, America's "lust for leading the world and its tendency of expansionism" naturally intensified. According to the director of the Strategy Department at the Academy of Military Sciences, Washington seeks to "build a unipolar world exclusively dominated by itself."[35] In order to do this, writes another expert, the United States must maintain its dominance in the making of international rules, preserve its lead in "the economic and technological fields," and retain its "overwhelming [military] superiority over any opponent." Above all, America must guard against "the emergence of a power or power bloc on the Eurasian continent that can comprehensively challenge [it]."[36]

China, of course, is the one nation that has the potential to someday pose such a challenge, and its rise therefore provokes anxiety and even fear in Washington. This is to be expected; it is the manifestation of what two scholars at China's National Defense University refer to as a "structural contradiction" or a "profound conflict between China's rising power and expanding interests . . . on the one hand and US plans to maintain hegemony on the other."[37] In this view, it is the simple fact of China's rise, rather than the specific character of its regime, that is at the root of American suspicion and hostility. While Washington wants to avoid the costs of open conflict, it "also always guards against China's development and seeks to contain or delay China's development by all means."[38]

As if these structural, power political forces were not enough, China's current rulers also see the United States as implacably hostile to them on ideological grounds. Although the two factors are often discussed separately, they are inextricably linked. As many Chinese analysts emphasize, ideology tends to reinforce and amplify the imperatives of power politics, making the Americans even more suspicious and aggressive in their attitudes toward China. The fall of the Berlin Wall and the worldwide retreat of communism left the People's Republic isolated and exposed as the most important remaining proponent of the "socialist way." Having brought the Soviet Union to its knees, the United States would now try to do the same thing to China. If there was any lingering doubt, the sharp American response to Tiananmen convinced China's leaders that they had lost a strategic partner and gained an ideological adversary.[39]

America's animus springs from its founding principles and basic beliefs. As Wang Jisi explains, "U.S. grand strategy is based on the very ideology and values it promotes." The United States cannot help but assert that its values are universal, nor can it refrain from "applying them to judge right and wrong in international relations and the internal affairs of other countries."[40] While there may be some variation in the degree to which different American administrations emphasize ideological factors, they will never be entirely abandoned, or even downplayed for very long. Seen in this light, the 1969–89 period of strategic alignment, during which the Americans were largely willing to overlook the character of the Chinese regime, appears as an aberration.

Ideology shapes America's goals but it also goes a long way to determining which nations it sees as enemies or strategic rivals. Unlike a state whose leaders are guided by pure realist principles, the United States judges others by the organization and internal behavior of their domestic regimes. For the Americans, writes an analyst from the Central Party School's Institute for Strategic Studies, "ideology is one of the most important markers for determining whether a state has hostile intent." In short, a "state pursuing an ideology that conflicts with freedom and democracy is [believed] more likely to have hostile intentions toward the United States." Whether or not a country meets "Western standards" for democratic governance will go a long way to determining whether the United States regards it as an enemy or a friend.[41]

It is thus not China's rise alone, but the nature of its political system, that is at the root of Washington's mistrust and hostility. Unless China stops growing, or embraces American-style democracy, this is not going to change. In a way that parallels the thinking of some U.S. analysts about the Islamic world, China's leaders appear to have concluded that the Americans hate and fear them not only, and perhaps not even primarily, for what they do, but for who they are and what they represent.

Chinese analysts believe that in light of this assessment, the United States has developed a coherent, deliberate strategy for dealing with their country, a "highly cohesive master plan" that it has been pursuing consistently since the end of the Cold War.[42] Sometimes referred to as a "two-handed" or "one hard hand, one soft hand" strategy, this approach is variously described as combining "cooperation plus containment," or "engagement plus containment."[43] According to a leading Chinese expert, "the U.S. has pursued a dual track post-Cold War policy toward China: a desire to exert pressure on China and to restrict the growth of China's national power and prestige coexists with a desire to preserve contact and co-operation."[44]

Since Tiananmen, China's leaders have regularly accused the United States of trying to promote what they call "peaceful evolution." Despite its benign ring, in the Communist Party's lexicon of political invective this term actually means something closer to "subversion" or "conquest from within." Together with its allies, the United States aims to "Westernize and divide" China. Under the guise of economic, cultural, and educational "engagement," the democracies are working to encourage dissent and discontent, undermine the legitimacy and authority of the Communist Party, and eventually bring about its demise.

Although the Americans claim to have the best interests of the Chinese people at heart, their true aim is to weaken China so that they can retain their dominant position in Asia and the world. A 2005 essay in a journal sponsored by the Ministry of Foreign Affairs laid out the most recent details of this nefarious American plot: using "non-governmental and religious organizations [the United States has] stepped up infiltration into China, promoted US-style 'democracy,' secretly supported dissidents and anti-government groups inside and outside China, and produced unstable elements within China."[45]

While foreigners might find this description far-fetched and even paranoid, it is certainly true that the U.S. government has regularly expressed sympathy for dissidents, support for religious freedom, and hope that China will someday become a liberal democracy. Indeed, as we have seen, American officials from the president on down have at times been remarkably candid in saying that the ultimate aim of the policy of engagement is to help speed the onset of far-reaching political reforms. They often seem blithely unaware of how threatening such changes would be for those who presently hold positions of privilege and power.

On this point, China's leaders are undeniably right; the United States *does* seek to encourage the political liberalization of their country. American officials may say that they favor a stable and prosperous China, but this part of their message falls on deaf ears. In their review of the personnel files of the Communist Party's fourth generation, Andrew Nathan and Bruce Gilley find no sign of any discussion of these reassurances. Evidently, they conclude, "Chinese analysts consider such statements to be too obviously deceptive to deserve attention."[46]

At the same time as it works to divide and weaken China from within, the United States is portrayed as being engaged in a determined and wide-ranging effort to block its rise and contain the expansion of its power and external influence. This aspect of American strategy is usually discussed in geographic terms. The United States is frequently accused of attempting to physically encircle China, establishing alliances and building positions of strength all along its periphery.[47]

Chinese analysts have watched as the United States has revitalized key Cold War alliances in the Western Pacific and redeployed air and naval forces into and across the region. They note with interest that especially since the turn of the century, and despite the distractions caused by 9/11, the United States has "improved strategic deterrence and forward strike capability," and used the supposed threat from North Korea as an excuse to "accelerate the development of a Theater Missile Defense system in east Asia," the true purpose of which is "to weaken China's military capability."[48] Taking careful note of every official reference to their country as a "peer competitor," Chinese observers have concluded, not unreasonably, that the United States is intent on countering and offsetting their own increasing military power.

The Chinese see that the Americans have also been hard at work bolstering their regional alliances. Japan and Australia are the northern and southern "anchors" of the U.S. position in the Asia Pacific. Albeit with limited success to date, some American and Japanese "rightists" have even tried to stitch together a coalition of Asian democracies, including India, Australia, and possibly South Korea. As viewed from Beijing it is clear that "curbing China" is the ultimate aim of all this diplomatic activity.[49]

Taiwan is also a crucial part of the U.S. containment plan. The Americans have backed away from the aggressive stance that George W. Bush adopted at the beginning of his administration, when he promised to do "whatever it takes" to help defend Taiwan. Despite its increased caution, however, Chinese analysts believe that Washington remains determined to perpetuate the present standoff and to exploit it for strategic advantage. Its goal is a condition of "U.S.-dominated relative peace" or "a permanent situation of no reunification" sustained by its own measured support for the island. America's efforts to maintain peace in the Taiwan Strait are in fact "an important new aspect of [its] meddling and interference."[50] Once again, Washington's protestations of benign intent are meant to conceal deeper and more sinister motivations.

During the era of containment Washington created a "crescent-shaped encirclement" along China's eastern coast, parts of which are now being revitalized. After 9/11 it went even further, achieving a "historic break-through" by penetrating into Central Asia. The Americans have cleverly "used antiterrorism . . . to establish new military bases and mobilization locations in Central Asia, South Asia and East Asia," thereby positioning themselves to apply pressure on China from all sides.[51] By combining its activities in the Pacific, with its new presence in Afghanistan and several Central Asian republics, and its burgeoning relationships with India and Mongolia, the United States is attempting to build a "complete contain-ment circle" around China.[52]

Chinese strategists are acutely sensitive to the possible links between efforts to contain them from without and schemes designed to weaken them from within. They note that the most serious threats to their security come from "those problems that are capable of turning 'external worries' into 'internal troubles.'" America's continuing attempts at "ideological and political penetration" of Chinese society are one such problem, but "under certain conditions, the threat posed by the extremism, separatism, and terrorism triggered by ethnic and religious problems may be [even] greater."[53]

Here too, the Americans can play a crucial, and dangerous, role. Chi-nese strategists believe that the so-called color revolutions that took place in 2005 in Georgia, the Ukraine, and Kyrgyzstan were part of a U.S.-backed scheme targeting Moscow, but they carried a clear warning for Beijing. Similar events in other parts of Central Asia could bring to power regimes that would pursue "one-sided pro-West policies." If this happens, countries on China's western border, as well as established rivals like India to the south, could become "forward bases for instigating separatism in Xinjiang and Tibet."[54] Internal movements with strong foreign support would weaken and divide China and could even pose a deadly threat to its stability and survival.

Containment is not merely a matter of building a physical cordon around China's frontiers. Even as they seek to profit from burgeoning ties of trade and investment, the United States and the other advanced industrial nations are also believed to be acting in ways intended to weaken their rival economically and retard its growth. Policies that Americans might explain as the product of interest group pressures and congressional grandstanding are often interpreted by Beijing as part of an overarching strategic plan. For example, demands that China revalue its currency and enforce intellectual property rights are seen as blatant attempts to "hold back and stifle our country." Controversies over whether to allow Chinese firms to invest in the U.S. energy, electronics, and telecommunications sectors reveal similar motives, as does the periodic tightening of American export control regulations.[55]

Some recent analyses suggest a direct link between America's trade policies and its desire to contain China. According to one scholar, Washington has been trying since the late 1990s to find ways of countering the challenge to its position in East Asia posed by China's rise. At first the Americans concentrated on strengthening their alliances and expanding their own military presence, but these traditional methods have proved to be costly and in some respects counterproductive. "After rethinking, the United States put its strategic focus on the economic domain," and began to sign free trade agreements (FTAs) with various countries in East Asia. Its goal is to form "an FTA sphere geo-economically surrounding China," containing Beijing's influence and ensuring that despite the fact that it is not truly an Asian nation, the United States would remain "East Asia's economic center."[56] Trade policy is, in short, a continuation of geopolitics by other means. Climate change negotiations, in which the United States and the other advanced industrial democracies are trying to force China to accept a disproportionate share of the costs of remediation, could provide another means of slowing its growth and undercutting its prestige.[57]

CONCLUSION

The basic Chinese assessment of American strategy has not changed substantially since the end of the Cold War. Washington is still pursuing a two-handed approach that seeks to combine engagement with containment. What may be shifting, in the view of at least some analysts, is the balance between those two elements. Discussion of this question is linked directly to the ongoing debate over the changing structure of the international system.

In the early 2000s, as they watched the United States project power into Central Asia, expand its activities in South and Southeast Asia, and nudge Japan toward greater assertiveness, some observers concluded that Washington was increasing "the weight of the 'containment' aspect of its China policy." "The 'hard aspect' has been strengthening," wrote another scholar, "which means that the elements of 'containment' have been increasing."[58] For a time this appears to have been the prevailing view in Beijing.

Starting in 2006, however, some more optimistic voices began to be heard. While the United States keeps up its "military guard against China, increases protectionist pressure," and pursues its "diplomatic rivalry with China in Asia," it has also become more attuned to Beijing's concerns and more accommodating of them.[59] There are many "problems and obstacles" to be overcome, but at least for the moment, "engagement and cooperation" are the dominant elements in U.S.-China policy, while the "negative factors of guarding against and containing China" seem unlikely to grow "into the main current of policy."[60]

Various factors can be cited to explain this favorable development, but the most obvious are also the most important: China is growing wealthier, more powerful, more influential, and less susceptible to external pressures. Because it now depends on China to help finance its debt, "the United States no longer dares threaten boycotts against China" as lightly it did in the 1990s.[61] By every conceivable measure "China's strategic weight . . . [has] markedly increased." The Americans are beginning to "realize that China's rejuvenation is unstoppable," and that their best option is thus "to avoid confrontation . . . practice peaceful coexistence, and strengthen cooperation."[62]

For how long will this favorable tendency in U.S. policy be sustained? Will bilateral relations grow ever-more stable as Washington comes to grips with China's rise, and its own relative decline? Some are less optimistic on this score than others. After a lengthy and generally measured assessment of all the various factors at play, one well-placed observer concludes that U.S.-China relations are likely to remain "steady but not stable."

The reasons for this assessment are clear: neither the structural nor the ideological drivers of suspicion and rivalry between the two nations have yet been fundamentally altered. The mere existence of China as a strong East Asian power poses a challenge to America's desire for regional dominance. Moreover, as China's interests expand and it seeks to project power in order to defend them, every move it makes beyond its borders "is bound to be interpreted as encroaching on US geostrategic space."

The "'natural antagonism' between a rising power and an established hegemonist" has not been, and cannot easily be, extinguished. Nor can the "massive" ideological differences between America and China be put aside. The United States has "never abandoned its efforts to 'Westernize' China," and the very success of "the development model of socialism with Chinese characteristics" in recent years has rekindled a sense of ideological rivalry. While in many respects the configuration of power is evolving in ways favorable to China, these tensions stand in the way of building a deep sense of mutual trust and leave the Sino-American relationship vulnerable to shocks and setbacks.[63]

Six

"HIDE OUR CAPABILITIES AND BIDE OUR TIME"

THE 24 CHARACTERS AND THE 3 AXIOMS

As seen from Beijing, the strategic situation is characterized by tenuous near-term stability, serious medium-term dangers, and expansive long-range possibilities. Although "the propensity of things" is essentially favorable, the course of history is by no means preordained. China is like a vessel being carried forward by strong currents into fast-flowing rapids. Only by navigating these dangerous waters successfully can it gain greater freedom of action and achieve safety on the other side. The task facing today's leaders is to steer their country unscathed through a period of turbulence and uncertainty. If they succeed, China will emerge stronger, more secure, and, perhaps most important from the perspective of the current regime, with the Chinese Communist Party still firmly at the helm.

While it sees itself confronting many challenges at home and abroad, the regime has no doubt that the United States represents the biggest and most dangerous external obstacle that it must face in negotiating the passage from weakness to strength. Due to a combination of ideological animus and power political paranoia, Washington remains profoundly suspicious and deeply hostile. Behind their pretense of friendship and goodwill, the Americans are pursuing a deliberate policy of attempting to slow China's rise and contain its power, while simultaneously seeking to undermine its domestic political stability. If their nation is to fulfill its destiny, China's leaders must find a way of countering this "two-handed" strategy. But how?

In this and the next chapter I offer an account, based on statements by strategists and policy makers, the pattern of observable Chinese behavior, and a fair amount of inference and speculation, of how Beijing has sought since the end of the Cold War to answer this question. I begin by identifying a set of basic strategic principles that appear to be generally accepted by Chinese decision makers and which I believe to have guided their actions since the early 1990s. These have set the broad general direction of policy without specifying a precise end point or identifying a unique path for attaining it. In chapter 7 I explore the question of how China's Communist Party rulers may define their long-term goals, and discuss in more detail the policies through which they appear to be pursuing them.

Complex military and diplomatic concepts are often reduced in Chinese writings to pithy slogans or "*tifa*" ("peace and development," "three no changes and three new changes," and so on). No such official summary statement of China's grand strategy or, somewhat more narrowly, of its strategy for dealing with the United States is known to exist. The closest thing to such a formulation is probably Deng Xiaoping's often-quoted admonition that China should "hide its capabilities and bide its time." These words were part of a slightly longer "24-character strategy" circulated to top party officials in the summer of 1991. By this time Communist Party rule had been overturned across Eastern Europe, the Soviet Union was on the verge of collapse and disintegration, and following the killings in Tiananmen Square, Deng and his fellow party leaders found themselves the target of sanctions and international opprobrium. Some in the regime favored abandoning domestic economic reforms and taking a much tougher and more confrontational stance toward the American "hegemonists" and their allies. Deng was determined to persevere, and in response to demands that he reverse course, he penned a new strategic directive.

Telegraphic and lacking in specifics, the "24-character strategy" nevertheless laid down some general guidelines for both foreign and domestic policy. The party and the nation should "observe calmly; secure our position; cope with affairs calmly; hide our capabilities and bide our time; be good at maintaining a low profile; and never claim leadership."[1] In short, China needed to deflect American pressure, stifle the temptation to lash out in righteous anger against foreign meddling and provocation, and stick to its long-term plan for achieving growth through "reform and opening up." Above all, as Deng subsequently warned, China must "persist in not seeking confrontation."[2]

Extrapolating only slightly from Deng's formulation, I would suggest that China's post–Cold War strategy for dealing with the United States, and with the outside world more generally, can be summed up in the following three axioms:

- "Avoid confrontation."
- "Build comprehensive national power."
- "Advance incrementally."

Just as the prevailing assessment of China's situation has remained remarkably stable over time, so too have these basic principles continued to guide virtually every relevant aspect of national policy. Deng's successors have thus far stayed on the path he set for them thirty years ago. Recognizing that a stable international environment is essential to sustaining growth and maintaining domestic stability, they have, for the most part, gone to great lengths to ease tensions and avoid disputes with other nations. At home and in their dealings with the outside world, the leadership has given top priority to the long-term task of cultivating national wealth and power. Despite its caution, however, Beijing has not been passive. Over the years it has sought to extend its influence and strengthen its position relative to potential rivals, both in Asia and, increasingly, in other areas of the world.

Reflecting the recent increase in optimism about the nation's long-term trajectory, there is some evidence of debate over whether China should abandon its diffidence and its preference for incrementalism in favor of a bolder, more assertive approach to the world. At least for the moment, the advocates of continued caution would appear to have won out.

"AVOID CONFRONTATION"

This first axiom remains, for now, the "prime directive" of China's grand strategy, the one rule that must not be broken under any but the most-dire circumstances. The injunction to avoid confrontation and conflict applies across the board, and certainly with respect to all the other major powers, but it obviously has special force as regards the United States. This essential axiom has been reiterated in various official formulations issued since the end of the Cold War, and its impact is evident in the overall pattern of Beijing's dealings with most of its neighbors and all of the other major powers.

In keeping with this principle, in the first half of the 1990s China took steps to improve relations with all of its neighbors. Beijing proceeded to recognize governments with which it had previously had no formal dealings (like Indonesia, Singapore, and South Korea), it normalized relations with some old enemies (like Vietnam), resolved or tabled long-standing border disputes with others (including Russia and India), and established good, "neighborly" relationships with the new Central Asian republics that had emerged along its western frontier from the wreckage of the Soviet empire.[3]

Despite these placatory gestures, some aspects of Chinese behavior continued to arouse concern. The rocket-rattling campaign of intimidation against Taiwan in 1995–96 stirred anxiety in Washington, as we have seen, but it also rang alarm bells in the region, most notably in Tokyo. Beijing's tough stance on the demarcation of maritime boundaries in Southeast Asia had similar effects. Recognizing that its assertiveness was proving counterproductive, in the mid-1990s Beijing announced its adoption of a "New Security Concept" designed to reassure the world of its peaceful intentions.[4] Having established or stabilized diplomatic relations with all its neighbors, the regime sought to further deepen and strengthen its bilateral ties by negotiating "partnership" agreements with key states. In addition to announcing such arrangements with Russia (in 1996 and again in 2001), Japan (1998), and South Korea (1998), it reached agreements of varying degrees of substance and specificity with France (1997), the United States (1997), the EU (1998), and Great Britain (1998).[5]

Alongside these bilateral moves, Beijing opened up a new, multilateral front. Chinese diplomats had to this point largely avoided participation in regional institutions, fearing that they would be isolated, outvoted, and subjected to lectures, sanctions, or worse. Now, as their strength and confidence grew, they began to see these organizations as additional venues for practicing the diplomacy of reassurance. Gingerly at first, Beijing began in the mid-1990s to take part in meetings of the Association of Southeast Asian Nations (ASEAN) Regional Forum, a committee of foreign ministers dedicated to discussing "confidence-building" and "conflict resolution" measures, as well as other security-related issues. These initial forays were followed by the signing of a "Good-neighborly Partnership of Mutual Trust" with ASEAN (1997), and by the creation of still more regional groupings, including "ASEAN Plus One" (China) and "ASEAN Plus Three" (China, Japan, and South Korea). Meanwhile, to its west, in 1996 Beijing founded what would become the Shanghai Cooperation Organisation, a body whose members eventually came to include all five newly independent Central Asian republics as well as Russia.[6]

Beijing also sought to burnish its credentials as a nonthreatening, unobtrusive "joiner" by signing on to various global arms control accords. These too had previously been seen as potential traps, mechanisms through which the superpowers intended to freeze their military advantages in place and to block the rise of any potential challengers. In the 1970s and 1980s China had refused to accept any constraints on its freedom to build and test new weapons, and to export whatever it wanted to foreign buyers. By the 1990s, however, the nation's leaders had become more certain of their growing capabilities, more concerned about cultivating a reputation for responsibility, and more willing to make concessions to ease American concerns. By acceding to the treaty on the Non-Proliferation of Nuclear Weapons (1992), the Missile Technology Control Regime (1992), the Chemical Weapons Convention (1993), and the Comprehensive Nuclear Test-Ban Treaty (1996), among others, Beijing hoped to remove a major source of friction in its relations with Washington.[7]

While Beijing's initiatives were generally welcomed by the West, Sino-American relations remained troubled through the turn of the century. Disputes over proliferation, human rights, accusations of espionage, charges of "hegemonism" and interventionism, and the 1999 Belgrade embassy bombing all played a role, but Taiwan remained the focal point for mistrust and suspicion. By the end of the decade, many Chinese analysts had become convinced that the United States was building up the military capability and the international legal rationale that it would need to intervene on behalf of a growing Taiwan independence movement. These concerns were heightened by the newly elected George W. Bush administration's initial identification of China as a "strategic competitor" and the president's April 2001 statement that he would do "whatever it took" to help Taiwan defend itself.

The task of avoiding confrontation with the United States was transformed almost overnight by the September 11, 2001, terrorist attacks. Within a matter of months the mood in Beijing went from watchful uncertainty to ebullient optimism. In November 2002, at the Sixteenth Party Congress, Jiang Zemin felt emboldened to declare that the first two decades of the twenty-first century would be a period of "strategic opportunity" for China.[8] Based on a "scientific assessment" of the "overall situation," Jiang exhorted his colleagues to "firmly grasp" the possibilities being presented to them and to use the time to "accomplish great things."[9]

Although high party officials did not say so directly, the importance of the first two decades of the new century was in large measure clearly due to a sudden change in the geopolitical environment. America's preoccupation with terrorism and the Middle East made it less inclined to confront Beijing and more willing to seek cooperation and stability. Jiang's declaration was therefore, among other things, an expression of relief that Washington's newfound concerns had created the possibility of a period of relative peace. But it was also a warning that China must not squander the period of strategic opportunity by provoking the United States.

As the twenty-first century began, China's continued economic progress and growing military strength were making it increasingly difficult to claim, as its spokesmen still tried to do at times, that it was just another developing country. A decade and a half into the post–Cold War era, Deng Xiaoping's strictures about hiding capabilities and avoiding leadership seemed to some to have outlived their usefulness.[10] But how could China acknowledge its strength and assert its influence without running an increased risk of alarming, antagonizing, and perhaps even colliding with other states?

In late 2003 and early 2004 newly elevated Communist Party leaders Wen Jiabao, Hu Jintao, and others close to them began to use the term "peaceful rise" to describe both the reality of China's changing circumstances and the essence of its preferred posture toward the world. Having concluded that it no longer made sense to try to deny the obvious, the new party leaders wanted to find a way to highlight their country's growing power, while at the same time easing some of the anxiety that they knew it was causing in Washington and throughout Asia. Because it was impossible to fully conceal China's growing capabilities, shaping how others viewed its intentions had become all the more important. This was not merely a matter of proclaiming purity of purpose. By expressing their understanding of the problems that previous rising powers had caused, China's leaders sought to convince the world that they had the self-awareness and the self-control necessary to avoid a repetition.

Peaceful rise was received more favorably abroad than at home. Hardliners cautioned that the new slogan might convey a sense of irresolution and perhaps an unwillingness to use force if necessary to decide the Taiwan issue or to defend other vital national interests. Others objected that to speak of China as a rising power lacked modesty and could stir national chauvinism. To judge from the eventual outcome of this debate, however, the decisive objections came from a mix of military officers, diplomats, and think-tank analysts who warned that the very use of the word *rise* would create "suspicion and wariness among other countries."[11] After its initial unveiling, "peaceful rise" quickly faded from the official lexicon, to be replaced eventually by "peaceful development," a tepid, nonthreatening invocation of Deng's original formula from the 1980s.[12]

Easing fears and avoiding confrontation remain essential goals of Chinese foreign policy. While the country's comparative success in weathering the aftereffects of the 2008–9 financial crisis may have encouraged a new self-confidence, and perhaps even a degree of cockiness in some quarters, official reaction has thus far followed a familiar pattern. Chinese strategists are clearly hopeful that recent upheavals will hasten the decline of America's power relative to their own, but they are also alive to the danger that disagreements over trade imbalances and exchange rates could lead to serious friction. China needs to stand up for itself, but it must also be careful to avoid being drawn into disputes that could escalate due to the unfortunate American tendency to let "nationalism and . . . differences in ideology, philosophy, and values" influence its handling of trade issues.[13] Despite recent progress, writes one analyst, "China should continue to adhere to the diplomatic principles of 'biding one's time, concealing one's strengths,'" and "it should be soberly aware of its own strengths without seeking to replace or equal America in the international economic order."[14] As they did after 9/11, China's leaders hope that they can turn this crisis to their advantage by taking it as an occasion, not merely to avoid confrontation, but to promote even closer cooperation. But Beijing cannot afford to drop its guard. The Americans have grown increasingly dependent on China for its help in managing the global economy, but they have not yet abandoned their "two-faced policy" of "guarding against, containing, and even holding back China."[15]

"BUILD COMPREHENSIVE NATIONAL POWER"

Avoiding conflict is no doubt a good thing for its own sake, but for Beijing, it is also a means to a larger end. As Deng was acutely aware, China needs time to build up every aspect of its comprehensive national power, "the combination of all the powers [essential to] the survival and development of a sovereign state."[16] Until it does so to a sufficient degree, it will not be able to provide reliably for its own security, let alone to pursue any wider and more ambitious goals.

Analysts at Chinese government-sponsored think tanks and research institutes have devised various schemes for measuring comprehensive national power, all of which include some mix of economic, military, and political components.[17] Of these, the first is universally acknowledged to be the most important. The Chinese people have learned from painful experience that wealth, rather than ideological enthusiasm, is the taproot of all other forms of strength. Political power may still spring in part from the barrel of a gun, as Chairman Mao insisted, but producing guns requires financial resources, scientific expertise, and industrial capacity. For as long as it continued to adhere to Maoist economic principles, China could not acquire these vital building blocks of comprehensive national power as efficiently as its capitalist rivals.

Since the start of the reform period, Chinese analysts have consistently described a three-step sequence that would carry them from the early 1980s to the middle of the twenty-first century. In the 1990s, observers spoke of an initial phase (1981–2000) during which the economy would quadruple in size and a second (2001–10) in which output would double again. The remainder of the growth necessary to achieve an acceptable level of prosperity would be accomplished in the subsequent four decades (2010–50).[18]

More recent commentary has stressed the critical importance of the years 2000–20, the "period of strategic opportunity," in China's rise to great-power status. Such an extended period of relative tranquility is, as one author notes, "rare and valuable" in Chinese history; it is "something that the . . . nation has not experienced in the past 150 years."[19] Unfortunately, this interlude cannot last forever. At some point, Washington will shift its attention away from the problems of terrorism and proliferation and back to the increasing challenge to its hegemonic position posed by China's rapid growth. When it does, China must be strong enough to resist renewed pressure, whatever form it takes. This is the reason why Beijing should feel "a sense of urgency" about sustaining economic growth, but also why it must take care at the same time to enhance its "national defense strength . . . national cohesiveness" and all the other elements of its comprehensive national power. In the words of one analyst, China must use the "period of strategic opportunity" to acquire "a more favorable position in the increasingly fierce competition in terms of overall national strength."[20]

In contrast to the economic domain, where it has laid out some quite specific numerical targets, Beijing has had relatively little to say about the eventual parameters of what is by now a two-decade-long military buildup. The government's periodic defense "white papers" are notable for their lack of specifics regarding future budgets and force posture. However, these policy statements do suggest a phased expansion in military power whose stages coincide roughly with those of the plan for overall economic development.

Chinese defense planners describe themselves as being in the middle of a three-step process that will culminate in the complete modernization of the nation's armed forces. According to the 2008 defense white paper, by 2020 China aims to complete the mechanization of its armed forces and to make "major progress" toward what is referred to as "informationization," the full integration of advanced computers and communication systems into all units and service branches. By "the mid-21st century" Beijing will "by and large" have completed the process of military modernization and will have an assured capacity for "winning local wars in conditions of informationization."[21]

Foreign observers have very little insight into the Chinese government's internal deliberations on defense issues. Still, at the periphery of the decision-making system there are signs that a debate is starting to get under way. There are certainly a significant number of well-placed critics who argue that China needs, and can afford, far more capability than it is currently building. Thus, one thorough study of comprehensive national power and grand strategy recommends that the government "raise sharply the percentage of defense spending in GDP."[22] Another author chastises the leadership for having failed thus far to build "sufficiently strong and comprehensively modern armed forces" and urges it to "accelerate efforts to build and improve military strength in all areas."[23] And a 2007 essay by two researchers at the National Defense University concludes on a similar note that "China's complex and grim security environment requires it to speed up its national defense modernization."[24]

None of these statements is authoritative, of course, but they do suggest the existence of a body of opinion favoring a still-bigger buildup and in all probability echoing the views of some high-ranking insiders. At this point, it is likely that Chinese policy makers have not definitively answered the question that their American counterparts put to themselves in the 1960s: "How much is enough?" The optimal size of the military component of China's comprehensive national power remains to be determined.

In addition to pursuing wealth and military strength, Beijing seeks prestige, respect, and political influence. With these ends in view, Chinese strategists have lately devoted considerable attention to the question of how they can best acquire and apply what the American political scientist Joseph Nye has labeled "soft power."[25] Their discussion of these issues tracks closely with the one now under way in the West. The seeming decline in America's influence and prestige since the start of the Iraq war, despite the absence of any measurable change in its "hard power," presents a puzzle to those "realists" inclined to focus only on material indicators of capability. Clearly there is something at work here that cannot be so easily measured, but that can amplify or diminish other elements of comprehensive national power. " 'Soft power,' if it is wielded properly, can turn 'hard power' from weak to strong," notes one Chinese analyst, but if it is incorrectly applied, "this will impair 'hard power' no matter how strong it is."[26] If China wants to take its rightful place on the world stage, in short, it will have to develop its soft power alongside its economy and armed forces.

Some argue that China can build respect and gain influence by exposing others to its language and its "profound and excellent culture," whether at overseas "Confucius Institutes" or on the campuses of its own universities. Culture aside, others assert that China's economic success and political stability can provide a model for other developing countries.[27] Close students of soft power note that America's is a by-product not only of material success but also of the universal appeal of the principles it purports to follow at home. This insight has led analysts to caution that until it can put its own house in order and build sturdier "systems for social equality and justice," China will not be able to close the present "soft power gap" with the United States.[28]

One recent attempt to rank China's overall comprehensive national power concludes that it "has not yet reached the superpower level" and remains, for the moment, "one of the major powers" in the same category with Japan, Russia, Britain, France, Germany, and India. Over the next decade, however, China is the only nation in this group that stands to gain in all three major categories of comprehensive national power. Together with the United States, therefore, China alone will have a "relatively balanced structure."[29]

By 2020, the end of the "period of opportunity," Chinese analysts expect that their country will rank second in the world in terms of comprehensive national power.[30] At that point its military capabilities will still lag behind America's, but the gap between the two countries' GDPs will have narrowed substantially and perhaps disappeared, and if it plays its cards right, China could match the United States in its ability to exert political influence. This overall judgment is widely shared and its implications are unmistakable: the process of building comprehensive national power is well under way, but there is much work yet to be done.

"ADVANCE INCREMENTALLY"

The account of China's strategy offered to this point seems inherently plausible, given the country's circumstances; it is also well supported by the available evidence from statements by party and government officials, think-tank analysis, and academic commentary. While in the 1990s the idea that Beijing had any kind of coherent grand strategy might have been controversial among Western China-watchers, it is far less so today. Indeed, a number of other Western analysts have painted pictures broadly similar to the one presented here. For example, in their 2000 RAND Corporation study, *Interpreting China's Grand Strategy*, Michael Swaine and Ashley Tellis argued that China is pursuing what they term a "calculative strategy." This approach emphasizes economic growth, military development, and, at least for the first several decades of the twenty-first century, diplomatic caution.[31] In 2001 Avery Goldstein sketched the outlines of a "largely implicit grand strategy" of "transition" intended to guide China through the dangers of unipolarity and back to the comparative safety of a multipolar world.[32] Similarly, in his 2008 book, *The Three Faces of Chinese Power*, scholar David Lampton described a "consensus strategy" under which China will follow a "nonconfrontational path in the short and medium term" in order to become "a major force in the world."[33]

Because of the gaps and silences in discussions of these issues, and the prevailing uncertainty regarding the future character of the Chinese regime, all of these interpretations leave open two very important and closely related questions: What will China do while it bides its time, hides its capabilities, and builds its comprehensive national power? And what might it seek to accomplish once it has grown sufficiently strong to abandon any pretense of humility and is ready to assume its rightful place as a great power?

Putting aside for the moment the question of ultimate goals, one way of interpreting Deng's 24-character strategy is as a call for a long interval of passivity, to be followed at some point by a period of decisive action. In this view, while it waits to grow strong, China should simply lie low, downplaying its capabilities and avoiding the limelight. Such an approach would have much to commend it. Maintaining an accommodating, low-profile posture could well provide the best chance of avoiding a confrontation with the United States or another major power. Given China's continued relative weakness, a premature showdown would either force it to retreat or cause it to be drawn into a war that it would stand a good chance of losing.

"Bide our time and build our power" is also a formula that should appeal to important elements of the Chinese elite. Just as is true in the United States, so also in China, those who presently enjoy the benefits of economic interdependence have a strong interest in continued peace and stability and an aversion to anything that risks conflict and disruption. At the same time, because it emphasizes building comprehensive national power in all of its dimensions, this strategy clearly demands high priority and growing budgets for the military and the security services, thereby rewarding key constituencies within the Chinese Communist Party and the People's Liberation Army. Finally, a two-stage strategy would have the benefit of deferring difficult decisions about long-term objectives. Discussion of these issues could conceivably be put off for years or even decades while the process of power-building proceeds.

In addition to its advantages, however, a sequential approach could also have serious liabilities. At some point it will become difficult if not impossible for China to conceal its growing capabilities. Persistent efforts to do so may begin to strike others as deceptive and disturbing rather than modest and reassuring. Indeed, Beijing has already started to encounter difficulty on this score. Depending on the nature of the opponent, a purely passive posture could also be counterproductive and even dangerous. If it is mistaken for weakness, caution might tempt aggression. Moreover, if China's opponents are pursuing an active, assertive strategy of their own, staying on the defensive could make it easier for them to achieve their objectives. While China is biding its time and hiding its capabilities, rival nations may be using theirs to weaken and defeat it.

Given their assessment of the situation they confront, and their perceptions of the aggressive character of U.S. strategy, Chinese planners have evidently concluded that they must strike a balance between boldness and caution. They recognize that the period of strategic opportunity is also a period of relative weakness and potential vulnerability. But they also believe that in order to survive it, China must successfully parry both parts of America's "two-handed" strategy with a two-handed strategy of its own.[34] In other words, while continuing to pursue the maximum gain from economic engagement, China's leaders need to fend off attempts to weaken their legitimacy. At the same time, while avoiding direct confrontation, they must block, circumvent, and defeat U.S.-led efforts to encircle China and prevent its rise. This second task, in particular, requires external action. Beijing may be on the defensive strategically, but in part for that reason, it must seek opportunities to seize and hold the tactical initiative.

As we shall see, this kind of reasoning has evidently informed Chinese policy *in practice* since the turn of the century, if not before. Support for a more assertive interpretation of Deng's dictum *in theory*, if not its frank abandonment, has also grown alongside perceptions of rising Chinese power. As one Chinese scholar explained in 2004, China has now "achieved tremendous success." While it needs to continue to act "without arrogance and impetuosity," it is no longer necessary, and could even be counterproductive, to "always [be] giving people the feeling that we are 'hiding our capacities and biding our time.'"[35] Some analysts suggest that the old approach is "now gradually fading from the stage of Chinese history."[36] Others, like conservative nationalist Yan Xuetong, favor giving it a push and replacing Deng's self-effacing slogan with something far more muscular, such as "wielding our comprehensive national power to defend our national interests."[37]

In any case, notes a well-placed America-watcher, hiding capabilities and biding time has become "harder to master in practice" and is no longer "sufficient to effectively defend China's national interests." China must act, but when it does so it should "retain a sense of proportion" and avoid advancing in a simple, crude, or rash fashion without regard to the "condition of national strength." Nevertheless, when circumstances demand and capabilities permit, "we must certainly do what we have to do."[38] China will continue to advance incrementally, but the increments will be bigger and the advances more bold as its power and self-confidence grow.

Seven

———◆———

"TO WIN WITHOUT FIGHTING"

WHAT DOES "CHINA" WANT?

For more than twenty years now, the three axioms just described have set a general direction for Chinese policy. Given the prevailing assessment of "the propensity of things," the belief that the nation was, for the time being at least, relatively weak and on the defensive, it has made good sense for China to avoid confrontation and accumulate power, even as it carefully expanded its influence and bolstered its geopolitical position.

But what of the longer term? Assuming that China continues to move from weakness to strength, how will its leaders attempt to use their increasing power to shape the world around them? To the extent that they do so in a form recognizable to Western counterparts, how are Chinese strategists likely to define their goals? And through what mix of policies, stratagems, and maneuvers do they anticipate being able to reach them?

Few questions are as important, as contentious, or as fraught with uncertainty as those regarding China's long-term objectives and strategy. Whether it is because they are being secretive, are disinclined for reasons of strategic culture to specify fixed ends, are divided among themselves, or are simply undecided, China's elites remain largely (though not entirely) silent on these issues. What is more, even if we knew what today's leaders wanted, we could not say with assurance that a future, sixth- or seventh-generation Communist Party regime, or perhaps even a post-Communist government would necessarily have the same goals. In light of all these complexities any analysis of China's long-term strategy cannot help but rest heavily on inference and speculation, and its conclusions should therefore be treated with appropriate skepticism.

That said, what China's current rulers appear to want and what their successors will almost certainly want as well, is to see their country become the dominant or preponderant power in East Asia, and perhaps in Asia writ large. It is toward such a position of advantage that Beijing most likely sees itself advancing, and believes it should continue to advance, even as it avoids conflict and accumulates power.

"Preponderance" is not a fixed end point but a sliding scale of possibilities. Its precise definition, and the extent to which it can be achieved at acceptable cost at any given moment, remain open to discussion and debate. In general, however, China's leaders appear intent on making their country the strongest and most influential in its neighborhood, capable of deterring attacks, threats, or other actions it deems contrary to its interests, resolving disputes over territory and resources according to its preferences, and coercing or persuading others to accede to its wishes on issues ranging from trade and investment, to alliance and third-party basing arrangements, to the treatment of ethnic Chinese populations, and, at least in some cases, the character and composition of their governments. Beijing may not seek conquest or direct physical control over its surroundings, but despite repeated claims to the contrary, it does seek a form of regional hegemony.

Such ambitions would hardly make China unique. Throughout history, there has been a strong correlation between the rapid growth of a state's wealth and potential power, the geographic scope of its interests, the intensity and variety of the perceived threats to those interests, and the desire to expand military capabilities and exert greater influence in order to defend them. Growth tends to encourage expansion, which leads to insecurity, which feeds the desire for more power. This pattern is well established in the modern age. Looking back over the nineteenth and twentieth centuries, Samuel Huntington finds that "every other major power, Britain and France, Germany and Japan, the United States and the Soviet Union, has engaged in outward expansion, assertion, and imperialism coincidental with or immediately following the years in which it went through rapid industrialization and economic growth."[1] As for China, Huntington concludes that "no reason exists to think that the acquisition of economic and military power will not have comparable effects" on its policies. The pursuit of regional hegemony by China would, he writes, be a "natural result of its rapid economic development."[2]

The past behavior of other states is suggestive, but it is hardly a definitive guide to the future. Just because other powers have acted in certain ways does not necessarily mean that China will do the same. Perhaps, in a world of global markets and nuclear weapons, the fears and ambitions that motivated previous rising powers are no longer as potent. China's leaders may also have learned from studying history that overly assertive rising powers typically stir resentment and opposition. With this cautionary lesson in mind they may be able to modulate their behavior, resist temptation, and avoid the mistakes of others.

China is not just any rising power, and its unique history provides an additional reason for believing that it will seek some form of regional preponderance. China is a nation with a long and proud past as the leading center of East Asian civilization and with a more recent and less glorious experience of domination and humiliation at the hands of foreign invaders. As a number of historians have recently pointed out, China is not so much "rising" as it is *returning* to the position of regional preeminence that it once held and which its leaders and many of its people still regard as natural and appropriate.[3] The desire to reestablish a Sino-centric system would be consistent with what journalist Martin Jacques describes as "an overwhelming assumption on the part of the Chinese that their natural position lies at the epicenter of East Asia, that their civilization has no equals in the region, and that their rightful position, as bestowed by history, will at some point be restored in the future."[4] Conservative scholar Yan Xuetong puts the matter succinctly: the Chinese people are proud of their country's glorious past and believe its fall from preeminence to be "a historical mistake which they should correct."[5] If anything, the "century of humiliation" during which China was weak and vulnerable adds urgency to its pursuit of power and its desire for regional preeminence. For a nation with China's history, regaining a position of unchallengeable strength is not seen as simply a matter of pride but rather as an essential precondition for continued growth, security, and, quite possibly, survival.

MAKING THE WORLD SAFE FOR AUTHORITARIANISM

It may well be that any rising power in China's geopolitical position would seek a substantial influence in its own immediate neighborhood. It may also be true that in light of its history, and regardless of how it is ruled, China will be especially concerned with asserting itself and being acknowledged by its neighbors as the first among equals. But it is the character of the nation's domestic political system that will likely be decisive in determining exactly how it defines its external objectives and how it goes about pursuing them. Just as for the United States, so also for an increasingly powerful China, external strategy will be shaped by ideological as well as geopolitical factors.

As historian Ross Terrill points out, when outsiders speak of "China's intentions" or "China's strategy," they are really talking about the aims and plans of today's top leaders or, as he describes them, "the nine male engineers who make up the Standing Committee of the Politburo of the Chinese Communist Party."[6] Everything that is known of these men suggests that they are motivated above all else by their belief in the necessity of preserving Communist Party rule. This is, in one sense, a matter of unadulterated self-interest. Today's leaders and their families enjoy privileges and opportunities that are denied others in Chinese society and that flow directly from their proximity to the sources of political power. The end of the Communist Party's decades-long reign would have immediate, painful, and perhaps even fatal consequences for those at the top of the system. Rising stars who hope one day to occupy these positions, and even junior officials with more modest ambitions, will presumably make similar calculations. This convergence of personal interests and a sense of shared destiny gives the party-state a cohesion that it would otherwise lack. Party members know that if they do not hang together, they may very well hang separately, and this knowledge informs their thinking on every issue they face.

But it would be unfair to be entirely cynical about the motivations of China's leaders. To the contrary, there is every reason to think that they and their colleagues are quite sincere in their beliefs about the Communist

Party's past achievements and future indispensability. It was the party, after all, that rescued China from foreign invaders, delivered it from a century of oppression and humiliation, and lifted it back into the ranks of the world's great powers. In the eyes of its leaders, and some portion of the Chinese people, these accomplishments in themselves give the party unique moral authority and legitimize its rule.

Looking forward, party officials believe that they are all that stands between continued stability, prosperity, progress, and an unstoppable ascent to greatness on the one hand, and a return to chaos and weakness on the other. An analysis of the secret personnel files of the fourth generation of Chinese leaders concludes that, on this question, there is no evidence of dissension or doubt. Hu Jintao and his colleagues are aware of the numerous internal and external challenges they face, but they are confident that they, and they alone, can find the solutions that will be needed to keep their country moving forward and enable it to achieve its destiny. Indeed, they believe that it is precisely the magnitude and complexity of the problems confronting China that make their continued rule essential.

Some intellectuals may dream of one day creating a liberal democracy, and a few party officials may be willing to entertain the idea of a softer, more responsive brand of authoritarianism. But such views have little resonance among China's ruling elite. According to Sinologists Andrew Nathan and Bruce Gilley, today's leaders, and their likely successors, "think that their society is too complex and turbulent to be governable by a truly open, competitive form of democracy. They think Chinese society needs strong guidance both for domestic development and for foreign policy. . . . They see themselves as a qualified managerial elite, uniquely able to manage their society's modernization. They believe the Communist Party should stay in power."[7]

The party's desire to retain power shapes every aspect of national policy. As regards external affairs, it means that Beijing's ultimate aim can best be understood as "making the world safe for authoritarianism," or at least for continued one-party rule in China. Over the last several decades this focus on regime security has led, first of all, to an emphasis on preserving the international conditions necessary for continued economic growth. The party's ability to orchestrate rapid improvements in incomes and personal welfare is its most tangible accomplishment of the past thirty years and the source of its strongest claim to the gratitude and loyalty of the Chinese people. Economic growth, writes leading China scholar Thomas Christensen, "provides satisfaction and distraction to the population, and, therefore garners domestic support for the Party (or at least reduces active opposition . . .)." Growth also generates revenues that the regime can use to "buy off opposition and to channel funds to poorer regions and ethnic minority areas to prevent violent uprisings."[8]

As China has grown richer and stronger, the regime's pursuit of security has also led it to seek an increasing measure of control over the nation's external environment. This outward push has both offensive and defensive motivations. As the steward of national greatness, the Communist Party has the responsibility for returning China to its rightful place at the center of Asia. The visible deference of others will provide evidence of the regime's success in this regard and will help to reinforce its legitimacy at home. Especially if economic growth should falter, "standing up" to traditional enemies and resolving the Taiwan issue and other disputes on Beijing's terms are likely to become an increasingly important part of the party's strategy for retaining its grip on power. China's leaders believe that the stronger their country appears abroad, the stronger their regime will be at home.

Conversely, the appearance of weakness or the widespread perception that the nation has been defeated or humiliated could be extremely dangerous to the party's prospects for continued rule. Underlying concerns about its legitimacy make the regime more sensitive to slights and setbacks, and even more determined to deter challenges and to avoid defeat, than it might otherwise be. The best insurance against such risks is for China to accumulate an overwhelming preponderance of power in the areas adjacent to it where danger is most likely to arise.

Beijing also has some more concrete reasons for wanting to be able to dominate its neighbors and control events across its borders. The Communist Party's hypersensitivity to what it sees as "separatism" is a direct result of its belief that it must retain tight central control in all places and at all times. Pleas for greater autonomy from Tibet or Xinjiang, to say nothing of the prospect of Taiwan independence, are thus seen as deadly threats to national unity and hence to continued Communist Party rule. The regime believes that if it loosens its grip, even a little, the entire country will fall apart, and it will be unseated.[9] In light of this fear, Beijing needs to be able to conduct a "defense in depth" around its continental perimeter, developing strength sufficient to deter its neighbors from providing aid and comfort to separatist groups that may seek to operate across its borders and building the capabilities needed to intervene directly should that become necessary.

Even as it grows stronger and, in certain respects, more self-confident, the Communist Party continues to dread ideological contamination. For the moment, with the exception of Mongolia, China does not share a readily passable border with a fully functioning democracy. Although physical boundaries may not matter as much in the digital age as in the past, they are still important avenues for the movement of information, people, and contraband of various kinds. Pliant, like-minded states along its borders are far more likely to help Beijing deal with this danger than flourishing liberal democracies with strong ties to the West. The desire to forestall "peaceful evolution" at home gives the regime another compelling reason to want to shape the political development of its neighbors.

The special importance that the current regime attaches to continued, rapid economic growth coupled with its ideologically rooted mistrust of the United States has given it one additional motive for achieving preponderance in East Asia and projecting its power beyond. China's deepening dependence on imports of energy, food, and raw materials has rendered it increasingly vulnerable to possible disruptions of supply, either at their source or in transit. The fact that the U.S. Navy controls the world's oceans is no source of comfort for Beijing, as it is for Japan, South Korea, and the other East Asian democracies, and as it could conceivably be for China if it were also to become democratic. If it wants to free itself from the lingering threat of interdiction, China is going to have to find a way to offset America's advantages at sea, starting with the waters of the Western Pacific. In addition, to the extent that it comes to rely on pipelines or other means of terrestrial transport as partial alternatives to the sea, Beijing will have another reason for wanting to wield overwhelming force on land.

To sum up: China's current rulers do not seek preponderance solely because they are the leaders of a rising great power or simply because they are Chinese. Their desire for dominance and control is in large measure a by-product of the type of political system over which they preside. A liberal democratic China would certainly seek a leading role in its region, and perhaps an effective veto over developments that it saw as inimical to its interests. But it would also be less fearful of internal instability, less threatened by the presence of strong democratic neighbors, and less prone to seek validation at home through the domination and subordination of others.

ESTABLISHING A "FAVORABLE PERIPHERAL ENVIRONMENT"

Chinese strategists are generally careful to speak in terms of the interests of "the nation," or "the people," rather than those of the Communist Party, and they specifically, repeatedly, and vociferously deny that their country will ever "seek hegemony." Despite this, the open source literature contains ample support for the idea that China should seek regional preponderance. In one sense, the belief that China is destined to become the leading power in its neighborhood is a logical corollary to prevailing views about the shifting structure of the international system. Under conditions of unipolarity, power is heavily concentrated in the hands of a single strong state. This "global hegemon" can bring overwhelming force to bear, not only in the areas adjacent to it, but anywhere on the planet. As unipolarity ebbs and other powers rise, the world will naturally segment into regions, each of which will tend to center around a dominant "pole."

In Asia the movement away from unipolarity is already well in train, or as one observer puts it, "the balance of forces between multipolar and unipolar is developing in a direction favorable to the former." No matter how hard it tries, Washington cannot forever hold back the consequences of the "multipolarization trend."[10] Despite its recent dominance, Chinese strategists regard America as an interloper in Asia, and note that its position in the region hinges on a handful of postwar alliance relationships. These have been "unequal right from the start," involving significant encroachments on the sovereignty of Washington's security partners. With the end of the Cold War, as Beijing notes with some satisfaction, many of these relationships have begun to weaken.[11]

For its part, thanks to its exceptional economic success, and its policy of "befriending one's neighbors, ensuring tranquility in one's neighbors, and enriching one's neighbors," China has seen "its influence in the surrounding region steadily rise."[12] At this point, unless it is willing to deliberately provoke an armed conflict that would derail China's progress, the United States is "basically incapable of doing anything in face of the natural growth of China's influence in the region." Over time, Washington will have to "accept the reality of China's growing influence" and a diminution in its own sphere of influence.[13] It is natural that as America's power recedes, China will emerge as the most powerful nation in Asia.[14]

Chinese preponderance in Asia is therefore likely, given "the propensity of things." As seen from Beijing it is also highly desirable, in light of the regime's perceptions of its own vulnerabilities and the requirements for the nation's future security and prosperity. As one analyst explains, "History has shown that the instability of its adjacent areas brings instability to China, and if the adjacent areas are stable and have friendly relations with China, China benefits from this stability and friendliness."[15] The areas surrounding China, both terrestrial and maritime, comprise a "life zone" for its security and development. These areas must serve as a "protective screen" against possible external threats. They should also constitute a "close-knit economic belt" that will serve the needs of China's development by permitting the easy outward flow of goods and capital and the unencumbered inward movement of critical materials.[16]

The disposition of its "peripheral environment" is thus a matter of the utmost significance, and America's continued presence there remains a serious threat to Chinese security. In addition to maintaining its own forces, bolstering its traditional allies, and establishing new quasi-alliance ties, Washington has been hard at work trying to spread the myth of the "China threat" throughout Asia, in hopes of "driving a wedge" between China and its neighbors."[17] If China is to secure its life zone, it must reduce America's presence and influence there, and ensure that no other hostile power takes its place.

Chinese analysts and officials are cautious about stating this point too bluntly. In addition to eschewing hegemony as a matter of principle, they typically assert that their country is simply too busy focusing on domestic development to attempt "to build its own sphere of influence" or to try to re-create a Sino-centric regional order.[18] While most who comment on these topics stick closely to the party line, there are occasional exceptions. Shi Yinhong, a scholar known for his sometimes controversial views, has suggested that Beijing should take advantage of the prevailing trends in the world today in order to establish a position of "superior or near superior political, military, diplomatic, and economic influence on China's periphery (especially in east Asia)."[19] Men Honghua, a strategic analyst affiliated with the Central Party School, goes even further. For him, regional preponderance is vitally important, but it is also the means to a larger end. Beijing's ultimate aim, he writes, should be to "gain global influence by becoming the dominant power in the Asia-Pacific region."[20] A book published in 2010 by Liu Mingfu of the National Defense University, who is a senior colonel in the People's Liberation Army, takes a similar line. China should abandon any pretense of restraint and "sprint to become world number one." Its "big goal in the 21st century" must be to become "the top power," displacing the United States. If it fails, then "inevitably it will become a straggler that is cast aside."[21]

Shi and Men are neither militarists nor extreme nationalists (although Colonel Liu appears to be both). Their prescriptions for policy are remarkable more for the candor with which they are expressed than for the reasoning that underpins them. The goals they recommend follow quite naturally from an analysis of "objective conditions" and China's interests that is shared by many others. Colonel Liu's outburst is unusual for its lack of discretion, but it reflects a point of view that doubtless is heard far more often behind closed doors than in public debate.

Chinese strategists probably agree about the desirability of achieving some form of regional preponderance but differ over precisely how far it is necessary, and possible, to go. The answers to these questions will be determined by events and by the responses of others, rather than set in advance according to some predetermined theory or plan. In this important sense, China's grand strategy remains a work in progress.

The key issue that will have to be addressed at some point is the question of America's continuing role in East Asia. In the early 1990s Beijing criticized U.S. alliances as relics of the Cold War and called for their prompt dissolution. Since the turn of the century, analysts and official spokesmen have tended to take a somewhat more relaxed attitude. Chinese strategists still believe that Washington's ultimate aim is to maintain its "hegemonist status," and that the primary purpose of its bases and alliance relationships is to contain and counter China. Nevertheless, U.S. forces stationed in the region are seen at present as having a "diversity of goals," some of which (like combating terrorism) are not inimical to China's interests.[22] Like it or not, the U.S. presence in the Asia-Pacific region is also "a historical reality" that cannot be expected to disappear overnight.[23] To the extent that American security guarantees discourage other countries (like Japan) from acquiring nuclear weapons or engaging in unconstrained conventional air and naval buildups, they can still be said, on balance, to serve a useful purpose.

These expressions of tolerance reflect the recognition that even if it wanted to, Beijing is presently in no position to push the United States out of its neighborhood. Trying to do so now would only stiffen American resolve, arouse the anxieties of the regional powers, and convince the world that China harbors aggressive intentions toward its neighbors. It is far better, for the moment, to accept the reality of the situation and to try to slow the development of hostile forces through diplomacy and economic inducements, rather than making things worse with futile attempts to overturn the status quo. In the long run, however, China cannot achieve preponderance, and the current regime can never truly rest secure, if the United States maintains anything resembling its present position in East Asia.

"TO WIN WITHOUT FIGHTING IS THE HIGHEST FORM OF EXCELLENCE"[24]

China seeks to displace the United States as the dominant player in East Asia, and perhaps to extrude it from the region altogether, while at the same time avoiding a potentially disastrous direct confrontation. Although there is probably agreement on the general direction of policy, the current regime does not appear to have a universally shared definition of its preferred objective, a timetable for achieving it, or even a fully articulated strategy for doing so.

Despite this seeming lack of clarity, an analysis of the pattern of recent

Chinese behavior, combined with an examination of the writings of some of its strategic analysts, suggests an approach consisting of four interrelated elements. First, consistent with its overarching desire to avoid confrontation, Beijing has sought to delay or diminish any possible American response to its initiatives by cultivating the appearance of close cooperation with Washington. Second, even as it emphasizes the importance of working together, China has begun to build new regional institutions that are designed to exclude the United States, thereby enhancing its own leverage. Third, at least for the time being, China has sought to stabilize what some refer to as its continental "rear areas" so that, fourth and finally, it can focus more attention on threats and opportunities arising in the maritime domain to its east. Here, since the end of the Cold War, Beijing has been trying to find the right mix of threats and inducements to weaken the foundations of the American regional alliance system.

Preserving good relations with Washington
If Beijing wants eventually to ease the Americans out of East Asia, Chinese strategists believe it must first hold them close. Washington's underlying suspicion of an emerging peer competitor and its ideological animosity toward the Communist Party regime can never be entirely erased. Still, it may be possible to keep America's hostility in check and, by so doing, to dampen and delay its response to China's rising power. Nothing is more important in this regard than sustaining and, if possible, further deepening the strong economic, educational, scientific, cultural, and personal ties that now exist between the two societies. Along with their more direct benefits, these links have helped to build a large, if loose coalition in the United States dedicated to preserving good relations with China. Given the openness of the American system, the members of this coalition have many opportunities to push for policies that they believe will help to achieve this end while opposing any they fear might endanger it. Chinese strategists are well aware that engagement is not a one-way street. Just as America tries to shape China's behavior and change the character of its regime, they believe that China must attempt to influence the United States "from within through various channels and means."[25]

Insofar as their formal diplomatic relationship is concerned, Chinese analysts believe that Beijing cannot be content merely to avoid conflict, but rather must seek to cast itself as Washington's indispensable partner. No American suggestion for possible cooperation should be dismissed out of hand. To the contrary, China should do its utmost to fill the agenda with proposals for high-level dialogues, working groups, discussions, and exchanges, all of them promising eventual progress on issues of importance to Washington. Where areas of overlapping interest exist, Beijing should not hesitate to pursue "win-win" approaches that benefit both parties. Even where the potential gains are less clear, in this view it is crucial to give the United States some of what it wants or, at a minimum, to hold out the prospect of future cooperation. Above all, China's diplomacy should seek to mute America's competitive impulses even as it pursues highly competitive policies of its own.

Satisfying the United States without sacrificing other interests will sometimes require a delicate balancing act. In general, China aims to win the greatest possible gratitude for the least costly, and most easily reversible actions. As we shall see in the next chapter, at times the regime clearly believes that it must make gestures to placate Washington (like voting to support UN sanctions against alleged nuclear proliferators) while at the same time taking other, less visible steps that offset their impact (such as expanding trade and aid with those same, targeted states). In such situations, the *appearance* of cooperation, and the goodwill it gains in Washington, are far more important than the paltry reality of the results.

Building alternative architectures
China presently has neither the capacity nor the desire to launch a frontal assault on the U.S.-dominated order in Asia. For the time being, it has chosen to adopt a circuitous or "indirect line," not challenging Washington's bilateral alliance system, and working through existing regional mechanisms, while at the same time building "a consolidated strategic support" that will eventually put it in "an unassailable position."[26] Beijing is attempting to "promote some new institutional arrangements in parallel with existing [ones] so as to advance its interests," all the while remaining careful "to avoid challenging directly U.S. power and influence."[27] Instead of trying to chop down the institutions that comprise the existing order, Beijing is planting the seeds of new ones that it hopes will eventually over-

shadow the older ones, sapping them of their vitality and causing them gradually to wither away.

China's institution-building project consists of several structures in varying stages of completion. To the west, Beijing has successfully established the Shanghai Cooperation Organisation as the primary multilateral venue for discussing Central Asian security issues. To the east, it is working to build the Association of Southeast Asian Nations (ASEAN) "Plus Three" into the "major framework" for regional cooperation on all issues.[28] With the United States notably absent, China has emerged as the most powerful member of both groups.

In addition to these two institutions, some in Beijing envision an overarching East Asian "community" with China at the center and the United States on the margins, if not excluded altogether. Chinese strategists and diplomats now point out with some regularity that while it may be a Pacific power, America is not truly an *Asian* nation.[29] For this reason, they claim, Washington has been trying to promote the somewhat awkward and artificial concept of "pan-Pacific integration," while opposing and attempting to sabotage plans for a more natural and rational form of East Asian integration. The Americans recognize all too clearly that greater regional cooperation on economic and strategic issues will weaken and may "finally break" the network of alliances on which their own presence depends.[30]

Despite Washington's objections, however, Chinese strategists believe that the idea of East Asian integration has an economic, political, geographic, and cultural logic to it, and clearly hope that it will acquire a self-sustaining momentum. In order to forestall American opposition, it may be desirable at some point to offer a consolation prize, perhaps making the United States a "part-member" or "special member" of the emerging East Asia community. If Washington is to be included at all, however, it must "accept certain preconditions" set by China and the other first-tier members that will codify its peripheral status and may restrict its freedom of action.[31] The Obama administration's 2009 decision to reverse previous policy and finally endorse ASEAN's "Treaty of Amity and Cooperation" may provide a model in this regard. Because the treaty requires signatories to renounce the threat or use of force, while promising not to interfere in the internal affairs of others, Beijing may hope that it can be used to counter future U.S. efforts to criticize it for domestic repression, provide support for Taiwan, or extend deterrence to America's regional allies.[32]

Preserving a "stable strategic rear area"[33]

Even as it begins to build a new regional architecture centered on itself, Beijing has been working hard to lock in the strategic opportunities presented by the dissolution of the Soviet empire. In addition to removing a potentially dangerous adversary from along its continental frontiers, the emergence of independent republics permitted China to expand its influence into Central Asia. Thanks largely to these developments, the view among Chinese strategists is that the "land security environment showed a marked trend toward easing." At the same time, due to events on Taiwan, the bolstering of U.S. forward-based forces, and the strengthening of the U.S.-Japan alliance, the "sea security environment" was becoming "tense and grim." This general condition of "land stable, sea changeable, land relaxed, sea tense" has persisted into the twenty-first century.[34]

Like other favorable trends, however, the stability of China's continental periphery cannot simply be taken for granted. Beijing must ensure that this condition persists so that it can devote the bulk of its resources and attention to the more challenging maritime domain. The resolution of boundary disputes and the formation of "strategic partnerships" with neighboring states during the 1990s were important steps in this regard. In addition, all along its land frontiers (with the exception of the extreme mountainous regions to its south) China has been pursuing what journalist Ross Munro calls a "soft-border policy" aimed at expanding its influence and reducing the emergence of possible future threats.[35]

Following the Soviet collapse, in most areas Beijing opened its frontiers and permitted essentially unrestricted outward movements of goods and people, while retaining tight control over anything flowing in the opposite direction. Given the overwhelming size of China's population and the dynamism of its economy in relation to most of its neighbors, these flows have resulted in an expansion in its physical presence, economic importance, and political influence in adjacent areas of Russia and Central and continental Southeast Asia. Millions of Chinese now live and work in the Russian Far East, and lesser but still significant numbers are active in Kazakhstan, Kyrgyzstan, Laos, and Burma. China has become a major importer of goods from these countries and the dominant supplier of low-cost consumer products and investment capital. Most of the projects in which Beijing invests are designed to ease the extraction and transport to its borders of much-needed raw materials. In some cases, as in Burma, China has helped to build roads, ports, and airfields that could also some-day be used for the projection of its military power.[36]

Munro claims that the visible and seemingly organic growth of China's role along its continental periphery has actually been stimulated in part by a set of "secret and illicit techniques," including bribery, the recruitment of local businessmen and government officials by the Chinese intelligence services, unequal agreements that compel its weaker neighbors to effec-tively dismantle their border controls, and the quiet but active promotion of Chinese emigration. Through the use of a variety of instruments, Bei-jing is in the process of establishing spheres of influence or buffer zones that will effectively push its strategic frontiers well out beyond its territo-rial boundaries.[37]

In addition to penetrating and placating its relatively poor and weak neighbors, preserving the stability of the "rear area" also requires careful cultivation of the two major Asian land powers. As long as Russia and India are not actively hostile, or too closely aligned with the United States, their proximity will not impose significant additional burdens on China and should not deflect it from its eastward focus. Maintaining good rela-tions with Moscow has proved thus far to be comparatively easy. The two powers have several convergent interests: Russia wants to sell arms and oil, while China wants to buy them; both fear violent Islamist movements originating in Central Asia; and especially since Moscow took a sharp turn toward authoritarianism under Vladimir Putin, both feel threatened by American efforts to spread democracy. In recent years the onetime adversaries have begun to act in many respects like actual allies, confer-ring periodically on strategy and even staging large-scale joint military exercises.[38]

Having a friendly neighbor at its back gives China additional strategic depth and reduces the risk of encirclement by a U.S.-led coalition. At least until China succeeds in developing a more broad-based and autonomous arms industry, good relations will also be necessary to keep the People's

Liberation Army supplied with top-of-the-line aircraft, naval vessels, and surface-to-air missiles, as well as spare parts for weapons it has already purchased. If the various pipelines that have been discussed in recent years pan out, Russian gas and oil could also provide China with a relatively secure, overland alternative source of supply for at least some of its energy needs. This could help to reduce, even if it cannot eliminate, China's dependence on oil and gas imported over long and vulnerable sea routes from the Middle East and Southeast Asia.[39]

Despite all the progress that has been made, Chinese strategists believe that Beijing must remain wary of a Russian backlash. In part because of the ongoing penetration of its Far Eastern provinces by Chinese migrants, and the continuing improvement in the People's Liberation Army's conventional power projection capabilities, Russia is still "vigilant with respect to China's incremental power and increasing influence."[40] As it continues to grow, Beijing will probably have to work harder to damp down the fears of its northern neighbor, and to ensure that Moscow continues to receive sufficient benefits from an increasingly unequal partnership.[41]

Sino-Indian relations have been slower to warm, and Chinese strategists realize that they are likely in the long run to prove more problematic. The history of hostility between the two powers is just as deep as that between China and Russia, if not more so, and the sources of their mutual mistrust remain very much alive. India resents China's continuing support for Pakistan, its domination of Tibet, and its recent encroachments into parts of Southeast Asia. Beijing worries about India's evolving strategic relationship with the United States, its emergence since 1998 as an acknowledged nuclear weapons state, and its obvious ambition to become a major world economic and military power in its own right.

Until recently, geography, political friction, and a general lack of economic compatibility have served to limit trade and investment flows between India and China. As this begins to change, Chinese analysts hope that the two will have "more interests in common" and that this should help to "facilitate stable overall bilateral relations."[42] Beijing may also seek to find ways to appeal to India's history of strategic independence and to its even longer tradition of political realism. Chinese strategies recognize that one way to do this is to point out that if Delhi aligns too closely with

Washington, it risks antagonizing China while at the same time losing leverage with the Americans. India would be better advised to play the field and let others compete for its affections.

One part of Beijing's strategy toward India, therefore, is to remind its leaders that they stand to gain most by keeping the United States "at arm's length" and avoiding a "completely antagonistic strategy" toward China.[43]

The generally favorable developments unfolding along China's land periphery were disrupted, at least for a time, by the 9/11 attacks and the subsequent American movement into Central Asia. Almost overnight U.S. forces and bases appeared on China's western frontier. Whether this was part of a deliberate plan, or merely the opportunistic exploitation of unforeseen events, it permitted Washington to take a significant step toward its presumed goal of encirclement. If they can place themselves astride possible overland energy transportation routes, the Americans will be in a far better position to "squeeze China's room for development" and to control its access to the outside world. In the event of some future conflict, the American military might even be able to use its newly acquired bases to launch attacks on China's vulnerable rear areas.[44]

America's "strategic offensive" in Central Asia poses a "tremendous strategic challenge" to Beijing.[45] While China too may benefit if the United States succeeds in suppressing radical Islamist groups, a long-term U.S. military presence in the region is clearly undesirable. Rather than risk a direct confrontation by seeking overtly to dislodge the United States, Beijing has again adopted a more patient, indirect strategy. In contrast to the Americans, with their criticism of alleged human rights violations and calls for political reform, the Chinese have cast themselves as the supportive, noninterventionist friend of existing regimes. The "similarity of national conditions," the fact that China, like its Central Asian neighbors, has an authoritarian government, is an important advantage, as is geography.[46] The United States is far away and has shown itself to be unreliable and prone to sudden shifts in policy. China portrays itself, by contrast, as a steady presence that could not disengage from the region even if it wanted to do so. As the American people tire of interventionism, and as their government runs short of funds to pay for it, the United States will recede from Central Asia while Beijing's influence continues to expand. For the time being, however, the struggle between "containment" and "anti-containment" along China's land periphery will continue.[47]

Securing the maritime domain

In spite of what has happened since the "9/11 incident," concludes one analyst, "the general stability of China's land strategic front has not been fundamentally changed." As has been true for some time, however, the situation "regarding the sea is more serious than the situation regarding land."[48] On its maritime periphery Beijing confronts a long-term strategic puzzle of daunting difficulty. If it is to establish itself in a position of unquestioned preponderance in East Asia, China must find a way to bring Taiwan back, and push America out, while keeping Japan down. In other words, Beijing must select a course of action that will compel Taipei to accept unification on its terms, and constrict America's military presence and diplomatic influence in the Western Pacific, without at the same time triggering resurgent Japanese militarism, or the formation of an anti-China coalition of Asian powers in which Japan might play a major role.

It is not obvious that a solution to this puzzle actually exists. For at least the next several decades, China may have to be prepared to accept a second-best outcome, perhaps one in which the Taiwan issue is smoothed over with ambiguous diplomatic formulations, Japan remains strategically dormant, even as its relative power continues to decline, and Washington and Beijing find ways either to cooperate and share regional leadership or to establish mutually agreeable spheres of influence. The question of whether they will have to settle for something less than clearcut preponderance is probably unresolved at this point in the minds of China's leaders. For now, they will likely continue to press ahead in maritime East Asia along several axes of advance. How far they are able to get will depend on many factors, not least among them the nature of the American response.

Strategists sitting in Beijing and looking east to the Pacific see a maritime "front" with two flanks and a center. To the north is the Korean peninsula, to the south are the island nations of Southeast Asia and Oceania, in the middle are Japan and Taiwan, and, behind it all, the United States. As compared to the center, where the United States has traditionally had friends who shared its concern about China's rise, the flanks of its position have appeared at times to be soft and potentially vulnerable. By weakening America's grip to the north and south, Beijing may hope to make it easier eventually to pry it loose from the center. At least in the near term, the object is not to peel away U.S. allies and bring them over to China's side, but rather to diversify their interests, complicate their calculations, blur their loyalties, and set the stage for further erosion in what were once rock-solid, diplomatically monogamous relationships.

Australia and South Korea used to be the southern and northern "anchors" of the U.S. position in Asia, but as one Chinese analyst observes optimistically, they are "no longer as 'iron' as before." America's " 'iron brothers' have 'drifted away' and are not reliable."[49] As elsewhere in the region, these developments are the product of China's "smile diplomacy" combined with the seemingly irresistible pull of its massive, fast-growing economy. In the case of South Korea, Beijing has some additional advantages that it has sought to parlay into even greater influence. Despite its initial reluctance to get involved, Beijing has discovered that it can use its position at the center of the multilateral negotiations over North Korea's nuclear programs to gain leverage with Seoul, as well as Washington. Because it is the only state that enjoys reasonably cordial relations with both the United States and North Korea, China has tried to portray itself as an "honest broker" between them, thereby enabling it to control the pace and direction of negotiations. As the only major power in close contact with both Koreas, China has also sought to position itself to play a decisive role in their eventual reunification.

The fact that South Korea and China share a troublesome neighbor, and would be most directly affected by its sudden collapse, has made them far more wary than either the United States or Japan about applying pressure to North Korea. The eruption of the nuclear issue in 2003 thus created a situation in which there have at times been more "points of consensus" between China and South Korea than between the two countries and their respective allies. Chinese strategists evidently hoped that this would open the possibility for a much higher degree of "contact and coordination" than would otherwise have been possible, clearing the way for closer interaction on a range of strategic as well as economic issues.[50]

In the long run, China seeks to shape the terms of any final settlement between North and South Korea. One issue of prime concern will be the disposition of U.S. forces on the Korean peninsula and the nature of the continuing relationship between the Americans and their longtime allies in Seoul. Scholar David Shambaugh writes that although its leaders are careful not to say so in public, "China tends to view the Korean peninsula as its natural sphere of influence—much as the United States views Latin America." Not surprisingly, he concludes from conversations with Foreign Ministry officials and military officers that "China's strong preference is that U.S. military involvement would no longer be an issue following unification and that the alliance would be naturally dissolved and troops withdrawn."[51]

Some Chinese strategists assess that a final resolution of the Korean problem will have even more far-reaching consequences, perhaps calling into question the rationale for a continuing American military presence, not only on the peninsula but also in Japan and throughout East Asia. As one notes, "Should the [North Korean] 'threat' be eliminated, this will shake the foundations of U.S. strategy in the entire Asia-Pacific region."[52] For now, Beijing has had to settle for less dramatic and potentially reversible gains, including South Korea's hesitation about allowing U.S. forces based on its soil to conduct operations off the peninsula, and to the south, Australia's reluctance to participate in a strategic dialogue with Japan, India, and the United States for fear that it might be seen as intended to "curb China."[53] While much work remains to be done, the flanks of the American position are no longer as solid as they once were.

As regards the center of the maritime front, whatever may have been true in the past, it is Japan, not Taiwan, that will increasingly become the focus of Chinese strategy. Taiwan could cause serious problems, and perhaps even a major war, if it were to make a last-ditch dash for independence. In itself, however, the island has neither the resources nor the diplomatic leverage to pose a challenge to Beijing's hopes for achieving regional preponderance.

After a rocky start, since the turn of the century Chinese strategists believe that they have made considerable progress in bringing Taipei to heel. Although there is always a danger that they will stage a comeback, pro-independence forces on the island appear to have passed the peak of their popularity. Albeit at some cost to its reputation as a peace-loving power, Beijing's threats of military action helped to keep the Democratic Progressive Party (DPP) in check and, perhaps more important, to get the attention of the United States. Because of its preoccupation with terrorism and its desire to win China's support in dealing with North Korea, and other pressing issues, after 9/11 the United States became far more sensitive to Beijing's concerns. Largely as a result, for a time arms sales and other forms of strategic cooperation with the island ground almost to a halt. Chinese analysts now acknowledge that Washington has joined in "constraining" the more radical elements on Taiwan through public statements and stern private warnings.[54] The electoral defeat suffered by the DPP in 2008 provides further proof that its strategy is working.

All of this creates more time for China to tighten the noose around Taiwan by continuing its military buildup opposite the island, promoting ever-deeper economic engagement, further constricting Taipei's diplomatic space, and cultivating friends among its political and business elite. Barring some disruptive event, the trends are all in China's favor, with "the mainland growing stronger and Taiwan growing weaker." These shifts are "not only irreversible; the widening of the gap is also accelerating."[55] Nor is this merely a matter of improvements in the China-Taiwan military balance. Chinese analysts believe that scandals and assassination attempts have tarnished the appeal of Taiwan's democracy even as it has lost its economic and technological edge over the mainland. Meanwhile, the gap between Chinese and American military capabilities in the Western Pacific continues to narrow.[56] Beijing has reason to hope that at some point, Washington will recognize that it can no longer afford to risk war over a tiny island, and that partly as a result, Taipei will realize that it has no choice but to cut the best deal it can with the mainland.

While they are generally careful not to appear to endorse such views themselves, Chinese writers are aware that some foreign observers believe the "loss" of Taiwan would have significant strategic implications for the United States. If Washington is seen to have abandoned Taiwan, even if unification is achieved without bloodshed, others will lose faith in its security guarantees, America's alliances and strategic partnerships will wither, and its foothold on "the eastern extremity of the Eurasian continent" will eventually be lost. In time, Washington will find that it has been "gradually exclude[d] . . . from east Asia."[57]

Even if China succeeds in pacifying its interior frontiers, wooing its maritime neighbors in Northeast and Southeast Asia, and bringing Taiwan back into the fold with a mix of threats and blandishments, it will still face the question of what to do about Japan. For as long as Tokyo and Washington remain close, Beijing's growing power in East Asia can still be balanced and its influence constrained. Should its alliance with the United States come to an end, Japan could still pose a threat, whether alone or in combination with other Asian powers like Russia and India. If it is to move toward preponderance, China must find a way to separate Japan from the United States without provoking it into other forms of assertive behavior.

Since the end of the Cold War, Beijing has tried two very different approaches to this problem. During the 1990s, and with increasing intensity through the early years of the new century, it adopted a bullying, hectoring stance that stood in marked contrast to its congenial approach to most other countries. This attitude may have reflected a deep and abiding hatred of Japan on the part of some high-level decision makers, but it also had an underlying strategic rationale. China's harsh criticisms were clearly intended to play on the once powerful strain of pacifism in Japan and to dissuade its government from expanding the armed forces, adopting a more "normal" international role, or cooperating more closely with the Americans. The vociferous Chinese response to offensive statements by nationalist politicians and in history textbooks also served to awaken unhappy memories elsewhere in Asia, leaving Japan alienated from many of its neighbors. Jiang Zemin's 1998 state visit, in which he publicly lectured his hosts about their lack of contrition for the Second World War, was a noteworthy, if clumsy, application of this approach.[58]

By the turn of the century China's tactics appeared to be backfiring. Instead of trying to placate Beijing, as they might have done in the past, astute Japanese politicians responded to a growing public sense of post–Cold War vulnerability and insecurity by appealing to long-dormant nationalist and patriotic sentiments. Gestures such as Prime Minister Junichiro Koizumi's annual visit to the Yakasuni Shrine following his election in 2001 were obviously meant to please right-wing supporters, but they were also intended to signal Japan's reemergence as a "normal nation" capable of honoring its war dead without guilt or shame. Koizumi's insistence on repeating this ritual in the face of intense objections from other governments demonstrated Japan's newfound willingness to "say no" to foreign critics, and especially to China. The increasingly harsh official responses from Beijing only fed Japanese anxieties, fueling an even tighter downward spiral in relations.[59]

Starting in late 2003, Chinese analysts began to question the effectiveness of existing strategy.[60] Jiang's retirement and the installation of a new leadership team doubtless made this self-scrutiny easier than it would have been otherwise. Widespread anti-Japanese rioting in 2004 and again in 2005 also highlighted the danger that harsh public rhetoric could arouse passions that might end up being turned inward against the regime. In any event, the announcement in early 2005 of further enhancements to the U.S.-Japan alliance made clear that Beijing's hard line was not working and might, in fact, be having an effect precisely opposite to the one intended.

Koizumi's resignation as prime minister in 2006 cleared the way for Beijing to change course without losing face, and the election in 2009 of a new coalition government with a more favorable attitude toward China helped solidify the trend toward more cordial relations, but the underlying causes of the shift had little to do with personalities or even political parties. Having tried for over a decade to browbeat Japan into passivity, Beijing now had the resources, the self-confidence, and the skill to try to win it over with diplomacy and trade. Although the stakes and the degree of difficulty were greater than in any other instance, China's Japan policy seemed finally to have been brought into alignment with the rest of its strategy for Asia.

As elsewhere, Beijing benefited economically from growing bilateral flows of trade and investment, but it also hoped to gain strategically by building strong diplomatic ties to a vital American ally. Chinese analysts were not shy in pointing out that "Japan's economic revival . . . has to a very great extent been due to its trade and investment with China."[61] The obvious but unspoken point here is that Japan's future prosperity will depend more than ever before on the maintenance of good relations with its fast-rising neighbor.

Following its reappraisal, Beijing sought to draw closer to Japan while at the same time driving a wedge between Tokyo and Washington. In the words of one strategist in the People's Liberation Army, China needed to learn to "deal separately with Japan and the United States . . . and correctly understand and get an appropriate handle on the contradictions and differences between the two."[62] At the same time as it quietly advised Washington that Japan was a country in decline, or an untrustworthy and dangerous revanchist power, or both, Beijing sought to feed Tokyo's fears of abandonment. "It is not unreasonable for Japan to worry that the U.S. will 'neglect' it." After all, Washington has never hesitated to go over and around its friends "for the sake of its self interest." As China has become wealthier and more powerful, it has also grown more important to the United States, and the relationship between the two has blossomed. "If things continue as they are, wouldn't Japan be 'marginalized'?" asked one author helpfully. "This is an issue Japan has to ponder carefully."[63]

In contrast to its past rebukes, Beijing now extended a welcoming hand. The time had come to put a check on the "mutual dislike and even hostility between very large numbers of Chinese and Japanese people."[64] After all, the two former rivals had a great deal in common. Both would, at times, wish to "unite . . . to constrain U.S. unilateralist tendencies." In addition, the rise of "non-traditional security" challenges like climate change and piracy meant that "people of foresight" were "more and more realizing the limitations of the Japan-U.S. alliance." To deal with these problems, China and Japan would have to work together more effectively, both by promoting regional cooperation in East Asia (which, in some forms, would exclude the United States) and by establishing a "mutually beneficial strategic military security relationship."[65] Chinese strategists disavowed any intention of pushing America out of the region, but they also noted that "U.S. influence in Asia can hardly avoid weakening if . . . China and Japan get closer and strengthen cooperation."[66]

THE MEANING OF "VICTORY"

In keeping with their inclination to discuss trends rather than goals, Chinese analysts do not describe a future "end state" for East Asia. Still, recent commentary hints at two possibilities. Using the language of Western political scientists and game theorists, some writers discuss the prospect of achieving a "non-zero-sum" relationship in which America and China are able to cooperate, to varying degrees, on different issues and in different areas.[67] In such a world, the United States might retain some semblance of its present posture in Asia, albeit most likely in a diminished form, and the U.S. and Chinese spheres of influence in the region would overlap to some extent.

The other image is starker. Conservative writer Yan Xuetong argues that China will emerge eventually at the center of a new regional order in which all the other nations of East Asia will have no choice but to accept its leadership. Japan might wish to remain outside this new order, but "over time the Chinese club will be so powerful that Japan will want to join it."[68] Although Yan does not say so in as many words, it seems clear that in this scenario America's alliances would either cease to exist or be drained of any military significance.

Another author suggested in 2007 that if China continues to rise, the United States will "tend more and more toward earnestly considering and perhaps even adopting some kind of peaceful 'final solution,' a distinction in the balance of power and influence in different . . . geographical regions." Among other things, Washington would have to accept China's "leading status" in terms of "combined diplomatic/economic/political influence in Asia" and its "military parity and even slight superiority with the United States in the coastal water region (with Taiwan's eastern coastal waters as the boundary line) together with peaceful or basically peaceful cross-strait reunification."[69]

Similar ideas have been floated in different channels by more influential figures. In 2008 Admiral Timothy Keating, commander of the U.S. Pacific Command, reported a conversation in which a senior Chinese naval officer suggested drawing a line down the middle of the Pacific: "You guys can have the east part of the Pacific, Hawaii to the states. We'll take the west part of the Pacific, from Hawaii to China."[70] The Chinese admiral was joking of course, but like many attempts at humor, his comment is revealing. Obscure academics are not the only ones conjuring with the idea of a new, Sino-centric order in East Asia.

Eight

———◆———

THE BALANCE OF INFLUENCE

WHO IS WINNING THE "CONTEST FOR SUPREMACY"?

China and America are locked in a multifaceted competition to determine which will be the preponderant power in East Asia. Despite changes in leadership on both sides and the continual ebb and flow of events, over the past two decades the strategies of the contestants have remained remarkably stable. Washington strives to maintain a favorable balance of power while seeking through engagement to "tame" China's foreign policy and ultimately to transform its domestic political system. For its part, Beijing aims to slow Washington's responses to its growing strength, to weaken America's alliances and constrict its presence, while working to expand its own power and influence and ultimately to replace the United States as the dominant regional player.

Which side is winning the contest for supremacy? Or, to put the matter more precisely, which nation is closer at present to achieving its strategic objectives, and given the prevailing trends, which seems more likely to be able to do so in the coming decades? I devote this and the next chapter to providing answers to these questions. I begin by looking at some of the "softer," less tangible aspects of the U.S.-China rivalry. Central to the strategies of both competitors is an effort to exert influence over one another and over third parties. After assessing how each is doing in this regard, I turn in chapter 9 to an analysis of the "hard power" portions of their contest: the increasingly intense military competition that is now unfolding in the Western Pacific, and the economic and technological factors that will help shape its eventual outcome.

Looking across all the various domains of the Sino-American competition leads to a mixed and conditional conclusion: China has done better thus far at constraining America's response to its rise than America has done in changing China. As a result, unless it begins to respond more effectively to Beijing's ongoing buildup, Washington is going to find itself on the wrong end of an increasingly unfavorable balance of military power in East Asia. This could undermine America's security commitments, weaken its alliances, and increase the odds that China will eventually be able to establish itself as the region's preponderant power.

Such an outcome would be deeply damaging to American national interests, and to those of Asia's democracies, but fortunately it is far from inevitable. If the United States can mobilize the necessary resources and take advantage of the natural inclination of its Asian friends and allies to want to maintain their freedom of action in the face of China's growing strength, it should be able to preserve a favorable power balance while it continues to wait for fundamental changes in the character of the Beijing regime. Although for the next decade or so the momentum of the situation appears to favor China, in the somewhat longer run the People's Republic is likely to have increasing difficulty in maintaining the high rates of economic growth that appear now to make it such a formidable competitor. If the United States can stay in the game, it should have a good chance to ultimately win. But if America and its allies permit their position to erode until it is too late to respond, they could yet lose the struggle for mastery in Asia.

WHO IS "SHAPING" WHOM?

At its core, the Sino-American competition is a mind game. Each contestant seeks via various channels to influence the other's perceptions and calculations, and through them its strategies and goals. Beijing wants to ease Washington's anxieties and to dull its competitive reflexes, preventing or at least slowing a vigorous response to China's growing power. The United States is trying to encourage China's leaders to adopt policies that align more closely with its own and to dissuade them from mounting any challenge to the existing, American-dominated international order. In the long run, Washington hopes that engagement will help speed China's domestic political transformation, closing the ideological gap that now divides the two countries and enabling the kind of stable, trusting relationship that is possible between democracies.

In different ways and to varying degrees, each side is trying to "shape" the other. Despite a certain superficial symmetry, however, American strategists have clearly set themselves more ambitious goals, and must confront steeper obstacles, than their Chinese counterparts. It should come as no surprise then that at least in this aspect of their overall competition, Beijing has done better to date than its rival.

Stripped of diplomatic niceties, the ultimate aim of the American strategy is to hasten a revolution, albeit a peaceful one, that will sweep away China's one-party authoritarian state and leave a liberal democracy in its place. This would be no small task even if the tools available to accomplish it were more powerful and the blueprint for applying them much clearer than is in fact the case. As recent experience in Iraq and Afghanistan suggests, even when one country occupies and physically controls another, it may find it very hard to promote the growth of democratic values and practices. Of course the United States has no intention of invading China to bring about "regime change." Its leverage is, at best, indirect. Through trade and investment it can contribute to China's economic growth and thus to the emergence of a middle class that may one day act as the standard bearer for political change. Through dialogue, exchange, and example it can try to ease the way for the adoption of institutions, like a stronger and more independent judiciary and a freer and more open press, that will nurture and protect the delicate seedlings of reform. For the most part, however, Washington can do little more than stand back and hope that the general theories of political development on which its policies are premised will prove applicable to China.

Far-reaching political change may yet come to the People's Republic, and when it does, it will doubtless owe something to America's longstanding policy of engagement. But that transformative moment is not yet at hand, and in many respects it appears further away today than it did a few decades ago. Although the Chinese government now permits ordinary citizens greater freedom to travel, choose their jobs, own property, and engage in at least certain forms of personal expression, it retains a stranglehold on political power that shows no sign of loosening. Fundamental criticism of the party or the state (as opposed to complaints about particular policies or lower-ranking officials) is still forbidden, as is the formation of independent opposition parties.

Small changes that were once heralded as harbingers of serious reform have thus far failed to pan out. In the 1990s many Western observers pointed hopefully to the initiation of "village elections" as an indication that the regime was beginning to experiment with democracy. But this practice has not been replicated at higher echelons of government, and even at the local level, it has not resulted in genuine competition or effective popular control. Similarly, although Beijing has taken some steps to strengthen the nation's legal system, courts remain highly politicized and limited in their authority. Most important, according to Sinologist Minxin Pei, the Chinese Communist Party is still "fundamentally unwilling to allow real judicial constraints on the exercise of its power."[1] Finally, despite predictions from many China-watchers that the fourth generation of party leaders would turn out to be liberalizing reformers, Hu Jintao and his colleagues quickly showed themselves to be staunch defenders of the party's monopoly on political power. There is no evidence to suggest that their successors will be any different.

Far from accepting the necessity or inevitability of change, China's rulers have instead chosen to redouble their efforts to maintain tight control over society. This may cost them dearly one day, but for the moment, what is most striking is how extensive and effective these repressive measures have been and how little they seem to have interfered with China's continuing economic boom. The government has permitted its people access to the Internet, but it has also spent billions on a system of electronic and human monitors that allow it to track communications and block "offensive" material. A vast and expensive network of closed-circuit television cameras now scans public squares and major thoroughfares in virtually every Chinese city. Since the bloody dispersal of student demonstrators at Tiananmen Square in 1989, the regime has increased the budget, size, and prestige of the People's Armed Police, a force devoted exclusively to preserving internal security.[2] While the number of urban and rural protests has risen sharply in recent years, Beijing has perfected tactics for isolating and crushing them with minimal violence.[3] It has also honed the techniques of what Pei calls "selective repression." Instead of brutalizing large numbers of people, the regime has learned to focus on key political activists, using a variety of tactics to "intimidate, control, and neutralize" those who pose the most serious threat.[4]

The forces of repression in China have proved to be tenacious and effective. But the forces of change have also not been nearly as strong as many expected. Despite predictions based on the experiences of other societies, China's new middle class has not yet shown itself to be a major source of pressure for reform. Indeed, to the contrary, the middle classes appear, on balance, to be a strongly conservative influence, resistant to wide-ranging political change and essentially supportive of the current regime. These attitudes are partly the result of a deliberate effort at co-optation. Starting in the early 1990s, the Chinese Communist Party began to woo intellectuals and young professionals with salary increases, good jobs, perks, and recognition. The party has also opened its rolls to entrepreneurs, offering the new business elite preferred access to government decision makers, commercial opportunities, and capital, while binding them more closely to the regime.[5]

Middle-class conservatism also reflects an understandable calculation of self-interest on the part of tens of millions of people who want nothing more than to be left in peace to enjoy their newfound prosperity. As it has in the past, political change could bring upheaval and violence to China. Moreover, in light of the fact that the vast majority of the country's population is still rural and impoverished, a more equitable distribution of political power could well result in confiscatory taxes and attempts to redistribute income. As Sinologist Edward Friedman explains, "The new middle class in urban China tends to imagine democracy as a system that would empower the rural poor. The urban middle class thinks of angry and suffering peasants as ignorant people who backed Mao's policies which kept China poor and miserable. Rather than empower purportedly economically irrational peasants, the middle class will go along with the party's commitment to continue economic reform while not loosening its monopolization of political power."[6]

It is hard to deny the effectiveness of Beijing's policies. As it has since the 1970s, China continues to rank among the most repressive countries in the world.[7] The regime's periodic experiments with what it calls "democracy with Chinese characteristics" seem designed to provide an acceptable outlet for popular discontent and to deflect demands for real political reform. In any event, none of the superficial changes in procedures for choosing leaders and setting policies that have been made in recent years permit any meaningful challenge to the regime's legitimacy or control. A 2008 report by the Congressional-Executive Commission on China summarizes the situation: "The Chinese Communist Party's monopoly on political power remains firmly intact. Reforms have not removed barriers to the formation of competing political parties or an independent judiciary. . . . Thirty years after the launch of the reform era and nearly 60 years after the founding of the People's Republic of China, the basic structure of China's government—an authoritarian political system controlled by the top leaders of the Communist Party—remains unchanged."[8]

Despite decades of rapid economic progress, there are no signs that China is any closer to the promised tipping point where increasing prosperity will give rise to effective demands for political rights. In fact, the Communist Party's ability to sustain growth without granting greater freedom has been so impressive that it has caused some in the West to reexamine their most cherished convictions about the relationship between market economics and democratic politics. Perhaps, as has been suggested, the world is witnessing the emergence of a new, and possibly quite durable model of "authoritarian capitalism."[9]

Whether or not this ultimately proves to be the case, for the moment Beijing has clearly found a workable way to combine economic dynamism with political repression. This uncomfortable fact has begun to raise questions about the rationale for the engagement portion of America's China strategy. James Mann, for example, warns that U.S. officials are clinging to a policy that is "based upon premises about China's future that are at best questionable and at worst downright false."[10] Nor does this critique apply only to American policy. A 2009 assessment by a leading center-left European think tank describes as "anachronistic" the belief that contact with the European Union will cause China to "liberalise its economy, improve the rule of law and democratise its politics."[11] China has certainly changed in the past thirty years, but its political system has not evolved in the ways that the architects of engagement had hoped and predicted.

Instead of being on the verge of extinction, the Chinese Communist

Party could have decades of more life left in it. As Mann points out, the "Soothing Scenario," in which China somehow morphs smoothly and easily into a liberal democracy, may prove to be a fantasy. Twenty or thirty years from now, he warns, China will likely be far richer and stronger than it is today, but it may still be ruled by a Leninist dictatorship that remains "hostile to dissent and organized political opposition," supportive of other oppressive regimes around the world, and sharply at odds with the United States.[12]

IS AMERICA "TAMING" CHINA?

Putting aside the promise of eventual regime transformation, engagement was supposed to produce meaningful cooperation on a wide range of practical policy problems and, beyond that, an increasing convergence of Chinese and Western views on questions of regional and global order. At least insofar as the most urgent challenges on the American national security agenda are concerned, these expectations have not yet been met. As regards terrorism, the proliferation of weapons of mass destruction, the nuclear ambitions of North Korea and Iran, and the egregious behavior of lesser "rogue states," China has been far less helpful than eager American officials are sometimes wont to claim. Nor is there compelling evidence to suggest that Beijing's acceptance of present international arrangements is other than partial, tentative, evanescent, and likely to evaporate as its power grows.

In the aftermath of 9/11, some distinguished commentators expressed the belief that America and China would henceforth be united by the threat of terrorism, much as they had once been drawn together by the looming presence of the Soviet Union.[13] This view found resonance at the highest levels of the U.S. government. And yet, despite high hopes that the "common danger" of terrorism, as President George W. Bush described it in his January 2002 State of the Union address, was "erasing old rivalries," Sino-American collaboration on this issue has turned out to be limited in scope and significance.[14] Except to the extent that it feels directly threatened, China has shown little interest in addressing the broader problem of Islamist extremism. Instead, its concerns have been parochial and its approach tactical. Beijing took the occasion presented by the 9/11 attacks to seek American support for its brutal suppression of alleged Uighur separatists in Xinjiang province. Declaring that the United States and China shared "a common understanding of the magnitude of the threat" and stood "side by side" in the war on terrorism, the Bush administration eventually agreed to label one group, the East Turkestan Islamic Movement, a terrorist organization.[15] The Chinese reciprocated by soft-pedaling their criticism of U.S. actions in Afghanistan and Iraq, moves that, in any event, they could have done very little to prevent.

Beyond this tacit, qualified acquiescence in each other's counter-terrorism policies, the two countries agreed after 9/11 to share intelligence on emerging threats. The full extent and substance of these exchanges have never been disclosed, but their impact on U.S. counterterror operations appears to have been minimal at best.[16] Soon after talks began, top American officials complained publicly that the information being provided by Beijing was too vague and general to be of any practical use. Since 2005, according to a report to Congress, "U.S. concerns about China's extent of cooperation in counterterrorism have increased." Over time, the "war on terror" has become yet another source of mutual annoyance and mistrust. Beijing's calls for the closure of post-9/11 U.S. bases in Central Asia have antagonized Washington, and its contributions to stabilizing Afghanistan have been limited and narrowly self-interested.[17] For its part, Beijing has been irritated by America's expressions of official sympathy for some Uighur dissidents and by its refusal to repatriate captured Chinese citizens with alleged links to al Qaeda.[18]

American efforts to encourage greater Chinese cooperation in combating proliferation have also met with only limited success. Prior to the mid-1980s China was an active, unabashed supporter of proliferation and denounced any attempt to restrict the spread of weapons technology as a conspiracy by the superpowers to retain their advantages over the less developed nations. Beijing did more than merely talk; its actions in the 1960s and 1970s set in motion a cascade of nuclear proliferation with which the world is still attempting to deal. Without its assistance, Pakistan and perhaps North Korea would never have gotten the bomb, and without help from those two Chinese clients, Iran would be further from the nuclear finish line and neither Libya nor Syria would have ever come close.[19]

Disputes over alleged transfers of nuclear, chemical, and missile technology became a major source of tension in the 1980s, with Washington repeatedly imposing sanctions on Chinese companies accused of selling sensitive items to third parties and Beijing responding with protestations of shock and outrage. As part of its new embrace of international institutions, and its ongoing effort to reduce friction with the United States, the Chinese government eventually signed on to an array of control regimes. At least as regards nuclear weapons (though not so clearly in the case of ballistic missiles and chemical weapons), this shift seems to have reflected a genuine reassessment of the danger further proliferation posed to Chinese interests. Even so, from an American perspective, Beijing's adherence to new, self-imposed restrictions on its behavior remained incomplete and problematic.[20]

After the September 11 attacks, the United States assigned top priority to stopping the further spread of weapons of mass destruction and pressed others to do the same. The Chinese government responded with considerable fanfare in 2002 by promulgating new domestic regulations that it claimed would prevent once and for all the export of dangerous dual-use technologies to potential proliferators. As with previous promises to "go straight," the results have been disappointing. According to a 2007 report to Congress, "In spite of China's multilateral and bilateral nonproliferation commitments, and its own domestic laws, there have been repeated episodes of Chinese proliferation."[21] These have been explained away by some observers as the result of individual greed or bureaucratic ineptitude rather than deliberate government policy. For its part, the Bush administration eventually concluded that the "recurring transfers of militarily-sensitive materials, products, and technologies by Chinese companies and government organizations" showed that, for whatever reason, these "serial proliferators" had "no fear of government controls or punishments."[22]

Beijing has made much of its commitment to nonproliferation, and it has demonstrated the capacity to enforce restrictions when it sees fit to do so. When its diplomatic and commercial interests demand, however, it remains willing to turn a blind eye to questionable transactions involving longtime customers and strategic partners like Pakistan, Iran, and North Korea. Unfortunately, these happen also to be precisely the countries whose actions are driving the latest wave of proliferation.

China's handling of North Korea in recent years reveals a familiar pattern of ostentatious gestures and quiet evasion. When the Bush administration demanded that China take greater responsibility for reining in Pyongyang's nuclear program, it agreed in 2003 to host multilateral talks on the subject. At the outset, and at several points along the way, Beijing applied just enough economic and diplomatic pressure to its erstwhile allies to keep them coming back to the negotiating table. But it never deployed more than a small fraction of its potential leverage as North Korea's only ally, principle trading partner, and sole fuel oil supplier.[23] To the contrary, as the United States worked to increase pressure on the North, China sought to alleviate it by increasing trade and economic assistance. This may have been due to fear of triggering the collapse of the Kim Jong-il regime, and the possible loss of a buffer zone between China and a prosperous democratic ally of the United States. The sudden disappearance of the North would also have interfered with Beijing's longer-term goals of weakening the U.S–South Korea alliance and eventually achieving a dominant influence on the Korean peninsula. Having observed the grateful American response to their initial intervention, Chinese strategists may also have reasoned that prolonging the crisis served their interests better than ending it.[24] While trying to contain North Korea's nuclear ambitions was no doubt a concern, as scholar David Shambaugh noted astutely at the start of the crisis, it was not "by any means the first issue on Beijing's agenda."[25]

China's leaders were ultimately able to have their cake and eat it too. On the one hand, they won effusive praise from Washington for their diplomatic "leadership" in convening the Six Party Talks; on the other, they managed both to sidestep American demands for even more pressure on the North and to avoid blame when it finally tested a nuclear weapon. Not surprisingly, Beijing has tried to replicate its earlier success by using similar tactics in dealing with Iran's nuclear program. A 2010 study by the independent Brussels-based International Crisis Group describes how the regime has worked to "delay and weaken" economic sanctions, loudly opposing such measures in principle and eventually supporting them in order to appease the United States, but only once they had been watered down sufficiently so as to pose no real threat to China's commercial partners in Tehran. Much as it did in the North Korean case, Beijing has sought to put itself in an intermediary position that "maximizes its bargaining power, since it leads both sides to offer incentives for its support."[26] China's true aim is evidently not to stop Iran from going nuclear, but rather to create a situation in which the Americans have little choice but to accept this once unthinkable outcome, while at the same time feeling grateful to Beijing for trying to prevent it.

China has shown similar inventiveness in dealing with other ugly but useful regimes under pressure from the West. In the Sudan and in Burma, for example, China has demonstrated an almost surgical precision in doling out the thinnest possible slices of cooperation, avoiding isolation and condemnation, while at the same time remaining close to useful, if unsavory, governments. As British foreign policy specialist Mark Leonard notes, Beijing has mastered the art of "delivering just enough progress to satisfy the West but not so much as to endanger the autocratic regimes which look to China for support."[27]

None of this is meant to suggest that China is uniquely disingenuous. Rather, it is a rational player in the game of international politics that happens to define its interests in ways that are significantly at odds with those of the United States. On terrorism, proliferation, and its dealings with assorted rogue states and repressive regimes, Beijing has sought to cultivate its image as a cooperative, "responsible" state committed to upholding global norms while at the same time pursuing its own narrowly self-interested agenda.

And what of the supposed transformative effects of engagement? Have its extensive dealings with the West "socialized" Beijing, transmuting it from a onetime advocate of world revolution into a staunch defender of the existing international order? Is China in fact becoming, as leading Sinologist Iain Johnston has suggested, a "status quo power"?[28]

Compared to its recent past, there can be no question that China today is far more accepting of existing rules and institutions. In the thirty years since the start of the era of "reform and opening up," it has become a member in good standing of virtually every significant regional grouping and international organization.[29] Abandoning its former radicalism, China has adopted the posture of a conservative, even in certain respects, a reactionary power. Chairman Mao favored overthrowing the existing system of nation-states. By contrast, since the end of the Cold War, with the advanced industrial democracies trying to devise new international legal rationales to justify their interventions in the internal affairs of other countries, Beijing has cast itself as the leading advocate and defender of traditional conceptions of sovereignty.[30]

In this case, as with its relatively recent interest in preventing the further spread of nuclear weapons, China's behavior reflects a calculation of what is in its national interest rather than any principled commitment to some abstract concept of international order. Thus a comparatively weak China opposes intervention on human rights grounds because it fears that such a rationale could be turned against it. A stronger state may well use similar arguments to justify future interventions in the affairs of its neighbors.

More broadly, China's acceptance of certain aspects of the status quo does not necessarily mean that it has become a "status quo power." The fact that Beijing, to quote Johnston, "is not trying as hard as it might" to oppose America's existing system of alliances, the continued presence of its forces and bases, or its status as Asia's preponderant power does not mean that it harbors no ambitions to change these key features of the contemporary regional order.[31] A more plausible explanation is that Chinese strategists have simply concluded that they do not yet have the power, or the urgent need, to push for such changes.

Even among those in the West who are most optimistic about the prospects that engagement will reshape the way China's leaders think about the world, there is an appropriate measure of caution about the extent to which this has already occurred or is imminent. To the contrary, it is precisely because these optimists fear that new, essentially liberal views about the role of force, the benefits of trade and international institutions, and the futility of pursuing regional hegemony are not widely held, and that those who advocate them are in a minority in China's high councils, that they warn against what they regard as excessively confrontational, "hard line" policies. If the United States adopts such a stance, it will supposedly strengthen the hands of the "hawks" on the other side, triggering an escalating spiral of mutual suspicion and hostility and undermining the arguments of "moderates" in both countries that favor increased cooperation. Aside from whatever substantive results it may produce in the short run, the underlying purpose of engagement is precisely to encourage the rise of such people in the Chinese system. As even the optimists admit, however, this process is still in its early stages, and its outcome is by no means assured.[32]

IS CHINA "LULLING" AMERICA?

Beijing's strategy does not require transforming the American regime, or altering the balance of power within it by helping "moderates" win out over "hawks." While they would certainly like to see a permanent, long-term shift in U.S. attitudes, the most pressing aim of Chinese policy makers is to dampen and delay any dramatic response to their rising power. To do this they must simply reinforce tendencies that are already present within the American political system.

China's rulers have been in the business of "perception management" for millennia. Over the centuries, these efforts were generally aimed at convincing other governments of China's awesome power and importance. Vestiges of past practices are still visible today. Foreign visitors no longer have to kowtow when they meet with government officials, but they are still ushered into vast halls with enormous murals designed to make even those with the sturdiest egos feel small.

The task for contemporary Chinese perception managers is more challenging than it was under the emperors or even as recently as when Henry Kissinger and Richard Nixon first visited Beijing. Instead of trying to appear strong, for the first fifteen years after the end of the Cold War, China was trying to "hide its capabilities" even as these were growing at a rapid pace. More recently, Chinese strategists have sought ways of acknowledging and even in certain respects highlighting their increasing strength, while at the same time continuing to reassure others about their intentions.

In contrast to the past, this is no longer merely a matter of shaping the perceptions of a handful of diplomats. As recently as thirty years ago most of the business transacted between China and the United States was handled by a small group of politicians and bureaucrats.[33] Their views were what mattered, and they were therefore the focus of Beijing's efforts to shape opinions and preferences. Today the points of contact between China and America are more numerous and varied than ever before.

Members of Congress, businesspeople, scholars, students, journalists, tourists, and even some military officers travel freely to and within China, and their counterparts reciprocate by visiting the United States. And this is to say nothing of the innumerable electronic channels through which information now flows into and out of China.

Controlling all of this and shaping it into a completely coherent and consistent message is clearly impossible. But this does not mean that Beijing has abandoned its attempts to shape the perceptions of foreigners. To the contrary, the regime appears to attach even greater importance than ever to what was once called propaganda but is now referred to more delicately as "publicity work." The primary purpose of this activity, according to analyst David Finkelstein, is "to allay fears and concerns that China's rise will pose a threat or that China's rise *de facto* makes it a revisionist power."[34]

Perception management starts with the formulation of slogans such as "peaceful rise" and "peaceful development" that are meant to encapsulate the regime's message to the outside world. The promulgation of these slogans also indicates the parameters of acceptable opinion at the lower levels of what is now undeniably a more diffuse and open system that includes think tankers and academics, as well as party officials and government bureaucrats. In their public statements and their private conversations with Western counterparts, Chinese analysts and commentators do more than merely mouth quotes from the "Little Red Book," as they did under Chairman Mao. But their comments do tend to reflect and reinforce certain basic themes and arguments.[35]

It is no longer sufficient, as it might have been in Mao's day, to simply blast slogans from Chinese media outlets and hope that they will be heard and accepted abroad. Today's perception managers speak openly of the importance of "influencing and setting the foreign media agenda" by giving foreign journalists "special treatment" and providing them with "specialized information." They emphasize the need to "influence the influential," seeking out "famous commentators and writers . . . foreign 'eloquent speakers'" who are "familiar with China" and can be "good assistants in China's public relations."[36]

Beijing has found no lack of "good assistants" in the United States. Indeed, in the last several decades, China has been in the enviable strategic position of being able to align its interests with those of some of the most influential actors in American society. Since the start of the reform era, but especially since the early 1990s, when true economic "take off" began, important parts of the American business community have come to see China as a new frontier whose conquest is vital to their continued success. U.S. companies in one sector after another, from the makers of toys, consumer appliances, and automobiles, to aerospace, telecommunications, and finance, have sought markets and made substantial investments there, and in a tradition as old as American democracy, they have lobbied hard in Washington to protect and advance their interests. While some executives have expressed concern in recent years that Chinese government regulations may restrict the prospects for future growth and profitability, most who are active there remain bullish on China.[37]

In 1994, when the issue was whether to deny China most favored nation trading status, and again in 2000 when the Clinton administration sought to bring it into the World Trade Organization, prominent executives, individual companies, and broad-based industry associations played a critical role in urging Congress to support greater openness. Similarly, when the federal government considered relaxing Cold War–era high-technology export controls in the 1990s and again during the Bush years, the affected industries also undertook vigorous, and largely successful, lobbying efforts in favor of liberalization.[38]

Beyond supporting specific pieces of trade legislation, American companies have also sought in a variety of less direct ways to promote better relations with China. Corporations and wealthy donors have sponsored research programs at universities and think tanks, fellowships and educational exchanges, art exhibits and television documentaries. As historian Ross Terrill describes the process, "A symbiosis occurs between Americans who benefit from business or other success with China and American institutions. Money may appear from a businessman with excellent connections in China and it is hard for a think tank, needing funds for its research on China, to decline it." As they have become more successful and more active internationally, Chinese companies have also gotten more directly involved, often making their own substantial donations to think tanks, universities, and other influential institutions in the United States and other Western countries.[39]

The titans of American industry and finance have been joined in their efforts to promote good relations by a mix of politicians and former policy makers from both major political parties, and by many of the nation's most respected academic experts. The members of this loose grouping of businessmen, politicians, and scholars (what one former State Department official has labeled the "Shanghai Coalition") have a range of motivations and goals, but they are united by the belief that closer Sino-American ties are in the best interests of both countries and indeed of the entire world.[40] The fact that some also derive personal and professional benefits from promoting friendship with China is not coincidental, but neither in most cases can it be said to be decisive in explaining an individual's views. Esteemed figures like Henry Kissinger, Zbigniew Brzezinski, and former president George H. W. Bush were strong proponents of a U.S.-China alignment well before there was any money to be made from it. For them, what probably matters most are the psychic rewards that come from believing that they are helping to promote peace and the gratification of being revered and well treated by Beijing. They would no doubt hold the same views regardless of whether they were earning generous fees advising American companies on how best to do business in China. That said, it is hard to disagree with James Mann's assertion that the strong, preexisting inclination of American elites to avoid criticism of China and to support good relations with it is "reinforced all the more by the influence of money."[41]

It is even possible that, perhaps unconsciously, the prospect of future career opportunities may be shaping the behavior of serving government officials. As Mann notes, the profitable path first cut by Kissinger and the other pioneers of today's U.S.-China relationship now beckons less prominent figures. Officials who develop a reputation for being favorably disposed toward China "can move on to lucrative careers as advisors, consultants, or hand-holders for corporate executives eager to do business in China."[42] Like those who have gone before them, today's bureaucrats and policy makers doubtless believe in the overriding importance of maintaining good relations with China. Still, they would be less than human if the benefits of being seen as a "friend of China" (and the potential costs of acquiring the contrary reputation) did not help add at least a small additional measure of conviction.

For some, of course, profit comes first, and enthusiasm for China a distant second. For these pragmatists, good bilateral relations are more a means than an end in itself, and there is little shame in adjusting one's words and deeds in order to grease the wheels of commerce. Computer software moguls who, in other settings, would be the first to profess their faith in the free flow of information have typically been silent on the subject when seeking business in China. U.S. telecom companies that would blanche at the thought of assisting their own government have been only too happy to help Beijing monitor the communications of its citizens.[43]

Scholars who pride themselves on their independence and are often fierce critics of U.S. government policy have their own reasons for caution when it comes to Beijing. Most do not have a direct, financial interest in China, and there is no cause to question the depth and sincerity of their views on how best to deal with that country. But there are often other, more subtle influences at work. Professor Perry Link, a leading authority on modern Chinese literature who was banned from entering the country for his involvement with human rights advocates, describes how the regime encourages self-censorship among scholars: "Everyone in the field knows that too much frank talk can land one on a visa blacklist or, even if one gets into China, cut off access to key people or important archives."[44] As a result, Link writes, senior academics sometimes decline to comment in public on sensitive topics, and younger scholars avoid working on subjects (like democratization) that may be difficult or risky to research. Concern for Beijing's sensibilities can sometimes even distort "the very language of China-watching," causing experts to avoid using certain words or phrases (like "Taiwan independence") that might raise objections from the regime.[45] The end result of all these pressures, according to another scholar, is that many "academics who study China . . . habitually please the Chinese Communist Party, sometimes consciously, and often unconsciously."[46]

The Shanghai Coalition is not a monolith; its members do not always agree, and even when they do, they do not always get what they want. Nevertheless, the existence and strength of this loose alliance have helped to sustain the forward momentum of engagement even when other forces have threatened to throw it off course. This is certainly the case on economic issues, where appeals for protection from threatened domestic industries and labor unions have generally been met by strong counter-vailing pressures for continued openness. But the implications extend beyond the realm of trade. When serious diplomatic crises erupt, as in May 1999 when demonstrators responded to the accidental bombing of the Chinese embassy in Belgrade by laying siege to the American embassy in Beijing, or in April 2001 when a Chinese fighter plane collided with a navy surveillance aircraft, distinguished figures in Washington are quick to council caution and urge calm. When China tests an antisatellite weapon, harasses American survey ships in international waters, undertakes the world's largest peacetime submarine building program, is found to have penetrated the Pentagon's computer networks, or announces yet another double-digit increase in defense spending, an assortment of scholars, analysts, former diplomats, and retired military officers invariably emerge to explain why such developments are not unusual for a rising power and, in any event, pose no particular threat to the United States.

By contrast, when the U.S. government expands defense cooperation with Japan or India, deploys more B-2 bombers and attack submarines to the Western Pacific, or contemplates the development of an expanded theater missile defense system or new long-range conventional precision strike weapons, many of the same experts can be relied on to urge restraint and to warn against the dangers of creating "self-fulfilling prophecies." Whatever one thinks of these arguments, there can be no question that the existence of the Shanghai Coalition reinforces engagement, while acting as a constraint on balancing.

The beauty of all of this, from the Chinese perspective, is that it does not require much by way of overt exertion. As in its overall strategy, China seeks to align itself with prevailing forces that it does not entirely control, but that act in ways that carry it closer to its goals. Americans who favor deepening engagement and worry about the destabilizing effects of stepped-up balancing are not cynical, self-interested tools of Beijing, nor are they its unwitting dupes. Nonetheless, through their influence on U.S. policy, they may be speeding the day when China will emerge as Asia's preponderant power.

BALANCING OR "BANDWAGONING"?

As they work to shape each other's perceptions and policies, both Washington and Beijing are also competing for influence in capitals across Asia. The American goal in this game is to preserve and strengthen existing alliances and to build new ties to other countries in the region that share its interest in balancing China's rising power. Beijing's objective, meanwhile, is to discourage its neighbors from aligning too closely with the United States, or with one another, for purposes of what it sees as "containment." China does not wish to construct competing alliances, but rather to bring about the eventual dissolution of those that have been built up over the years by the United States and to forestall the creation of any new countervailing coalition among the Asian powers that might emerge to take their place.

Both parties recognize that this diplomatic contest is a pivotal part of their rivalry. American strategists have concluded, correctly, that they cannot prevent Chinese hegemony in Asia without the help of local friends and allies. Their counterparts in Beijing meanwhile understand that China will not achieve what they regard as its rightful place in the region until America's alliances have dwindled to insignificance, if not disappeared altogether.

The underlying forces at work in the diplomatic domain are mixed, with some flowing Washington's way and others toward Beijing. Thanks in part to simple institutional inertia, the network of alliances that America built up in Asia during the Cold War continued to function after its end even though, for a time, many of them lacked a clear rationale. If Washington had tried to create an entirely new alliance system to prepare for a potential, but as yet ambiguous, challenge from a rising China, the obstacles would have been insurmountable. Domestic critics would doubtless have warned against the danger that "provocative" gestures could produce a hostile response. In capitals across the region, friendly governments would have hesitated to act for fear of antagonizing Beijing. Thanks to the carryover from the Cold War, however, no dramatic departures were necessary. Instead, over time, existing structures were able to evolve quietly from their original functions to a more direct, though still discreet, focus on China. Inertia alone cannot indefinitely sustain America's alliances, but as in the past, it can help them to survive through future periods of turmoil and uncertainty.

The United States also stands to gain from the underlying geopolitical dynamics of the situation in Asia and, paradoxically, from the fact that it is far removed from the region's geographic core. Assuming for the moment that Asian nations are governed by the same principles of international politics that have applied over the centuries in Europe, we should expect them to try to balance against China's rising power. Because none is strong enough to do this on its own, they will have to collaborate with one another and, to the extent possible, with outside powers to achieve this end. If America were close at hand, some in the region might feel threatened by its proximity. Instead, because it is both strong and far away, the United States is an ideal balancing partner for nations looking to preserve their independence and freedom of action.

To the extent that ideological affinity plays a role in determining patterns of alignment, Washington should also benefit, at least in maritime East Asia and parts of South Asia, where the biggest and most dynamic players (Japan, South Korea, Taiwan, Australia, Indonesia, and India) are democracies. By contrast, the ideological factor favors China along its continental frontiers, where its immediate neighbors are mostly ruled by autocratic regimes (including North Korea, Russia, the Central Asian republics, Burma, Laos, and Vietnam).

Both in peripheral areas and across the region more broadly, there are a number of other forces that, in the long run, could work to Beijing's advantage. What appears at this point to be a geopolitical liability for China as compared to the United States could ultimately prove to be a significant source of strength. The country's sheer size and its presence at the very heart of Asia make it a potential threat to virtually all of its neighbors. On the other hand, unlike the United States, China has no option to withdraw from the region. This fact alone cannot help but give pause to any smaller nation that might contemplate defying Beijing's will. Rather than risk being left alone eventually to face a powerful, displeased neighbor, local governments could conclude at some point that their interests would be better served by pursuing a policy of accommodation and appeasement.

China has always been big, but in the modern era it has never been rich. As its economy has expanded, it has begun to exert a powerful gravitational tug on the countries around it, drawing in raw materials and other imports to feed its growth, attracting customers for the goods that it is able to produce in huge volume and at comparatively low cost, and pumping out aid and investment capital to many of the countries on its periphery. If concern for their security and sovereignty causes its neighbors to lean toward the United States, the pursuit of prosperity is pulling them toward China.

China's increasing wealth is also giving it access to the instruments of "soft power." In addition to its appeal as a trading partner, China can now present itself to its poorer neighbors as a model of successful development and the wave of the future in Asia if not the entire world. Beijing has more money to spend on training first-class diplomats and opening "Confucius Institutes" to encourage the study of China's language and culture, to say nothing of sponsoring the eye-popping 2008 Olympic Games that served as a spectacular showcase for its achievements. Some analysts believe that since the late 1990s China has been engaged in a "charm offensive" that is intended, at least in part, to draw other countries toward it and away from the United States.[47]

There is one final factor that could tilt the field decisively in China's favor. It is possible that Asia will turn out, in fact, to be very different from Europe. In his book *The Clash of Civilizations and the Remaking of World Order*, Samuel Huntington argues that the pattern of politics *among* nations in different regions of the world has tended historically to mirror the varying patterns of politics *within* them. In the West, kingly authority was checked, first by an increasingly assertive aristocracy and then by the empowerment of the masses. Thus in Europe the balancing of power with power was long thought to be "natural and desirable," internationally as well as domestically.[48]

In large parts of Asia, by contrast, where authority continued until the modern era to be concentrated in the hands of omnipotent rulers, hierarchy was seen as appropriate and normal. As a result, Huntington concludes, "a functioning balance of power system . . . was foreign to Asia," and until the mid-nineteenth century, "East Asian international relations were Sinocentric with societies arranged in varying degrees of subordination to, cooperation with, or autonomy from Beijing."[49] Huntington predicts that these deep-seated inclinations and long-standing patterns of behavior will ultimately reemerge. The nations of Asia will choose eventually to follow the lead of a rising China, "bandwagoning" with it, in the language of contemporary Western international relations theory, rather than trying to balance against it.[50]

THE DIPLOMATIC BALANCE SHEET

At least for the moment, geography and ideology are overpowering any potential Asian cultural predisposition toward bandwagoning. Instead the diplomatic rivalry now under way has begun to divide the region into two nascent blocs. On one side is a largely maritime grouping, extending in an arc from Northeast to South Asia and composed primarily (though not exclusively) of liberal democracies. The members of this loose coalition include America's longtime treaty allies (Japan, South Korea, Australia, Thailand, and the Philippines), a quasi-ally (Taiwan), and several states with which it has developed significant strategic ties since the end of the Cold War (Singapore, India, and Mongolia). All fear being overshadowed and overmatched by their fast-growing neighbor but (with the exception of Mongolia) are separated from it by expanses of ocean, high mountains, or the intervening presence of one or more buffer states. Albeit to varying degrees, these states have chosen for now to cooperate with the United States in trying to counterbalance China's rising power. This grouping could be joined in the future by others, including Indonesia and Vietnam.[51]

On the other side of the equation is a continental coalition of poor, authoritarian, and comparatively weak states ranged around China's periphery. Whether it is because they see no alternative given their proximity and limited power, hope to benefit from China's economic growth, are happy to receive the protection of a like-minded regime, or some combination of all three, these countries have tended to align themselves with Beijing. China's neighbors include its only allies (North Korea and Pakistan) and countries that are either already its clients (Laos and Cambodia) or which it seeks to draw increasingly into its economic and diplomatic

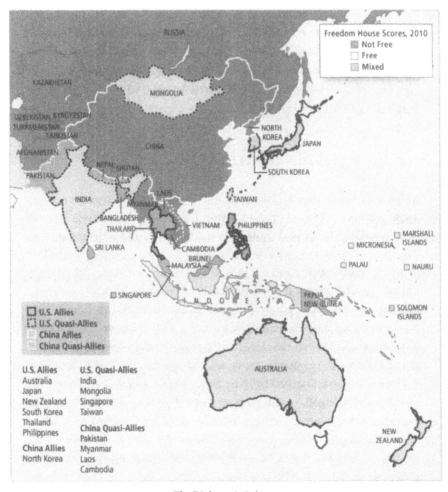

The Diplomatic Balance.
Information from Freedom House, 2010.

orbit (Burma, Tajikistan, Kyrgyzstan, and Kazakhstan). Despite its size, prior stature, and residual military strength, Russia is a shadow of its former self, and especially following its own turn toward authoritarianism, its leaders have chosen to cast in their lot with China. For the moment, Moscow's relative weakness, and the absence of any clear alternatives, have led it to ignore the potential long-term threats to its interests from a rising

China in favor of the immediate benefits of diplomatic backing against the West and the profits from sales of arms and energy.[52]

The risk of internal unrest in Xinjiang and Tibet remains a major worry, as does the possible emergence of radical Islamic regimes across China's borders in Central Asia. At least insofar as traditional threats from hostile nation-states are concerned, however, Beijing has thus largely succeeded in stabilizing its continental "strategic rear area." The one significant potential exception to this generally favorable picture is India. Because of the importance assigned by the Bush administration to building an Indo-U.S. partnership, China was forced to play catch-up for most of its two terms in office. This put New Delhi in the enviable position of being able to improve its two most significant bilateral relationships simultaneously, and despite clear evidence of deepening strategic ties to Washington, it left open the possibility that India might continue to "play the field," rather than drawing ever closer to the United States.

The election of a new American president in 2008 with different priorities than his predecessor seemed for a time as if it would result in a significant slowdown in the development of Indo-U.S. ties. Barack Obama's expressed desire to bolster the Non-Proliferation Treaty, eliminate nuclear weapons, withdraw expeditiously from Afghanistan, downplay the "global war on terror," ease back on "democracy promotion" and "values-based diplomacy," and push hard for climate change agreements together resulted in a distinct cooling of relations with India. The new administration's apparent eagerness to "reassure" China and its seeming lack of sensitivity to India's anxieties over status and security did not help matters. After nearly a decade of dramatic progress, the question on the minds of some observers in both countries was whether the economic, strategic, and societal ties between the United States and India were sufficiently strong to weather a potentially protracted period of comparative neglect, if not open diplomatic discord.[53]

Thanks to the strength of the underlying forces pushing them together, China's own clumsiness, and the Obama administration's somewhat belated recognition of India's importance, the movement toward a closer Indo-U.S. alignment has recently been renewed. Whether as part of a general trend toward greater assertiveness, a more specific calculation that

Beijing's leverage over New Delhi had increased due to developments in Washington, or as a result of heightened anxiety over Tibet following riots there in 2008, China chose in 2009–10 to step up pressure on a number of outstanding border issues with India. These moves had the effect, surely unintended, of feeding Delhi's fears about China's long-term intentions and strengthening the pro-American factions in Indian politics.[54] Meanwhile, concern about increasing Chinese assertiveness in the western Pacific helped to restore Washington's enthusiasm for building stronger relations with India.[55]

Turning to the maritime domain, since the 1990s Beijing has sought to use its growing economic weight, diplomatic skill, and perceived future power to reach across the physical gap that separates it from the states of the region in an attempt to shape their policies and, to the extent possible, to begin to ease them away from the United States. For China the objective is to dissuade its maritime neighbors from taking part, whether actively (through the provision of their own forces) or passively (by granting U.S. forces access to bases and facilities on their territory) in American-led efforts to balance its power in peacetime and to defeat its forces in war. Although it is too early to judge the eventual results, by this standard, China's exertions have been, at best, only partly successful.

Two of America's five Asian alliances are arguably weaker today than they were during the Cold War, though only in one case can this shift be directly attributed to China. Since the turn of the century both Thailand and the Philippines have been preoccupied with problems of internal stability resulting from Islamist insurgencies and elite political conflicts. Since the 1990s both have deepened their trade relationships with China and have also developed strategic ties of various kinds to Beijing, including purchases of Chinese arms and equipment and military-to-military dialogues and exchanges.

In 1992, for reasons having nothing to do with China, the Philippines requested the complete withdrawal of U.S. forces from their massive naval and air bases at Subic Bay and Clark Field. Prior to the obvious emergence of China as a strategic competitor, the loss of these facilities was not seen to have great significance. Today, it is clear that renewed access to bases in the Philippines could add depth and diversity to America's military presence in the Western Pacific and would contribute greatly to its ability to counter

China's buildup opposite Taiwan. While it has not yet shown any inclination to invite the Americans back, the Philippine government has taken steps to restore closer defense ties. These moves were motivated, initially, by concerns over a growing domestic insurrection, elements of which have links to Middle Eastern Islamist terror groups. Although Manila is focused for the moment on internal security, a recent assessment concludes that it "clearly perceives an external security threat in growing Chinese power."[56] Filipino leaders are worried that Beijing will someday use its growing power projection capabilities to settle outstanding claims over the control of territory and resources in the South China Sea. Recent statements that these represent "core national interests" of China have done nothing to lessen the anxieties of its maritime neighbors. Despite enhanced economic and diplomatic ties, increased Chinese assertiveness on these issues will likely cause Manila to seek more help from Washington.[57]

Thai foreign policy has often been described as "bending with the wind," adjusting to shifts in the international distribution of power in order to preserve its independence and freedom of action. Given this tradition of accommodation, Thailand's relative proximity and potential vulnerability to China, and the increasing volume of goods and capital flowing between them (most notably, substantial Chinese investments in Thai infrastructure), it is hardly surprising that Bangkok has been tilting toward Beijing in recent years.[58] Although the Thai government is now trying to straddle between its two "strategic partners," there are growing doubts on the American side that it could be relied on to fulfill its treaty obligations in the event of a confrontation with China.[59] The fact that since a 2006 coup Thailand has been wracked by increasingly deep and violent domestic divisions has further weakened its perceived utility as a U.S. ally.[60] Especially if Bangkok were to deny access in the midst of a crisis, when there would be little time to find alternatives, loss of the use of ports, airfields, and supply depots in Thailand could greatly complicate American efforts to project military power into South and Southeast Asia.

If Thailand and the Philippines are at one end of the range of outcomes in the ongoing diplomatic rivalry between Washington and Beijing, Australia is at the other. America and Australia are long-standing partners in defense, diplomacy, and intelligence. Still, as the economic relationship between Australia and China has grown, there have been moments when it appeared Canberra might be trying to sidle away from its traditional ally to curry favor with its newfound friend. At the turn of the century some Australian strategists appeared to be more worried about possible American belligerence than about the continuing growth of Chinese power. Fears of being forced to choose between Washington and Beijing were heightened in 1999 when future Bush administration official Richard Armitage told an audience that in the event of a conflict, the United States expected Australia to do its share of the "hard, dirty, and dangerous work" of defending Taiwan. Several years later, with exports to China up by a factor of three, Foreign Minister Alexander Downer reopened the issue while on a visit to Beijing by emphasizing that the security treaty between Australia, New Zealand, and the United States, also called the ANZUS Treaty, did not require Australia's *automatic* participation.[61] In a similar vein, in 2008 Canberra helped kill a nascent four-way strategic dialogue with Japan, the United States, and India for fear that it would be seen as openly anti-Chinese.[62]

These incidents caused anxiety in Washington, but in retrospect, it seems clear that they signaled a new level of caution about unnecessarily provoking Beijing rather than a major shift in strategic direction. Like everyone else, including the United States, Canberra wants to continue to reap the economic benefits of engagement with China and certainly has no stomach for confrontation. At the same time, like many others in its region, Australia has become more concerned about the seemingly ceaseless growth and increasingly open exercise of Chinese power. Emboldened by a sense of its own growing importance, and by Canberra's minor diplomatic concessions, Beijing proceeded to overplay its hand. When a Chinese official warned publicly against invoking ANZUS, many Australians seem to have concluded that, as one analyst summarized, "'the more you give, the more Beijing asks for.'"[63] Subsequent controversies over the defection of a senior Chinese diplomat who oversaw espionage operations in Australia, the suicide of a dissident returned to China by the Australian government, scuffles between pro-Tibet and pro-China protestors during the passage of the Olympic torch through Canberra, and the trial of an Australian mining company executive on charges of spying against China all contributed to a cooling of public attitudes and a stiffening of government resolve. By the end of the decade some Australians were even beginning to question the wisdom of ever-deeper economic entanglement with the PRC.[64]

The most telling and significant indication of this tougher new stance is the text of the government's 2009 defense "white paper," in which it spells out long-term priorities and the assumptions that underlie them. In addition to reaffirming the importance of its alliance with the United States, the white paper calls for a major expansion in Australia's own capabilities. At the top of the list of needs are submarines, jet fighters, and modern surface combatants of the sort needed to wage high-intensity warfare against a sophisticated opponent, whether in Australia's maritime approaches or in combination with allied forces at considerable distance from its shores. The document leaves little doubt that the only conceivable enemy in such a fight would be China, the country on track to become "the strongest Asian military power, by a considerable margin."[65]

The Australian white paper is something of a "good news/bad news" story for the United States. On the one hand, Canberra is now prepared to take some significant additional steps to preserve a favorable balance of power in the Western Pacific, and it is evidently untroubled by the prospect of Beijing's inevitable response. On the other, the Australians are characteristically blunt in expressing their concern that at some point the United States will find itself "preoccupied and stretched in some parts of the world such that its ability to shift attention and project power into other regions . . . is constrained."[66] It is precisely because they are uncertain of America's future regional role that the Australians are stepping up their own defense programs.[67]

South Korea's response to China's rise places it somewhere between the incipient bandwagoning of Thailand and the redoubled balancing of Australia. The fact that Beijing and Seoul did not even recognize one another until 1992 makes the rapid progression of their relationship all the more remarkable. In the course of a decade and a half, China has grown to become the largest consumer of South Korean exports and the leading destination for its investment capital. Their relative proximity (nearby, but separated by an essentially impermeable barrier), cultural links, and comparatively positive shared past have helped ease the development of close educational, societal, and diplomatic connections. At the same time, the rise of a younger generation of Koreans more susceptible to anti-Americanism, the

election at the turn of the century of left-wing governments suspicious of
Washington and eager to pursue détente with Pyongyang, and heightened
tensions over the North Korean nuclear issue and the stationing of American troops in the South during the Bush administration, all seemed to
presage a major downgrading of the U.S.–South Korean alliance.[68] In 2005
President Roh Moo-hyun suggested that South Korea needed to pursue a
more self-reliant posture, perhaps even going so far as to assume a balancing role between Washington and Beijing.[69] While this never amounted to
more than idle talk, throughout the Bush years, South Korea's burgeoning
relationship with China did appear to be having a discernible restraining
impact on its strategic cooperation with the United States. Seoul's reluctance to participate in an expanded U.S.-led regional missile defense system, or to give advanced authorization for the use of facilities on its soil to
support operations away from the Korean peninsula, reflected what was
described at the time as a "conspicuous . . . sensitivity toward perceived
Chinese interests."[70]

Despite this, China's continued rise has clearly begun to cause anxiety
in Seoul. This may be in part due to a growing awareness that China has no
intention of helping to denuclearize the North and a concern that, far from
promoting unification, China may actually be using commercial penetration to establish a buffer zone and virtual colony in the portions of the
North directly opposite its borders. The Chinese government's reluctance
to criticize or sanction Pyongyang, even after its unprovoked sinking of
the South Korean naval vessel *Cheonan* in early 2010, added to a growing
skepticism about its long-term intentions.[71]

After a period of infatuation with Beijing, and disillusionment with
Washington, the essentially pro-Western, pro-American orientation of the
South Korean people appears to be reasserting itself. Public opinion polls
conducted at the end of the Bush administration found that compared to
their American counterparts, a larger percentage of South Koreans were
worried that China may someday become a military threat (74 percent of
South Koreans versus 70 percent of Americans), and a smaller percentage
were comfortable with the idea that China will eventually be "the leader
of Asia" (21 percent versus 27 percent). South Koreans also assigned more
importance to their economic relationship with the United States than

did citizens of any other Asian nation, and they were more worried than anyone else that an American military withdrawal from East Asia could trigger a dangerous arms race between China and Japan.[72]

The election in 2008 of conservative Lee Myung-bak as president was accompanied by a clear tilt away from Beijing and back toward Washington. The new government in Seoul pressed the Obama administration to complete a free trade agreement, citing, among other benefits, its contribution to offsetting China's growing regional influence.[73] Even before the torpedoing of the *Cheonan*, Washington and Seoul had begun to discuss ways of reinvigorating their defense cooperation. This incident provided the occasion for a further tightening of military ties and what one observer described as a major effort by President Lee to "distance his country from China [and] establish it as America's full geopolitical partner in North Asia."[74] Instead of pondering how best to balance between these two giants, Seoul was once again focused on the task of engaging China while working with the United States to provide a counterweight to its growing power.[75]

Throughout the second half of the 1990s and into the 2000s, China's approach to its maritime domain took the form of a pincer movement. Beijing adopted an accommodating, nonthreatening approach to South Korea on the one hand, and Australia, the Philippines, and the other Southeast Asian nations on the other, while taking a tough, even aggressive stance toward Taiwan and Japan. While these methods yielded some gains on either flank, they failed to bring China closer to its goals at the center. Moreover, even where it was initially successful, Beijing's soft touch did not produce lasting, significant shifts in the orientation of America's traditional friends and allies in either Northeast or Southeast Asia.

Toward the close of the Bush administration, China began to reverse course in its dealings with both Japan and Taiwan. As discussed briefly in the last chapter, Beijing's move toward a more accommodating stance was made easier by political changes in Tokyo and Taipei. The 2009 defeat of the long-dominant Liberal Democratic Party by the Democratic Party of Japan ushered in a new era of unprecedented flux and uncertainty regarding Japan's foreign relations. The new ruling coalition's willingness to risk a crisis by reopening negotiations over the location of U.S. military facilities on Okinawa, and its apparent desire to seek greater independence from Washington while cultivating better relations with Beijing, contributed for a time to the sense that Japan might be in the process of edging "from America towards China."[76] By the close of 2010, however, Beijing's resort to bullying tactics and the emergence of a new, more obviously pro-American leadership team at the top of the Democratic Party of Japan helped to ease these fears.[77]

If American policy makers were initially concerned over the apparent drift in Japanese policy, many were delighted by the return to power of Taiwan's Kuomintang or Nationalist Party after eight years of turbulence. Despite years of bloody warfare, and defeat at the hands of the Chinese Communist Party, the Nationalists have never abandoned their commitment to the idea that there is only "one China." While they have clearly given up hope that they will someday rule it, the Nationalists (many of whom are descended from those who came to the island in the aftermath of the civil war) continue to have an emotional attachment to the mainland. In contrast to their opponents, who think of themselves primarily as Taiwanese, the Nationalists have been more receptive to Beijing's entreaties and more interested in pursuing negotiations that might eventually lead to some kind of mutually agreeable settlement.

China still has chances to solidify its position at the center of the maritime domain, and to weaken America's. How fully it will be able to capitalize on the opportunities before it remains to be seen. The fact that Taiwan is a democracy in which only a fraction of the people favor unification (or independence, for that matter) limits how far any government can legitimately go in satisfying Beijing's demands. If Chinese strategists believe they are finally on the verge of bringing Taiwan back into the fold, they are likely to be sorely disappointed. Frustration over a continuing stalemate could cause them to shift back toward a more coercive approach.

Tokyo's flirtation with China in 2009–10 and its somewhat standoffish attitude toward the United States seems to have more to do with domestic politics, and the desire of a new coalition government to differentiate itself from its predecessors, than with any profound rethinking of Japan's strategic options. In spite of Beijing's attempts to convey warmth, suspicion of its motives runs very deep, as does fear of how China might act if it were ever to succeed in displacing the United States and emerge as East Asia's preponderant power. Beijing's bullying behavior during the 2010 dispute over the use of the waters off the Senkuku (or, as the Chinese prefer, the Diaoyutai) Islands served as a reminder of what might lie in store.[78] The realignment of Japanese politics could delay the further development of its military capabilities, slow its already painful progress toward a more mature and effective alliance with the United States, and complicate American-led efforts to counter China's growing strength, but it does not appear likely at this point to result in a fundamental shift in the balance of power. Japan may try to edge away from America, but unless it is willing to accept even greater constraints on its autonomy, it is unlikely to go very far.

To sum up: China's efforts to weaken U.S. alliances have thus far met with only limited success. Even in those cases where existing relationships have grown weaker, the reasons are complex and change cannot be credited entirely to Beijing. Moreover, the brute fact of China's growing power, and the anxiety this has produced in many of its neighbors, have more than offset the gains that it has derived from any subtle strategic influence campaign.

Two caveats are in order here. First, these are early days in what will likely prove a protracted competition. In part because it fears provoking an even stronger reaction, and perhaps also because it is confident that its ability to shape events will grow in time along with its power, Beijing has not tried very hard, to this point, to split America from its allies. Instead it has been content to insert a wedge, developing economic ties and political constituencies that will help to constrain balancing in other countries much as they are already doing in the United States.

Looking to the future, the willingness of America's friends and allies in Asia to continue working with it will depend, in some measure, on their reading of its capabilities and intentions. To the extent that the United States is seen as being in a long-term decline relative to China, or, even worse, if it appears irresolute, incompetent, unwilling, or simply unable to fulfill its security commitments, other governments could well conclude that they have no choice but to reconsider their national strategies. Some would probably try to build up their own defenses, perhaps acquiring nuclear weapons in hopes of deterring aggression and preserving a measure of independence. Others, demoralized and overmatched, might decide to distance themselves from the United States and cut the best deal they can with Beijing. Either way, America's influence in Asia would be drastically reduced, and its run as the dominant player in the region would finally be at an end.

Nine

———◆———

THE BALANCE OF POWER

THE "HARD POWER" RIVALRY

In a world in which states must still ultimately look to their own defenses, "hard power"—the capacity to coerce, deter, defend, and destroy—remains the essential currency of international politics. While they work to influence one another, and to shape the perceptions and policies of third parties, the United States and China are also engaged in an increasingly intense and focused military competition. In this chapter I examine three critical dimensions of that rivalry: China's attempts to dissuade or prevent the United States from projecting conventional air and naval power into the Western Pacific; its efforts to eat away at the credibility of the nuclear deterrent "umbrella" that the United States has long extended over its Asian allies, and to deter the United States from ever using nuclear weapons against it, even in the face of conventional defeat; and its nascent search for ways to defeat or circumvent America's overwhelming superiority at sea.

Having assessed the evolving balance of military capabilities between the two powers, I then turn to an examination of two factors that will help shape the course of their competition over the next several decades. The enormous advantages that the United States now enjoys are the product of its long-standing lead in the development and deployment of new technologies, and the unmatched ability of its huge and dynamic economy to carry the costs of military primacy. Whether it will continue to enjoy these advantages in a long-term strategic rivalry with China is by no means obvious.

THE CONVENTIONAL MILITARY BALANCE:
"POWER PROJECTION" VERSUS "ANTI-ACCESS"

America's strategic position in Asia is built on a foundation of military power. Since the end of the Second World War, the United States has bound itself to others (and others to it) by extending security guarantees, offering defense assistance, and, in some cases, stationing its forces on foreign soil. The credibility of U.S. promises to come to the aid of its friends, and the willingness of others to accept them, are direct results of its perceived strength and its reputation for resolve. If these erode, the superstructure of alliances and overseas bases that rests on them may persist for a time, but it cannot do so forever. Whether the end takes the form of a graceful decoupling or a sudden, catastrophic collapse will depend largely on chance and circumstance.

In the more than twenty years that have elapsed since the end of the Cold War, the American military has enjoyed an interval of unmatched global prowess but it has also seen the beginnings of a sharp decline in its margin of advantage in East Asia. Unless it acts soon to counter recent Chinese advances, the United States will find it increasingly dangerous in a future crisis to deploy its air and naval forces across a wide swath of the Western Pacific. A dawning recognition that this is the case cannot help but diminish the credibility of America's guarantees, thereby weakening the network of alliances and strategic partnerships on which its Asian presence depends.

Alone among the major powers, the United States today has the ability to bring military force to bear at virtually any point on the earth's surface. This expeditionary orientation is a natural outgrowth of the fact that America is an essentially insular nation that rose to prominence without strong and menacing neighbors. Instead of expending resources on coastal defenses and border fortifications, it has been free through much of its history to focus on projecting power into other regions. By contrast, even at its peak, the Soviet Union was a continental empire preoccupied with proximate threats and possessed of very limited means for deploying or using its armed forces beyond the boundaries of Eurasia.

During the latter stages of the Cold War the United States pressed home its advantages to the very shores of the Soviet Union by threatening to sink Russian surface ships and submarines before they could even sail clear of their ports at Murmansk and Vladivostok into the open waters of the Atlantic and the North Pacific.[1] Although the U.S. Navy and Air Force would have eventually won these battles, the Soviet fleet, backed by land-based naval aviation, would have at least given them a run for their money. By the early 1990s, with the vestiges of Soviet naval power rotting at bases in the Russian Far East, the Pacific had been transformed into an American lake. Japan, the only other substantial maritime power in the region, was a U.S. ally. China, meanwhile, had barely begun to prepare to fight "limited wars under high-tech conditions" off its coasts.

With the collapse of the Soviet Union, American forces could operate with complete impunity throughout the Western Pacific. Using forward-deployed ships, aircraft, and troops, as well as those that could be dispatched from Hawaii and the West Coast, and staging out of bases in South Korea, the Japanese home islands, Okinawa, Thailand, the Philippines (until 1992), and Singapore (after 1990), the United States could defend its friends, deter potential enemies, and move its forces freely across the region. American air and naval units conducted routine deployments and reconnaissance missions just outside (and at times no doubt *within*) China's airspace and territorial waters without fear of harassment or interdiction, while U.S. satellites passed overhead, unseen and unmolested.

Given China's limited ability to project power, virtually the only place where a clash with the United States would have been physically possible at this time was in the immediate vicinity of Taiwan. Here, had it chosen to do so, the United States could have used surface ships and submarines, along with aircraft flying off the decks of carriers and from nearby bases, to help defend the island against invasion, blockade, or attack from the air. American intervention would likely have been decisive in determining the outcome of any confrontation, and barring the occasional lucky shot, or a drastic decision by Beijing to escalate to the use of nuclear weapons, victory could have been achieved at comparatively low cost to the United States. In their own backyard, and on a matter of utmost importance,

China's rulers had no plausible plan for countering an opponent coming from half a world away. This humiliating reality, underscored by the 1996 Taiwan Strait crisis, helped spur the military buildup that is still in progress.[2]

Since the mid-1990s the People's Liberation Army has made steady and significant improvements in its ability to threaten to attack Taiwan. As part of its overall strategy for bringing the island to heel, Beijing has also deployed forces that are designed to deter, and if necessary to defeat, any attempt by the United States or other outside powers to intervene in what it regards as a strictly internal affair. American defense analysts have been slow at times to acknowledge the scope and seriousness of these developments. Since the turn of the century, however, it has become impossible to ignore the fact that China is not simply preparing for a traditional, cross-strait invasion of Taiwan; rather it is putting in place the pieces of what Pentagon planners refer to as an "anti-access" or "area denial" capability aimed squarely at the United States.[3]

The best way of highlighting the extent to which the balance of power has shifted in recent years is to compare the emerging situation to the one prevailing at the start of the post–Cold War era. Twenty years ago the PLA lacked the means with which to acquire timely information about what was happening even a relatively short distance from its own shores. The Americans, on the other hand, had satellites, electronic listening posts, and other "national technical means" that enabled them to track developments deep inside China, as well as along its periphery. The United States was close to all-seeing while China was effectively blind, an asymmetry that would likely have been decisive in determining the outcome of any conflict between them.

Today the balance between the two sides' "situational awareness" is much closer to being equal, and in the future, it could begin to tilt in Beijing's favor. China now has its own constellation of reconnaissance, communication, and navigation satellites that permit it to target fixed facilities like airbases, ports, command bunkers, fuel depots, weapons storage sites, and communications facilities anywhere in East Asia. Meanwhile, space-based surveillance systems, combined with onshore "over-the-horizon" radars, unmanned aerial vehicles, and small craft disguised as commercial vessels, enable the People's Liberation Army Navy (PLAN) to track surface ships hundreds of miles out to sea. According to press reports, the Chinese navy has also begun to install a network of underwater listening devices designed to help it locate approaching American submarines.[4]

In addition to being able to spot distant targets, China increasingly has the ability to disable or destroy them. The PLA's search for plausible options against Taiwan has led it to deploy over one thousand short-range ballistic missiles along its southeastern seaboard, and the numbers continue to grow. Unlike high-performance manned aircraft, these are relatively easy and cheap to build, maintain, and use, but they can be very difficult and expensive to defend against. Armed with increasingly accurate and sophisticated conventional warheads, Chinese missiles are poised to strike a devastating initial blow that would weaken Taiwan's defenses, disrupt its industry and trade, shut down its communications systems, demoralize its population, and perhaps decapitate its political and military leadership. The opening salvo in a war could come with little or no warning, overwhelming Taiwan's antimissile systems, disabling many of its airfields, fighters, and air defense radars, and permitting the Chinese air force to gain control of the skies within a matter of hours or, at most, a few days.[5]

The ability of the United States to sustain its forces in East Asia is heavily dependent on a relative handful of regional bases, most of them on the territory of its allies. Since the 1960s Beijing has had at least some capacity to strike at these targets with nuclear weapons, but it has only recently acquired the means to do so effectively using precision conventional munitions. Having found a method of attack that promises quick results against nearby Taiwan, China now seeks to apply the same approach throughout Northeast Asia. The range, accuracy, and number of medium-range ballistic and cruise missiles in China's arsenal will soon give it the option of hitting every major American and allied base in the region with warheads that could put craters in the middle of runways, smash through concrete aircraft shelters, and shut down ports, power plants, and communications networks. What is new and significant here is that all of this can now be done without radioactive fallout, huge civilian casualties, and the virtual certainty of an equally devastating nuclear response from the United States.[6]

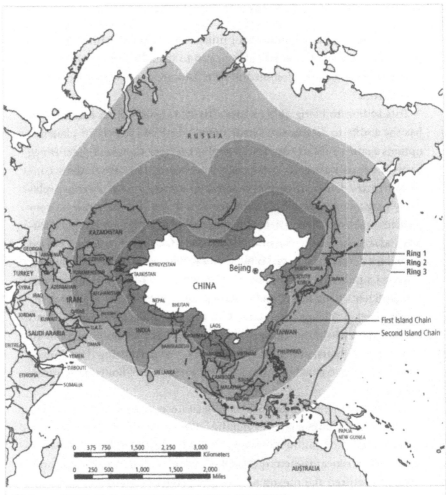

Conventional Anti-access Capabilities.

This map shows the increasing range at which China can strike targets throughout Asia, including aircraft, ships, ports, and airfields, using conventional weapons launched from Chinese territory. The weapons systems listed here include surface-to-air missiles (SAMs), short-range ballistic missiles (SRBMs), medium-range ballistic missiles (MRBMs), anti-ship ballistic missiles (ASBMs), antiship cruise missles (ASCM), land-attack cruise missles (LACMs), and manned aircraft (FB-7 and B-6).

Office of the Secretary of Defense, Annual Report to Congress: Military and Security Developments Involving the People's Republic of China, 2010 (Washington, D.C.: Department of Defense, 2010), p. 32.

With or without local bases, the tip of the spear of America's unique ability to project power is its navy and, in particular, its aircraft carriers. These massive, awe-inspiring vessels can be deployed virtually anywhere in the world, and once on station, they can show the flag, provide air cover to friendly nations, or deliver thousands of tons of conventional ordnance, with great precision, against targets on shore. The greatest limitation of existing carrier-based aircraft is their comparatively short range. Unless launched from within a few hundred miles of where they are needed, these planes will not be able to reach their targets or to linger over them long enough to be effective. It follows that for a country that fears carrier-based air strikes, the best defense is a good offense. If it can credibly threaten to engage, disable, and possibly sink these costly symbols of American power, China may be able to neutralize them by forcing them to operate far out to sea.

Rather than betting everything on one approach, the PLAN has experimented with a variety of different ship-killing weapons and modes of attack. Quieter submarines armed with Russian-designed high-speed torpedoes and hypersonic cruise missiles may be able to get close enough to unleash a deadly attack on American surface vessels. Russian-built destroyers are intended to carry out similar missions, even at risk of their own destruction. In recent years China has also begun to build significant numbers of a new type of small, high-speed, stealthy patrol boat. With their wave-piercing catamaran hulls, these ships are capable of traveling at extremely high speeds and carry long-range, supersonic antiship cruise missiles.[7]

Most novel and in the long run most worrisome are the land-based antiship ballistic missiles that Beijing is now set to deploy. Using information from land and space-based tracking systems, these could be launched from hundreds of miles away toward the last known location of high-value targets like aircraft carriers. Upon reentering the atmosphere, the missile's warheads would use onboard sensors to steer them toward their aim points, releasing a spray of explosive "submunitions" seconds before impact or triggering devices designed to destroy nearby command and control systems with a powerful pulse of electromagnetic energy. Antiship ballistic missiles have been described as a potential "game changer" that could force the U.S. Navy to pull its carriers and other surface combatants far back from China's coasts, drastically reducing their effectiveness and fundamentally altering the balance of power in the Western Pacific.[8]

Even the deadliest and most successful preemptive strike on U.S. carriers and regional bases would not protect China from possible retaliation. Assuming that the United States chose not to respond with nuclear weapons, it could still hit back with conventionally armed, long-range bombers stationed outside the reach of Chinese missiles, as well as cruise missiles launched from hard-to-detect submarines. Since the first Gulf War, PLA planners have paid close attention to the ways in which the United States has used precision-guided munitions fired from stealthy platforms to cripple its opponents.[9] In order to protect themselves against such strikes, they have begun to make large investments in defenses of various kinds. If American planes and cruise missiles can be tracked with antistealth radars or other detection systems, it should be possible to engage them using People's Liberation Army Air Force (PLAAF) fighters and surface-to-air missiles.[10] Hardened and dispersed command posts and buried fiber-optic communication cables (instead of, or in addition to, radio and microwave systems that are easier to intercept and disrupt) would provide another layer of protection against attack from the air.[11] Locating some critical facilities far inland could put them outside the range of existing conventional systems, forcing an American president to choose between doing nothing and risking all-out war by escalating to the use of nuclear-armed intercontinental ballistic missiles.

While it works to defend its own interior lines of communication, Beijing has been looking for ways to attack the long and potentially vulnerable lines of its opponent. China's much publicized 2007 test of a rudimentary antisatellite weapon is the most visible part of an effort that may eventually include more sophisticated "direct ascent" weapons that can destroy satellites by colliding with them or unleashing a pulse of electromagnetic energy, ground-based lasers, and other directed energy weapons designed to "dazzle" and disable American satellites, and perhaps even the use of saboteurs and special forces against vulnerable antennas and ground stations.[12]

Because satellites have limited "bandwidth," the Pentagon also uses undersea cables to transmit vast volumes of information between its forward bases and power projection forces and their ultimate sources of command and control back home. The American military depends on cyberspace for virtually everything it does, and as the chief of Naval Operations pointed out in a 2009 address, "Cyberspace is on the ocean floor."[13] As suggested by incidents in which earthquakes and errant ships have occasionally wreaked havoc on global communications, fiber-optic cables can be severed accidentally. Using submarines, divers, or unmanned underwater vehicles, China might try to produce similar results, temporarily disrupting American operations at the outset of a conflict with a few carefully targeted attacks. The immediate damage to world trade and to China's economy from such an event would no doubt be substantial, but because its own military would be operating close to home and independent of transoceanic cables, the potential strategic gains might appear to be well worth the price.

Compared to cutting cables and destroying satellites, introducing malicious code into U.S. and allied computer networks would be an act of comparative subtlety, but the results might be even more dramatic. A successful cyberattack could bring down systems used by the military, intelligence agencies, and top civilian decision makers to confer, gather data, transmit orders, coordinate logistics, and direct combat operations. Even if some of these networks proved too tough to crack, attacks on domestic banks, power grids, and air traffic control computers could cause chaos, sowing panic, distracting leaders, and snarling efforts to mobilize U.S. forces and deploy them to where they are needed.

PLA strategists have written at length about the potential use of computer network attacks to throw an enemy off balance, even before fighting has commenced. Indeed, the very sophistication of the American defense establishment has been identified as its greatest potential vulnerability. China's interest in cyberwarfare has already advanced well beyond the stage of abstract speculation. Since the turn of the century, official spokesmen in Washington and other friendly capitals have complained publicly about repeated intrusions into government computer networks that, when traced to their source, appear to originate in China. While the precise purpose of these probes cannot be known with certainty, one thing seems clear: the first "battle" in any future conflict between the United States and China will take place in cyberspace. Whoever wins that exchange may well have won the war before the shooting even starts.[14]

China's investments in its anti-access/area denial strategy, sustained over a period of two decades, have begun to bear fruit. By pursuing a number of different paths and experimenting with new weapons and concepts of operation, the PLA is approaching the point where it may have (or its leaders may *believe* that they have) a real chance of knocking U.S. forces out of the Western Pacific, at least in the opening stages of a war, using only conventional weapons and without hitting targets on America's home soil. While some of the details are classified, a number of war games and other studies suggest that without appropriate remedial action, this could soon be the case. A recent RAND Corporation study concludes, for example, that the threat to Taiwanese and U.S. airbases from Chinese conventional ballistic missiles is "sufficiently grave that a credible case can be made that the air war for Taiwan could essentially be over before much of the Blue air forces have even fired a shot."[15] Another finds that with as few as thirty-four ballistic missiles armed with submunitions, the PLA will soon be able to "damage, destroy or strand 75 percent of aircraft based at Kadena [on Okinawa]." If it does this, while at the same time sinking or compelling the withdrawal of American aircraft carriers, China could force the United States to rely on airbases as many as fifteen hundred miles away from the Taiwan Strait. Maintaining air superiority from such distances would require vastly more fighters and tankers than the U.S. Air Force presently has the money to build.[16] Military war games reportedly reach more optimistic conclusions, but only because they assume that the United States will harden existing airbases, disperse its forces to others across the region in the event of crisis, buy more tankers, minimize its vulnerability to cyberwarfare, and preserve its existing advantages in stealth technology.[17]

To sum up: despite their vast cost, past success, and impressive appearance, America's power projection forces in East Asia are in danger of becoming "wasting assets."[18] Unless it is willing to make substantial investments of its own, the United States may soon find that its promises to use conventional force to defend its regional friends lack credibility and its threats have lost their persuasiveness.

THE NUCLEAR BALANCE: EXTENDED DETERRENCE VERSUS COUNTER-DETERRENCE

During the 1940s and 1950s, if faced with the prospect of defeat on the ground in Western Europe, the United States could have responded by threatening to attack Russia and its Eastern bloc allies with nuclear weapons. This threat was most credible when the Soviet Union did not have a sizable nuclear arsenal of its own and, even as it began to accumulate one, when it still lacked the ability to strike American soil. As late as the early 1960s, when the Soviets began to deploy a handful of intercontinental ballistic missiles (ICBMs), there was a good chance that the United States could have destroyed them in a preemptive strike, minimizing damage to itself while laying waste to its enemy. Although the Soviets might still have been able to strike at U.S. allies and bases along their periphery using shorter-range missiles and aircraft, America itself would have remained out of reach. Under these conditions the idea that a president might decide to initiate the use of nuclear weapons rather than accept the conquest of Western Europe did not appear absurd; certainly the Kremlin could not assume that it was.

By the early 1970s, however, Soviet nuclear forces had grown so large and diverse that they provided what strategists refer to as a "secure second-strike capability." No matter how hard it was hit, the Soviet Union would have retained a sufficient number of weapons to inflict massive damage on the United States in return. Once this point was reached, the threat of nuclear escalation in response to conventional defeat lost most of its remaining credibility. The United States and its allies toyed with the idea of using lower-yield, battlefield or tactical nuclear weapons to blunt an invasion, but ultimately concluded that they had no choice but to expand their nonnuclear forces, despite the costs and difficulties that this entailed.

Until very recently, the relationship between American and Chinese nuclear forces in many respects resembled that between U.S. and Soviet forces at the time of the 1962 Cuban missile crisis. Like the Soviet Union, even after it got the bomb China did not initially possess missiles or aircraft capable of delivering them against the continental United States. In fact it was only as the Cold War drew to a close that Beijing began to deploy what would eventually grow to be a force of around twenty, 13,000-kilometer-range DF-5A ICBMs, the number that still exists today. Although they represented a major advance for China, by superpower standards these weapons were quite primitive. Like the very first U.S. and Soviet missiles, they took hours to fill with volatile liquid fuel, were initially based above ground rather than in hardened silos, and carried only one large warhead instead of several smaller, more accurate ones.[19]

Assuming that they could be found, China's ICBMs would have been easy to destroy in a first strike. In fact, as the United States deployed more and better long-range conventional precision strike weapons during the 1990s, some analysts claimed that it could have eliminated the small long-range Chinese nuclear force without itself using nuclear weapons.[20] As was true for the Soviets during the Cold War, however, even if it lost its small force of intercontinental-range missiles, China would likely have retained at least some of its considerably larger stock of shorter-range weapons, and it could have used them to launch nuclear strikes against Washington's regional allies. This possibility would no doubt have weighed heavily on the minds of U.S. decision makers, restraining them from attacking China's nuclear forces in all but the most extreme circumstances. But its relative invulnerability would have given Washington a significant psychological and strategic advantage in any direct confrontation with Beijing.[21]

Whatever edge the United States may have once had in this domain is about to evaporate. China is now in the process of building its own secure second-strike force by fielding two new types of intercontinental-range ballistic missiles. In addition to a family of land-mobile, solid-fueled ICBMs (the DF-31 and DF-31A) that can strike targets in the continental United States, the PLAN will soon deploy submarine-launched missiles (the JL-2) that will afford similar coverage, provided that they can reach mid-ocean launch points. Both new missiles may eventually carry multiple warheads, and compared to their predecessors, both types will be extremely difficult for an enemy to find and destroy.[22] The fact that these deployments will come as the United States is striving to further reduce the size of its arsenal, with the stated goal of eventually reaching "nuclear zero," means that the gap between the two forces will narrow even more rapidly than would otherwise be the case.

China's Growing Nuclear Deterrent*

	EARLY 1980S	2010	2020 ESTIMATE
Land	DF-5: < 20 missiles	DF-5: 20 missiles DF-31A: 10–15 missiles	DF-31A: 35–100 missiles
Sea	None	JL-2: Developmental	JL-2: 60
Total no. of warheads	< 20	30–35	95–640*

Sources

Estimates of JL-2 numbers from "Annual Report to Congress: Military Power of the People's Republic of China, 2009," Office of the Secretary of Defense, p. 24. Estimates on MIRV capabilities of the JL-2 from Christopher McConnaughy, "China's Undersea Nuclear Deterrent," in Andrew S. Erickson, Lyle J. Goldstein, William S. Murray, and Andrew R. Wilson, eds., *China's Future Submarine Force* (Newport, RI: Naval Institute Press, 2007), pp. 77–113.

Data and estimates on the DF-5 and DF-31A from "Annual Report to Congress: Military Power of the People's Republic of China, 2010," Office of the Secretary of Defense, p. 34; information on MIRV capability from *Jane's Strategic Weapons Systems*, issue 50, ed. Duncan Lennox (Surrey: Jane's Information Group, January 2009), pp. 27–29.

*All figures are for numbers of "strategic" or long-range nuclear weapons capable of striking targets in the continental United States. The low-end estimate for 2020 assumes that China will deploy only the number of missiles now publicly predicted by the U.S. intelligence agencies, and that each will carry only one warhead. The high-end estimate assumes that it will deploy more DF-31As and that each will carry four multiple independently retargetable reentry vehicles. In addition, this estimate assumes that China will build five submarines, each capable of carrying twelve JL-2 missiles, and that each of these will carry three or four warheads.

Unless it builds a national missile defense system larger and more effective than the one currently envisioned, or develops techniques for locating and preemptively destroying land-mobile and undersea missiles far superior to those that presently exist, the United States will soon enter a world in which it is more vulnerable to Chinese nuclear attack than it has ever been in the past. Exactly what this will mean for its position in Asia is open to debate. If the history of the Cold War is any guide, however, this shift will lead to questions about the credibility of American security guarantees, pressure in some countries to develop independent nuclear forces, increased attention (at least among American defense planners) to the importance of maintaining a satisfactory balance of *conventional* forces with China, and debates between the United States and its allies over the extent to which this is really necessary and, if it is, how to share the resulting fiscal, strategic, and domestic political burdens.

In sum, the impending loss of any semblance of a meaningful nuclear advantage, coinciding as it does with the growing challenge to America's ability to project conventional power into the Western Pacific, cannot help but raise further doubts about its future role in the region.

COMMAND OF THE SEAS

There is a third, global arena in which military competition is only just starting to get under way. Now and for some time to come, the farther one moves from China's coasts, the greater the margin of U.S. advantage will be. Without a true, oceangoing surface fleet of its own, or a significant number of nuclear-powered attack submarines that can cruise for thousands of miles without refueling, the PLAN is poorly positioned to challenge America's command of the world's oceans beyond the Western Pacific.[23] In the event of a crisis or war, the United States and its partners could seize or sink Chinese commercial vessels at critical chokepoints or on the high seas, and there would be very little that Beijing could do about it. Because of its rapidly growing need for imported oil and other raw materials, the great bulk of which reach it by water, China is already vulnerable to the effects of a naval blockade, and it will become even more so as its economy grows. Unless a future conflict were to end very quickly, Beijing would face the prospect of being brought to its knees by the U.S. Navy, much as the British Royal Navy hobbled Germany's economy during the First World War.[24]

China today is in a historically anomalous and strategically precarious position. In the past, sea power and commerce have tended to develop in tandem. As rising states became more deeply engaged in foreign trade, investment, and empire-building, they also acquired navies to protect their far-flung interests and to defend the sea lanes that connected them to the mother country. This was generally a reciprocal process in which trade created the demand for navies whose existence encouraged more trade, and it was often played out over a period of centuries.

By contrast, in less than thirty years, China has emerged from virtual autarky to become one of the world's largest trading nations. In addition to its reliance on vital flows of imports and exports, its investors now own copper mines, oil wells, and smelting plants in foreign lands, and thousands of its workers toil to build roads, railways, ports, and telecommunication systems in Southeast Asia, the Middle East, Africa, and Latin America. Almost overnight China has acquired interests in virtually every corner of the earth, yet it currently has no means of protecting them or of guaranteeing its access in the event of war. What is worse, the nation that now enjoys unchallenged command of the global commons is not an ally and protector, but one that Beijing regards as its greatest rival and deadliest potential enemy.

Chinese strategists are painfully aware of this situation and of the dangers it entails, but they do not yet have an agreed response. No doubt there are some who believe, along with many in the West, that the threat of maritime blockade is no more than a theoretical possibility, rendered virtually unthinkable in a world of nuclear weapons and economic inter-dependence, or a phantasm conjured up by bureaucratic and industrial interests to justify vast new spending programs. But there are clearly oth-ers, including some top civilian and military officials, who take the danger very seriously and believe that China must develop the capabilities needed to secure its vital sea lines of communication. One recent survey of Chi-nese writings concludes that there is a growing "maritime faction" which believes, in the words of one of its more prominent theorists, that "if a nation lacks sea power, its development has no future."[25] Nor is this a prob-lem whose solution can be indefinitely delayed. As another Chinese writer puts it, "Regarding the problems . . . of sea embargo or oil lanes being cut off . . . China must . . . 'repair the house before it rains.' "[26]

For now, at least as regards ensuring its access to energy, Beijing is pursu-ing a variety of approaches, most of which do not rely on a rapid expansion in naval capabilities, and none of which yet provides a plausible solution to the basic problem. Cross-border pipelines to Russia and Central Asia will afford some protection against a maritime blockade, but are them-selves exposed to interdiction and, in any event, are unlikely ever to supply more than a fraction of total national needs. Additional pipelines through Burma and Pakistan, or a canal across the isthmus of Thailand might per-mit Chinese ships to avoid what President Hu Jintao has reportedly referred to as "the Malacca Dilemma," the necessity of passing through the narrow straits opposite Singapore. But these massive engineering projects would do nothing to alleviate the vulnerability of Chinese shipping farther to the West, in the Indian Ocean and the Persian Gulf. China would be in a better position to defend the flow of energy from suspected undersea reserves in the South China Sea, close enough to home to be protected, in

China's Critical Sea Lanes.
From *Military Power of the Peoples' Republic of China*, 2009, p. 4.

part, by land-based forces. But the production facilities themselves would be vulnerable to attack by the United States and its allies. Finally, the strategic petroleum reserve that China has built up in recent years will enable the PLA to keep fighting in the event of an American blockade, but only for a matter of weeks or, at best, a few months.

Some analysts believe that China's involvement in the construction of ports and airfields in Burma, Pakistan, and Sri Lanka is part of a deliberate plan to construct a "string of pearls" extending all the way to the Persian Gulf.[27] After first dismissing the idea out of hand as Western propaganda, some Chinese naval officers recently floated the suggestion that it might in fact be "appropriate" to acquire fixed bases "for supplies and maintenance" in areas where they plan to conduct extended operations.[28] If it were to deploy ships, submarines, and reconnaissance systems and strike aircraft to such facilities (and perhaps someday to others in Iran or some other friendly state), the PLAN could project power into the Indian Ocean and adjacent seas without developing a true, long-range "blue water" navy. This kind of capability might be useful in dealing with lesser threats, from pirates, for example, but it would also present a serious opponent with an array of soft, fixed targets that could be quickly destroyed in the opening stages of any conflict.

It is difficult to believe that the present Beijing regime will accept indefinitely a situation in which its fate could depend on American forbearance, and hard to see how it can escape that condition without building a much bigger and more capable navy. As a first step, China may develop its own commerce raiding capability in the hopes that this will deter the United States and its allies from ever initiating a naval blockade.[29] Some of what the PLAN is already doing, rapidly expanding its fleet of attack submarines and building new bases on its southern coast, including a huge new facility on Hainan Island, may be intended in part to serve this purpose. If it can close off the northern exits from the South China Sea with the threat of mines and torpedoes, Beijing can constrict the energy lifelines of Japan and South Korea. Building large numbers of antiship ballistic missiles would also enable it to strike oil tankers and other commercial vessels from shore, instead of reserving these weapons only for American aircraft carriers or other high-value targets. If the mainland ever succeeds in absorbing Taiwan and can base sensors, aircraft, missiles, and submarines there, it will be able to extend its reach even farther to the east and north. With the island in its possession, Beijing would be well positioned to impose a blockade of its own on Japan or South Korea.

One drawback of this approach is that while it would pose a grave challenge to America's Asian allies, it would not do much to threaten the United States itself. If Chinese naval strategists wish to do that, or merely to have some realistic chance of defending their own sea lines of communication against hostile action, they are going to have to venture much farther afield. If it models itself on its main rival, the PLAN will eventually deploy carriers, missile-carrying surface ships of various sizes to help protect them, and nuclear-powered attack submarines. Like the U.S. Navy, it will also seek access to ports closer to the areas it wishes to patrol.

A twenty-first-century contest for command of the seas could also have some novel aspects, including substantial reliance on unmanned aerial and underwater vehicles to gather intelligence and conduct attacks, and a greatly expanded role for long-range antiship ballistic missiles. Based on land, and perhaps also on ships and submarines, these could expand the geographical scope of naval warfare in much the same way that carrier-based aircraft did in the 1940s. If this is the direction in which the competition moves, the PLAN may have some significant advantages. China already has more than a decade of experience in developing long-range antiship ballistic missiles. For its part, the United States continues to labor under the constraints imposed by the Cold War–era Intermediate-Range Nuclear Forces Treaty, which prohibits it from developing or deploying land-based ballistic or cruise missiles with ranges between 300 and 3400 miles. These are precisely the sorts of weapons on which a new, missile-based naval strategy would depend. Because of its vast investments in large surface vessels over many decades, and their centrality to its existing doctrine and concepts of operation, the U.S. Navy also has much more to lose if missiles make such ships obsolete.

Whatever its precise form, the next several decades are going to see an intensifying naval rivalry among the United States, China, India, Japan, South Korea, Australia, and perhaps others that will shape the forces and strain the budgets of all who take part in it.

THE SHRINKING TECHNOLOGY GAP

The ability of the United States to maintain a technological edge over the Soviet Union was a crucial part of its strategy for winning the Cold War. The superior performance of many major U.S. weapons systems enabled them to offset considerably larger numbers of Soviet tanks, submarines, and aircraft. Over time, the gap between East and West grew so wide that the United States was able to deploy some weapons the Soviets simply could neither match nor readily counter. This shift is signified by the fact that while in the 1940s and 1950s both superpowers could produce ballistic missiles and nuclear bombs, the most advanced weapons of the day, by the 1980s only one could manufacture stealthy aircraft and high-accuracy precision-guided conventional munitions. The Kremlin's unsuccessful efforts to keep pace with Western technology diverted scarce resources from the civilian sector, further slowing economic growth. This poor performance, plus the realization that Russia was falling further behind in the qualitative arms race, deepened the demoralization of the Soviet elite and helped set the stage for the desperate, and ultimately disastrous experiments of the Gorbachev era.

Today's rivalry is already taking a very different course. Instead of widening, the overall gap in technical sophistication between the American and Chinese economies has narrowed considerably since the end of the early 1990s, and it is likely to continue to do so in the years ahead. In terms of military capability, the United States still holds a sizable lead in most areas, but China is beginning to make rapid progress in several. Of course, China does not have to be America's equal in every respect in order to compete with it militarily. As Thomas Christensen pointed out in 2001, the PLA can "pose problems without catching up," and, indeed, that is precisely what it has done in the intervening decade.[30] None of China's ships, submarines, or aircraft is yet comparable to their American counterparts nor, considered individually, are most of the sensors and missiles that combine to support its anti-access strategy. Nevertheless, in light of the disparate aims of the two combatants, and the geography of the Western Pacific "battlespace," the PLA has managed to knit these systems together in a way that poses a serious challenge to U.S. power projection forces. But the game has only just begun. Unless it chooses simply to opt out, the United States will have to find ways of better masking the location of its surface ships, extending the range of its conventional strike systems, and defending both fixed and moving targets from barrages of ballistic missiles. If China is to defeat these countermeasures, and to compete more broadly in undersea warfare, air and missile defenses, and precision strike, it will have to work even harder to close the technological gap that still separates it from its rival.

There are a number of reasons for believing that China can do this and none to suggest that it will not try. Beijing certainly recognizes the centrality of science and technology to every aspect of its program for building "comprehensive national power." Starting with the so-called 863 Program (so named because it was announced in March 1986), it has periodically put forward plans with the stated aim of catching and, in the most recent iteration, surpassing the West across a wide range of scientific and technological fronts, especially those of direct military importance.[31]

Since the mid-1990s, the government has put its money where its mouth is. Total national spending on research and development has grown even faster than the economy as a whole, increasing its share of GDP from around .3 percent in 1998 to 1.34 percent in 2005, with a goal of reaching 2.5 percent by 2020. Other "inputs" to the innovation process have increased as well, including the numbers of scientists and engineers engaged in R&D in China, students enrolled in college and graduate school, and those receiving doctoral degrees in science and engineering fields.[32] Given all the resources being pumped into the system, it is hardly surprising to find that some of the common measures of national scientific and technological "output" have also begun to move sharply upward. Included among these are patent applications by Chinese residents and publications by Chinese authors in scholarly journals.[33] The National Science Foundation and other organizations have combined hard indicators such as these with expert judgments about other, less easily quantifiable factors to rank nations according to their "technological competitiveness." While there are differences among such assessments, all show the same general trend: China is not yet in America's league, but it continues to move up rapidly through the ranks of the world's most advanced countries.[34]

More significant than any of these numerical measures are changes in the structure of Chinese institutions. Drawing lessons from the shortcomings and failures of the Soviet Union, and some of the more obvious virtues of the American "military-industrial complex," Beijing has taken steps to restructure its system for the design and manufacture of advanced weaponry. Defense enterprises are no longer under the often-stifling control of the military services they supply, and research institutes no longer labor in isolation from arms manufacturers. In addition to their own in-house laboratories, manufacturers can seek the best new ideas, products, and techniques by entering into partnerships with universities and other research institutes. Last but not least, government contracts are now awarded on the basis of competitive bidding between enterprises. All of these changes are meant to break the rigid and wasteful, Soviet-style, top-down process of the Maoist era and to increase incentives for efficiency and, above all, innovation.[35]

One major distinction between the U.S. and Soviet systems was the absence, in the latter case, of a vibrant commercial sector. This did not make a significant difference during the opening decades of the Cold War, when both sides were focused on producing weapons and other military systems (like thermonuclear weapons and ballistic missiles) for which there was no civilian analog. In the United States, some of the breakthroughs achieved in the course of developing these weapons (such as digital computers) were "spun off" into the economy as a whole, where they formed the basis of new products and entire industries. Competition for customers and market share then took over as the spur to further innovation, first in the United States and then across the advanced industrial world. Eventually "spin-off" was overshadowed in importance by "spin-on." In critical areas like microelectronics, commercially developed technology surpassed and then was fed back into the defense sector, enabling the manufacture of new and better weapons. It was only in the 1970s and 1980s that the profound differences between the market-based U.S. economy and that of its state-centric opponent began to have a decisive impact on their military-technical rivalry.[36]

As with the evolving structure of its defense industry, in this regard too China today looks more like the United States than it does the Soviet Union. In the last thirty years China's economic development has been driven by the manufacture of commercial products, and under the banner of "Locating Military Potential in Civilian Capabilities," Beijing has recently given top priority to encouraging the flow of technology from civilian industry to the military.[37] Efforts to promote the development and incorporation of dual-use technologies have met with considerable success. Indeed, a 2005 study of the Chinese defense industry notes that it is precisely in those sectors where civil-military linkages are the strongest (shipbuilding and information technology) that the achievements have been the most dramatic. In other areas (missiles and especially aviation) China has been slower to move forward, and its newest weapons platforms are often still the lineal descendants of systems developed in the 1960s and 1970s.[38] Here too, however, the incorporation of dual-use items from the commercial information technology sector has resulted in major improvements in accuracy, reliability, and command and control. Simply by buying what the U.S. Department of Defense describes as "commercial off-the-shelf technologies" such as computer network switches and routers from top Chinese companies, the PLA is now able to acquire "state-of-the-art telecommunications equipment."[39]

All of this points to the single most significant difference between the Chinese and Soviet systems, and to the factor that has played the greatest role in helping China close the technological gap that still separates it from America. Whereas Russia (and Maoist China) sought isolation from global markets, since the late 1970s the PRC has embraced them with unparalleled ardor. Unlike the Soviet Union, which purchased very little from outside its bloc and had little to offer in return, China has both the desire and the ability to trade. Its massive exports of consumer goods have fueled economic growth and enabled it to purchase sophisticated weapons from advanced suppliers like Russia and Israel, which it has sought to "reverse engineer" in order eventually to be able to build its own. In addition, Chinese companies, many with direct links to the military, have used both legal and illicit transactions to purchase a wide array of dual-use items, including guidance and control systems, turbine engines, precision machine tools, software, computers, and semiconductors.[40]

Vital though imports have undoubtedly been, it is foreign direct investment that has served as the "decisive catalyst" propelling China up the high-tech ladder.[41] Backed by Beijing, Chinese firms have driven hard bargains with foreigners seeking access to their country's vast potential market and its supply of skilled, low-cost labor. In return for the right to build assembly plants, foreign companies have been required to transfer technology and know-how to their Chinese partners. To this point, writes James Kynge, "it is globalization rather than R&D that is the main catalyst behind China's reemergence as a technology power."[42] But, especially in areas of direct military relevance, the government's stated aim is to build an indigenous capacity to develop and apply cutting-edge technologies.[43]

China's integration into the world economy and the global scientific community provides it with innumerable opportunities to get what it needs to move closer to this goal. The Soviet Union made its own attempts to acquire Western technology, usually covertly via intermediaries in Europe or Asia. But Soviet graduate students rarely studied in American universities, Soviet and East bloc nationals did not work in Western laboratories, and private (or quasi-private) Soviet commercial enterprises certainly did not buy up American companies or join them in ventures to develop new products. Nor was the Soviet Union connected to a worldwide communications network that afforded it access to the information systems of governments, corporations, and individuals throughout the West.

Trade, investment, legitimate exchange, and espionage will help China to continue closing the technological gap with the United States. Whether it will actually be able to surge ahead, not merely copying but truly innovating on its own, remains to be seen.[44] In addition, even as China advances, America and its allies will hardly be standing still. Despite this, it would be imprudent to assume that the United States will be able to rely on the same margins of technical superiority that permitted it to preserve its position, at manageable cost, in the past. China has already shown that it can "cause problems without catching up"; it will be able to cause even bigger ones as it begins to do so.

RESOURCES FOR THE "LONG HAUL"

It has been more than a century since the United States faced a strategic competitor with a GDP equal to its own. Imperial Japan and Nazi Germany did not come close, and, as we now know, even at its peak the Soviet Union's total output was probably only a third to a quarter that of its capitalist rival.[45] The superior size of the American economy permitted it to sustain large defense expenditures at lower levels of exertion (i.e., with a smaller fraction of total output) than its rivals. In peacetime this meant there were ample resources remaining to support high levels of private consumption, business investment, and other forms of government expenditure, all of which contributed, albeit in varying degrees, to fueling economic growth. Over the course of the Cold War the United States was able to remain strong and economically dynamic while at the same time providing a steadily improving quality of life for its citizens. The Soviet Union, by contrast, sacrificed welfare and ultimately growth in order to continue building military power.

If current trends hold, by the middle of this century, if not sooner, China will finally displace the United States from its position atop the global

GDP tables. Despite its undeniable symbolic and psychological impact, however, this transition is unlikely to herald an accompanying shift in the distribution of military power. As was true in the early nineteenth century, when it was also the world's largest economy, this fact alone will not transform China into the world's most powerful nation. In fact, depending on a variety of other factors, the United States may actually find it easier to prosecute a strategic rivalry with China several decades hence than it does today.

High growth rates have thus far enabled Beijing to finance a large, sustained military buildup without concomitant increases in the defense burden. To the contrary, instead of rising, the PLA's share of GDP actually *fell*, by some estimates, from an average of just under 5 percent in the early 1990s, to under 4 percent in the first years of the twenty-first century.[46] Beijing has not yet had to face a guns-versus-butter dilemma.

Because of its geopolitical circumstances and strategic priorities, China has also had the luxury since the end of the Cold War of being able to focus on a comparatively limited range of capabilities and contingencies. The collapse of the Soviet Union and the warming of relations with Russia freed Chinese military planners from their costly preoccupation with large-scale land warfare and permitted them to focus on devising limited options for dealing with Taiwan. The fact that Beijing could direct a widening stream of resources against a more narrowly defined set of potential missions permitted it to make rapid progress in altering the balance of power in the Western Pacific.

At the turn of the century, just as the Chinese buildup was beginning to gain traction, the United States found itself more than usually distracted and constrained. Prior to 9/11, as described in chapter 4, the Pentagon was poised to devote more attention and more money to East Asia. The attacks, and the subsequent wars in Afghanistan and Iraq, pushed China well down on the list of strategic priorities. These events also provided members of the Shanghai Coalition with powerful new arguments against doing anything that might antagonize Beijing. September 11 did not avert an escalating Sino-American rivalry, as some observers hoped, it merely deferred it; or rather, it held the United States back from responding to Chinese initiatives as vigorously as it might otherwise have done.

What was once known as the "global war on terrorism" will have a lingering impact on America's willingness and ability to compete with China. The enormous costs of recent "irregular" conflicts have squeezed out spending on capabilities better suited for waging high-intensity conventional war against a technologically sophisticated opponent. Some top civilian officials, including Robert Gates, secretary of defense under Presidents Bush and Obama, have declared that the armed forces should explicitly shift emphasis from the latter kind of warfare, which they now regard as highly improbable, toward the purportedly greater likelihood of yet more irregular conflicts.[47] The Obama administration's first quadrennial defense review, completed in early 2010, took a similar tack, urging more investment in forces suitable for combating terrorists and insurgents while, according to some experts, largely discounting the "urgency of investments needed to address emerging challenges, such as growing anti-access/area-denial (a2/aD) threats, nuclear-armed regional powers, and sustaining access to, and use of, space and cyberspace."[48] If these recommendations are followed, the Defense Department will end up spending a smaller fraction of its overall budget on the kinds of weapons needed to deter, or fight, China.

Other restraints are less tangible. The human and financial cost of the wars in Afghanistan and Iraq, and the political controversies surrounding them, have left a portion of the public exhausted and eager to disengage from world affairs. A poll conducted in 2009 found, for example, that nearly half of those questioned agreed with the proposition that the United States should "mind its own business internationally." This was the highest positive response to a probe of isolationist sentiment since the aftermath of Vietnam and the highest ever since the same question was first asked in 1964.[49]

While the same polls also find the American people expressing long-term concerns about the growth of Chinese power, recent events will make it more difficult to rouse them to support an active response.[50] The intelligence failures of the past decade have decreased the credibility of yet more warnings about dire threats to national security. Satellite photographs of alleged military installations and solemn words of caution from top government officials no longer carry the weight they once did. Barring some galvanizing crisis, those who seek popular support for a more competitive stance toward China will continue to face indifference and skepticism.

As if all this were not enough, the 2008–9 financial crisis, the deep, protracted recession that followed, and the ballooning price tag for the bailouts and stimulus packages meant to ameliorate its effects have combined to impose tight new constraints on defense spending. According to the Congressional Budget Office, in 2009 the federal budget deficit stood at close to 10 percent of GDP, while debt had jumped to 60 percent of GDP. Not since the end of the Second World War has Washington wallowed in so much red ink.[51]

But the worst is yet to come. As the crisis recedes and interest rates rise, so too will the cost of debt servicing. The Congressional Budget Office predicts that between 2010 and 2020, government spending on interest will more than triple in nominal terms (from $203 billion to $723 billion) and more than double as a share of GDP (from 1.4 percent to 3.2 percent).[52] By 2017, in one estimate, annual interest payments could exceed outlays for national defense.[53] Together with the rising costs of health care and Social Security associated with the aging of the "Baby Boom" generation, these obligations will create an atmosphere of fiscal stringency and put strong downward pressure on the defense budget.[54] Like their British counterparts in the aftermath of the First World War, American strategists may be tempted to adopt a "10 Year Rule," under which they simply declare for planning purposes that no major conflict can break out during the coming decade. Assuming a problem out of existence is not the same as solving it, of course. Nevertheless, despite the growth in PLA capabilities that has occurred in the interim, there is less appetite in the U.S. government today for a stepped-up military rivalry than there was at the turn of the century.

Growth is the time-honored American remedy for debts and deficits. As happened after the Second World War and more recently, albeit on a smaller scale, in the 1990s, the United States will eventually work its way out of the tight fiscal spot in which it now finds itself. In this case, however, the process may turn out to be especially protracted because the aftereffects of the crisis are likely to impose an enduring drag on growth. While opinions vary, most experts agree that the U.S. economy will expand more slowly during the 2010s and perhaps beyond than it has been able to do in previous decades.[55] Engaging in a major expansion in defense budgets under such circumstances will not be impossible, but it will be painful.

Like the rest of the world, China suffered an economic slowdown in the wake of the 2008–9 financial crisis. Because of its comparatively limited exposure to the global banking system, the effects were mostly indirect, taking the form primarily of a sharp drop in demand for Chinese exports. Ever wary of the possible social and political effects of unemployment and economic dislocation, the authorities responded by wheeling out a stimulus program of truly heroic proportions. Despite warnings from some Western economists that it was setting the stage for overcapacity, inflation, and a more serious setback a few years down the road, in the short run at least Beijing's policies were an undeniable success.[56] After reaching a peak of 13 percent in 2007, the annual growth rate was cut almost in half (to around 7 percent on a year-on-year basis) during the initial stages of the global crisis.[57] By 2009 it had climbed back to around 9 percent and, within another year, was headed back to near pre-crisis rates of 10 or 11 percent.[58]

At least for the moment, China is clearly better situated to sustain the momentum of its buildup than the United States is to redirect and accelerate its own military programs. Fast-forward another twenty years, however, and the picture could look markedly different. By that point the United States will probably have withdrawn most, if not all of its forces remaining in Europe, and while it will continue to have a strong interest in the stability of the region, it will likely have pulled back considerably from the Middle East and Southwest Asia as well. Even allowing for the possibility of heightened security challenges in the Western Hemisphere, a far greater fraction of the total American military and intelligence effort will be devoted to the Western Pacific, and to the area that extends from the Strait of Hormuz, in the Persian Gulf, through the Indian Ocean to the Strait of Malacca.

Even as Washington is narrowing down, Beijing will be broadening its strategic vision. In another couple of decades, regardless of what happens to Taiwan, the PLA will probably be fully engaged in building up its power projection capabilities, the better to defend the nation's sea lanes and far-flung interests. China will have become a player on the global stage, with both the benefits and the burdens that this implies. Meanwhile, closer to home, its security environment may not be as favorable as it is today. A souring relationship with Russia, India, or Vietnam, a messy end to North Korea, growing turmoil in Central Asia, and increasing concern over securing cross-border energy supplies could necessitate an expansion of PLA ground forces. Trouble in Xinjiang, Tibet, and major urban centers across the nation may lead to further investments in the People's Armed Police. At the same time that they are expanding in size, China's armed forces will also be increasing in cost. As it becomes a wealthier and more advanced society, the price of both manpower and new weapons will rise, making additional increments of military power more expensive than those that came before.

By 2030 the capacity of the two contestants to carry forward their rivalry may be moving in opposite directions. The challenges that the United States will face in recovering from the financial meltdown, working off the resulting debt and deficits, maintaining increased savings rates, and reforming its health and social welfare policies are substantial; meeting them will require some tough, politically difficult decisions. But America also has some enduring advantages that should stand it in good stead. Some of these (including political stability, a rich endowment of natural resources, strong protections for property rights, deep capital markets, a commitment to free enterprise, the world's leading university system) are so familiar that they are sometimes overlooked or taken for granted. Others, in particular the nation's demographic profile, have only begun to get the attention they deserve.[59]

With the partial exception of the United States, all of the advanced industrial nations are set to experience a rapid aging of their societies over the next several decades. Falling birth rates and increasing longevity are combining to produce shrinking workforces, higher "dependency ratios" (the ratio of elderly to younger, working-age citizens), increased spending on pensions and health care and, in all likelihood, slower economic growth.[60] The United States too will have to cope with the consequences of an aging population, but the challenges it faces will be much less severe. Thanks to its unusually high birth rates and (assuming this continues) its traditional openness to immigration, America's workforce will continue to grow, its dependency ratio will remain relatively low, and it will have a better chance of sustaining GDP growth at or near historic averages. Other things equal, a nation whose GDP is growing at 3 or 3.5 percent in real terms will have an easier time caring for its elderly, while at the same time maintaining its geopolitical position, than one with an economy advancing at 2 percent. As Nicholas Eberstadt puts it, if U.S. power declines in the coming decades, "it won't be because of demography."[61]

Despite its present dynamism, China faces serious and perhaps intractable long-term problems in this regard. Assuming that it can find ways around all of the other potential obstacles to its growth (weak financial markets and property protections, inefficiencies due to corruption and the continuing outsized role of the state in economic decision making, rising dependence on imported commodities and raw materials, the accumulating costs of environmental degradation), China will still have to deal with shifts in its population profile of unprecedented speed and magnitude. As discussed in chapter 1, the economic miracle of the last thirty years has been fueled by a vast supply of young workers eager for employment in industry and willing to work for low wages. In part due to the "one child policy," this flow is going to shrink dramatically over the course of the next several decades. As it does, the average age of China's population, the absolute size of its elderly cohort, and the ratio of non-working-age to working-age citizens will increase.[62]

The impact of these demographic developments on growth rates is impossible to predict with precision, but they seem certain to be negative. As labor becomes scarcer, wages will rise and Chinese exports may become less competitive on global markets. Aging populations generally save less, meaning that capital will become scarcer, making investment in the technologies needed to increase the productivity of a dwindling supply of labor more costly. At the same time, unless they are to be left to die in penury, someone, either their government or their children, is going to have to pay for the care of the elderly. Preserving the rudiments of a decent society will require redirecting some of its resources from other purposes, most likely putting downward pressure on both private investment and government expenditures for national defense.[63]

The rapid aging of China's population will probably cause its rate of economic growth to fall sooner and faster than would otherwise have been the case. Just as the scope of its national interests is expanding, and the costs of its armed forces are growing, the resources available to fund them will start to become scarcer. Demographers note that China faces the challenge of "getting old before it gets rich." It may also turn out that China will have gotten old, and less dynamic, before it has had the chance to consolidate its position as a truly global power.

Ten

ALTERNATIVE STRATEGIES

"ALTERNATIVE CHINAS"

P rudent planners hope for the best but prepare for the worst. As preceding chapters have made plain, if China continues along its present path, growing richer and stronger but continuing under one-party authoritarian rule, it will pose a mounting strategic challenge. Daunting though it may be, the United States has no choice but to take this prospect seriously and to prepare for it accordingly. Indeed, it is precisely because it would be so stressful and difficult that this scenario demands urgent and sustained attention from American strategists.

Before turning to a detailed consideration of what will be required to meet the challenge of a fast-rising, authoritarian China, I briefly consider two other possibilities. Twenty years from now China's economy could still be humming along at a world-beating pace, and the country may finally have begun, or perhaps even completed, its long-anticipated transition to a more open and democratic form of government. On the other hand, due to a combination of factors, including unfavorable demographic trends, the nation's economic growth may have slowed dramatically, social unrest could be ratcheting upward, and the political system may have mutated into a new form of populist, hyper-nationalist, quasi-fascist authoritarianism. It is even conceivable that, as has happened before in its own history, and as happened twenty years ago to the Soviet Union, China's central government could be tottering on the brink of collapse.[1] Certainly this is a scenario that the nation's current rulers take very seriously and are working tirelessly to prevent.

What are the implications of these two broad possibilities—a nation that is weaker, less stable, but still authoritarian, or one that is rich, strong, and increasingly democratic—for U.S. strategy?

Weak, unstable China

An "alternative China" that is poorer and less stable may be a less effective competitor in certain respects, but it could also prove to be less predictable, more aggressive, and hence even more dangerous and difficult for the United States and its allies to manage. Today's Chinese leaders are sometimes described as so deeply preoccupied with internal problems and challenges that they barely have time to attend to external affairs. As their troubles mount, they may become even more inward focused and less concerned with grand schemes and lofty goals. Like ordinary people, national leaders who have to worry about day-to-day survival generally lack the energy for long-term planning or the patience to implement careful, incremental strategies.

Beyond merely deflecting their attention, internal weakness could render China's rulers more pliant and accommodating in their dealings with other powers. A study by political scientist Taylor Fravel finds that Beijing has been more likely to compromise with its neighbors over disputed borders when faced with the threat of serious domestic unrest. On a number of occasions since 1949, timely tactical shifts have alleviated tension and reduced the likelihood that others might try to take advantage of temporary Chinese weakness, opened the way for much-needed trade and economic assistance, and enabled the government to shift resources from defense to domestic development. If this pattern holds, then a future leadership that finds itself beset by strikes, ethnic unrest, and violence in the countryside could turn out to be highly accommodating and conflict averse.[2]

A nation with a persistently weak and faltering central government is also likely to have fewer resources with which to pursue its external ambitions. Minxin Pei argues that while the Communist Party regime may be tough and adaptable enough to hang on to power for decades yet to come, its corruption and inefficiency will inevitably lead to slower growth. As time passes, political and economic stagnation will reinforce one another, eroding what remains of the party's legitimacy and yielding further increases in "lawlessness, corruption, and social disorder." Stuck in what Pei terms an "incomplete transition," China may simply be incapable of becoming a peer-competitor of the United States, still less of "mounting a real challenge for global preeminence."[3]

There are darker possibilities, certainly for China's people and perhaps for the rest of the world. State failure could lead to disease, famine, civil warfare, floods of refugees, and a loss of control over nuclear weapons.[4] Even if it has not yet reached the brink of collapse, a regime beset by rising internal troubles could respond violently to perceived external challenges in an attempt to shore up its sagging legitimacy. Weak leaders might even seek confrontation with foreign enemies to rally domestic support and fend off pressures for political change. In the words of Sinologist Susan Shirk, it may be "China's internal fragility, not its growing strength that presents the greatest danger."[5]

Unfortunately, Beijing's past willingness to pursue external accommodation when faced with internal unrest may not provide an accurate indication of how it will behave in the future. For one thing, China is far stronger today than it was during previous periods of turmoil, such as the Cultural Revolution and the Great Leap Forward. After decades of military investment the regime may believe it has options that its predecessors lacked, and if hard-pressed, it may choose to exercise them rather than adopt a softer stance. Mao and Deng Xiaoping were towering figures who were much stronger in relation to any potential domestic rivals than their successors, and who did not have to think twice about how their policies would be received by "the masses." Today's party leaders are less substantial and less secure than their predecessors, and those who come after them are likely to be even less awe inspiring. Sensitivity to public criticism, and the desire to avoid being labeled as "soft" by domestic critics, may already be pushing the regime toward adopting more provocative postures in its dealings with foreign powers.[6] If China's elite politics become more openly competitive, even if they do not become truly democratic, these tendencies are likely to grow more pronounced in the years to come.

Two other features of Chinese strategic thought and behavior round out what is already a troubling picture. As we have seen, Beijing is inclined to see the hand of sinister foreign forces behind episodes of domestic unrest. Should these become severe and sustained, the regime may be prone to conclude that its foreign foes have thrown caution to the winds and are at last trying openly to overthrow and destroy it. Under these circumstances, with their own lives and fortunes and those of their families at stake, the leadership might be willing to take extraordinary risks to fend off disaster, perhaps including the use of armed force against foreign powers believed to be aiding and abetting internal unrest.[7]

In past crises, China has shown a propensity to initiate the use of force by striking sharp, stunning blows, not primarily for purposes of achieving concrete military objectives but rather as a way of signaling toughness and resolve and warning its enemies to stand down. Since its founding, the PRC has launched surprise attacks on the United States (1950), India (1962), Russia (1969), and Vietnam (1979).[8] As RAND analysts Mark Burles and Abram Shulsky point out, Beijing has been willing to strike first even when the overall balance of military power seemed to be heavily weighted in favor of its opponent. Indeed, from a Chinese perspective, the fact that the other side believed itself to be in an advantageous position may actually have been seen as heightening the shock value of a surprise attack.[9]

In the context of today's peacetime competition, Beijing can afford to be cautious and calculating, painstakingly accumulating marginal advantages in the hopes that these will eventually put it in a position to "win without fighting." Under severe duress, however, with its back to the wall, the regime may revert to a very different mode of behavior, one that, while still rational, could be extremely risky. The best that the United States and its allies can do to prepare for such an eventuality is to be aware of Beijing's heightened sensitivities so as to avoid unintended provocations, to reduce their own vulnerabilities, and to build up sufficient strength so that even at moments of deep crisis, preemptive attack will not appear to be a promising option.

The passage from strength to weakness, from a situation like today's, in which China's leaders have reason to think that time is on their side, to one in which they believe they are watching the future ebb away, promises to be especially demanding and dangerous. Under these conditions Beijing's preference for methodically "crossing the river by feeling the stones" could give way to a desperate, headlong dash for regional preponderance. Yet it may be that China will have to pass through such a period of instability before its people can rid themselves of Communist Party rule and place their country firmly on the path to liberal democracy.

Strong, democratic China

It is in part for fear of what might be unleashed that the United States has long eschewed any thought of trying directly to weaken or destabilize China. To the contrary, current policy is premised on the belief that a stable and strong, albeit also a *democratic* China is very much in America's interests. Such a country would presumably have goals and values that overlap those of the United States and its allies, and if the past history of relations among democracies is any guide, it would be far less likely to use force against them.

Not everyone is convinced of this optimistic forecast. Some self-styled "realists" assert that the interests and objectives of a democratic China will not be much different from those of today's authoritarian state. In this view, domestic reforms may make China richer, stronger, more stable, and hence a more potent competitor, without deflecting it from its desires to dominate East Asia and settle scores with some of its neighbors.[10] Even if, in the long run, China becomes a stable, peaceful democracy, its passage could prove rocky. The opening of the nation's political system to dissent and debate is likely to introduce an element of instability into its foreign policy as new voices are heard and aspiring leaders vie for popular support. As one observer ruefully points out, "An authoritarian China has been highly predictable. A more open and democratic China could produce new uncertainties about both domestic policy and international relations."[11]

Nationalism, perhaps in its most virulent and aggressive form, is one factor likely to play a prominent role in shaping the foreign policy of a democratizing China. Thanks to the spread of the Internet, and the relaxation of restraints on at least some forms of "patriotic" political expression, the current regime already finds itself subject to public criticism whenever it takes what some regard as an overly accommodating stance toward Japan, Taiwan, or the United States. Beijing has sought at times to stir up patriotic sentiment, but fearful that anger at foreigners could all too easily be turned against it, the regime has also gone to great lengths to keep popular passions in check. A democratically elected government might be far less inhibited. American-based political scientist Fei-Ling Wang argues that a post-Communist regime would actually be more forceful in asserting its sovereignty over Taiwan, Tibet, and the South China Sea. As he explains, "A 'democratic' regime in Beijing, free from the debilitating concerns for its own survival but likely driven by popular emotions, could make the rising Chinese power a much more assertive, impatient, belligerent, even aggressive force, at least during the unstable period of fast ascendance to the ranks of a world-class power."[12]

The last proviso is key. Even those who are most confident of the long-term pacifying effects of democratization recognize the possibility of a turbulent transition. In his book *China's Democratic Future*, Bruce Gilley acknowledges that democratic revolutions in other countries have often led to bursts of external aggression, and he notes that since the start of the twentieth century, pro-democracy movements in China have also been highly nationalistic. Despite these precedents, Gilley predicts that after an interval of perhaps a decade, a transformed nation will settle into more stable and cooperative relationships with the United States as well as its democratic neighbors.[13]

Such an outcome is by no means certain, of course, and would be contingent on events and interactions that are difficult to anticipate and even harder to control. If initial frictions between a fledgling democracy and its more well-established counterparts are mishandled, resulting in actual armed conflict, history could spin off in very different, and far less promising, directions than if they are successfully resolved. Assuming the transition can be navigated without disaster, however, there are good reasons to believe that relations will improve with time. One Chinese advocate of political reform summarizes the prospects well. Whereas a "nationalistic and authoritarian China will be an emerging threat," a liberal, democratic China will ultimately prove "a constructive partner."[14]

This expectation is rooted in more than mere wishful thinking. As the values and institutions of liberal democracy become more firmly entrenched, there will begin to be open and politically meaningful debate and real competition over national goals and the allocation of national resources. Aspiring leaders and opinion makers preoccupied with prestige, honor, power, and score-settling will have to compete with others who emphasize the virtues of international stability, cooperation, reconciliation, and the promotion of social welfare. The demands of the military and its industrial allies will be counterbalanced, at least to some degree, by groups who favor spending more on education, health care, and the elderly. The assertive, hyper-nationalist version of China's history and its grievances will be challenged by accounts that acknowledge the culpability of the Communist regime in repressing minorities and refusing to seek compromise on questions of sovereignty. A regime obsessed with its own survival and with countering perceived threats from foreign powers will be replaced by a government secure in its legitimacy and with no cause to fear that the world's democracies are seeking to encircle and overthrow it.

Conversely, because others are less likely to see it as a threat, a liberal democratic China should find it easier to get along with Japan, India, and South Korea, among others. The trust and mutual respect that eventually develop between democracies, and the diminished fear that one will use force against another, should increase the odds of attaining negotiated settlements of outstanding disputes over borders, offshore islands, and resources. A democratic government in Beijing would also stand a better chance of achieving a mutually acceptable resolution to its sixty-year standoff with Taiwan. In contrast to today's Communist Party rulers, a popularly elected mainland regime would have little to gain from keeping this conflict alive, it would be more likely to show respect for the preferences of another democratic government, and it would be more attractive to the Taiwanese people as a partner in some kind of federated arrangement that would satisfy the desires and ease the fears of both sides.[15]

In the long run, the United States can learn to live with a democratic China as the preponderant power in East Asia, much as Great Britain came to accept America as the dominant power in the Western Hemisphere. With the resolution of local quarrels and the reduction of uncertainty, mistrust, and tension, the rationale for retaining large and expensive U.S. forces in East Asia will eventually evaporate. While the United States will no doubt remain engaged in the region, and while its long-standing alliances may persist in some form, as in Europe, a large American force presence will cease to be necessary. Having kept the peace, encouraged the transition of all the major regional players from authoritarianism to democracy, and overseen the reemergence of Asia as a leading center of world wealth and power, Washington will be free to call home its legions.

ALTERNATIVE STRATEGIES

For two decades now the United States has pursued a strategy toward China that combines a shifting blend of engagement and containment, or balancing. The aim of this mixed approach has been to preserve a balance of power favorable to U.S. interests while awaiting the eventual liberalization of China's domestic political institutions. But suppose over the next two decades that China continues to grow richer and stronger without undergoing fundamental domestic political change. If this happens, future American administrations may choose (or be compelled) to abandon a mixed approach, moving much closer to one end of the spectrum of possibilities or the other. Alternatively, Washington could choose (or be constrained) to continue following the same basic formula, fine-tuning as circumstances demand by adjusting the mix of elements it contains.

Confrontation and appeasement
Neither of the more extreme alternatives appears either desirable or necessary at this point, and neither has significant support from serious strategists or influential political figures. A reversion to early Cold War–style containment is inconceivable in the near future, barring some major collision between the two Pacific powers. Only if U.S. and Chinese forces clash over Taiwan, or on the Korean peninsula, or off the coasts of Japan is it possible to imagine Washington doing the kinds of things that it did in the 1950s and 1960s: suspending diplomatic ties, imposing sanctions and embargoes, unleashing a major military buildup, or initiating a deliberate campaign to destabilize the Beijing regime. Even in the event of a severe crisis, the pressures for de-escalation, reconciliation, and a return to business as usual would be intense, certainly on the American side and perhaps on the Chinese as well.

A small handful of "realists" do believe that regardless of its domestic politics, a rising China will someday come to blows with the United States.

Their brutal prescription follows directly from this conviction: if a conflict is coming, Washington would be well advised to try to delay or derail China's rise, perhaps even going so far as to trigger a confrontation while the balance of power is still tilted in its favor.[16] At its furthest extreme, containment thus becomes a prescription for preventive war.

Fortunately in the real world there is no chance that any American president would follow such advice. An unprovoked shift from congagement to pure containment would face insurmountable domestic political obstacles, but there are sound strategic reasons for rejecting it as well. An unremittingly hostile American stance would guarantee an escalating competition on all fronts, raising the risks of war and possibly frightening some U.S. allies into neutrality. Adopting an openly confrontational posture would confirm the Beijing regime's most pessimistic claims about America's true intentions, lending credence to those within it who support a more militaristic, aggressively nationalistic approach to foreign policy and a less liberal course at home, and alienating many ordinary Chinese who might otherwise have been favorably disposed toward the United States. Reverting to containment before it becomes absolutely necessary would also preclude the possibility that history might eventually follow other, more gradual and less dangerous paths. It would be a tragic example of the worst kind of strategic folly, what Prussian foreign minister Otto von Bismarck (hardly a starry-eyed idealist) is said to have referred to as "committing suicide for fear of death."

Taking the engagement out of congagement yields a strategy of pure containment; subtracting containment leaves what can only be called a policy of appeasement. This approach too is premised on the assumption of China's inevitable rise. Rather than attempting to stop it, however, with all the dangers that this would entail, in this view the United States will simply have to learn to live with it. Trying openly to block China's emergence would be fruitless, and even if it did not result in war, it could poison trans-Pacific relations for decades. Instead of clinging sentimentally to old friends, alliances, and ways of doing business, Washington needs to focus on negotiating a new modus vivendi with Beijing, one that more accurately reflects the changed power relationship between them.

Given that America's relative power is waning, advocates of this approach argue that the best outcome that can reasonably be expected is some kind of bipolar condominium arrangement under which the two powers agree to jointly manage issues of mutual concern, leaving each dominant in its own sphere of influence. The key questions in this case would be where Beijing wished to draw the line and where America's present alliances and positions of strength would fall in relation to it. A sphere extending out to what Chinese strategists call the "first island chain" would leave Japan, the Philippines, Malaysia, Indonesia, and points east on one side, and the Korean peninsula, Taiwan, and the South China Sea on the other. By contrast, a line drawn through the "second island chain" would leave the tiny island of Guam as the westernmost outpost of American power in the Pacific.

As with unadulterated containment, the strategic and domestic political objections to appeasement are obvious and, at this point, overwhelming. Should China's growth falter and its behavior become erratic, there will be less strategic pressure on the United States to pull back from Asia and more reason than ever for it to remain engaged. Despite claims that it would reduce the risk of war, cutting a deal over the heads of democratic allies with a strong, authoritarian China would strike many Americans as both imprudent and immoral. Giving way in the face of demands from such a regime might simply embolden it to press for more and, by signaling U.S. weakness, could encourage aggressive behavior by other authoritarians in Asia and elsewhere. In light of America's long history of coming to the aid of fellow democracies, a decision that could be construed as abandoning some of them to their fates would also be controversial and politically risky at home, to say the least.

The same kinds of geopolitical considerations that caused American strategists to conclude in the early twentieth century that they had a vital interest in preventing the domination of Eurasia by potentially hostile powers are still applicable today. Unchecked Chinese domination of East Asia could give it preferred access to, if not full command over, the region's vast industrial, financial, natural, and technological resources. From a secure base, China could project power into other regions, much as the United States was able to do from the Western Hemisphere throughout the twentieth century. It is only if China liberalizes as it grows strong that Americans may conclude eventually that they no longer need to maintain a powerful presence in East Asia. Until that day there is little chance that

Washington will simply abandon its efforts to preserve a balance in the region in favor of a deliberate policy of appeasement.

Enhanced engagement

Eliminating the extremes at either end of the continuum of potential strategies leaves less radical variations on the theme of congagement. Logically speaking there are two broad alternatives, with many possible permutations of each: either the United States can intensify engagement, while holding steady or cutting back on anything that appears intended to counter Chinese power; or it can move in the opposite direction, maintaining or partially constricting engagement while stepping up balancing. The first option, a policy of "enhanced engagement," was essentially the one adopted during the opening years of the Obama administration. Notwithstanding its flaws and potential dangers, and despite its evident failure to induce better behavior from Beijing, this is still the approach favored by many American analysts, academics, and policy makers. After identifying the inadequacies of this approach, I close in the next, and final, chapter by making the case for an alternative strategy of "better balancing."

The views of mainstream China-watchers are spelled out in articles in prominent publications, and in a series of lengthy reports from prestigious think tanks that appeared in the waning days of the Bush administration and at the start of the presidency of Barack Obama. These doubtless deserve a close reading. For those wishing to save time, however, their essential message is captured in the title of an earlier essay by Elizabeth Economy of the Council on Foreign Relations: "Don't Break the Engagement."[17]

Even its most enthusiastic advocates would not claim that this aspect of American strategy has been a thoroughgoing success. If pressed, most would acknowledge that despite decades of rapid economic growth, political liberalization and respect for human rights in China have (in the understated words of one distinguished task force) "lagged behind expectations."[18] And it is hard to deny that despite intense and continuous interaction on a wide range of issues, Washington and Beijing remain divided by what another report labels a barrier of "strategic mistrust."[19]

Most of those who purport to speak with authority on China policy believe that the cure for what ails engagement is, simply, more engagement. In other words, the preferred response to the policy's disappointments is not a reexamination of the assumptions on which it is based but rather its intensification. Engagement's defenders believe that American officials must fend off critics and skeptics at home, while searching for ways to broaden and deepen communication and cooperation across the Pacific. If efforts to combat terrorism and control proliferation have failed to build a new strategic alliance, and if economic relations have become a cause for friction and tension as well as a source of mutual benefit, then the world's two greatest powers must raise their sights and expand their horizons. Such cooperation is more urgently needed now than ever before, because what is at stake in the twenty-first century may be nothing less than the survival of the human race. Advocates of enhanced engagement argue that the United States and China must work together to promote "the global good," and above all, they must cooperate to forestall the potentially catastrophic effects of climate change brought about by the accumulation of greenhouse gases.[20] This task is hugely important in its own right, but it also presents another opportunity to build a "far more cooperative foundation for U.S.-China relations as a whole."[21] In short, global warming has now replaced al Qaeda and the Soviet Union as the common enemy that China and America must join together to confront.

As it expands collaboration into new fields, the United States must also, in this view, take steps to deepen and improve the quality of engagement in areas where it is already under way. In the security domain Washington needs to acknowledge Beijing's great power aspirations while finding ways to "signal that it is prepared to welcome a growing role for China in regional and global security affairs." If it wants Beijing to become more "transparent" about defense budgets and force planning, the Pentagon must take steps of its own to soothe the anxieties of the People's Liberation Army by inviting observers to military exercises and exploring possibilities for collaboration in humanitarian relief, peacekeeping, and combating piracy. Above all, the U.S. government should attempt to build "habits of cooperation and coordination" and to reduce "mutual suspicions" by initiating a sustained high-level dialogue on military issues to complement similar talks that are already ongoing in the area of economic policy.[22]

As to trade and finance, the ties between the two nations are now so dense, so complex, and so vital to the well-being of both partners that they require something more than periodic talks between top officials. Toward this end, a number of analysts have suggested that the United States and China join together in a "Group of Two" that will provide "effective joint leadership of the world economy."[23] Such an arrangement would formalize what is already true in fact, and would bind the "G-2" together more tightly than ever before.

In addition to links between governments, believers in "soft power" argue that Washington should do whatever it can to promote ever-deeper personal and cultural connections between the two societies. American colleges and universities already host many Chinese students, and a smaller but growing number of young Americans now seek similar experiences in China. In addition, the federal government should ease visa restrictions on Chinese visitors, open consulates in more parts of China, and encourage Beijing to do the same in the United States, especially in midsize cities where "urban dwellers have few opportunities to learn about China."[24]

Enhancing engagement also requires taking active steps to avoid unnecessary friction. Nothing has been more problematic in this regard than recurrent American attempts to encourage political reform, starting with increased protections for human rights, especially freedom of religion and speech. While some observers stress how far China has come since the Maoist era, most acknowledge that U.S. efforts to promote political change "have not been highly successful."[25] It is time for Washington to reexamine this long-standing aspect of its policy toward China.

To the most fervent advocates of engagement, the question is not how best to sharpen and refine the tactics for encouraging reform, but rather how far to back away from the entire project of democracy promotion. There are varying views on this question. All agree that the United States should "rededicate itself to leading by example," and avoid "overheated rhetoric" or unduly confrontational public diplomacy.[26] Most favor a mix of "quiet diplomacy" and occasional public comment in multilateral forums regarding China's adherence to "global norms."[27]

Others are ready to go even further. A 2009 report by one prominent think tank makes virtually no mention of human rights or political reform and emphasizes instead the importance of "displaying respect" for China, while constructing "a new narrative" of Sino-American relations that will help the people of both countries to "gain a deeper appreciation for the overall success of engagement."[28] Dissenting from an earlier report that urged continued, mild pressure for reform, influential financier Maurice ("Hank") Greenberg objected to the "persistent urging of democracy in China." If the country is to liberalize, writes Greenberg, "it has to be their own choice."[29] The implication is obvious: the United States and its allies should let the subject drop. While few would go quite this far, most experts now agree that outsiders can have, at best, an indirect impact on China's political trajectory. In light of the demonstrated resiliency of the Communist Party regime, the United States should concentrate on working with it to solve pressing problems and integrating it into the existing international system, rather than trying to transform it.

Such an attitude is not logically incompatible with a tough stance on balancing, but, in practice, the advocates of enhanced engagement generally do not favor such an approach. Because they take a fairly relaxed view of Chinese power, these analysts and policy makers tend to be more concerned with reassuring Beijing than with bolstering deterrence. Thanks to its ongoing military buildup (generally referred to less menacingly as a process of "military modernization"), China's strength is growing, but it continues to trail the United States in most important respects. According to a 2007 study by the Council on Foreign Relations (co-chaired by Admiral Dennis Blair, former commander of U.S. forces in the Pacific and a future director of national intelligence in the Obama administration), "The United States enjoys space, air, and naval superiority over China and it will continue to do so for some time to come. The military balance today and for the foreseeable future strongly favors the United States and its allies." It will be decades before China can hope to become a true "peer competitor."[30]

There is, writes one scholar, no cause for either "alarm [or] exaggerated assessments" of Chinese power. Of course Washington should continue to keep a close eye on regional military developments, maintain its forces, bases, and alliances in East Asia, and, on occasion, provide defensive arms to Taiwan. But "Beijing's strategic advances do not require a major change in Washington's defense or regional security policy."[31] In fact, the real danger is not that the United States will do too little to preserve its position in the Western Pacific, but that it will try to do too much. American overreaction would feed China's insecurity, provoke it into an even more rapid buildup, and confirm the warnings, and enhance the influence, of the most retrograde elements in the national leadership.[32]

Avoiding such a spiral of mutual mistrust demands what Deputy Secretary of State James Steinberg referred to in a 2009 speech as a policy of "strategic reassurance." This involves more than simply being "transparent" about defense budgets and military programs. According to Steinberg, it requires the recognition of a "core, if tacit, bargain": "just as we and our allies must make clear that we are prepared to welcome China's 'arrival' . . . as a prosperous and successful power, China must reassure the rest of the world that its development and growing global role will not come at the expense of [the] security and well-being of others."[33]

Some worry that by continuing to combine balancing (or hedging) with engagement, the United States is already behaving in an unnecessarily hostile and aggressive fashion. In the words of John Podesta, former chief of staff to President Clinton and a respected voice in Democratic Party policy circles, the United States needs to "move beyond the 'engage and hedge' framework for China policy—an approach openly premised on mistrust and suspicion—to a strategy that maximizes opportunity" while also, in some unspecified fashion, "managing risk."[34]

For some, the alleged necessity of continued balancing is primarily a figment of the imagination of what retired U.S. ambassador Chas Freeman describes as a "military-industrial complex [that] has acquired a vested interest in demonizing China." Certainly once the Taiwan issue has been resolved, the possibilities for Sino-American cooperation will expand, while the prospects for conflict, and the need for the United States to maintain a strong military presence in Asia, dwindle. The sooner this happens, the better for all concerned. China's rise to power, its absorption of an island of only twenty-three million people, and its emergence as the preponderant player in Asia are inevitable. And, writes Freeman (quoting Edmund Burke), "The heart of diplomacy is to grant graciously what you no longer have the power to withhold."[35] Taken far enough, enhanced engagement thus becomes indistinguishable from appeasement.

The problem with this approach is not so much what it includes as what it leaves out. Enhancing engagement without doing more to maintain a favorable balance of power amounts to doubling down on an already risky bet. It is like pushing more and more chips onto a single square at the roulette wheel, or building a new addition to a house that sits astride a geological fault line, while simultaneously cutting back on homeowner's insurance.

Will the gamble pay off? Broadening and deepening engagement could lead to greater cooperation on some issues of concern to both Washington and Beijing, but recent experience suggests that Americans should not get their hopes up. The reason why the United States and China have failed to work more closely on combating terrorism, countering proliferation, disciplining "rogue regimes," and reducing their bilateral trade deficit is not a shortage of dialogue but a divergence of interest. To believe that more, higher-level talks will persuade Beijing to see things Washington's way, accept its rules, and follow its lead, even as China's power grows and its options expand, is either naive or condescending, and quite possibly both.

Given the differing interests of states at very different stages of industrial development, it also seems fanciful to suggest that the struggle to control carbon emissions can, in itself, provide the cornerstone of a new, improved Sino-American relationship. Indeed, this problem seems at least as likely to be another source of contention between the Pacific powers as it is to be the seed from which a new entente will grow. Cooperation on climate change is no doubt desirable, but that does not mean it will be achieved, still less that confronting this danger will transform the character of world politics.

Even if the engagers' fondest dreams come true, and dialogues of every shape and size spring forth, the mixed, and mutually mistrustful, relationship between the United States and Communist-ruled China will remain fundamentally unchanged. Americans will still look askance at a government they see as repressive, secretive, and lacking in democratic legitimacy, and they will continue to worry that as its power grows, the current Chinese regime will seek to displace the United States as the dominant power in Asia. For their part, China's rulers will no doubt welcome the chance to draw closer to Washington and they will be delighted to receive fewer lectures about human rights. But they will continue to see America as a nation determined to cling to its hegemonic privileges and driven by its ideology to seek their eventual removal from power.

If the efforts of outsiders to promote political change in China have thus far accomplished little, it is hard to see how doing *less* in this regard will achieve more. Some of the "enhanced engagers" do not appear to care very much about this. Their goal, stated with varying degrees of candor, is to build the best possible ties with China regardless of how it is ruled. Others continue to harbor hopes of change but believe that the United States can do more to hinder it, by taking steps that hard-liners can cast as hostile or disrespectful to the Chinese people, than to speed it along. Conversely, more engagement, more deference, more reassurance, and less criticism should help to undercut the arguments of conservative hyper-nationalists and bolster those of the more liberal, cosmopolitan, and reform-minded members of the Chinese elite.

This is a pleasing theory, but one that has virtually no empirical evidence to back it up. The idea that China's leadership contains hawks and doves, liberals and conservatives, "good guys" and "bad guys" seems plausible to Americans familiar with their own patterns of domestic politics. Indeed, there may be people among the think tankers and university professors who now opine publicly on questions of foreign and domestic policy to whom these labels could reasonably be applied. Within the Chinese governing elite, however, there appears to be far more unanimity than difference. Here, as senior CIA analyst Paul Heer points out, "the hard-liners versus moderates dichotomy is a false one." Certainly since the purges that followed the 1989 Tiananmen "incident," the range of acceptable debate on domestic questions has become much narrower. On these issues, writes Heer, China's leaders are "all moderates, and they are all hard-liners." On economic policy, there has been no serious challenge to Deng Xiaoping's market-oriented reforms. Regarding politics, however, "Chinese rulers are all hard-liners, since they retain a commitment to socialism, albeit with Chinese characteristics, and to Communist Party rule."[36]

Supposing that factions of some kind do exist, it is by no means obvious how their influence would be affected by external events. The notion that a low-key, nonconfrontational American approach will favor China's "moderates" has an intuitive appeal. But the opposite is at least equally plausible. If Washington adopts a softer, more acquiescent stance, Chinese "hard-liners" will no doubt try to take the credit, arguing that the change was a direct result of tough policies, like the sustained military buildup, that they championed. Attempts at accommodation could wind up strengthening precisely the groups and individuals it was intended to weaken.

Regardless of how wide the gap between their military capabilities is at present, the combination of Chinese momentum and American restraint cannot help but accelerate the pace at which the divide narrows. If the optimists are wrong, and the balance is already close or, regardless of the objective reality, if China's leaders *believe* it to be, then unilateral restraint could turn out to be a very dangerous policy indeed. While most advocates of enhanced engagement pay lip service to the importance of preserving a favorable military balance, their reading of the current situation, combined with their strong desire to avoid antagonizing Beijing, inclines them toward inaction rather than action. When the time comes to make decisions, they are likely to be wary of deploying additional forces to the Western Pacific, developing new weapons specifically designed for a possible conflict with China, going "too far" in tightening defense ties with U.S. friends and allies, or creating new multilateral mechanisms to enhance strategic cooperation among Asia's democracies. If their arguments carry the day, the shift in the regional balance of military power toward China will accelerate.

There are several dangers here. Because of the long lead times involved in designing, building, and deploying new capabilities, it is hard to quickly reverse unfavorable trends in the balance of military power. If today's leaders fail to make sound decisions when conditions are reasonably tranquil, their successors may find it very difficult to respond in a timely fashion in the future if the Sino-American relationship unravels or if China becomes unstable and unexpectedly aggressive.

An unduly muted reaction to China's ongoing buildup could also increase the risk of misperception, miscalculation, and unintended conflict. Washington's seeming passivity could be taken, not as a sign of self-confidence, but as an indication of a waning commitment to some or all of its longtime friends and allies in Asia. Depending on how they assess the military balance, planners in the People's Liberation Army may already be more optimistic about their capabilities than outsiders realize. Even if they are not, absent a vigorous American response, their sense of assurance can only grow with time. In some future showdown with a third party, Beijing might assume that Washington was disinterested, deterred, or both, only to find out too late that it was neither. The fact that the U.S. government has a history of not always being clear, even in its own collective mind, about how it would respond until confronted by aggression makes this an even more plausible, and worrisome, scenario.[37]

As it works to reassure Beijing by not overreacting to its initiatives, the United States may also succeed, albeit inadvertently, in demoralizing its own friends. There are already signs of anxiety emanating from some Asian capitals about America's willingness and ability in the long run to maintain its position of regional military preponderance. What seems like a prudent, measured response could appear from the other side of the Pacific as an indication of resignation and the start of a slow retreat. Overreaction doubtless has its dangers, but underreaction could wind up triggering a cascade of appeasement that will hasten the very outcome that American strategists are now trying to prevent.

Eleven

CAN AMERICA KEEP
ITS BALANCE?

GETTING ENGAGEMENT RIGHT

Along with all its other aspects, China's rise presents an intellectual challenge to the American people and their leaders. For much of the past century the United States has had the luxury of being able to divide the world neatly into two clear-cut camps. Its most important friends and military allies have tended to be democracies with whom it did the great bulk of its business, while its strategic rivals were authoritarian regimes with whom it talked little and traded less. China has shattered this mold and rearranged the pieces into an unfamiliar and disconcerting pattern: it is neither a friend nor, at this point, an avowed enemy, and despite the repressive character of its government, it is among America's most important commercial partners.

Dealing effectively with this novel and ambiguous situation requires first of all that Washington find accurate and realistic language with which to describe it. This is not as easy as it might seem. Since the days of Richard Nixon and Henry Kissinger, American political leaders, diplomats, and China specialists have been strongly inclined to "accentuate the positive," playing up actual or potential accomplishments and areas of agreement, describing the relationship in the most glowing and optimistic terms, and generally understating or ignoring deeply rooted problems and enduring differences. This tendency has been the product of an evolving mix of considerations: a desire to reassure China and to sustain what was at first a fragile bilateral diplomatic process; the perceived need to defend a sometimes-controversial policy from domestic critics, to justify it to the

American people, and to claim credit for its achievements; and a deep and genuine belief on the part of many policy makers that engagement was, and is, the only path to peace.

Unfortunately, the endless stream of diplomatic happy talk emanating from Washington has done very little to change Beijing's perceptions of U.S. intentions and strategy; these are as hardnosed and skeptical as ever. However, the impact of such language on America's domestic discourse has been substantial and problematic. Praising China unduly in hopes that its accomplishments will someday live up to Washington's lofty rhetoric risks raising public expectations to unrealistic levels, thereby setting the stage for disappointment and a possible future backlash. Even more important, ceaselessly exaggerating the quality of Sino-American relations can only make it harder for U.S. political leaders to win support for the costly and difficult measures that will be needed to maintain a favorable balance of power in Asia. "If things are so good," an astute taxpayer might well ask, "why do we need to spend billions on arms, bases and alliances in the Western Pacific?"[1] Why indeed?

Squaring this circle will demand greater candor about past accomplishments, current challenges, and emerging threats. In addition to praising Beijing when it does the right thing (agreeing to orchestrate talks over North Korea's nuclear program), American leaders ought to feel free to express their disappointment when it falls short (failing to apply sufficient pressure to actually bring Pyongyang to heel) and their disapproval when it does wrong (supporting repressive regimes in Southeast Asia, Africa, and Latin America). Failing to speak frankly gives a free pass to a Beijing regime that is often surprisingly sensitive to public criticism. More important, it conveys an unrealistic and incomplete picture of a complex and evolving relationship to the American people and to its strategic partners. China is not an ally, nor is it a trusted friend; it is an increasingly powerful and important country with which the United States seeks cooperation wherever possible, but it is also a nation that, under its present leadership, has interests and objectives that are at times in direct opposition to America's own.

As regards China's military buildup, official commentary should not be confined to obscure annual reports read only by specialists, or occasional cryptic remarks in speeches by admirals or defense secretaries. The ongoing accumulation of arms by Beijing is a development with far-reaching and potentially dangerous implications. U.S. leaders should not pretend otherwise by seeming to downplay or ignore it. They should make clear in their pronouncements that America does not seek confrontation with China and, indeed, is eager to avoid it. But hard experience has taught that the best way to keep the peace is by preserving a favorable balance of power. For as long as China keeps augmenting its strength, the United States and its allies will feel compelled to respond in kind. Saying this will not shock or offend Beijing, and among other benefits, it will have a salutary effect on domestic discussion of long-term defense needs, especially as the United States begins to reduce its commitments to Iraq and Afghanistan.

Washington also needs to rethink what it says and does about the Chinese government's continuing refusal to grant basic political freedoms and civil liberties to its citizens. In place of the existing grab bag of initiatives, reports, and speeches, Washington needs a more deliberate and well-integrated approach to this problem. The place to start, once again, is with a healthy dose of reality. Despite the fond hopes of theorists and policy makers, economic growth has not yet led to political reform in China, nor are there any signs that it is about to. What the world has learned over the past two decades is that in the face of determined and clever opposition, the link between economic change and political progress is not as direct, nor as strong, as was once assumed. American officials should be candid in acknowledging this fact, but they should present it as a challenge rather than an unalterable truth. The question is not whether the United States should continue trying to encourage political reform in China, but how it can do so more effectively.

The answer must inevitably involve a mix of words and deeds. Public hectoring may be useless or even counterproductive, but silence would send a resounding signal of resignation and retreat. As its wealth and influence have grown, Beijing has been increasingly successful in using threats of economic retaliation to intimidate other governments into toning down or abandoning their criticisms of its abysmal human rights record. The Chinese authorities would like nothing more than to bend Washington to their will in similar fashion. If the United States can be induced to back further away from its earlier, outspoken stance, it will only confirm what

Beijing has said all along: that America's alleged concern for democracy and personal liberties is a cynical sham, designed to serve its own selfish interests while humiliating China and holding it down. The Americans talk a good game, but now that there is a price to be paid for their outspokenness, they turn out to be no different, and certainly no more principled, than anyone else.

Questions of sincerity aside, a shift in policy that is widely seen as a response to China's growing stature can only serve to weaken America's long-term position in Asia. If Washington has to trim its sails and watch its words, others will be forced to draw the logical conclusions, not only regarding their own stance on human rights, but also about the shifting balance of power. In the face of what it can only regard as a signal of dwindling American strength, Beijing will no doubt do the same.

Soft-pedaling talk of freedom will not reassure China's leaders as much as it will embolden them, and it will be deeply demoralizing to those in China (like the brave signatories of the recent "Charter o8" document) who continue to believe in, and to take risks for, real reform.[2] Whatever it says publicly about general principles and specific abuses, the U.S. government should be looking for ways to help these people. Most will not even have an explicitly political agenda. Groups that campaign against corruption and the continued destruction of the natural environment, or for old-age pensions, improved health care, worker's rights, impartial courts, and freedom of worship will be able to do more in the near term to push China toward responsive and accountable government than those who advocate a multiparty political system or a free press. The U.S government, nongovernmental organizations, universities, churches, and private foundations can all play a part in assisting these advocates of social change.

To say, as some Western analysts do, that reform is ultimately the responsibility of the Chinese people is both obvious and deeply disingenuous. No outside power could impose alien and unwelcome institutions on a nation of 1.3 billion souls, nor is any sane person advocating such a policy. But the great bulk of China's population has few rights, little power, and no say in their country's future. To suggest that when they are ready, these people can simply choose democracy gravely understates the obstacles and dangers they face, while conveniently absolving outsiders of any obligation to try to help them.

Beijing's strategy for domestic control depends on keeping its many critics atomized and isolated. The Chinese Communist Party knows full well that if the individuals and groups that object to various aspects of its rule can communicate easily across regions and issues, they may be able to form a critical mass that will be impossible to repress or ignore. It follows that the most valuable thing the United States and the other advanced democracies can do to promote the cause of reform is to enable the freest possible flows of information into, out of, and within China. The best way to do that, in turn, is to encourage the development of software and other tools that will permit users to evade the state's efforts to track their communications or block their access to global information networks. A game of measure-versus-countermeasure is already well under way in cyberspace, and American involvement in it need not be directed specifically at Beijing, but rather at any regime that engages in similar repressive practices.[3] As a complement to these measures, the U.S. government, along with nongovernmental organizations like the Electronic Frontier Foundation and stockholders associations, should also make it embarrassing, and perhaps illegal, for American companies to assist China's security services.[4] The decision by search engine giant Google to withdraw from China rather than continue to submit to government restrictions on politically sensitive content was an admirable gesture, even if it has not yet inspired many imitators.[5] At a minimum, America's private sector, like its government, should seek to avoid doing anything that will hurt the cause of freedom.

The reluctance of policy makers and pundits to speak ill of China stems, in part, from a fear that doing so will fan the flames of irrational Sinophobia at home and play into the hands of those who, for ideological or other nefarious reasons, seek to derail relations with Beijing. Since the "Red Scare" of the 1950s there has been a sense among specialists that China policy should be shielded as much as possible from the vicissitudes of normal politics and the unruly passions of the American public.[6] The use of political advertisements blaming China for America's economic woes in the 2010 congressional elections has helped to stir these fears anew.[7] And yet, to judge by opinion polls, popular attitudes toward China have tended to be at least as subtle, and arguably more sensible, than those of "elites."

Thus, for example, a recent survey found that while on balance the public had favorable attitudes toward China (50 percent favorable versus 38 percent unfavorable), a majority (53 percent) also recognized that its growing power could pose a threat to the United States. By comparison only 21 percent of the members of the Council on Foreign Relations acknowledged this danger, while 58 percent took the optimistic view that China was destined to grow in importance as a "partner or ally" of the United States. What is more, fully 43 percent of council members expressed no concern over the possibility that China might grow to equal America's military power, a situation that only 29 percent of the public found acceptable. Where China is concerned, the American people seem more balanced, more prudent, and better able to hold two seemingly contradictory ideas in their minds than the nation's elites.[8]

The truth is that China is too important to be left to the China hands. The incentives and inhibitions at work in the academic and business worlds and, to some extent, within government itself have led to an artificial and unwholesome narrowing in the range of views that are considered to be acceptable by the self-selected guardians of "responsible" opinion. And yet, many of the most important questions are those to which no one can honestly claim to have definitive answers: Does China, in fact, have a grand strategy, and if so, what are its aims? Can the Communist Party preserve its power while maintaining economic growth, and if so, for how long? What will be the impact of coming demographic shifts on economic performance and social stability?

It is not the case that any perspective on these issues is as good as the next, but it is certainly true that there is a wider range of plausible possibilities than much of the expert discourse in recent years has been prepared to acknowledge. As they weigh long-range strategies and near-term decisions, policy makers and planners need to be sure that they are exposed to alternative interpretations of events and the full panoply of forecasts about the future. Under the present dispensation they are simply not going to get such diversity from the fraternity of established China-watchers. Someone, most likely a mix of government agencies and private foundations, is going to have to fund the research of serious analysts who take a range of underrepresented (and often unpopular) alternative views on key strategic issues. The purpose of this activity is not necessarily to displace or discredit what is now mainstream opinion, but rather to supplement and challenge it in ways that can help reduce the risk of error and surprise.[9]

Because the stakes are so high, the economic dimension of engagement continues to be the most important. For the same reason, it is also the area in which it is most difficult to reevaluate and readjust policy in ways that better reflect the interests of the United States as a whole, as opposed to those of particular sectors, companies, or individuals. Here special pleading is rife, and it is usually wrapped in lofty appeals to principle. Alongside those who profit from engagement but support it with references to world peace and free trade, are others who fear commercial competition from China yet cast their opposition in terms of the imperatives of national security. Neither can be said to occupy the moral high ground.

In such a charged atmosphere, dispassionate analysis and careful calibration of policy are difficult, to say the least. To complicate matters further, the available instruments—tariffs, sanctions, restrictions on investment, export controls—are imprecise, clumsy, and capable of doing much harm if misapplied. For this reason, and because, on balance, economic engagement with China continues to serve U.S. interests, policy makers should incline toward gradual adjustments rather than major, sudden shifts in direction.

As regards trade, Washington should concern itself primarily with the net balance in flows of goods, services, and capital between the two countries, rather than with the specific composition of those flows or their absolute level. In other words, while pleas for protection from specific industries should be regarded with skepticism, China's huge bilateral trade surpluses, and its continued accumulation of dollar-denominated assets, are a legitimate cause for concern. The latter phenomenon, in particular, carries real strategic risks. If the United States wants to maintain the greatest possible freedom of action, it cannot allow itself to remain deeply indebted to any one country, let alone the nation that is emerging as its primary geopolitical rival.[10]

The present lopsided relationship, in which the United States imports more than it exports from China and pays the difference in dollars, has more to do with America's economic policies than with the undeniable fact that China is employing various unfair trading practices. The most effective way to correct the problem is not to impose tariffs on specific Chinese goods, but rather to reduce the overall gap between what America imports and what it exports. A revaluation of the yuan, which Beijing continues to hold at artificially low levels by buying dollars, would certainly help. Ultimately, however, the solution lies closer to home. If the American people want to shrink the trade deficit and reduce their dependence on foreign capital, they and their government are going to have to consume less and save more.

If the 2008–9 financial meltdown has a silver lining, it is that it has forced Americans to alter their spending habits and has produced at least a temporary jump in personal savings. Unfortunately, in its attempts to mitigate the effects of the crisis, the federal government has simultaneously engaged in massive "dis-saving," running huge deficits and accumulating debts whose effects will linger for many years to come. It may take some novel and potentially controversial long-term measures, such as the introduction of a national consumption tax or a tax on energy use, to ensure that personal savings remains up while the budget deficit comes down. Regardless of the means by which it is achieved, however, such a correction is essential.[11]

A change in American patterns of savings and consumption could help induce China to make matching adjustments of its own. With the dissolution of many state-owned enterprises, most Chinese workers no longer have guaranteed jobs or pensions. Acting rationally in the face of these uncertainties, they have become remarkably frugal, often saving as much as 20 percent of their incomes to guard against the day when they are too old or sick to work.[12] In order to sustain growth as exports to the United States decline, Beijing is going to have to find ways to stimulate domestic demand by diverting some of these savings into consumption. The most obvious way of doing that, in turn, is to create some kind of social safety net, funded with a mix of public and private contributions, which will provide protection against becoming destitute in old age.

In addition to reducing its vulnerability to financial pressure, a rebalancing of the bilateral trade relationship could have several additional economic and strategic benefits for the United States. If Beijing permits exchange rates to rise and encourages domestic consumption, American exporters should benefit. As China becomes a more consumer-oriented society, in which individuals not only have rising incomes but also are less insecure and able to exercise an ever-widening range of personal choice, it may also see an increase in demands for political rights. Robust social welfare programs will absorb a larger fraction of the national budget and will therefore compete with the military and the security services for scarce resources. Public enthusiasm for displays of military power and assertive external policies may be tempered by the knowledge that these come at the expense of less generous pensions or publicly provided health care. In short, a "rebalanced China" would be a more humane, and possibly a more democratic society, and there is a good chance that it would also be a less vigorous and committed strategic competitor than it is today.

High-tech trade and investment is one area of the overall economic relationship that deserves special attention from policy makers. Over the next several decades the United States and China are likely to be engaged in an intense military-technical rivalry, one in which the United States will have to work hard to sustain a margin of advantage over its increasingly capable competitor. Staying ahead will require both that the United States continue to move forward in the design and development of new military systems, and that it does nothing that makes it easier for China to close the gap that currently separates the two countries.

The latter problem has several aspects, some old and relatively familiar and others quite new. Since the end of the Cold War, the U.S. government has wrestled with the question of whether it should keep trying to control exports of products or knowledge that might help potential enemies develop sophisticated new weapons. Representatives of the business and scientific communities have long argued that in a globalized economy, in which U.S.-based firms no longer have a monopoly on the development of critical technologies, controls are useless, if not positively harmful to American competitiveness. In today's "flat" world it is no longer possible to contain innovation within national boundaries.[13]

Sweeping generalizations about the futility of export controls need to be reexamined in light of the emerging strategic competition with China. Even skeptics acknowledge that there are some areas of American advantage (including stealth and encryption) where unilateral controls continue to make sense.[14] In addition, if several other technology leaders (including India, Japan, and South Korea) have reason to fear that improved Chinese weapons will be aimed at them, there may be new possibilities for some types of multilateral controls.

The only way the Soviets could get their hands on sensitive Western technology was by stealing it. China too engages in extensive scientific and industrial espionage, using both the time-honored techniques of bribery and theft, and the newer and often more effective methods of cyber-penetration and exploitation. In addition to slipping past firewalls, however, China has the option of simply walking in through the front door. Acting on their own or at Beijing's direction, Chinese firms now have the wherewithal to buy foreign companies that will either give them direct access to what they need or put them in a better position to penetrate other, more closely protected enterprises.

The prospect of cash-rich foreigners buying up American brand names and coveted landmarks aroused anti-Japanese fears in the mid-1980s, and twenty years later, it has provoked similar worries in some quarters about China. Much of this anxiety is misplaced. The purchase by Chinese investors of Maytag or IBM's computer manufacturing division, and the attempted takeover of a major U.S. oil concern, all stirred controversy in the mid-2000s, but none posed a real danger to national security.[15]

Not all transactions will be so innocuous, however. Permitting Chinese companies to sell next-generation telephone switching equipment to one of America's biggest service providers might make it easier for China's intelligence services to tap into sensitive U.S. and allied communications.[16] Similarly, Chinese ownership of a chip manufacturing firm that supplies components for high-end IT products could create opportunities for Beijing to penetrate or sabotage other governments' computers, communications systems, and even weaponry.[17] Despite a tendency in some quarters to dismiss all such scenarios as science fiction, or the products of an outdated, Cold War mindset, some will turn out to be all too real. The challenge for policy makers will be to separate genuine threats from imaginary ones, and to resist pressures for action (or inaction) that are motivated by the pursuit of profits, rather than a genuine concern for the nation's security.

In the long run, the only way to maintain a technological edge is not by holding others back but by continuing to move forward. The blueprint for doing this is no secret, nor has it changed substantially since it was drawn up in the wake of the Second World War. The foundations are formed by a first-class educational system, a society open and attractive to talented and ambitious immigrants, and generous public and private support for basic scientific research. Vibrant civilian industries, with ready access to capital, and a tax and legal code that reward innovation provide the scaffolding. A flexible, diverse, and competitive array of defense manufacturers, serving a well-funded and forward-looking defense establishment, complete the structure. China is now trying to adapt key elements of this scheme to its own purposes. Whether the United States still has the ability and the seriousness of purpose to follow its own design remains to be seen.

PRESERVING A FAVORABLE BALANCE OF POWER

Even as it continues to engage China, the United States must work with its friends and allies to maintain a margin of military advantage sufficient to deter attempts at coercion or aggression. Assuming that China's power continues to grow, this will require even greater exertion and closer cooperation in the future than it has in the past.

Once again, it is important to begin with words. In this case, what matters most is not what Washington says, but how it responds to what *Beijing* says. Chinese spokesmen can be relied on to react with great vehemence to any attempt at stepped-up balancing, whether in the form of new force deployments, arms sales to U.S. friends, or closer cooperation with regional allies. If it senses a chance to delay or derail a major initiative, Beijing will unleash a full-blown influence campaign in which public statements are accompanied by private warnings to both the United States and its local partners. Similar messages will be delivered via seemingly independent but mutually reinforcing channels: one-on-one conversations with trusted interlocutors, and unofficial "Track II" dialogues involving academics and think-tank analysts, as well as formal diplomatic *demarches*.[18] The bottom line in every case will be the same: "what you are contemplating is a dangerous and unnecessary provocation that endangers peace and stability, and risks triggering an arms race, if not an actual war."

Eager to sustain the forward momentum of engagement, and hopeful of undercutting Chinese "hard-liners" in imagined internal debates, American policy makers have at times been too quick to take such warnings at face value. This is a serious mistake. If they wish to retain their freedom of action, U.S. officials are going to have to become much more discerning and tough-minded in responding to, and at times simply ignoring, Chinese rhetoric. Beijing needs to be broken of the habit of trying to use blood-curdling warnings to dissuade the United States from doing what it deems essential to defend its interests and support its allies.

Without active cooperation from its regional partners, Washington cannot hope in the long run to balance against a rising China. On the other hand, without strong tokens of its continuing commitment and resolve, America's friends may grow fearful of abandonment, perhaps eventually losing heart and succumbing to the temptations of appeasement. A serious response to China's military buildup is therefore vital both for its own sake and for its potentially spine-stiffening effects on others.

The Pentagon's top priority over the course of the coming decade must be to find cost-effective ways to blunt, counter, sidestep, and defeat the rapidly maturing anti-access/area denial capabilities of the People's Liberation Army. The reasons should be readily apparent. If Beijing comes to believe that it can destroy U.S. forces and bases in the Western Pacific in a first strike, using only conventional weapons, there is a chance that it will someday try to do so. Such an attack would obviously carry with it grave risks. The decision to launch it would therefore come, not from the clear blue sky, but at a moment of extreme duress, when China's leaders had convinced themselves that inaction or delay would mean defeat, humiliation, and a possible loss of power. Should such a moment ever arrive, the U.S. position in Asia must appear so strong and so resilient that Beijing will ultimately choose to stand down rather than risk everything on a "cosmic roll of the dice."[19]

It is important to remember that both China's political elites and its military establishment would approach the prospect of war with the United States with even more than the usual burden of doubt and uncertainty. Unlike Mao, Deng, and their contemporaries, the present generation of party leaders has no experience of war, revolution, or military service. Perhaps more important, the PLA itself has no recent history of actual combat. Unlike the U.S. military, which has fought repeatedly since the end of the Cold War, China's armed forces have not engaged in large-scale operations since 1979, when they turned in a less-than-impressive performance against Vietnam. This fact, combined with its rapid modernization, means that the PLA is increasingly armed with weapons that it has never used in combat, and led by officers who have never heard a shot fired in anger.

The effects on political-military decision making of this unusual situation are by no means clear. A healthy degree of uncertainty and doubt on the part of generals and party officials could make both even more reluctant to pull the trigger than they might otherwise be. On the other hand, untested military men of questionable stature may be more prone to displays of overconfidence, and perhaps more reluctant to tell their superiors that despite massive investments over many years, they still lack usable options. For their part, inexperienced political leaders may be more inclined to accept without question the judgment of their military advisors.

The United States and its allies should aim to reinforce doubts within China about the likely effectiveness of new weapons systems, war plans, and concepts of operation. Among other things, this will require striking a balance between drawing the attention of domestic and allied audiences to PLA advances, without at the same time encouraging Chinese observers to exaggerate the capabilities of their own forces. It may also require, on occasion, that the U.S. government reveals some of what it knows about the PLA's weaknesses and vulnerabilities, rather than holding back every scrap of information against the day when it might be needed to fight and win a war. There are clearly opportunities here for disinformation and deception on both sides, coupled with real risks of misperception and miscalculation.

China's anti-access strategy depends on its ability to use nonnuclear weapons to strike U.S. and allied forces, facilities, and capabilities throughout the Western Pacific. Deterring such an attack will require taking visible steps to reduce its chances of success by dispersing, hardening, or otherwise defending the targets at which it would be directed. Some of the necessary measures will be expensive, but many would also be relatively simple. Reinforcing aircraft hangars and command posts, investing in runway repair kits, or surveying dozens of "expedient" airfields on small Pacific islands would not advance the frontiers of military science.

But such steps could reduce the PLA's confidence in its ability to gain control of the skies in the early stages of a future war. Hardening satellites and computer networks, and preparing rapid "work-arounds" or replacements, would be more challenging and costly, but should help make U.S. forces resilient in the face of even the most sophisticated first strike. Even if they are less than perfect, defenses against incoming ballistic and cruise missiles could also complicate the task of those hoping to score quick kills against land bases or ships at sea. In the case of the latter, new techniques for disabling or deceiving an enemy's land, sea, and space-based sensors could help to improve the survivability and extend the utility of aircraft carriers and other surface combatants.[20]

Modern wars are not won on the defensive, however, nor can they be deterred reliably by adopting a purely passive and reactive posture. As China improves its ability to attack targets off its eastern coast, the United States and its allies are going to have to find new ways of threatening to conduct conventional counterstrikes against the mainland. Because of the widening reach of Chinese military operations, this will require concealing the platforms from which strikes are launched and extending the range of the weapons that carry them out. Moving in this direction is certain to stir controversy on several counts. New systems for projecting power will be costly and time-consuming to develop, and they will divert resources from the kinds of weapons traditionally preferred by the armed services. Instead of more massive aircraft carriers and sleek manned fighter jets, the evolving strategic situation requires some mix of long-endurance unmanned aerial vehicles, submerged or low-observable "arsenal ships" loaded with precision weapons, long-range conventional ballistic missiles, and perhaps a new intercontinental-range stealthy manned bomber.[21]

Beijing will denounce the acquisition of these new offensive capabilities as aggressive and destabilizing, a charge that can be answered in part by pointing out that it was *China's* deployment of hundreds of ballistic missiles and other offensive weapons over many years that finally forced the United States and its regional allies to respond in kind. The United States and its allies aim to strengthen deterrence by restoring a balance upset by China's relentless buildup. Public rhetoric aside, PLA planners and serious observers across Asia must be made to understand that should China hit U.S. forces or the territory of its allies with conventional weapons, the United States has the option of ordering proportionate and militarily effective counterattacks of its own. The prospective scope and scale of these strikes must be sufficiently large so as to disrupt or destroy key components of Beijing's anti-access/area denial capability, including weapons and ground-based sensors and satellite links, as well as potentially threatening the functioning of its economy and perhaps of its mechanisms for maintaining domestic political control. Mere pinpricks against coastal targets, of the sort that the United States can carry out today, using a relative handful of comparatively short-range manned aircraft and sea-launched cruise missies, will not do the job.[22]

The contribution of nonnuclear offensive and defensive capabilities to deterrence will grow as the credibility of the American nuclear guarantee dwindles. As China's intercontinental-range nuclear arsenal becomes larger and less vulnerable, the likelihood that the United States would respond to conventional aggression with nuclear attacks, never large, will fall even further. As happened during the Cold War, the emergence of a durable nuclear stalemate is going to force the burden of deterrence down to lower levels of conflict. Rather than investing scarce resources in trying to recapture its earlier advantages (by deploying a "thick" national missile defense system or trying to acquire the capability to locate and destroy all of China's land- and sea-based ballistic missiles before they could be launched), Washington would be wiser to focus on improving the survivability and offensive power of its conventional forces.

Despite its dwindling credibility, the United States should not abandon the threat of nuclear escalation altogether by signing on to a "no first use" pledge. Assuming that such a paper promise had any impact at all on PLA planners, it would be to weaken deterrence by taking away a residual source of uncertainty about the potential risks of a conventional attack. On the other hand, because the United States has never before been willing to forgo the option of escalation, agreeing to no-first-use would be correctly perceived by its allies as a major change in policy. Such a shift, coming in obvious response to China's increasing strength, could not help but raise questions about the future viability of American security guarantees.

Even as Washington abandons any thought of maintaining a meaning-ful margin of nuclear advantage, U.S. planners need to be certain that their Chinese counterparts do not come to believe that they can somehow acquire an edge of their own. This may appear fanciful in a world in which the United States continues to deploy thousands of nuclear weapons while China has hundreds, only a fraction of which can reach American terri-tory. But if the Obama administration is serious about its pledge to seek the abolition of nuclear weapons, and about its desire to make deep cuts in the current arsenal as a step in that direction, the situation could change. If Washington builds down while Beijing builds up, the balance could narrow further and faster than now appears plausible.

The aspect of America's present position of military advantage that is likely to have the greatest geopolitical payoff in the long run is its com-mand of the global commons and, in particular, of the world's oceans. Assuming that current trends continue, over the next several decades China is going to become even more heavily dependent on seaborne imports of energy and raw materials than it is today. Beijing is already spending a great deal on pipelines and other projects designed in part to mitigate the strategic vulnerability that results from these circumstances, and it has begun to take steps toward acquiring elements of an oceangoing navy that might eventually enable it to defend its sea lines of communica-tion and perhaps also to threaten those of its neighbors.

For a mix of geographic, economic, technical, and historical reasons, however, Beijing is unlikely to be able to improve its situation any time soon. Assuming that it cannot supply its needs from sources accessible by land, China is going to have to continue to import energy and other resources by sea, using ships that must travel great distances, along routes that pass through narrow choke points and close to the shores of several major competitors, before arriving at a comparative handful of large ports along its eastern coast.[23] And even if it could somehow reduce its reliance on imported resources, the vitality of the Chinese economy will continue to depend on its ability to import and export manufactured products by sea. Like it or not, in the last thirty years China has become a maritime nation. In contrast to India, Japan, and Australia, however, to say nothing of the United States, it has virtually no experience in building, training, maintaining, or operating a blue water navy. It has no modern seafaring tradition and, at least until quite recently, showed few signs of having a political-naval-industrial complex of the sort that has propelled the acquisition of sea power in other rising states.[24]

Unless they believe that they can fight, win, and resolve a war very quickly, Chinese planners will have to reckon for some time to come with the disruptive and potentially devastating consequences of a prolonged naval blockade. If only because most conflicts are begun on the assumption that they will be over "before the leaves fall," there is no guarantee that this will deter war; but it should certainly help.

There is one potential wildcard in the deck that American strategists have only recently begun to ponder. If, in the next few years, Taiwan is absorbed by the mainland, whether through coercion or consent, and if China is able to use the island for military purposes, the naval situation could change to its advantage. Using eastward-looking sensors, antiship missiles whose range would now extend farther out to sea, and submarines able to slip easily into the deep waters of the Pacific, Beijing might be able to impose a counterblockade of its own. Threatening to disrupt shipping flowing north, to Japan and South Korea, or east, across the Pacific to the Western Hemisphere, would not solve all of China's problems, but it would put it in a better position to dissuade others in East Asia from taking sides with the United States.[25] While it might appear desirable on other grounds, a premature resolution of the Taiwan issue could thus turn out to be damaging, not only to the Taiwanese people but also to the security and autonomy of the region's other democracies.[26]

It is these countries that ultimately form the hard core, or rather the sturdy outer rim, of the American position in Asia. Far from being obsolete, the so-called hub-and-spokes arrangement that took shape during the Cold War remains indispensable. Whatever else it does, Washington needs to tend to its bilateral ties with democratic treaty allies (Japan, South Korea, Australia, and, to the extent possible, Thailand and the Philippines) and quasi-allied democracies (Taiwan, Mongolia, and, above all, India). Over time, it should seek to establish a similarly close and cooperative relationship with Indonesia. All of these actors share a commitment to democratic governance and, despite their increasingly tight economic integration, a common desire not to be dominated by China. Asia's democracies are America's true friends and enduring strategic partners, and America's leaders should not be afraid to say so.

Since the early 1990s, the United States has developed good relations with one key quasi-democratic state (Singapore), and in the future it may move toward closer cooperation with several plainly authoritarian regimes with which it nevertheless shares strong strategic interests. Despite lingering ideological bonds between the two countries, Vietnam has a deep and long-standing fear of China and a history of at times bloody resistance to its rule. While there are obviously limits to how far they can prudently go, the United States, Japan, and India all have reason to want to see Hanoi retain its strategic independence. Certainly if China had access to naval bases and airfields along the Vietnamese coast, the People's Liberation Army Navy would be in a much stronger position to regulate maritime traffic through the South China Sea, as well as to control the resources that may lie beneath its surface.

Russia is the biggest prize in any contest for the allegiance of Asia's nondemocratic powers. For two decades now, Beijing has enjoyed the considerable benefits of good relations with its neighbor to the north: ready access to energy and arms, and freedom from the necessity of having to defend a long and inhospitable frontier. In time, however, China's growing power and increasing assertiveness may cause Moscow to reconsider its orientation and perhaps to seek reassurance from the West. A warier and more distant relationship with Russia could complicate Beijing's strategic planning problems, not least by reducing its confidence that, in a crisis, it could count on ready access to energy, replacement weapons, and spare parts. Pulling Russia out of China's orbit would thus have a positive impact on the balance of power in Asia, just as prying China away from the Soviet Union did in the 1970s. Even as it works to block Russian revanchism in Europe, Washington should try to avoid doing anything that would foreclose this possibility.

In addition to strengthening bilateral links, the United States must seek to integrate Asia's democracies more closely with one another. The absence of a region-wide grouping of some kind is an historical anomaly, the result of distance and a divergence in strategic perspective between Northeast and Southeast Asia, as well as an abiding postwar animosity in both regions toward Japan. Lack of strategic coordination is a luxury that the democracies can no longer afford; if they hope to balance China's growing power, they are going to have to find ways to resolve their differences, pool their resources, and align their policies.[27]

Some of the proposed mechanisms for achieving these ends, such as an Asian equivalent of NATO, are not presently feasible. Uncertainty about China's future and reasonable concerns over provoking it unnecessarily make this suggestion a nonstarter, at least for the moment. A "community of Asian democracies" would have a softer edge and could conceivably be part of a broader global coalition of like-minded states. The democracies certainly have a good deal to talk about that has little directly to do with China, including how best to coordinate their diplomacy, investment, and foreign aid so as to promote the spread of liberal norms across the region. Those who object to this idea on the grounds that it would be "divisive" or offensive to authoritarian regimes should recall that the European Union is an international organization with strict political entry requirements. The fact that China has established its own club for authoritarians in Central Asia (the Shanghai Cooperation Organization) should also help ease concerns about creating a loose league of Asian democracies.

Toward this end, the United States should focus in the near term on promoting communication and cooperation among the various bilateral and "mini-lateral" groupings that have already sprung up across the region. A logical place to start is by revitalizing the idea of a pan-Asian "quad." The United States is allied to Japan and Australia; Japan and India have begun to consult with one another on naval issues and other sensitive topics, as have India and the United States, Australia and Japan, and India and Australia. It makes perfect sense for the four countries to meet together on occasion to compare notes and share information. Similarly, Washington should do everything in its power to encourage reconciliation and a resolution of recent tensions between Japan and South Korea. The on-again, off-again trilateral meetings of defense officials should be put on a firmer footing. If Australia or others from outside Northeast Asia wish to be included in these discussions, so much the better.

The goal of all this communication and cooperation would be to promote candid discussion among like-minded governments and to set up regular multilateral mechanisms for sharing information, discussing options in various contingencies, and establishing common procedures for communication and possible joint military operations. In the event that it becomes necessary to solidify these ties into something more closely resembling a traditional alliance, much of the necessary groundwork will already have been laid. China will not like any of this, to be sure, but that should not inhibit the democracies from defending themselves and securing their interests.

What about more inclusive, region-wide institutions that would incorporate nations regardless of the character of their regimes? Various structures have been proposed in recent years, including an East Asian Community modeled on the European Economic Community and a concert of Northeast Asia's major powers that would include at least five of the six participants in the Six Party Talks (the United States, China, Japan, Russia, and South Korea). Beijing has put its weight behind "ASEAN Plus Three," a grouping that consists of the Southeast Asian nations, plus Japan, South Korea, and China.

While it cannot prevent their formation, Washington should discourage its friends from placing undue reliance on organizations that deny it a place at the table. More generally, it should favor institutions that are trans-Pacific and pan-Asian (i.e., including India) rather than exclusively East Asian in membership. Given the degree of economic integration among these regions, and the transregional character of many of the non-economic problems that need to be addressed, more open structures make a good deal of sense. Not coincidentally, they also happen to have the virtue of being more difficult for Beijing to dominate.

Openness should also be the theme of America's trade policy, both at home and in Asia. Resisting protectionism is essential to maintaining the best possible relationship with China, but it is also vital to countering the growing gravitational pull of China's economy. If the United States were to close its market to Asian exports and investments, the region would become even more heavily dependent on China. Beyond providing economic benefits for all concerned, American openness will undercut Chinese efforts to put itself at the center of an exclusive regional economic bloc.

Much the same goes for flows of people. As China continues to build successful universities, laboratories, and cutting-edge industries, it will become a magnet for people of talent and ambition throughout Asia and the world. If anti-immigrant sentiment and fear of terrorism result in permanent high barriers to entering the United States, it could deprive itself of the steady influx of talented, ambitious men and women that has always been one of its most valuable advantages in the global competition in science and technology.

America's place as an Asian power rests not only on economic and strategic interests but also on enduring ties of family, faith, and personal experience. For many decades these have bound the United States closely to South Korea, Japan, Australia, and the Philippines. Today they are linking it to India and to China as well. If these connections are to flourish, they must be constantly refreshed. For America, continued openness is not only an expression of self-confidence, it is an enduring source of national strength. The surest way for the United States to keep its balance in Asia and in the world is to remain true to its finest traditions.

Appendix: Sources and Methods

My account of Chinese strategy, particularly in the period since the turn of the century, is based largely on English translations of some seventy articles published in nearly two-dozen professional journals, newspapers, and magazines, all of which are available either online or at libraries in the United States.[1] The great majority of the articles cited here appeared in a handful of publications linked to one of China's major think tanks or research institutes. These organizations, in turn, are typically sponsored either directly or indirectly by an agency of the state or the party.

Of the sources listed in table 1, five account for over half of the citations:

Xiandai Guoji Guanxi [Contemporary International Relations] is published by the State Council's Chinese Institutes of Contemporary International Relations, a think tank linked to the Ministry of State Security, China's main civilian intelligence agency.

Heping Yu Fazhan [Peace and Development] is published by the Peace and Development Research Center, which is affiliated with the People's Liberation Army.

Guoji Wenti Yanjiu [Journal of International Studies] is published by the China Institute for International Studies, which is linked to the Ministry of Foreign Affairs.

Dangdai Yatai [Contemporary Asia-Pacific] is published by the Chinese Academy of Social Sciences, Institute of Asia-Pacific Studies. The Academy of Social Sciences is administered by the State Council.

Zhanlue Yu Guanli [Strategy and Management] was the journal of the

Chinese Society for Strategy and Management, an organization founded in 1989 by several prominent party officials, including members of the State Council and the military. The journal was closed in 2004 by the Propaganda Department, allegedly because it published articles critical of North Korea and prematurely favorable to improved relations with Japan.

With the partial exception of *Strategy and Management*, these are respected publications that generally reflect the main currents of "responsible" opinion on a range of topics. None carries articles by extreme nationalists, for example, such as those that can be found on various websites. In certain respects, these journals convey information similar to what can be gleaned from reading their American equivalents: *Foreign Affairs, Foreign Policy*, the *Washington Quarterly*, the *National Interest*, combined with opinion pieces published in major newspapers like the *New York Times* and the *Washington Post*. Taken together they give a sense of which issues are receiving the most attention from the community of Chinese strategists and foreign policy analysts, indicate the array of positions on those issues, suggest the areas where there seems to be a broad consensus, and point to at least some where there are divergences of opinion.

One obvious and important difference between the public discussions of foreign policy in the two countries is that in China debate is closely monitored and controlled by the authorities. As a result, in striking contrast to the United States, there are no attacks on the wisdom or competence of top officials and few direct criticisms of current policy. Certain options are also notable by their absence and appear to have been ruled outside the bounds of acceptable public discussion. Internal debates, in which many of the same analysts take part, and which are sometimes conducted in the pages of restricted-circulation journals, are reportedly freer and more wide-ranging.

As in the American case, with a few exceptions, articles in open publications represent the views of people who are not actually in the government. The extent to which any given author's opinions reflect or have an influence on the thinking of policy makers cannot therefore be determined with certainty. Some of those cited here are known to have access to the inner circles of the party and state.[2] While access does not necessarily imply influence, it is probably safe to assume that their opinions carry more weight than those who are less well known, are less senior, or are affiliated with less prestigious institutions. In order to help the reader make judgments about the relative weight to attach to any given piece of writing, I have included a list of all of the authors cited (table 2), along with their titles and affiliations. In most cases, these were current as of the date of publication.

Table 1. List of Sources

PUBLICATION	ENGLISH	TYPE OF PUBLICATION	DESCRIPTION	ACCESS
China Daily Online	China Daily Online	Daily newspaper's web edition	The website of China's official English-language newspaper.	http://www.chinadaily.com.cn
Dangdai Yatai	Contemporary Asia-Pacific	Monthly journal	Published by the Chinese Academy of Social Sciences, Institute of Asia-Pacific Studies. Articles focus on political, economic, and security issues related to the Asia-Pacific region.	Available through East View, China Academic Journals Full-Text Database, http://china.eastview.com: 1994–present
Guoji Luntan	International Forum	Bimonthly journal	Published by Beijing Foreign Studies University.	Available through East View, China Academic Journals Full-Text Database, http://china.eastview.com
Guoji Wenti Yanjiu	Journal of International Studies	Bimonthly journal	Published by the China Institute of International Studies, which is linked to the Ministry of Foreign Affairs. Prints articles on foreign policy, especially on the Asia-Pacific region.	Most issues available at George Washington University's Global Resources Center: 2000–2, 2004, 2006–present
Guoji Xianqu Daobao	International Herald Leader	Weekly newspaper	Published through Xinhua's Cankao Xiaoxi (Reference News) with many articles focusing on foreign policy.	Available at http://www.xinhuanet.com/herald/

(continued)

Table 1 (*continued*)

PUBLICATION	ENGLISH	TYPE OF PUBLICATION	DESCRIPTION	ACCESS
Guoji Zhanwang	World Outlook	Semimonthly journal	Published by the Shanghai Institute of International Studies. Publishes articles largely on domestic events in foreign countries, but sometimes covers international issues.	Available through East View, China Academic Journals Full-Text Database, http://china.eastview.com: 1994–present
Guoji Zhengzhi Yanjiu	International Studies Quarterly	Quarterly journal	Published by Peking University's Institute for International Relations. Publishes articles on international relations and international politics.	Available through East View, China Academic Journals Full-Text Database, http://china.eastview.com: 1980–present
Heping Yu Fazhan	Peace and Development	Quarterly journal	Sponsored by the Peace and Development Research Center. Usually prints articles on foreign policy issues. Sometimes prints translations in English.	Some issues available at George Washington University's Global Resources Center: 1999–2003; for more recent items, see East View, China Academic Journals Full-Text Database, http://china.eastview.com: contains 1994–present
Huanqiu Shibao	Global Times	Daily online	Newspaper published by Renmin Ribao and published online on Huanqiu Wang. Focuses on international relations and politics, as well as foreign views of China.	Available at http://www.huanqiu.com; English edition available at http://www.globaltimes.cn
Liaowang	Outlook Magazine	Weekly journal	Published by Xinhua. Often carries general articles on political, economic, social, cultural, and foreign policy topics.	Available through World News Connection, http://wnc.dialog.com/
Qiushi	Seek Truth Journal	Semimonthly journal	Published by the CCP Central Committee. Publishes social, economic, and political articles.	Available at http://www.qsjournal.cn
Renmin Ribao Online	People's Daily Online	Daily newspaper's web edition	The website of China's official newspaper, *Renmin Ribao* [People's Daily].	Available at http://www.people.com.cn/

PUBLICATION	ENGLISH	TYPE OF PUBLICATION	DESCRIPTION	ACCESS
Shiji Jingji Baodao	Twenty-first Century Business Herald	Daily newspaper's web edition	Daily website of Guangdong Provincial CCP Committee's daily newspaper, *Nanfang Ribao.*	Available at http:// www.nanfangdaily .com.cn
Shijie Jingji Yu Zhengzhi	World Economics and Politics	Monthly journal	Published by the Chinese Academy of Social Sciences, Institute of World Economics and Politics. Focused on international political and economic issues.	Available through the Chinese Electronic Periodical Service, http://www.ceps.com: 2005–present
Shijie Zhishi	World Affairs	Semimonthly journal	Published by the World Affairs Publishing House, which is under the Chinese Ministry of Foreign Affairs. Prints pieces on international issues and foreign policy.	Most issues available at Princeton University East Asian Library: 1955–2008, some 2009. Available also through East View, China Academic Journals Full-Text Database, http:// china.eastview.com: 1994–present
Waijiao Pinglun	Foreign Affairs Review	Bimonthly journal	Published by the China Foreign Affairs University.	Most issues available at George Washington University's Global Resources Center: 1993–94, 1997, 2001–5. Additional issues may be available through East View, http:// china.eastview.com.
Xiandai Guoji Guanxi	Contemporary International Relations	Monthly journal	Published by the State Council's Chinese Institutes of Contemporary International Relations (CICIR). Generally publishes articles focusing on foreign policy and the Asia-Pacific region.	Most issues available at George Washington University's Global Resources Center: 1981–97, 2001–present
Zhanlue Yu Guanli	Strategy and Management	Bimonthly journal	Defunct (as of 2004) journal that published foreign policy articles considered controversial or beyond the scope of acceptable debate.	Issues referenced in this book are available at George Washington University's Global Resources Center: 1998–2000, 2003–4

(continued)

Table 1 (*continued*)

PUBLICATION	ENGLISH	TYPE OF PUBLICATION	DESCRIPTION	ACCESS
Zhongguo Dangzheng Ganbu Luntan	Chinese Cadres Tribune	Monthly journal	Sponsored by the CCP Party School. Contains articles on political, economic, and CCP-related issues, often authored by Party School professors, members of the State Council, and ministerial and provincial officials.	Most issues available at George Washington University's Global Resources Center: 1997–98, 2000–present
Zhongguo Junshi Kexue	China Military Science	Quarterly journal	Published by the PLA Academy of Military Science and the China Military Science Association.	Most issues available at George Washington University's Global Resources Center: 1992–93, 1995–97 [in storage], 2005–present.
Zhongguo Pinglun	China Review	Monthly magazine	Published in Hong Kong. Pro-PRC with articles focused on the PRC, Taiwan, Hong Kong, and overseas Chinese issues.	Available online at http://gb.chinareview news.com
Zhongguo Qingnian Bao	China Youth Daily	Daily newspaper	Published by the Communist Youth League of the CCP Central Committee. Publishes articles on political, economic, and social issues, as well as public opinion.	Available at http://www.cyd.com.cn and also http://www.zqb.cyol.com

CCP, Chinese Communist Party; PLA, People's Liberation Army; PRC, People's Republic of China.

Table 2. List of Authors

AUTHOR	AFFILIATION
Bian Qingzu	Former secretary-general, Chinese People's Association for Friendship with Foreign Countries
Chai Liu	Reporter, CCTV Overseas Center
Chang Shanshan	PhD student at the China Institutes of Contemporary International Relations
Chen Xulong	China Institute of International Studies
Chi Diantang	MA student, Institute of Southeast Asian Studies, Jinan University
Chu Shulong	Professor at Qinghua University
Cui Liru	President, China Institutes of Contemporary International Relations
Da Wei	Associate researcher of the Institute of American Studies, China Institutes of Contemporary International Relations
Dong Manyuan	Fellow at the China Institute of International Studies
Feng Zhaokui	Former deputy head of the Japanese Studies Institute of the Chinese Academy of Social Sciences, research fellow at the Chinese Academy of Sciences
Fu Mengzi	Director of the Institute of American Studies at the China Institutes of Contemporary International Relations
Gao Yiwei	Graduate student, College of International Relations, China Institutes of Contemporary International Relations
Gao Zhenyuan	Senior research fellow, China Institute of International Studies
Gao Zichuan	Associate Professor at the Naval Command College
Gao Zugui	Research fellow, Division of Security and Strategic Studies, China Institutes of Contemporary International Relations
Guo Yuli	Deputy director and professor, Institute of International Strategy and Development
Hou Songling	Associate professor, Institute of Southeast Asian Studies, Jinan University
Hu Angang	Chair Professor and Director of the Center for China Studies at Tsinghua University
Hu Xiaowen	Writer for *Beijing Shijie Zhishi*
Jin Canrong	Assistant dean at School of International Relations, China People's University; deputy director at the Center for American Studies
Li Hongmei	Columnist, People's Daily Online
Li Xiaohua	PhD student at the World Economics and Politics Department of the Chinese Academy of Social Sciences Graduate School
Li Yonghui	Dean of the School of International Relations at Beijing Foreign Studies University
Lin Limin	Director and researcher, Center for Strategic Studies, China Institutes of Contemporary International Relations
Lin Xinzhu	PhD student at the Institute of International Strategy and Development at Qinghua University

(continued)

Table 2 (*continued*)

AUTHOR	AFFILIATION
Liu Huaqiu	Director of the State Council Foreign Affairs Office
Liu Jianfei	Professor and deputy director, The Institute of International Strategic Studies, the Central Party School of the CCP
Lu Gang	Master's researcher, Strategic Studies Institute, National Defense University
Ma Zhengang	Director, Chinese Institute for International Studies
Men Honghua	Professor at the Institute of International Strategic Studies, China's Central Party School
Ni Shixiong	Former dean of the School of International Relations and Public Affairs and former director of the Center for American Studies at Fudan University
Niu Jun	Professor of International Relations, Peking University
Niu Xinchun	Associate researcher, China Institutes of Contemporary International Relations; guest researcher, Center for Peace and Development Studies
Qin Yaqing	Vice dean and professor of China Foreign Affairs University
Shang Hong	Research fellow with the China Institute for International Strategic Studies
Shi Yinhong	Professor of International Relations and director of Center on American Studies at Renmin University of China
Song Guoyuo	Lecturer at the Center for American Studies, Fudan University
Tang Shiping	Institute of Asia-Pacific Studies, Chinese Academy of Social Sciences
Tang Yongsheng	Deputy director of the Strategy Institute at China's National Defense University
Wang Jisi	Dean of the School of International Studies at Peking University and director of the Institute of International Strategic Studies at the Party School of the Central Committee
Wang Wanzheng	Postdoctoral scholar with the Central Compilation and Translation Bureau, and chief editor of *Current Affairs*
Wang Wenfeng	Associate researcher of the Institute of American Studies, China Institutes of Contemporary International Relations
Wang Yusheng	Department of International Studies, executive director of the Chinese Foundation for Strategic Research Center
Xu Jian	Former Chinese ambassador to Romania
Xu Ping	Associate professor, Contemporary International Relations Center, Jilin University
Xu Wangsheng	International Studies Division, Foreign Language Institute, People's Liberation Army
Yan Xuetong	Director of the Institute of International Studies, Tsinghua University
Yang Yi	Admiral and director of Institute of Strategic Studies, National Defense University
Yao Youzhi	Major general, director of the Department of Strategic Studies at the Academy of Military Sciences
Ye Zicheng	Professor, Institute of International Relations, Peking University

AUTHOR	AFFILIATION
Yin Chengde	Fellow, of China Institute of International Studies
Yu Xintian	Director, Shanghai Institute for International Studies
Yuan Jirong	Scholar, Institute of American Studies, Chinese Academy of Social Sciences
Yuan Peng	Director of Institute for American Studies, China Institutes of Contemporary International Relations
Zhang Wenling	Academic committee member of the Chinese Academy of Social Sciences and director of the academic committee of the International Department
Zhang Yunling	Director and research fellow of the Institute of Asia-Pacific Studies, Chinese Academy of Social Sciences
Zhao Changqing	Deputy director and senior researcher, Institute for Euro-Asia Social Development Studies at the State Council's Center for Development Studies
Zhao Huasheng	Director, Center for Russia and Central Asia Studies, Center for Shanghai Cooperation Organization Studies, Fudan University
Zhao Qinghai	Associate researcher, China Institute of International Studies
Zheng Yu	Researcher at the Institute of East European and Central Asian Studies, Chinese Academy of Social Sciences

Notes

INTRODUCTION: A CONTEST FOR SUPREMACY

1. Jed Babbin and Edward Timperlake, *Showdown: Why China Wants War with the United States* (Washington, D.C.: Regnery, 2006).
2. Interview with Lee Kuan Yew, October 22, 2009, *Charlie Rose*, http://www.charlie rose.com/download/transcript/10681.

CHAPTER 1: MEANS OF ASCENT

1. Several observers have described this process as one in which the center of gravity of the international system is shifting to the Pacific. See, for example, Henry Kissinger, "A Global Order in Flux," *Washington Post*, July 9, 2004, p. A19.
2. J. H. Parry, *Europe and the Wider World, 1415–1715* (London: Hutchinson's University Library, 1949), pp. 42–43. The exploits of the Portuguese explorers are discussed in Robert D. Kaplan, *Monsoon: The Indian Ocean and the Future of American Power* (New York: Random House, 2010), pp. 47–66.
3. K. M. Panikkar, *Asia and Western Dominance: A Survey of the Vasco da Gama Epoch of Asian History, 1498–1945* (London: George Allen and Unwin, 1959).
4. Of course, it was precisely these advantages that allowed Europe to lay the ground for its eventual domination of Asia, as well as much of the rest of the world. As historian Carlo Cipolla points out, "The gunned ship developed by Atlantic Europe in the course of the fourteenth and fifteenth centuries was the contrivance that made possible the European saga." Carlo M. Cipolla, *Guns, Sails, and Empires: Technological Innovation and the Early Phases of European Expansion, 1400–1700* (New York: Minerva Press, 1965), p. 137. Overall, notes one survey, "the technological superiority of the east over the west" continued until the late Middle Ages when "the balance began to swing, and the technological superiority of western Europe to emerge." A. R. Hall, "The Rise of the West," in Charles Singer et al., eds., *A History of Technology*, vol. 3: *From the Renaissance to the Industrial Revolution, c 1500–c 1750* (Oxford: Clarendon Press, 1957), p. 709. Historian William H. McNeill refers to the period from 1000 to 1500 as "the era of Chinese predominance." See William H. McNeill, *The Pursuit of Power: Technology, Armed Force, and Society since A.D. 1000* (Chicago: University of Chicago Press, 1982), pp. 24–62.

5. John K. Fairbank, Edwin O. Reischauer, and Albert M. Craig, *East Asia: The Modern Transformation* (Boston: Houghton Mifflin, 1965), p. 10.

6. Parry, *Europe and the Wider World*, pp. 42–43.

7. P. O'Brien, "Europe and the World Economy, 1492–1789," in Hedley Bull and Adam Watson, eds., *The Expansion of International Society* (New York: Oxford University Press, 1984), p. 60.

8. Panikkar, *Asia and Western Dominance*, p. 315.

9. Angus Maddison, *Chinese Economic Performance in the Long Run* (Paris: Organisation for Economic Co-operation and Development, 1998), pp. 40–41.

10. E. J. Jones, *The European Miracle: Environments, Economies and Geopolitics in the History of Europe and Asia* (New York: Cambridge University Press, 1987), p. 41.

11. David S. Landes, *The Wealth and Poverty of Nations: Why Some Are So Rich and Some So Poor* (New York: W. W. Norton, 1998), p. 186.

12. Gale Stokes, "Why the West? The Unsettled Question of Europe's Ascendancy," *Lingua Franca* vol. 11, no. 8 (November 2001), pp. 508–525; David D. Buck, "Was It Pluck or Luck That Made the West Grow Rich?" *Journal of World History* vol. 12, no. 2 (1999), pp. 413–430.

13. Kenneth Pomeranz, *The Great Divergence: China, Europe, and the Making of the Modern World Economy* (Princeton: Princeton University Press, 2000), p. 207. For respectful but skeptical analyses of Pomeranz's arguments, see P. H. H. Vries, "Are Coal and Colonies Really Crucial? Kenneth Pomeranz and the Great Divergence," *Journal of World History* vol. 12, no. 2 (2001), pp. 407–446; J. Bradford DeLong, "China's Advocate: A Review of Ken Pomeranz's *The Great Divergence*," March 2000, at http://econ161.berkeley.edu/TotW/pomeranz.html.

14. Landes, *Wealth and Poverty of Nations*, p. 175.

15. Max Weber, *The Religion of China: Confucianism and Taoism*, trans. Hans Gerth (Glencoe, Ill.: Free Press, 1951); Mark Elvin, "Why China Failed to Create an Endogenous Industrial Capitalism: A Critique of Max Weber's Explanation," *Theory and Society* vol. 13 (1984), pp. 379–391.

16. Richard A. Easterlin, "Why Isn't the Whole World Developed?" *Journal of Economic History* vol. 41, no. 1 (March 1981), p. 17.

17. See, for example, Douglass C. North and Robert Thomas, *The Rise of the Western World: A New Economic History* (New York: Cambridge University Press, 1973).

18. Jones, *European Miracle*, pp. 67, 119.

19. Ibid., p. 107.

20. Jared Diamond, *Guns, Germs, and Steel: The Fates of Human Societies* (New York: W. W. Norton, 1999), pp. 414–416.

21. Daniel R. Headrick, *The Tools of Empire: Technology and European Imperialism in the Nineteenth Century* (New York: Oxford University Press, 1981), p. 130.

22. Despite this rough technological parity, comparatively small European forces were sometimes able to achieve victory, thanks to superior organization, discipline, and doctrine. Thus advantages in military "software," rather than "hardware," were critically important in permitting the British to consolidate their control over much of India in the 1770s and 1780s. Gayl D. Ness and William Stahl, "Western Imperialist Armies in Asia," *Comparative Studies in Society and History* vol. 19 (1977), pp. 2–29. William McNeill notes that from 1700 to 1850, Europe's expansion was enabled by a mix of superior organization and firepower. Thereafter it

was driven by advances in "steam transport and the associated transformation of the metallurgical industries . . . quick-firing, long-range firearms . . . [and] the growth of medical knowledge" that permitted Europeans to survive in hostile climates. See Michael Howard, "The Military Factor in European Expansion," in Bull and Watson, eds., *Expansion of International Society*, pp. 33–43. Quote from p. 38.

23. Headrick, *Tools of Empire*, p. 84.

24. François Godemont, *The New Asian Renaissance: From Colonialism to the Post–Cold War* (New York: Routledge, 1997), p. 25.

25. D. K. Fieldhouse, *The Colonial Empires: A Comparative Survey from the Eighteenth Century* (New York: Delacorte Press, 1967), pp. 190–201.

26. Richard A. Pierce, *Russian Central Asia, 1867–1917: A Study in Colonial Rule* (Berkeley: University of California Press, 1960), p. 19.

27. David J. Dallin, *The Rise of Russia in Asia* (New Haven: Yale University Press, 1949), pp. 17–30, 123–150.

28. Panikkar, *Asia and Western Dominance*, p. 129.

29. Harry G. Gelber, *Nations out of Empires: European Nationalism and the Transformation of Asia* (London: Palgrave, 2001), p. 3.

30. Paul Kennedy, *The Rise and Fall of Great Powers: Economic Change and Military Conflict from 1500 to 2000* (New York: Random House, 1987), pp. 148–149.

31. Rupert Emerson, "Introduction," in Rupert Emerson, Lennox A. Mills, and Virginia Thompson, *Government and Nationalism in Southeast Asia* (New York: Institute of Pacific Relations, 1942), p. 11.

32. For the details of one such relationship, see Peter Duus, *The Abacus and the Sword: The Japanese Penetration of Korea, 1895–1910* (Berkeley: University of California Press, 1995), pp. 245–288.

33. Maddison, *Chinese Economic Performance*, pp. 25, 40.

34. Ibid., p. 40.

35. Efforts to improve military capabilities often led to more wide-ranging changes in economic and political organization. See David B. Ralston, *Importing the European Army: The Introduction of European Military Techniques and Institutions into the Extra-European World, 1600–1914* (Chicago: University of Chicago Press, 1990).

36. Rupert Emerson, *From Empire to Nation: The Rise to Self-Assertion of Asian and African Peoples* (Boston: Beacon Press, 1960), p. 26.

37. James Mayall, "Nationalism and the International Order," in Michael Leifer, ed., *Asian Nationalism* (New York: Routledge, 2000), p. 188.

38. Gelber, *Nations out of Empires*, p. 147.

39. Quoted in David B. Abernathy, *The Dynamics of Global Dominance: European Overseas Empires, 1415–1980* (New Haven: Yale University Press, 2000), p. 119.

40. Fairbank et al., *East Asia*, p. 773.

41. Ellen Hammer, "Indochina," in Lawrence K. Rosinger and associates, *The State of Asia: A Contemporary Survey* (New York: Alfred A. Knopf, 1951), p. 221.

42. John Keay, *Last Post: The End of Empire in the Far East* (London: John Murray, 1997), p. 245.

43. Abernathy, *Dynamics of Global Dominance*, pp. 148–150.

44. Niall Ferguson, *The War of the World: Twentieth-Century Conflict and the Descent of the West* (New York: Penguin Press, 2006), pp. lxviii–lxix.

45. Lawrence K. Rosinger, "The State of Asia," in Rosinger and associates, *State of Asia*, pp. 9–10.
46. The five waves, and the links among them, are discussed in Shigehisa Kasahara, "The Flying Geese Paradigm: A Critical Study of Its Application to East Asian Regional Development," United Nations Conference on Trade and Development, Geneva, Discussion Paper 169, April 2004, http://www.unctad.org/en/docs/osgdp20043_en.pdf.
47. John Page et al., *The East Asian Miracle: Economic Growth and Public Policy* (New York: Oxford University Press, 1993), p. 101.
48. Hugh Patrick and Henry Rosovsky, "Japan's Economic Performance: An Overview," in Hugh Patrick and Henry Rosovsky, eds., *Asia's New Giant: How Japan's Economy Works* (Washington, D.C.: Brookings Institution, 1975), p. 45.
49. For two views, see Shadid Yusuf, "The East Asian Miracle at the Millennium," in Joseph E. Stiglitz and Shadid Yusuf, eds., *Rethinking the East Asian Miracle* (New York: Oxford University Press, 2001), pp. 1–53; Robert Wade, *Governing the Market: Economic Theory and the Role of Government in East Asian Industrialization* (Princeton: Princeton University Press, 1990), pp. 8–72.
50. Danny M. Leipziger, ed., *Lessons from East Asia* (Ann Arbor: University of Michigan Press, 1997), pp. 4–5.
51. Bruce Cumings, "The Origins and Development of the Northeast Asian Political Economy: Industrial Sectors, Product Cycles, and Political Consequences," *International Organization* vol. 38, no. 1 (Winter 1984), pp. 26–28.
52. See Anne Booth, "The Economic Development of Southeast Asia: 1870–1985," *Australian Economic History Review* vol. 31, no. 1 (March 1991), pp. 21–52.
53. These shifts are summarized in Page et al., *East Asian Miracle*, pp. 123–156. See also Jomo K. S. et al., *Southeast Asia's Misunderstood Miracle: Industrial Policy and Economic Development in Thailand, Malaysia and Indonesia* (Boulder, Colo.: Westview Press, 1997).
54. Stephen Cohen, *India: Emerging Power* (Washington, D.C.: Brookings Institution, 2001), p. 99.
55. Finance Minister Manmohan Singh's 1992 speech making the case for reform is quoted in John Williamson and Roberto Zagha, "From the Hindu Rate of Growth to the Hindu Rate of Reform," Stanford University Center for Research on Economic Development and Policy Reform, Working Paper 144, July 2002, p. 8, http://scid.stanford.edu/pdf/credpr144.pdf.
56. Gurchuran Das, quoted in J. Bradford DeLong, "India Since Independence: An Analytic Growth Narrative," April 2001, p. 5, http://econ161.berkeley.edu/Econ_Articles/India/India_Rodrik_DeLong.pdf.
57. Arvind Virmani, "India's Economic Growth: From Socialist Rate of Growth to Bharatiya Rate of Growth," Indian Council for Research on International Economic Relations, Working Paper 122, February 2004, p. 31, http://www.icrier.org/pdf/wp122.pdf.
58. Maddison, *Chinese Economic Performance*, pp. 40, 97.
59. Gregory Chow, *China's Economic Transformation* (Malden, Mass.: Blackwell, 2007), pp. 24–41.
60. Jung Chang and Jon Halliday, *Mao: The Unknown Story* (New York: Alfred A. Knopf, 2005), pp. 438, 547.

61. Maddison, *Chinese Economic Performance*, p. 56.

62. Barry Naughton, *Growing out of the Plan: Chinese Economic Reform, 1978–1993* (New York: Cambridge University Press, 1995), p. 74.

63. The timing and content of China's reforms are summarized in Organisation for Economic Co-operation and Development, *OECD Economic Surveys: China* (Paris: OECD, 2005), p. 29.

64. The question of the extent of state ownership is more complex than it might appear at first glance. While the number of state-owned enterprises has dwindled since the start of the reform period, many of those that remain are very large in terms of the value of the assets they control. Moreover, some nominally private firms have complex ownership structures that give government officials a substantial say in their operations. See Gao Xu, "State-Owned Enterprises in China: How Big Are They?" East Asia & Pacific on the Rise, blogs.worldbank.org, January 19, 2010, http://blogs.worldbank.org/eastasiapacific/state-owned-enterprises-in-china-how-big-are-they.

65. Justin Yifu Lin, Fang Cai, and Zhou Li, *The China Miracle: Development Strategy and Economic Reform* (Hong Kong: China University Press, 2003), p. 139.

66. Naughton, *Growing out of the Plan*, p. 274.

67. The term "supergrowth" is Angus Maddison's. Maddison, *Chinese Economic Performance*, p. 55.

68. Organisation for Economic Co-operation and Development, *OECD Economic Surveys: China*, p. 32.

69. "The Dragon and the Eagle," *Economist*, October 2, 2004, p. 4.

70. See Dominic Wilson and Roopa Purushothaman, "Dreaming with BRICs: The Path to 2050," Goldman Sachs, Global Economics Paper 99, October 2003, pp. 1–24.

71. The difference reflects the use of either market exchange rates to convert all GDP figures into current dollar values or the so-called purchasing power parity method that seeks to correct for distortions in exchange rates by comparing the cost of similar baskets of goods in each country. In China's case, where exchange rates are artificially low due to government intervention, the latter method produces the higher estimate. See World Bank, *World Development Indicators* (2009); http://siteresources.worldbank.org/DATASTATISTICS/Resources/GDP_PPP.pdf and http://siteresources.worldbank.org/DATASTATISTICS/Resources/GDP.pdf.

72. See Wilson and Purushothaman, "Dreaming with BRICs," pp. 1–24; Albert Keidel, "China's Economic Rise—Fact and Fiction," Carnegie Endowment for International Peace, Policy Brief 61, July 2008, http://carnegieendowment.org/files/pb61_keidel_final.pdf; Jim O'Neill, "The New Shopping Superpower," *Newsweek*, March 21, 2009, http://newsweek.com/2009/03/20/the-new-shopping-superpower.html. Robert Fogel, "$123,000,000,000,000," *Foreign Policy* (January/February 2010), http://www.foreignpolicy.com/articles/2010/01/04/123000000000000.

73. See "China's Investment Boom: The Great Leap into the Unknown," Pivot Capital Management, August 2009, pp. 1–10, http://invest.3888388.com/wp-content/uploads/2009/12/Chinas_Investment_Boom.pdf; "Realty Trouble in the Offing," *Xinhuanet*, July 24, 2010, http://news.xinhuanet.com/english2010/indepth/2010-07/24/c_13412718.htm.

74. See Richard Jackson and Neil Howe, *The Graying of the Middle Kingdom: The*

Demographics and Economics of Retirement Policy in China (Washington, D.C.: Center for Strategic and International Studies, 2004).

75. See World Bank Office, Beijing, *China Quarterly Update—June 2010*, p. 3, http://sitesources.worldbank.org/CHINAEXTN/Resources/318949-1268688634523/Quarterly_June_2010.pdf.

76. For useful surveys of these problems, see Charles Wolf Jr., K. C. Yeh, Benjamin Zycher, Nicholas Eberstadt, and Sung-Ho Lee, *Fault Lines in China's Economic Terrain* (Santa Monica, Calif.: RAND, 2003); C. Fred Bergsten, Bates Gill, Nicholas R. Lardy, and Derek Mitchell, *China: The Balance Sheet* (New York: PublicAffairs, 2006), pp. 18–72.

CHAPTER 2: ROOTS OF RIVALRY

1. Perhaps proving the point that great minds think alike, this witticism, usually attributed to Yankee's great Yogi Berra, was apparently first coined by Nobel Prize–winning physicist Niels Bohr.

2. For further discussion of these issues, see Aaron L. Friedberg, "The Future of U.S. China Relations: Is Conflict Inevitable?" *International Security* vol. 30, no. 2 (Fall 2005), pp. 7–45.

3. These observations form the basis for the so-called realist approach to the study of international relations. For contemporary statements see Hans Morgenthau, *Politics among Nations* (New York: McGraw-Hill, 1985); and Kenneth Waltz, *Theory of International Politics* (New York: McGraw-Hill, 1979).

4. Thucydides, *History of the Peloponnesian War*, trans. Rex Warner (Harmondsworth, U.K.: Penguin, 1972), p. 23.

5. The correlation between increasing power and expanding interests is discussed in Robert Gilpin, *War and Change in International Politics* (New York: Cambridge University Press, 1981), pp. 22–23.

6. See Michael D. Swaine and Ashley J. Tellis, *Interpreting China's Grand Strategy: Past, Present, and Future* (Santa Monica, Calif.: RAND, 2000), pp. 197–229. See also Randall L. Schweller, "Managing the Rise of Great Powers: Theory and History," in Alistair Iain Johnston and Robert S. Ross, eds., *Engaging China: The Management of an Emerging Power* (New York: Routledge, 1999), pp. 7–17.

7. According to the original study of this topic, "One could almost say that the rise of . . . a challenger guarantees a major war." A. F. K. Organski, "The Power Transition" (1958), reprinted in James Rosenau, ed., *International Politics and Foreign Policy* (New York: Free Press of Glencoe, 1961), p. 360.

8. Samuel P. Huntington, "America's Changing Strategic Interests," *Survival* vol. 33, no. 1 (January/February 1991), p. 12.

9. John Mearsheimer, *The Tragedy of Great Power Politics* (New York: W. W. Norton, 2001), p. 400.

10. Michael Doyle, "Kant, Liberal Legacies and Foreign Affairs, Part 2," *Philosophy and Public Affairs* vol. 12, no. 3 (Summer 1983), pp. 325–326.

11. See Mark Burles and Abram N. Shulsky, *Patterns in China's Use of Force: Evidence from History and Doctrinal Writings* (Santa Monica, Calif.: RAND, 2000).

12. Jack Levy, "The Diversionary Theory of War: A Critique," in Manus Midlarsky, ed., *Handbook of War Studies* (London: Unwin-Hyman, 1989), pp. 259–288.

13. A 2007 UPI poll found that a majority of Americans (53.5%) believed the United States has a responsibility to defend Taiwan if the island is attacked by China. "UPI Poll: U.S. Responsibility to Taiwan," United Press International, May 28, 2007, http://www.upi.com/Zogby/UPI_Polls/2007/05/28/upi_poll_us_responsibility_to_taiwan/4667/. A plurality also believe that taking a strong stand on Taiwan, by force, if necessary, is more important than maintaining relations with Beijing. "Most Americans Say Tibet Should Be Independent," CNN, February 18, 2010, http://politicalticker.blogs.cnn.com/2010/02/18/cnn-poll-most-americans-say-tibet-should-be-independent/.

14. Joshua Cooper Ramo, "The Beijing Consensus," Foreign Policy Centre (London, May 2004), pp. 1–61, http://fpc.org.uk/fsblob/244.pdf.

15. Anthony Lake, "From Containment to Enlargement," address at the School of Advanced International Studies, Johns Hopkins University, Washington, D.C., September 21, 1993, http://www.mtholyoke.edu/acad/intrel/lakedoc.html; George W. Bush, "Second Inaugural Address," Washington, D.C., January 20, 2005, http://georgewbush-whitehouse.archives.gov/news/releases/2005/01/20050120-1.html.

16. Michael Doyle, *Ways of War and Peace: Realism, Liberalism, and Socialism* (New York: W. W. Norton, 1997), pp. 250–301.

17. Niall Ferguson and Moritz Schularick, "Chimerica and the Global Asset Market Boom," *International Finance* vol. 10, no. 3 (2007), pp. 215–239; Zachary Karabell, *Superfusion: How China and America Became One Economy and Why the World's Prosperity Depends on It* (New York: Simon and Schuster, 2009).

18. For the liberal view on the pacifying potential of trade, see Richard Rosecrance, "War, Trade and Interdependence," in James N. Rosenau and Hylke Tromp, eds., *Interdependence and Conflict in World Politics* (Aldershot, U.K.: Avebury, 1989), pp. 48–57; for objections to the liberal view, see Robert Gilpin, "Economic Interdependence and National Security in Historical Perspective," in Klaus Knorr and Frank N. Trager, eds., *Economic Issues and National Security* (Lawrence, Kans.: University of Kansas Press, 1978); Barry Buzan, "Economic Structure and International Security: The Limits of the Liberal Case," *International Organization* vol. 38, no. 4 (Autumn 1984), esp. pp. 610–623; see also Anne Uchitel, "Interdependence and Instability," in Jack Snyder and Robert Jervis, eds., *Coping with Complexity in the International System* (Boulder, Colo.: Westview Press, 1993), pp. 243–264.

19. Prior to the outbreak of war, Britain was Germany's second-largest trading partner and its leading export market—absorbing 14.2% of German exports in 1913. For Britain, trade with Germany was greater than with allies like France and Russia. For more on Anglo-German economic interdependence and complementarity, see Paul M. Kennedy, *The Rise of the Anglo-German Antagonism, 1860–1914* (London: Allen and Unwin, 1982), pp. 291–305.

20. These anxieties are discussed in Aaron L. Friedberg, *The Weary Titan: Britain and the Experience of Relative Decline, 1895–1905* (Princeton: Princeton University Press, 1988), pp. 37–38.

21. This point is made in Waltz, *Theory of International Politics*, pp. 129–160.

22. For a discussion of the impact of the 2008–9 crisis on disputes over trade, exchange

rates, and investment, see Aaron L. Friedberg, "Implications of the Financial Crisis for the US-China Rivalry," *Survival* vol. 52, no. 4 (August–September 2010), pp. 31–54.

23. The plausibility of these scenarios is assessed in Daniel W. Drezner, "Bad Debts: Assessing China's Financial Influence in Great Power Politics," *International Security* vol. 34, no. 2 (Fall 2009), pp. 7–45.

24. See Bruce Stokes, "Prime the Foreign Investment Pump," *National Journal*, April 3, 2010, pp. 48–49.

25. For an extreme example, see George Friedman and Meredith Lebard, *The Coming War with Japan* (New York: St. Martin's Press, 1991).

26. Niall Ferguson and Moritz Schularick, "The End of Chimerica," Harvard Business School, Working Paper 10-037, October 2009, pp. 1–31, http://www.hbs.edu/pdf/10-037.pdf. China's apparent attempts to use its near monopoly over production of certain so-called rare earth elements for diplomatic leverage suggests another way in which economic links can contribute to heightened tensions. See Keith Bradsher, "Amid Tension, China Blocks Vital Exports to Japan," *New York Times*, September 22, 2010, http://nytimes.com/2010/09/23/business/global/23rare.html_r=1.

27. For useful overviews, see Miriam Fendius Elman, "The Need for a Qualitative Test of the Democratic Peace Theory," in Miriam Fendius Elman, ed., *Paths to Peace: Is Democracy the Answer?* (Cambridge: MIT Press, 1997), pp. 1–57; and Bruce M. Russett and John R. Oneal, *Triangulating Peace: Democracy, Interdependence, and International Organizations* (New York: W. W. Norton, 2001), pp. 81–124.

28. Henry S. Rowen, "The Short March: China's Road to Democracy," *National Interest* vol. 45 (Fall 1996), pp. 61–70.

29. Bruce Gilley, *China's Democratic Future: How It Will Happen and Where It Will Lead* (New York: Columbia University Press, 2004), pp. xii, 32.

30. See Edward D. Mansfield and Jack Snyder, *Electing to Fight: Why Emerging Democracies Go to War* (Cambridge: MIT Press, 2005); and Jack Snyder, *From Voting to Violence: Democratization and Nationalist Conflict* (New York: W. W. Norton, 2000). Quote from p. 158.

31. For a more pessimistic view, see Denny Roy, "China's Democratised Foreign Policy," *Survival* vol. 51, no. 2 (April–May 2009), pp. 25–40.

32. By one count, the PRC's membership in formal, international governmental organizations more than doubled between 1977 and 1997 (from 21 to 52), while its membership in international nongovernmental organizations soared during the same period, from 71 to 1,163. David M. Lampton, *Same Bed, Different Dreams: Managing U.S.-China Relations, 1989–2000* (Berkeley: University of California Press, 2001), p. 163.

33. Robert B. Zoellick, "Whither China: From Membership to Responsibility?" remarks to National Committee on U.S.-China Relations, New York City, September 21, 2005, http://www.ncuscr.org/files/2005Gala_RobertZoellick_Whither_China1.pdf.

34. For a careful explication of this view by its leading advocate, see Alastair Iain Johnston, *Social States: China in International Institutions, 1980–2000* (Princeton: Princeton University Press, 2008).

35. See Robert Kagan, "The Illusion of 'Managing' China," *Washington Post*, May 15, 2005, p. BO7.

36. This claim about the pacifying effects of nuclear weapons is developed at length in Robert Jervis, *The Nuclear Revolution* (Ithaca: Cornell University Press, 1989).

37. Avery Goldstein, "Great Expectations: Interpreting China's Arrival," *International Security* vol. 22, no. 3 (Winter 1997/98), p. 70.

38. Some of the more alarming episodes are discussed in Scott D. Sagan, *The Limits of Safety: Organizations, Accidents and Nuclear Weapons* (Princeton: Princeton University Press, 1993); and Gordon S. Barrass, *The Great Cold War: A Journey through the Hall of Mirrors* (Stanford: Stanford University Press, 2009).

CHAPTER 3: FROM CONTAINMENT TO ALIGNMENT

1. Karl Marx, *The 18th Brumaire of Louis Bonaparte* (Rockville, Md.: Wildside Press, 2008), p. 15.

2. In 1949, State Department director of policy planning George Kennan went so far as to suggest that the only way to deny Taiwan to the Communists might be to depose Chiang Kai-shek and his corrupt regime and have U.S. forces take control until some kind of plebiscite could be arranged. See David M. Finkelstein, *Washington's Taiwan Dilemma, 1949–1950: From Abandonment to Salvation* (Fairfax, Va.: George Mason University Press, 1993), pp. 178–181.

3. "PPS/39: United States Policy toward China," October 13, 1948, in *Foreign Relations of the United States* [hereafter *FRUS*], *1948*, vol. 8: *The Far East: China* (Washington, D.C.: GPO), p. 150.

4. NSC 48/1, "The Position of the United States with Respect to Asia," December 30, 1949, in U.S. Department of Defense, *United States–Vietnam Relations*, vol. 8 (Washington, D.C., 1971), p. 227. In 1899, the U.S. government circulated diplomatic notes to all the major imperial powers requesting that they do nothing to prevent others from trading in the spheres of influence they had established within China. This is generally seen as the first serious attempt by the United States to intervene on the Asian mainland, and the first in a series of efforts to prevent others from monopolizing Asia's resources. See A. Whitney Griswold, *The Far Eastern Policy of the United States* (New York: Harcourt, Brace, 1938), pp. 36–86.

5. NSC 48/1, "Position of the United States with Respect to Asia," December 30, 1949, p. 228.

6. This is the characterization of a 1949 CIA report, quoted in Melvyn Leffler, *A Preponderance of Power: National Security, the Truman Administration, and the Cold War* (Stanford: Stanford University Press, 1992), p. 298.

7. NSC 48/1, "The Position of the United States with Respect to Asia," p. 253.

8. Ibid., p. 262.

9. Ibid., p. 245.

10. The crossing of the Yalu by Chinese forces has been described as the event that "consummated America's failure to draw China away from the Soviet Union." David Allan Mayers, *Cracking the Monolith: U.S. Policy against the Sino-Soviet Alliance, 1949–1955* (Baton Rouge: Louisiana State University Press, 1986), p. 94.

11. Townsend Hoopes, *The Devil and John Foster Dulles* (Boston: Little, Brown, 1973), p. 222. The 1954 Geneva Conference was called to deal with the consequences of the French defeat in Vietnam.

12. NSC 166/1, "U.S. Policy towards Communist China," November 6, 1953, in *FRUS*, *1952–54*, vol. 14: *China and Japan*, p. 305.

13. Patrick Tyler, *A Great Wall* (New York: PublicAffairs, 2000), p. 56.

14. Hoopes, *Devil and John Foster Dulles*, pp. xiii–xiv.

15. NSC 166/1, "U.S. Policy towards Communist China," pp. 280–281.

16. Ibid., p. 282. Covert operations against the mainland are described in Frank Holober, *Raiders of the China Coast: CIA Covert Operations during the Korea War* (Annapolis: U.S. Naval Institute Press, 1999).

17. Ethnically and religiously distinct, and geographically isolated from the rest of China, Tibet had first been brought under Chinese suzerainty by the Qing emperors. At the beginning of the twentieth century the Tibetans took advantage of China's weakness to reclaim their independence. During the civil war both the Nationalists and the Communists had pledged to bring what they regarded as a renegade province back under Beijing's direct control. In 1950 Chairman Mao made good on his promise by dispatching several divisions of the People's Liberation Army to Tibet. Armed resistance continued for over two decades, and political opposition to Chinese rule persists to the present day. The CIA's operations in Tibet are described in Kenneth Conboy and James Morrison, *The CIA's Secret War in Tibet* (Lawrence: University of Kansas Press, 2002); and John Kenneth Knaus, *Orphans of the Cold War: America and the Tibetan Struggle for Survival* (New York: PublicAffairs, 1999).

18. NSC 166/1, "U.S. Policy towards Communist China," p. 304.

19. Quoted in Shu Guang Zhang, *Economic Cold War: America's Embargo against China and the Sino-Soviet Alliance, 1949–1963* (Stanford: Stanford University Press, 2001), p. 194.

20. For an overview of public opinion on China during this period, see Leonard A. Kusnitz, *Public Opinion and Foreign Policy: America's China Policy, 1949–1979* (Westport, Conn.: Greenwood Press, 1984), pp. 23–94.

21. For a brief review of the Sino-Soviet split, see Doak Barnett, *China and the Major Powers in East Asia* (Washington, D.C.: Brookings Institution, 1977), pp. 32–79.

22. Ibid., pp. 34–37.

23. Undersecretary of State for Political Affairs George McGhee to Assistant Secretary of State for Public Affairs Robert Manning, "Program to Influence World Opinion with Respect to a Chicom Nuclear Detonation," September 24, 1962, with decision memorandum by Secretary of State Rusk attached, dated September 20, 1962, Secret. http://www.gwu.edu/~nsarchiv/NSAEBB/NSAEBB38/document4.pdf.

24. These deliberations are described in William Burr and Jeffrey T. Richelson, "Whether to 'Strangle the Baby in the Cradle,'" *International Security* vol. 25, no. 2 (Winter 2000/1), pp. 54–99. The declassified documents on which this analysis is based can be found at the website of the National Security Archive. See William Burr and Jeffrey T. Richelson, eds., "The United States and the Chinese Nuclear Program," January 12, 2001, http://www.gwu.edu/~nsarchiv/NSAEBB/NSAEBB38/.

25. The dramatic story of the revolution in U.S.-China relations has been told many times, from a variety of perspectives, including that of the major U.S. participants. For a recent treatment that focuses on the initial encounter between the nations'

leaders, see Margaret Macmillan, *Nixon and Mao: The Week That Changed the World* (New York: Random House, 2007).

26. Jeremi Suri, *Henry Kissinger and the American Century* (Cambridge: Harvard University Press, 2007), pp. 161–163.

27. For information on the Soviet buildup and Soviet military strategy, see William E. Odom, "Soviet Military Doctrine," *Foreign Affairs* vol. 67, no. 2 (Winter 1988), pp. 114–134.

28. The origins, unfolding, and devastating impact of the Cultural Revolution are described in all of their brutal detail by Roderick MacFarquhar and Michael Schoenhals, *Mao's Last Revolution* (Cambridge: Harvard University Press, 2006).

29. For a discussion of these events, and how they were interpreted in Washington, see Henry Kissinger, *White House Years* (Boston: Little, Brown, 1979), pp. 171–191.

30. Ibid., p. 192.

31. Kerry B. Dumbaugh and Richard F. Grimmett, *U.S. Arms Sales to China*, Report 85-138F (Washington D.C.: Congressional Research Service, July 8, 1985), p. 3.

32. See U.S. State Department Memorandum of Conversation, "US Reaction to Soviet Destruction of CPR [Chinese People's Republic] Nuclear Capability; Significance of Latest Sino-Soviet Border Clash," August 18, 1969, Secret/Sensitive, http://www.gwu.edu/~nsarchiv/NSAEBB/NSAEBB49/sino.sov.10.pdf.

33. U.S. Embassy Tehran airgram A-383 to State Department, "Soviet Chicom Hostilities," September 4, 1969, Secret, http://www.gwu.edu/~nsarchiv/NSAEBB/NSAEBB49/sino.sov.16.pdf.

34. Kissinger, *White House Years*, p. 182.

35. Ibid.

36. Kissinger's comments are recorded in "Minutes of the Senior Review Group Meeting; Subject: U.S. Policy on Current Sino-Soviet Differences (NSSM 63)," November 20, 1969, in *FRUS, 1969–1976*, vol. 17: *China, 1969–1972*, p. 133.

37. Ibid., p. 138.

38. Kissinger, *White House Years*, p. 183.

39. Ibid., p. 910.

40. Kissinger's comments are recorded in "Memorandum of Conversation: Wednesday, February 23, 1972, 9:35 a.m. – 12:34 p.m.," in *FRUS, 1969–1976*, vol. E-13, *Documents on China, 1969–1972*, Document 92, p. 3, http://history.state.gov/historicaldocuments/frus1969-76ve13/d92.

41. Tyler, *Great Wall*, p. 179.

42. "Memorandum of Conversation: July 6, 1973," in *FRUS, 1969–1976*, vol. 18: *China, 1973–1976*, p. 293.

43. "Memorandum of Conversation, November 13, 1973," in William Burr, ed., *The Kissinger Transcripts: Top Secret Talks with Beijing and Moscow* (New York: New Press, 1998), pp. 203–204.

44. Tyler, *Great Wall*, p. 174.

45. Regarding the impact of domestic political factors during this period, see Robert G. Sutter, *The China Quandary: Domestic Determinants of U.S. China Policy, 1972–1982* (Boulder, Colo.: Westview Press, 1983), pp. 17–69.

46. "PRM/NSC-10, Military Strategy and Force Posture Review, Final Report," Department of Defense, June 1977, pp. 29–30, http://www.jimmycarterlibrary

.gov/documents/prmemorandums/prm10.pdf. In addition to this study of military requirements, the National Security Council staff, under the direction of Professor Samuel Huntington of Harvard University, prepared a "comprehensive net assessment" of all aspects of U.S. and Soviet power. This part of the study remains classified.

47. Ibid., pp. 31–32.

48. Presidential Review Memorandum/NSC 24, "People's Republic of China," April 5, 1977, http://jimmycarterlibrary.org/documents/prmemorandums/prm24.pdf.

49. Harry Harding, A Fragile Relationship: The United States and China since 1972 (Washington, D.C.: Brookings Institution, 1992), p. 87.

50. Sutter, China Quandary, p. 9.

51. Harding, Fragile Relationship, p. 89.

52. Kevin Pollpeter, U.S.-China Security Management (Santa Monica, Calif.: RAND, 2004), p. 9.

53. Ibid.

54. In the spring of 1980, Chinese officials reportedly presented a list of items that they wanted to buy, including ground-to-air missiles and antitank missiles. This request was rejected. See Harding, Fragile Relationship, p. 93.

55. Tyler, Great Wall, pp. 298, 307.

56. Report by the J-5 to the Joint Chiefs of Staff on United States–China Security Relationship, JCS 2118/292-2, April 17, 1981, p. 1, http://www.dod.gov/pubs/foi/reading_room/928.pdf.

57. Ibid., p. 6.

58. See the chronology in Kerry Dumbaugh and Larry Q. Nowels, China-U.S. Cooperation: Military Sales, Government Programs, Multilateral Aid, and Private-Sector Activities, Report 89-355 F Washington, D.C.: Congressional Research Service, July 14, 1989), p. 4.

59. Dumbaugh, U.S. Arms Sales to China, pp. 17–20.

60. Thomas L. Wilborn, Security Cooperation with China: Analysis and a Proposal (Carlisle, Penn.: U.S. Army War College, 1994), p. 5.

61. Tyler, Great Wall, p. 338.

62. See Report by the J-5 to the Joint Chiefs of Staff on United States–China Security Relationship, pp. A-7–A-10. The last two measures were described as representing the "culmination" of the security relationship, likely to be undertaken only "under conditions of impending conflict" with the Soviet Union.

63. Harding, Fragile Relationship, p. 166.

64. Ibid., pp. 168–169.

65. See table A-1 in Harding, Fragile Relationship, p. 363.

CHAPTER 4: "CONGAGEMENT"

1. The high-level deliberations leading up to the crackdown are described in a fascinating collection of internal documents leaked to the West, translated, and published in 2001: Zhang Liang, Andrew Nathan, and Perry Link, The Tiananmen Papers (New York: PublicAffairs, 2001).

2. Nixon's comment to Mao is quoted in James Mann, *About Face: A History of America's Curious Relationship with China, from Nixon to Clinton* (New York: Alfred A. Knopf, 1999), p. 236.

3. The term appears to have been coined by Zalmay Khalilzad, RAND analyst and future U.S. ambassador to Afghanistan, Iraq, and the United Nations. See Zalmay Khalilzad, *Congage China*, Issue Paper IP-187 (Santa Monica, Calif.: RAND, 1999), http://www.rand.org/pubs/Issue_papers/IP187/IP187.html.

4. See George H. W. Bush, "Remarks at the Yale University Commencement Ceremony in New Haven, Connecticut May 27, 1991," *Public Papers of the Presidents of the United States: George H. W. Bush, 1989–1993* (Washington, D.C.: GPO, 1991), book 2, pp. 565–568. See also George H. W. Bush, "Message to the House of Representatives Returning without Approval the United States–China Act of 1992," in ibid., book 2, pp. 1689–1690. William J. Clinton, "Remarks by the President to the Pacific Basin Economic Council," May 20, 1996, http://www.fas.org/spp/starwars/offdocs/w960520.htm.

5. Mann, *About Face*, p. 228.

6. See, for example, the issues listed in a speech by Barack Obama, "Remarks by the President at the U.S./China Strategic and Economic Dialogue," Washington, D.C., July 27, 2009, http://www.whitehouse.gov/the_press_office/Remarks-by-the-President-at-the-US/China-Strategic-and-Economic-Dialogue/.

7. David M. Lampton, *Same Bed, Different Dreams: Managing U.S.-China Relations, 1989–2000* (Berkeley: University of California Press, 2001), p. 45.

8. Under Secretary of State Peter Tarnoff, quoted in Robert S. Ross, "Engagement in U.S. China Policy," in Alastair Iain Johnston and Robert S. Ross, eds., *Engaging China: The Management of an Emerging Power* (New York: Routledge, 1999), p. 190.

9. Ibid., p. 184.

10. Robert B. Zoellick, "Whither China: From Membership to Responsibility?" remarks to National Committee on U.S.-China Relations, September 21, 2005, http://www.ncuscr.org/files/2005Gala_RobertZoellick_Whither_China1.pdf.

11. These events are well described in Mann, *About Face*, pp. 292–314.

12. "Message to the House of Representatives Returning without Approval the United States–China Act of 1992," September 28, 1992, in *Public Papers of the Presidents of the United States: George H. W. Bush, 1989–1993*, book 2, pp. 1689–1690.

13. Bill Clinton, "Remarks by the President in Address on China and the National Interest," October 24, 1997, http://clinton4.nara.gov/WH/New/html/19971024-3863.html.

14. Quoted in James Mann, *The China Fantasy: How Our Leaders Explain Away Chinese Repression* (New York: Viking, 2007), p. 2.

15. George W. Bush, "President Bush's Address in Bangkok, Thailand," August 7, 2008, http://georgewbush-whitehouse.archives.gov/news/releases/2008/08/20080807-8.html.

16. The "Base Force" review was mainly the work of the Joint Staff, under the direction of the Joint Chiefs of Staff chairman General Colin Powell. It was intended to head off congressional demands for even deeper cuts in defense spending once the Cold War came to an end. The study was completed on the eve of Saddam Hus-

sein's invasion of Kuwait in August 1990, and was subsequently adopted as the basis for future planning in 1991. See Lorna S. Jaffe, *The Development of the Base Force, 1989–1992* (Washington, D.C.: Joint History Office, July 1993).

17. For an account of the leaked report, see Barton Gellman, "Keeping the U.S. First; Pentagon Would Preclude a Rival Superpower," *Washington Post*, March 11, 1992, p. A1. Various declassified drafts can be found in a collection of documents available online from the National Security Archive under the heading "The Making of the Cheney Regional Defense Strategy, 1991–92," http://www.gwu.edu/~nsarchiv/ nukevault/ebb245/index.htm. One of the later versions of the report includes a single redacted page on "regional threats and risks" in East Asia. The final version of this study, titled "Defense Strategy for the 1990s: The Regional Defense Strategy," was published in January 1993, as the first Bush administration was about to leave office. This document can also be found at the Security Archive website.

18. See James Woolsey, "World Threat Assessment Brief," testimony before the Senate Select Committee on Intelligence, 104th Congress, 1st session, January 10, 1995.

19. The political background to the crisis is described in Alan D. Romberg, *Rein in at the Precipice: American Policy toward Taiwan and US-PRC Relations* (Washington, D.C.: Stimson Center, 2003), pp. 155–175.

20. Regarding planning for a possible conflict by the Pacific Command in Hawaii, see Patrick Tyler, *A Great Wall* (New York: PublicAffairs, 2000), p. 27. As serious as they undoubtedly were, these preparations were only for a limited conflict in which the United States helped Taiwan defend itself against an attack from the mainland, as opposed to a possibly protracted struggle between Chinese and American air and naval forces.

21. Mann, *About Face*, p. 334. The precise wording and context of this remark have been a subject of some controversy, but its essential meaning seems clear enough.

22. For the first of these reports, see Office of the Secretary of Defense, Report to Congress Pursuant to the FY2000 National Defense Authorization Act, *Annual Report on the Military Power of the People's Republic of China*, June 2000, http:// www.defense.gov/news/Jun2000/china06222000.htm.

23. "Worldwide Threat Assessment Brief: Worldwide Threat Assessment Brief to the Senate Select Committee on Intelligence by the Director of Central Intelligence, John M. Deutch," February 22, 1996, https://www.cia.gov/news-information/ speeches-testimony/1996/dci_speech_022296.html.

24. CIA Annual Threat Assessment 1997, "Current and Projected National Security Threats: Statement by Acting Director of Central Intelligence George J. Tenet before the Senate Select Committee on Intelligence Hearing on Current and Projected National Security Threats to the United States," February 5, 1997, https://www.cia .gov/news-information/speeches-testimony/1997/dci_testimony_020597.html.

25. CIA Annual Threat Assessment 1998, "DCI before the Senate Select Committee on Intelligence: Director of Central Intelligence, George J. Tenet, before the Senate Select Committee on Intelligence Hearing on Current and Projected National Security Threats," January 28, 1998, https://www.cia.gov/news-information/ speeches-testimony/1998/dci_speech_012898.html.

26. Department of Defense, *Report of the Quadrennial Defense Review*, May 1997, p. 5, http://www.dod.gov/pubs/qdr/.

27. Department of Defense, *Report of the Quadrennial Defense Review*, September 30, 2001, p. 4, http://www.defense.gov/pubs/pdfs/qdr2001.pdf.

28. Ibid.

29. For early rumblings of concern from within the military about where the quadrennial defense review (QDR) and the newly appointed secretary of defense might be headed, see Thomas E. Ricks, "Rumsfeld Outlines Defense Overhaul," *Washington Post*, March 23, 2001, p. A1; Michael R. Gordon, "Pentagon Review Puts Emphasis on Long-Range Arms in Pacific," *New York Times*, May 17, 2001, http://www.nytimes.com/2001/05/17/world/pentagon-review-puts-emphasis-on-long-range-arms-in-pacific.html; Nicholas Lemann, "Dreaming about War," *New Yorker*, July 16, 2001, http://www.comw.org/qdr/0107lemann.html.

30. Department of Defense, *Quadrennial Defense Review Report*, February 6, 2006, pp. 27–28, http://www.defense.gov.qdr/report/report20060203.pdf.

31. Ibid., pp. 29–31.

32. The 100,000-man floor was initially announced in 1995, following what would prove to be only the first act in the long-running confrontation with North Korea over its nuclear program. It was reiterated in 1998. The figure was not entirely arbitrary but represented roughly the manpower of the U.S. Eighth Army and Seventh Air Force in Korea, the Third Marine Expeditionary Force and Fifth Air Force in Japan, and the U.S. Seventh Fleet. See Department of Defense, "The United States Security Strategy for the Asia-Pacific Region," 1998, pp. 10–11, http://www.dod.gov/pubs/easr98/easr98.pdf.

33. See Committee on Armed Services, United States Senate, *The Global Posture Review of United States Military Forces Stationed Overseas: Hearing before the Committee on Armed Services, United States Senate*, 108th Congress, 2nd session, September 23, 2004 (Washington, D.C.: GPO, 2005). Also Senior Administration Officials, "Defense Department Background Briefing on Global Posture Review," August 16, ·2004, http://www.globalsecurity.org/military/library/news/2004/08/mil-040816-dod02.htm.

34. The rationale for building up Guam is described in Andrew S. Erickson and Justin Mikolay, "Anchoring America's Asian Assets: Why Washington Must Strengthen Guam," *Comparative Strategy* no. 25 (2005), pp. 153–171.

35. Admiral William J. Fallon, quoted in a briefing by Lieutenant Colonel Kevin Wong, U.S. Air Force, "U.S. Pacific Command: Perspective on the Pacific," February 28, 2007.

36. Ronald O'Rourke, *China Naval Modernization: Implications for U.S. Navy Capabilities—Background and Issues for Congress*, Report RL33153 (Washington, D.C.: Congressional Research Service, April 16, 2008), pp. 60–61, http://fpc.state.gov/documents/organization/104703.pdf.

37. Richard Halloran, "The New Line in the Pacific," *Air Force Magazine* (December 2007), pp. 34–39.

38. Pacific Command commander Admiral Timothy J. Keating, quoted in ibid., p. 34.

39. Richard Halloran, "PACAF between War and Peace," *Air Force Magazine* (August 2008), p. 31.

40. For the background to these developments, see Richard J. Samuels, *Securing Japan:*

Tokyo's Grand Strategy and the Future of East Asia (Ithaca: Cornell University Press, 2007).

41. See David J. Richardson, "U.S.-Japan Defense Cooperation: Possibilities for Regional Stability," *Parameters* (Summer 2000), pp. 94–104.

42. See Secretary of State Rice, Secretary of Defense Rumsfeld, Minister of Foreign Affairs Machimura, and Minister of State for Defense Ohno, "Security Consultative Committee Document, U.S.-Japan Alliance: Transformation and Realignment for the Future," October 29, 2005, Ministry of Foreign Affairs of Japan, http://www.mofa.go.jp/region/n-america/us/security/scc/doc0510.html.

43. On the background of U.S.-Japan cooperation, see Patrick M. O'Donogue, *Theater Missile Defense in Japan: Implications for the U.S.-China-Japan Strategic Relationship* (Carlisle, Penn.: Strategic Studies Institute, 2000).

44. For an analysis of the Japanese response to 9/11, see Daniel M. Kliman, *Japan's Security Strategy in the Post-9/11 World* (Washington, D.C.: Center for Strategic and International Studies, 2006), pp. 67–92.

45. The 1996 declaration, and Beijing's response to it, are described in Avery Goldstein, *Rising to the Challenge: China's Grand Strategy and International Security* (Stanford: Stanford University Press, 2005), p. 103.

46. Evan S. Medeiros, "Strategic Hedging and the Future of Asia-Pacific Stability," *Washington Quarterly* vol. 29, no. 1 (Winter 2005–6), p. 152.

47. See the joint U.S.–Republic of Korea statement on the launch of the Strategic Consultation for Allied Partnership in U.S. Department of State, Office of the Spokesman, "United States and Republic of Korea Launch Strategic Consultation for Allied Partnership," January 19, 2006, http://seoul.usembassy.gov/rok20060119 .html.

48. For an overview of U.S.-Taiwan defense cooperation during the 1990s and early 2000s, see Michael Pillsbury, *The US Role in Taiwan's Defense Reforms*, report to the U.S.-China Economic and Security Review Commission, February 29, 2004, http://www.uscc.gov/researchpapers/2004/04_05_24_dr_pspeechintaipei_final1 .php.

49. Douglas J. Gillert, "Cohen's Visit Produces Harbor Promises," American Forces Press Service, January 21, 1998, http://www.defenselink.mil/news/newsarticle .aspx?id=41223.

50. Evelyn Goh, "Singapore and the United States: Cooperation on Transnational Security Threats," paper prepared for 26th Annual Pacific Symposium, Honolulu, Hawaii, June 8–10, 2005, http://www.ndu.edu/inss/symposia/Pacific2005/goh .pdf.

51. For developments under the Bush administration, see Jane Perlez, "U.S. Takes Steps to Mend Ties with Indonesian Military," *New York Times*, February 7, 2005; and Brendan Murray and Richard Keil, "Bush Seeks Better Ties with 'Young Tiger' Vietnam," *Bloomberg*, November 17, 2006, http://www.bloomberg.com/apps/news ?pid=newsarchive&sid=apfiDb9LA7io&refer=home. For more recent developments, see Elisabeth Bumiller and Norimitsu Onishi, "U.S. Lifts Ban on Indonesian Special Forces," *New York Times*, July 22, 2010, New York edition, p. A6; Mark Landler, "Offering to Aid Talks, U.S. Challenges China on Disputed Islands," *New York Times*, July 23, 2010, New York edition, p. A4; Jay Solomon, "U.S., Hanoi in

Nuclear Talks," *Wall Street Journal*, August 3, 2010, http://online.wsj.com/article/ SB10001424052748704741904575409261840078780.html.

52. For a description of the early stages of this process by one of the central participants see Strobe Talbott, *Engaging India: Diplomacy, Democracy, and the Bomb* (Washington, D.C.: Brookings Institution, 2004). For a concise statement of the case for an expanded strategic partnership, see an essay by the Bush administration's first ambassador to New Delhi: Robert Blackwill, "The India Imperative," *National Interest* no. 80 (Summer 2005), pp. 9–17.

53. U.S. Department of State, Office of the Spokesman, "Background Briefing by Administration Officials on U.S.-South Asia Relations," March 25, 2005, http:// www.fas.org/terrorism/at/docs/2005/StatePressConfer25mar05.htm.

54. Mann, *About Face*, pp. 386–387.

55. See the Wisconsin Project on Nuclear Arms Control, *U.S. Exports to China 1988– 1998: Fueling Proliferation* (April 1999), http://www.wisconsinproject.org/pubs/ reports/1999/execsumm.html.

56. Details of the various allegations are contained in *Report of the Select Committee on U.S. National Security and Military/Commercial Concerns with the People's Republic of China*, House Report 105-851 (Washington, D.C.: GPO, June 1999), http:// www.gpo.gov/congress/house/hr105851-html/index.html. The FY 2000 National Defense Authorization Act required that all the relevant departments prepare a collective annual report to Congress on the "transfer of militarily sensitive technologies to countries and entities of concern" and a review of the "adequacy of export control policies and procedures." Offices of Inspector General of the Commerce, Defense, Energy, Homeland Security, State and the Central Intelligence Agency, *Interagency Review of Export Controls for China, Volume I*, Report D-2007-050, January 2007, http://www.dodig.mil/audit/reports/FY07-050.pdf.

57. For brief overviews of the contending positions in this debate, see David Shambaugh, "Lifting the EU Arms Embargo On China: An American Perspective," and Gudrun Wacker, "Lifting the EU Arms Embargo on China: U.S. and EU Positions," in Bates Gill and Gudrun Wacker, eds., *China's Rise: Diverging U.S.-EU Perceptions and Approaches* (Berlin: Stiftung Wissenschaft und Politik, 2005), pp. 23–29, 30–36.

58. See U.S. Department of Commerce, Office of Inspector General, Bureau of Industry and Security, *U.S. Dual-Use Export Controls for China Need to Be Strengthened*, Final Report IPE-17500, March 2006, http://www.oig.doc.gov/reports/2006/BIS-IPE-17500.pdf.

59. Remarks by Christopher A. Padilla, Assistant Secretary of Commerce for Export Administration, "The Future of U.S. Export Controls on Trade with China," Shenzhen, China, January 29, 2007, http://www.bis.doc.gov/news/2007/padilla02012007 .htm.

60. Hillary Rodham Clinton, Secretary of State, "U.S.-Asia Relations: Indispensible to Our Future," remarks at the Asia Society, New York, February 13, 2009, http:// www.state.gov/secretary/rm/2009a/02/117333.htm.

61. Originally proposed by economist C. Fred Bergsten, this idea was given wide attention by Zbigniew Brzezinski, former national security advisor to President Jimmy Carter and an advisor to the 2008 Obama presidential campaign. Edward Wong,

"Former Carter Adviser Calls for a 'G-2' between U.S. and China," *New York Times*, January 2, 2009, http://www.nytimes.com/2009/01/12/world/asia/12iht-beijing.3.19283773.html?_r=1.

62. "Clinton: Chinese Human Rights Can't Interfere with Other Crises," CNNPolitics .com, February 22, 2009, http://www.cnn.com/2009/POLITICS/02/21/clinton .china.asia/.

63. John Pomfret, "Obama's Meeting with the Dalai Lama Delayed," *Washington Post*, October 5, 2009, http://www.washingtonpost.com/wp-dyn/content/article/ 2009/10/04/AR2009100403262.html.

64. Deputy Secretary of State James B. Steinberg, "Keynote Address," Center for a New American Security, Washington, D.C., September 24, 2009, http://www .cnas.org/files/multimedia/documents/Deputy%20Secretary%20James%20 Steinberg%27s%20September%2024,%202009%20Keynote%20Address%20 Transcript.pdf. Like the G-2 proposal, the idea of "strategic reassurance" lacked adequate support within the administration and soon disappeared from view.

65. Robert Gates, "A Balanced Strategy: Reprogramming the Pentagon for a New Age," *Foreign Affairs* vol. 88, no. 1 (January/February 2009), pp. 28–40.

66. Bill Powell, "The Chinese Navy: How Big a Threat to the U.S.?" Time.com, April 21, 2009, http://www.time.com/time/world/article/0,8599,1892954,00.html.

67. Clinton's remarks were triggered by a confrontation between the Chinese government and the American-based Internet search engine giant Google. See Secretary of State Hillary Rodham Clinton, "Remarks on Internet Freedom," Washington, D.C., January 21, 2010, http://www.state.gov/secretary/rm/2010/01/135519.htm.

68. Helen Cooper, "U.S. Arms for Taiwan Send Beijing a Message," *New York Times*, January 31, 2010, http://www.nytimes.com/2010/02/01/world/asia/01china.html.

69. Joseph Curl, "Obama–Dalai Lama Meeting 'Closed Press,'" *Washington Times*, February 19, 2010, http://www.washingtontimes.com/news/2010/feb/19/obama-dalai-lama-meeting-closed-press/.

70. Mark Landler, "Offering to Aid Talks, U.S. Challenges China on Disputed Islands," *New York Times*, July 23, 2010, http://www.nytimes.com/2010/07/24/world/ asia/24diplo.html.

71. "China Shuns U.S. Mediation in Its Island Dispute with Japan," CNN.com, November 3, 2010, http://www.cnn.com/2010/WORLD/asiapcf/11/03/china.japan .disputed.islands/.

72. "U.S.-Korean Defense Leaders Announce Exercise Invincible Spirit," July 20, 2010, http://www.globalsecurity.org/military/library/news/2010/07/mil-100720-afps05 .htm; "They Have Returned," *Economist*, April 12, 2010, http://www.economist .com/node/16791842.

73. See Ambassador John V. Roos, "The Enduring Importance of Our Security Alliance," Waseda University, Tokyo, January 29, 2010, http://japan.usembassy.gov/ e/p/tp-20100129-71.html.

74. Among other steps, the 2010 Quadrennial Defense Review stressed the need to "develop a joint air-sea battle concept . . . expand future long-range strike capabilities . . . exploit advantages in subsurface operations . . . increase the resiliency of U.S. forward posture and base infrastructure . . . assure access to space and the use of space assets . . . enhance the robustness of key [command and control] capabilities . . . [and] defeat enemy sensor and engagement systems," Depart-

ment of Defense, *Quadrennial Defense Review Report*, February 2010, pp. 32–34, http://www.defense.gov/qdr/qdr%20as%200f%2029jan10%201600.pdf.

75. See U.S. Department of Defense, Office of the Assistant Secretary of Defense (Public Affairs), "DoD Background Briefing with Senior Defense Officials from the Pentagon," News Transcript, April 19, 2010, http://www.defense.gov/transcripts/transcript.aspx?transcriptid=4610.

76. Jeffrey Ball, "Summit Is Seen as U.S. versus China," *Wall Street Journal*, December 14, 2009, http://online.wsj.com/article/SB126074144005789473.html; Kim Chipman and Nicholas Johnston, "Obama Snubbed by Chinese Premier at Climate Meeting," *Bloomberg*, December 18, 2009, http://www.bloomberg.com/apps/news?pid=newsarchive&sid=a5uY22AnevM4.

77. Since the 2008–9 global financial crisis, persistent high unemployment rates have fueled frustration with China's trade policies. But, to date, these sentiments have not translated into popular enthusiasm for increased defense budgets to counter China's military buildup.

78. Joseph Nye, quoted in Jim Mann, "U.S. Starting to View China as a Potential Enemy," *Los Angeles Times*, April 16, 1995.

CHAPTER 5: "THE PROPENSITY OF THINGS"

1. Winston Churchill, "The First Month of the War," in *Blood, Sweat, and Tears* (New York: G. P. Putnam's Sons, 2007), 173.

2. For a sophisticated analysis of an increasingly complex process, see Linda Jakobson and Dean Knox, *New Foreign Policy Actors in China* (Stockholm: Stockholm International Peace Research Institute, 2010). For a useful compendium of the vast array of materials now available on military topics, see Taylor Fravel, "The Revolution in Research Affairs: Online Sources and the Study of the PLA," and Evan Medeiros, "Undressing the Dragon: Researching the PLA through Open Source Exploitation," in James C. Mulvenon and Andrew N. D. Yang, eds., *A Poverty of Riches: New Challenges and Opportunities in PLA Research* (Santa Monica, Calif.: RAND, 2003), pp. 49–118, 119–168.

3. François Jullien, *A Treatise on Efficacy: Between Western and Chinese Thinking* (Honolulu: University of Hawai'i Press, 2004), p. 38.

4. Ibid., p. 20. This point is so important, and so familiar, that the great Chinese strategist Sun Tzu presents it as a piece of conventional wisdom: "Thus it is said that one who knows the enemy and knows himself will not be endangered in a hundred engagements." Ralph D. Sawyer, *Sun Tzu: The Art of War* (New York: Basic Books, 1994), p. 179.

5. The idea of "peace and development" was introduced in speeches by Deng Xiaoping and Premier Zhao Ziyang. Ren Xiao, "The International Relations Theoretical Discourse in China: A Preliminary Analysis," Sigur Center Asia Papers, No. 9, Sigur Center for Asian Studies, Washington, D.C., 2000, pp. 2–3, http://www.gwu.edu/~sigur/assets/docs/scap/SCAP9-Xiao.pdf.

6. The conservative critique is described in Joseph Fewsmith, *China since Tiananmen* (New York: Cambridge University Press, 2001), pp. 21–43.

7. For a discussion of this debate in the wider context of Chinese strategic thought at

the turn of the century, see Gilbert Rozman, *Chinese Strategic Thought toward Asia* (New York: Palgrave Macmillan, 2010), pp. 89–107.

8. For an incisive analysis, see David M. Finkelstein, "China Reconsiders Its National Security: The Great Peace and Development Debate of 1999," Center for Naval Analysis, CME D0014464.A1, December 2000, http://www.cna.org/documents/D0014464.A1.pdf.

9. Ren Xiao, "The International Relations Theoretical Discourse in China: One World, Different Explanations," *Journal of Chinese Political Science* vol. 15, no. 1 (November 2009), p. 6.

10. Ibid., p. 3.

11. The debates over multipolarity and the imminence of U.S. decline are described in Michael Pillsbury, *China Debates the Future Security Environment* (Washington, D.C.: National Defense University Press, 2000), pp. 3–105.

12. Wang Jisi, quoted in Yong Deng, "Hegemon on the Offensive: Chinese Perspectives on U.S. Global Strategy," *Political Science Quarterly* vol. 116, no. 3 (2001), pp. 343–365.

13. From *Renmin Ribao* [People's Daily], quoted in Pillsbury, *China Debates the Future Security Environment*, p. 28.

14. Ibid.

15. Finkelstein, "China Reconsiders Its National Security," pp. 24–25. This shift from optimism to resignation is described in more detail in Yong, "Hegemon on the Offensive"; Biwu Zhang, "Chinese Perceptions of American Power, 1991–2004," *Asian Survey* vol. 45, no. 5 (September/October 2005), pp. 667–686.

16. Post-2001 developments in Chinese thinking are analyzed in Peter Hays Gries, "China Eyes the Hegemon," *Orbis* vol. 116, no. 3 (Summer 2005), pp. 401–412; Andrew Erickson and Lyle Goldstein, "Hoping for the Best, Preparing for the Worst: China's Response to US Hegemony," *Journal of Strategic Studies* vol. 29, no. 6 (December 2006), pp. 955–986; Rozman, *Chinese Strategic Thought toward Asia*, pp. 109–130.

17. Wang Jisi, "Zhongmei guanxi: Xunqiu wending de xinkuangjia [Sino–US relations: seeking a new framework for stability]," *Zhongguo Dangzheng Ganbu Luntan* [Chinese Cadres Tribune], no. 202 (January 2005), pp. 37–39.

18. Xu Jian, "Four Main Trends in Changes in Asia-Pacific Situation," *Liaowang* [Outlook Magazine], October 10, 2005, NewsEdge Document Number: 200510241477.1_3a360651fdce75b1.

19. Shi Yinhong, "Yilake zhanzheng yu zhongmei guanxi taishi [The Iraq war and the state of Sino-US relations]," *Xiandai Guoji Guanxi* [Contemporary International Relations] (May 2007), pp. 16–17.

20. Niu Xinchun and Gao Yiwei, "Zhongmei guanxi kewang chixu wending [Sino-USA relations can be expected to remain stable]," *Heping Yu Fazhan* [Peace and Development] no. 2 (May 2008), pp. 10–12, 69.

21. Shi Yinhong, "Meiguo quanshi, zhongguo jueqi, shijie zhixu [US power, China's rise and world order]," *Guoji Wenti Yanjiu* [Journal of International Studies] (May 2007), pp. 28–31.

22. Quotes from Shang Hong, "Jinrong weiji dui meiguo baquan diwei de chongji [Impact of the financial crisis on America's hegemonic position]," *Xiandai Guoji Guanxi* (April 2009), pp. 32–33; Guo Yuli, Lin Xinzhu, and Chu Shulong, "Meigo,

zhonguo de fazhan bianhua yu shije geju [Developmental Changes in China, United States: What they mean for world framework]," *Xiandai Guoji Guanxi* (August 2009), pp. 37–40; Wang Wanzheng, "Keep Sino-US 'Soft Conflicts' Under Control," *China Daily Online*, February 4, 2010, http://www.chinadaily.com.cn/opinion/2010-02/04/content_9425268.htm.

23. Li Hongmei, "US Hegemony Ends, Era of Global Multipolarity Enters," *Renmin Wang* [People's Daily Online], February 24, 2009, http://english.peopledaily.com.cn/90002/96417/6599374.html.

24. Dong Manyuan and Chen Xulong, "In the Face of the Pressure of All-Round Challenges," *Liaowang*, December 14, 2009, NewsEdge Document Number: 200912241477.1_5dce07a60a106f04.

25. Li Yonghui, "Jinrong weiji, guoji xin zhixu yu zhongguo de xuanze [Financial crisis, new world order and China's choice]," *Xiandai Guoji Guanxi* (April 2009), p. 37.

26. Guo, Lin, and Chu, "Developmental Changes in China, United States."

27. Qin Yaqing, "Guoji tixi zhuanxing yiji zhongguo zhanlue jiyu qi de yanxu [Transformation of the international system and continuation of the period of strategic opportunities for China]," *Xiandai Guoji Guanxi* (April 2009), pp. 35–37.

28. Shi Yinhong, "Zhongmei guanxi yu zhongguo zhanlue [Sino-US relations and China's strategy]," *Xiandai Guoji Guanxi* no. 1 (January 2007), pp. 35–36.

29. Lin Limin and Chang Shanshan, "Guanyu zhongguo chengzhang wei shijie dier da jingji tihou de guoji zhanlue sikao [Some thoughts on international strategy after China grows to become world's second largest economy]," *Xiandai Guoji Guanxi* (October 2008), pp. 32–40.

30. Wang Jisi, quoted in "Bingfei G2 geju: Zhongmei weilai shi nian [No G2 in future China-US relations]," *Shiji Jingji Baodao* [Twenty-first Century Business Herald], January 26, 2010, http://nf.nfdaily.cn/epaper/21cn/content/20100126/ArticelJ23002FM.htm.

31. Wang Yusheng, "Qie wu wangyan 'zhongmei G2 shidai' [Talk of 'Sino-US G2 era' unrealistic]," *Zhongguo Qingnian Bao* [China Youth Daily], February 27, 2009, http://zqb.cyol.com/content/2009-02/27/content_2558126.htm.

32. Guo, Lin, and Chu, "Developmental Changes in China, United States."

33. Jin Canrong, "Ruhe renshi guoji da qushi [How to view major international trends]," *Xiandai Guoji Guanxi* (September 2008), pp. 3–5.

34. Hu Jintao, quoted in Andrew J. Nathan and Bruce Gilley, *China's New Rulers: The Secret Files* (New York: New York Review of Books, 2003), p. 235. Mao and his revolutionary colleagues represent the founding generation of Chinese leaders; Deng, the second generation; Jiang, the third; and Hu Jintao, the fourth. If all goes according to plan, a new group of leaders will be named at the 18th National Party Congress in 2012. Although surprises are always possible, everything that is known about their background and views suggests these people will be very similar in outlook to their predecessors. See Cheng Li, "China's Fifth Generation: Is Diversity a Source of Strength or Weakness?" *Asia Policy* no. 6 (July 2008), pp. 15–54.

35. General Chen Kaizeng and Yao Youzhi, both quoted in David Shambaugh, *Modernizing China's Military: Progress, Problems, and Prospects* (Berkeley: University of California Press, 2002), p. 297.

36. Jin Canrong, "Weibei chuantong dailai de bu queding xing [Uncertainties brought

about by going against tradition]," *Xiandai Guoji Guanxi* (August 2003), pp. 19–21.

37. Tang Yongsheng and Lu Gang, "Zhongmei guanxi de jiegouxing, maodun, jiqi huajie [Structural contradictions in Sino-US relations, and their resolution]," *Xiandai Guoji Guanxi* no. 6 (June 2007), pp. 52–60.

38. Fu Mengzi, "'Zhongguo weixie' haishi weixie zhongguo ['China threat' still threatening China]," *Shijie Zhishi* [World Affairs], September 1, 2005, pp. 38–39.

39. Andrew J. Nathan and Robert S. Ross, *The Great Wall and the Empty Fortress: China's Search for Security* (New York: W. W. Norton, 1997), p. 72.

40. Wang Jisi, "Zhongguo de guoji zhanlue yanjiu: fanshi de fansi goujian [Some thoughts on building a Chinese international strategy]," *Guoji Zhengzhi Yanjiu* [International Studies Quarterly] (Winter 2007), pp. 1–5.

41. Liu Jianfei, "Zhongguo minzhu zhengzhi jianshe yu zhongmei guanxi [The building of democratic politics in China and Sino-US relations]," *Zhanlue Yu Guanli* [Strategy and Management] no. 2 (March 2003), pp. 76–82.

42. Yong Deng, "Hegemon on the Offensive," p. 349.

43. Li Xiaohua, "Jiechu de xiandu: meiguo zhanlue sixiang de pinkun yu duihua zhengce liangnan [Limits of engagement: poverty in the US strategic thinking and difficulties in its China policy]," *Shijie Jingji Yu Zhengzhi* [World Economics and Politics] no. 8 (August 2002), pp. 10–15.

44. Wang Jisi, quoted in Phillip C. Saunders, "China's America Watchers: Changing Attitudes towards the United States," *China Quarterly* no. 161 (March 2000), pp. 41–65.

45. Fu, "'Zhongguo weixie' haishi weixie zhongguo ['China threat' still threatening China]."

46. Quoted in Nathan and Gilley, *China's New Rulers*, p. 237.

47. Regarding China's perceptions of encirclement and efforts to defeat it, see John W. Garver and Fei-Ling Wang, "China's Anti-encirclement Struggle," *Asian Security* vol. 6, no. 3 (2010), pp. 238–261.

48. Gao Zichuan, "Zhongguo zhoubian anquan huanjing jiben taixi jixi [An analysis of the basic situation of China's peripheral security environment]," *Dangdai Yatai* [Contemporary Asia-Pacific] no. 1 (January 2004), pp. 4–10.

49. Wang Yusheng, "Zhongmeiri sanjiao guanxi de yanbian he qianjing [Evolution, prospects of Sino-US-Japanese trilateral relations]," *Heping Yu Fazhan* no. 3 (July 2008), pp. 35–37.

50. Gao Zhenyuan, "Zhongmei guanxi de taiwan wenti: bianhua yu yingxiang [The Taiwan issue in Sino-US Relations: changes and impact]," *Guoji Wenti Yanjiu* no. 118 (March 2007), pp. 20–25.

51. Ni Shixiong, "Meiguo duihua xin zhanlue ji zhongguo dui mei zhanlue tiaozheng [The United States' new China strategy and China's US strategy adjustment]," *Zhongguo Pinglun* [China Review] no. 56 (August 2002), pp. 73–77.

52. Gao, "Zhongguo zhoubian anquan huanjing jiben taixi jixi [An analysis of the basic situation of China's peripheral security environment]."

53. Wang Jisi, "Dui woguo guoji huanjing he meiguo zhanlue zouxiang de ji dian guji [Some evaluations of China's international environment and US strategic direction]," *Xiandai Guoji Guanxi* no. 11 (November 2002), pp. 1–3.

54. Zheng Yu, "'Yanse geming' yu zhong e mei sanjiao guanxi ['Color revolution' and

Sino-Russia-US trilateral relations]," *Heping Yu Fazhan* no. 4 (October 2007), pp. 12–15.

55. Fu, "'Zhongguo weixie' haishi weixie zhongguo ['China threat' still threatening China]."

56. Song Guoyuo, "Meiguo de dongya FTA zhanlue jiqi dui diqu zhixu de yingxiang [America's East Asia FTA strategy and its impact on regional order]," *Dangdai Yatai* no. 11 (November 2007), pp. 34–40.

57. A leaked Chinese report written immediately following the UN Climate Change Conference in Copenhagen reveals such concerns. Jonathan Watts, Damian Carrington, and Suzanne Goldenberg, "China's Fears of Rich Nation 'Climate Conspiracy' at Copenhagen Revealed," *Guardian* (London), February 11, 2010, http://www.guardian.co.uk/environment/2010/feb/11/chinese-thinktank-copenhagen-document.

58. Hou Songling and Chi Diantang, "Dongnanya yu zhong ya: Zhongguo zai xin shiji de diyuan zhanlue xuanze [Southeast Asia and Central Asia: China's geostrategic options in the new century]," *Dangdai Yatai* no. 4 (April 2003), pp. 9–15. Li, "Jiechu de xiandu: meiguo zhanlue sixiang de pinkun yu duihua zhengce liangnan [Limits of engagement: poverty in the US strategic thinking and dilemmas in its China policy]."

59. Shi, "Zhongmei guanxi yu zhongguo zhanlue [Sino-US relations and China's strategy]."

60. Yin Chengde, "Sino-US Relations Move towards Benign Interaction," *Liaowang*, April 20, 2006, NewsEdge Document Number: 200604201477.1_f26304a829da4577.

61. Niu and Gao, "Zhongmei guanxi kewang chixu wending [Sino-USA relations can be expected to remain stable]."

62. Yin, "Sino–US Relations Move towards Benign Interaction."

63. Yuan Peng, "Zhanlue yu huxin zhanlue wending: Dangqian zhongmei guanxi mianlin de zhuyao wangwu [Strategic mutual trust and strategic stability: principal tasks facing Sino-US relations]," *Xiandai Guoji Guanxi* no. 1 (January 2008), pp. 30–38.

CHAPTER 6: "HIDE OUR CAPABILITIES AND BIDE OUR TIME"

1. Allen S. Whiting, "Chinese Nationalism and Foreign Policy after Deng," *China Quarterly* no. 142 (June 1995), p. 301.

2. Ibid., p. 310.

3. Diplomatic developments during this period are well covered in Andrew J. Nathan and Robert S. Ross, *The Great Wall and the Empty Fortress: China's Search for Security* (New York: W. W. Norton, 1997).

4. The best discussions of these developments are Evan S. Medeiros and M. Taylor Fravel, "China's New Diplomacy," *Foreign Affairs* vol. 82, no. 6 (November/December 2003), pp. 22–35; and Bates Gill, *Rising Star: China's New Security Diplomacy* (Washington, D.C.: Brookings Institution, 2007).

5. David M. Finkelstein, "China's New Security Concept: Reading between the Lines," Center for Naval Analysis, Project Asia Issue Paper, April 1999, p. 3.

6. Gill, *Rising Star*, pp. 21–73.

7. Ibid., pp. 74–103.

8. Jiang Zemin, "Remarks to the 16th National Congress of the Communist Party of China," November 8, 2002, http://www.china.org.cn/english/features/49007 .htm.

9. Liu Jianfei, "Zhongguo minzhu zhengzhi jianshe yu zhongmei guanxi [The building of democratic politics in China and Sino-US relations]," *Zhanlue Yu Guanli* [Strategy and Management] no. 2 (March 2003), pp. 76–82.

10. See, for example, Ye Zicheng, "Zai xin xingshi xia dui Deng Xiaoping waijiao sixiang de jicheng, fazhan, he sikao [Carrying forward, developing and pondering Deng Xiaoping's foreign policy thinking in the new situation]," *Shijie Jingji Yu Zhengzhi* [World and Economics and Politics] no. 11(November 2004), pp. 8–14.

11. Bonnie S. Glaser and Evan S. Medeiros, "The Changing Ecology of Foreign Policy-Making in China: The Ascension and Demise of the Theory of 'Peaceful Rise,' " *China Quarterly* vol. 190 (June 2007), pp. 291–310.

12. See Robert L. Suettinger, "The Rise and Descent of 'Peaceful Rise,' " *China Leadership Monitor*, no. 12 (Fall 2004), http://www.hoover.org/publications/clm/ issues/2903986.html; see also ibid.

13. Wang Jisi, "Bingfei G2 geju: Zhongmei weilai shi nian [No G2 in future China-US relations]," *Shiji Jingji Baodao* [Twenty-first Century Business Herald], January 26, 2010, http://nf.nfdaily.cn/epaper/21cn/content/20100126/ArticelJ23002FM.htm.

14. Shang Hong, "Jinrong weiji dui meiguo baquan diwei de chongji [Impact of the Financial crisis on America's hegemonic position]," *Xiandai Guoji Guanxi* [Contemporary International Relations] no. 4 (April 2009), pp. 32–33.

15. Dong Manyuan and Chen Xulong, "In the Face of the Pressure of All-Round Challenges," *Liaowang* [Outlook Magazine] (December 14, 2009), NewsEdge Document Number: 200912241477.1_5dce07a60a106f04.

16. Hu Angang and Men Honghua, "The Rising of Modern China: Comprehensive National Power and Grand Strategy" (first published in *Strategy and Management* no. 3 [May 2002]), http://irchina.org/en/xueren/china/pdf/mhh3.pdf.

17. Michael Pillsbury, *China Debates the Future Security Environment* (Washington, D.C.: National Defense University Press, 2000), pp. 203–258.

18. Wu Xinbo, "China: Security Practice of a Modernizing and Ascending Power," in Muthiah Alagappa, ed., *Asian Security Practice* (Stanford: Stanford University Press, 1998), p. 143.

19. Liu Huaqiu, "Ji bixu jin jin zhua zhu you keyi dayouzuowei—tan 'zhongyao zhanlue jiyu qi' [Discussing important period of strategic opportunity]," *Renmin Ribao Online*, April 14, 2003, www.southcn.com/NEWS/ztbd/llb/gn/200304140345 .htm.

20. Ibid.

21. Information Office of the State Council of the People's Republic of China, "China's National Defense in 2008," January 2009, http://www.gov.cn/english/ official/2009-01/20/content_1210227.htm.

22. Hu and Men, "Rising of Modern China," p. 33.

23. Shi Yinhong, "Zhongguo de waibu kunnan he xin lingdao jiti mian dui de tiaozhan—guoji zhengzhi, waijiao zhengce, taiwan wenti [China's external difficulties and challenges faced by the new leadership—international politics, foreign policy, and the Taiwan issue]," *Zhanlue Yu Guanli* no. 3 (May 2003), pp. 34–39.

24. Tang Yongsheng and Lu Gang, "Zhongmei guanxi de jiegouxing, maodun, jiqi huajie [Structural contradictions in Sino-US relations, and their resolution]," *Xiandai Guoji Guanxi* no. 6 (June 2007), pp. 52–60.

25. See Joel Wuthnow, "The Concept of Soft Power in China's Strategic Discourse," *Issues & Studies* vol. 44, no. 2 (June 2008), pp. 1–28. See also, Joseph Nye, *Soft Power: The Means to Success in World Politics* (New York: PublicAffairs, 2004).

26. Yu Xintian, " 'Ruan shili' duanxiang [Random thoughts on 'soft power']," *Waijiao Pinglun* [Foreign Affairs Review] no. 97 (August 2007), pp. 35–36.

27. Ma Zhengang, "Lixing kandai zhongguo de guoji yingxiangli [Viewing China's international influence in rational way]," *Qiushi* [Seek Truth], no. 5, (March 1, 2006), http://theory.people.com.cn/GB/40534/4155285.html.

28. Yan Xuetong, "Zhongmei ruanshili bijao [A soft power comparison between China and the United States]," *Xiandai Guoji Guanxi* no. 1 (January 2008), pp. 24–29.

29. Yan Xuetong, "The Rise of China and Its Power Status," *Chinese Journal of International Politics* vol. 1 (2006), pp. 19–21.

30. Yan estimates that China will rank second by 2015, when it will have become a "semi-superpower." Ibid., p. 31. Others calculate that China is already number two in total comprehensive national power. Hu and Men, "Rising of Modern China," p. 23.

31. Michael D. Swaine and Ashley J. Tellis, *Interpreting China's Grand Strategy: Past, Present, and Future* (Santa Monica, Calif.: RAND, 2000), pp. 97–150.

32. Avery Goldstein, *Rising to the Challenge: China's Grand Strategy and International Security* (Stanford: Stanford University Press, 2001), pp. 20, 38.

33. David M. Lampton, *The Three Faces of Chinese Power: Might, Money, and Minds* (Berkeley: University of California Press, 2008), pp. 27–32. Quote on p. 29.

34. For a discussion of China's two-handed strategy, see Chai Liu and Chu Shulong, "Zhongguo dui mei zhanlue de lishi yanbian yu weilai qushi [China's U.S. strategy, historical trends and future evolution]," *Xiandai Guoji Guanxi* no. 6 (June 2006), pp. 18–23, 63.

35. Ye Zicheng, "Zai xin xingshi xia dui deng xiaoping waijiao sixiang de jicheng, fazhan, he sikao [Carrying forward, developing and pondering Deng Xiaoping's foreign policy thinking in the new situation]."

36. Yuan Jirong, "Zhongguo waijiao zhanlue xu da tiaozheng ma? [Does Chinese diplomacy require a strategic adjustment?]," *Huanqiu Shibao* [Global Times], January 6, 2009, http://world.huanqiu.com/roll/2009-01/336411.html.

37. Interview with Yan Xuetong, "Dialogue: China Should Maintain Balance between Power and Responsibility—Yan Xuetong," *Guoji Xianqu Daobao* [International Herald Leader], December 30, 2009.

38. Yuan Peng, " 'Hexie shiji' yu zhongguo 'xinwaijiao' ['Harmonious world' and China's 'new diplomacy']," *Xiandai Guoji Guanxi* no. 4 (April 2007), pp. 1–8.

CHAPTER 7: "TO WIN WITHOUT FIGHTING"

1. Samuel P. Huntingon, *The Clash of Civilizations and the Remaking of World Order* (New York: Simon and Schuster, 1996), p. 229.

2. Ibid.

3. See, for example, Wang Gungwu, "The Fourth Rise of China," *China: An International Journal* vol. 2, no. 2 (September 2004), pp. 311–322.

4. Martin Jacques, *When China Rules the World* (New York: Penguin Press, 2009), p. 176.

5. Yan Xuetong, quoted in Mark Leonard, *What Does China Think?* (London: Harper Collins, 2008), p. 83.

6. Ross Terrill, "What Does China Want?" *Wilson Quarterly* (Autumn 2005), pp. 50–61.

7. Andrew J. Nathan and Bruce Gilley, *China's New Rulers: The Secret Files* (New York: New York Review of Books, 2003), p. 263.

8. Thomas J. Christensen, "China," in Richard J. Ellings and Aaron L. Friedberg, eds., *Strategic Asia 2001–02: Power and Purpose* (Seattle: National Bureau of Asian Research, 2001), pp. 32–33.

9. This concern is discussed at length in Ross Terrill, *The New Chinese Empire* (New York: Basic Books, 2003), pp. 205–252.

10. Xu Jian, "Four Main Trends in Changes in Asia-Pacific Situation," *Liaowang* [Outlook Magazine], October 10, 2005, NewsEdge Document Number: 200510241477.1_3a360651fdce75b1.

11. Bian Qingzu, "Bushi zhengfu de yatai zhanlue [Asia-Pacific strategy of the Bush administration]," *Heping Yu Fazhan* [Peace and Development] no. 2 (May 2007), pp. 15–19.

12. Xu Ping and Zhao Qinghai, "Zhongguo zhoubian anquan huanjing touxi [Analysis of China's peripheral security environment]," *Guoji Wenti Yanjiu* [Journal of International Studies] no. 2 (March 2007), pp. 26–31.

13. Niu Jun, "Zhongmei: yicun he jingzheng zhizhong [China and the United States: between interdependence and competition]," *Shijie Zhishi* [World Affairs] no. 1 (January 2003), pp. 13–14.

14. See the estimates of comprehensive national power for Russia, Japan, India, and China in Hu Angang and Honghua Men, "The Rising of Modern China: Comprehensive National Power and Grand Strategy" (first published in Strategy and Management no. 3, 2002), pp. 22–24, http://irchina.org/en/xueren/china/pdf/mhh3.pdf.

15. Zhang Wenling, "Goujian zhongnguo yu zhoubian guojia zhijian de xinxing guanxi [Constructing China's new relations with neighboring countries]," *Dangdai Yatai* [Contemporary Asia-Pacific] no. 11 (November 2007), pp. 3–11.

16. Zhang Yunling, "Ruhe renshi zhongnguo zai yatai diqu mianlin de guoji huanjing [How to understand the international environment China faces in the Asia-Pacific region]," *Dangdai Yatai* no. 6 (June 2003), pp. 3–14.

17. Xu and Zhao, "Zhongguo zhoubian anquan huanjing touxi [Analysis of China's peripheral security environment]."

18. Zhang, "Goujian zhongguo yu zhoubian guojia zhijian de xinxing guanxi [Constructing China's new relations with neighboring countries]."

19. Shi Yinhong, "Zhongguo jinqi zhuyao duiwai zhanlue wenti—jiantan changqi xing jiben zhanlue jiyu [Major strategic issues of Chinese foreign policy in the short run—and basic strategic opportunities in the long run]," *Zhanlue Yu Guanli* [*Strategy and Management*] no. 6 (November 2003), pp. 21–25.

20. Men Honghua, "Zhongguo guoji zhanlue liyi de tuozhan [Expansion of China's national strategic interest]," *Zhanlue Yu Guanli* no. 2 (March 2003), pp. 83–89. Interestingly, both this article and the one cited in note 19 appeared in a now-defunct journal that had a reputation for publishing controversial essays that sometimes went beyond the scope of acceptable debate.

21. Chris Buckley, "China PLA Officer Urges Challenging U.S. Dominance," Reuters .com, March 1, 2010, http://www.reuters.com/assets/print?aid=USTRE6201C C20100301.

22. Yan Xuetong, "Meiguo tiaozhan haiwai zhujun de zhanlue dongxiang [Strategic Trend of US adjustment of its armed forces stationed overseas]," *Zhongguo Junshi Kexue* [China Military Science] no. 4 (August 2003), pp. 136–138.

23. Yu Xintian, "Zhanzheng yu heping de xin tedian [New characteristics of war and peace]," *Guoji Zhanwang* [World Outlook] no. 2 (May 2004), pp. 16–19.

24. Ralph D. Sawyer, *Sun Tzu: The Art of War* (New York: Basic Books, 1994), p. 92.

25. Niu, "Zhongmei: yicun he jingzheng zhizhong [China and the United States: between interdependence and competition]."

26. Tang Yongshong, "Goujian jianshi de diyuan zhanlue yituo [Building a solid global strategic support]," *Xiandai Guoji Guanxi* [Contemporary International Relations] no. 5 (May 2008), pp. 20–21.

27. Zhang W., "Goujian zhongguo yu zhoubian guojia zhijian de xinxing guanxi [Constructing China's new relations with neighboring countries]."

28. Zhang Y., "Ruhe renshi zhongguo zai yatai diqu mianlin de guoji huanjing [How to understand the international environment China faces in the Asia-Pacific region]."

29. Author's conversations in Washington with a high-ranking Chinese diplomat (in spring of 2004) and in Tokyo with a top expert on the United States (in fall of 2007). As is often the case, these comments do not appear to be random expressions of personal opinion but rather probes, or trial runs of possible new diplomatic formulations, intended to test the sensitivities and responses of the listener.

30. Lin Limin, "Meiguo yu dongya yiti hua de guanxi xilun [An analysis of relations between the United States and an increasingly integrated East Asia]," *Xiandai Guoji Guanxi* no. 10 (October 2007), pp. 1–6.

31. Ibid.

32. For a review of these issues, see Mark E. Manyin, Michael John Garcia, and Wayne M. Morrison, *U.S. Accession to ASEAN's Treaty of Amity and Cooperation (TAC)*, R40583 (Washington, D.C.: Congressional Research Service, July 13, 2009), http://www.fas.org/sgp/crs/row/R40583.pdf.

33. Zhao Huasheng, "Zhongmei zai zhongya nengfou hezuo [Can China, Russia, and the United States cooperate in Central Asia]?" *Zhanlue Yu Guanli* no. 2 (March 2004), pp. 94–107.

34. Gao Zichuan, "Zhongguo zhoubian anquan huanjing jiben taishi jiexi [An analysis of the basic situation of China's peripheral security environment]," *Dangdai Yatai* no. 1 (January 2004), pp. 4–10.

35. Ross Munro, *China's Strategy towards Countries on Its Land Borders*, Final Report to Director, Net Assessment, Office of the Secretary of Defense (McLean, Va.: Booz Allen Hamilton, August 2006).

36. See "China's Myanmar Dilemma," Asia Report 177, International Crisis Group, September 14, 2009, http://www.crisisgroup.org/~/media/Files/asia/north-east-asia/177_chinas_myanmar_dilemma.ashx.

37. Munro, *China's Strategy towards Countries on Its Land Borders*, pp. 2, 4.

38. China and Russia staged joint military exercises in 2005 and again in 2009. Nick Childs, "China-Russia War Games Underway," BBC News, August 15, 2005, http://news.bbc.co.uk/2/hi/asia-pacific/4161660.stm; Toni Vorobyova, "Russia, China Stage War Games in Central Asia," Reuters, April 18, 2009.

39. Andrew Erickson and Gabriel B. Collins, "China's Oil Security Pipe Dream: The Reality, and Strategic Consequences, of Seaborne Imports," *Naval War College Review* (March 2010), pp. 89–112.

40. Zhang W., "Goujian zhongguo yu zhoubian guojia zhijian de xinxing guanxi [Constructing China's new relations with neighboring countries]."

41. Stephen Kotkin, "The Unbalanced Triangle: What Chinese-Russian Relations Mean for the United States," *Foreign Affairs* vol. 88. no. 5 (September/October 2009), pp. 130–138. See also Rajan Menon, *The China-Russia Relationship: What It Involves, Where It Is Headed, and How It Matters for the United States*, Century Foundation Report (New York: Century Foundation, 2009), http://tcf.org/publications/pdfs/pb690/menon.pdf.

42. Tang Shiping, "2010–2015 niande zhongguo zhoubian anquan huanjing [China's peripheral security environment in 2010–2015—decisive factors, trends and prospects]," *Zhanlue Yu Guanli* no. 5 (October 2002), pp. 34–45.

43. Ibid.

44. Hou Songling and Chi Diantang, "Dongnanya yu zhongya: zhongguo zai xin shiji de diyuan zhanlue xuanze [Southeast Asia and Central Asia: China's geostrategic options in the new century]," *Dangdai Yatai* no. 4 (April 2003), pp. 9–15.

45. Gao Zugui, "Zhongmei zai 'xixian' de zhanlue guanxi fenxi [An analysis of Sino-US strategic relations on the 'Western Front']," *Xiandai Guoji Guanxi* no. 12 (December 2004), pp. 1–7.

46. Zhao Changqing, "Daguo zai zhongya de liyi jiaozhi [The interwoven interests of the great powers in Central Asia]," *Heping Yu Fazhan* no. 2 (May 2007), pp. 36–39.

47. Gao, "Zhongguo zhoubian anquan huanjing jiben taishi jiexi [An Analysis of the basic situation of China's peripheral security environment]."

48. Ibid.

49. Wang Yusheng, "Zhongmeiri sanjiao guanxi de yanbian he qianjing [Evolution, prospects of Sino-US-Japanese trilateral relations]," *Heping Yu Fazhan* no. 3 (July 2008), pp. 35–37.

50. Cui Liru, "Chaoxian bandao anquan wenti: zhongguo de zuoyong [The question of security on the Korean peninsula: China's role]," *Xiandai Guoji Guanxi* no. 9 (September 2006), pp. 42–47.

51. David Shambaugh, "China and the Korean Peninsula: Playing for the Long Term," *Washington Quarterly* vol. 26, no. 2 (Spring 2003), pp. 50–51.

52. Bian Qingzu, "Bushi zhengfu de yatai zhanlue [Asia-Pacific strategy of the Bush administration]," *Heping Yu Fazhan* no. 2 (May 2007), pp. 15–19.

53. Wang, "Zhongmeiri sanjiao guanxi de yanbian he qianjing [Evolution, Prospects of Sino-US-Japanese trilateral relations]."

54. Guo Zhenyuan, "Zhongmei guanxi zhongde taiwan wenti: bianhua yu yingxiang [The Taiwan issue in Sino-US relations: changes and impact]," *Guoji Wenti Yanjiu* no. 2 (March 2007), pp. 20–25.

55. Ibid.

56. Hu Xiaowen, "Sui niujun, jin canrong, ganshou taiwan [Experiencing Taiwan with Niu Jun and Jin Canrong]," *Shijie Zhishi* no. 1 (January 2005), pp. 52–54.

57. Hou and Chi, "Dongnanya yu zhongya: zhongguo zai xin shiji de diyuan zhanlue xuanze [Southeast Asia and Central Asia: China's geostrategic options in the new century]."

58. Valerie Reitman, "Japan, China Renew Ties; War Apology Clouds Talks," *Los Angeles Times*, November 27, 1998, http://articles.latimes.com/1998/nov/27/news/mn-48266. For an overview of shifting Chinese thinking on how best to deal with Japan, see Gilbert Rozman, *Chinese Strategic Thought toward Asia* (New York: Palgrave Macmillan, 2010), pp. 155–176.

59. Richard Samuels, *Securing Japan: Tokyo's Grand Strategy and the Future of East Asia* (Ithaca: Cornell University Press, 2007), pp. 135–158.

60. Feng Zhaokui, "Dui re guanxi de jiannan qiusuo [A difficult search in relations with Japan]," *Shijie Jingji Yu Zhengzhi* [World Economics and Politics] no. 5 (May 2004), pp. 26–31.

61. Ibid.

62. Xu Wangsheng, "Lun rimei tongmeng zhuanbian: cong 'lengzhanhou' dao 9.11 hou [Transformation of the Japan-US alliance: from 'post Cold War' to 'post September 11],' *Guoji Luntan* [International Forum] no. 6 (November 2005), pp. 7–11.

63. Wang, "Zhongmeiri sanjiao guanxi de yanbian he qianjing [Evolution, prospects of Sino-US-Japanese trilateral relations]."

64. Shi, "Zhongguo jinqi zhuyao duiwai zhanlue wenti—jiantan changqi xing jiben zhanlue jiyu [Major strategic issues of Chinese foreign policy in the short run—and basic strategic opportunities in the long run]."

65. Yang Yi, "Zhongri zhanlue huhui wu yao wu buyao" [Five desirables and five undesirables in mutually beneficial strategic relations between China and Japan]," *Huanqiu Shibao* [Global Times] (August 2007), p. 11.

66. Feng Zhaokui, "Guoji zhengzhi huanjing bianhua yu zhongri guanxi [Changes in the international political environment and Sino-Japanese relations]," *Shiji Jingji Yu Zhengzhi* no. 6 (June 2006), pp. 24–30.

67. Da Wei and Wang Wen Feng, "Quanqiu fankong zhanzheng yu meiguo dui hua zhanlue guanzhu [Paying attention to global war on terror, US strategy toward China]," *Xiandai Guoji Guanxi* no. 1 (January 2008), pp. 39–43.

68. Yan Xuetong, quoted in Leonard, *What Does China Think?* p. 113.

69. Shi Yinhong, "Meiguo quanli, zhongguo jiqi yu shijie zhidu [US power, China's rise and world order]," *Guoji Wenti Yanjiu* no. 3 (May 2007), pp. 28–38.

70. Admiral Timothy J. Keating, Commander, U.S. Pacific Command, testimony before the House Armed Services Committee, 110th Congress, 1st session, March 12, 2008, https://www.pacom.mil/speeches/sst2008/080312-hasc-keating_testimony.pdf.

CHAPTER 8: THE BALANCE OF INFLUENCE

1. Minxin Pei, *China's Trapped Transition: The Limits of Developmental Autocracy* (Cambridge: Harvard University Press, 2006), p. 65. Pei's book was one of the first to explain China's lack of progress toward democracy.

2. Some estimate the size of the People's Armed Police at 1.5 million members, though the Chinese government put their number at 666,000 in 2006. See Michael Wines, "China Approves Law Governing Armed Police Force," *New York Times*, August 27, 2009, http://www.nytimes.com/2009/08/28/world/asia/28china.html.

3. Murray Scot Tanner, "Chinese Government Responses to Rising Social Unrest," testimony presented to the U.S.-China Economic and Security Review Commission, April 14, 2005 (RAND CT-240), p. 8, http://rand.org/pubs/testimonies/CT240/index.html.

4. Pei, *China's Trapped Transition*, p. 82.

5. Ibid., pp. 88–95.

6. Edward Friedman, "Authoritarian China as a World Power: Democracy in the Balance," mimeograph (2005), p. 9.

7. The most authoritative, independent annual assessment of political conditions around the world continues to place China at or near the bottom of its lowest category of "unfree" countries. Freedom House ranks countries on a 1 (high) to 7 (low) scale depending on its provision of political rights and civil liberties. In its 1999 report it shifted China's score on the latter issue from 7 to 6 to take account of the "easing in state intrusion into the personal lives of its citizens," but there has been no improvement since then. Robert L. Bartley and Roger Kaplan, *Freedom in the World: The Annual Survey of Political Rights and Civil Liberties, 1998–1999* (New York: Transaction, 1999), p. 133.

8. Congressional-Executive Commission on China, *Annual Report: 2008* (Washington, D.C.: GPO, 2008), p. 147. Also available from http://www.cecc.gov/.

9. Azar Gat, "The Return of Authoritarian Great Powers," *Foreign Affairs* vol. 86, no. 4 (July/August 2007), pp. 59–69. China's evolution in this direction is explained by Kellee S. Tsai, *Capitalism without Democracy: The Private Sector in Contemporary China* (Ithaca: Cornell University Press, 2007).

10. James Mann, *The China Fantasy: How Our Leaders Explain Away Chinese Repression* (New York: Viking, 2007), p. 101. The response to this argument from prominent Sinologists has been fourfold: Mann is right about the absence of deep political reform, but he understates the progress that *has* occurred, is too impatient and, in any event, has no alternative policy to offer Western governments. See David M. Lampton, "*The China Fantasy* Fantasy," *China Quarterly* vol. 191 (September 2007), pp. 745–749.

11. John Fox and François Godement, *A Power Audit of EU-China Relations* (London: European Council on Foreign Relations, 2009), p. 1.

12. Mann, *The China Fantasy*, p. 27.

13. See, for example, Richard Holbrooke, "A Defining Moment with China," *Washington Post*, January 2, 2002, p. A13; David Shambaugh and Robert S. Litwak, "Common Interests in a Hazardous World," *New York Times*, October 17, 2001, p. A31.

14. See George W. Bush, "State of the Union Address of the President to the Joint Session of Congress," January 29, 2002, http://www.c-span.org/executive/transcript .asp?cat=current&code=bush_admin&year=2002.

15. "Transcript: President Bush, China's Jiang Zemin Meet in Shanghai," October 19, 2001, Department of State Washington File, EPF501, http://usinfo.org/wf-archive/2001/011019/epf501.htm.

16. One highly favorable assessment claimed in 2003 that U.S.-China intelligence sharing had led to several "major international criminal arrests," but acknowledged that these involved heroin smuggling and fell "outside the realm of strict counterterrorism cooperations." David Lampton and Richard Daniel Ewing, *The U.S.-China Relationship Facing International Security Crises: Three Case Studies in Post-9/11 Bilateral Relations* (Washington, D.C.: Nixon Center, 2003), p. 8.

17. Robert Kaplan, "Beijing's Afghan Gamble," *New York Times*, October 6, 2009, http://www.nytimes.com/2009/10/07/opinion/07kaplan.html?_r=1. As in other parts of the developing world, China has been primarily interested in extracting raw materials, including, in this case, copper.

18. For an overview, see Shirley Kan, *U.S.-China Counter-Terrorism Cooperation: Issues for U.S. Policy*, Report RL33001 (Washington, D.C.: Congressional Research Service, May 7, 2009), http://assets.opencrs.com/rpts/RL33001_20090507.pdf. Quote from p. 3.

19. The publicly available evidence regarding China's support of Pakistan's nuclear program (and, albeit on a more limited scale, Iran's), and Pakistan's support for Iran, Libya, and North Korea is summarized in Matthew Kroening, "Exporting the Bomb: Why States Provide Sensitive Nuclear Assistance," *American Political Science Review* vol. 103, no. 1 (February 2009), pp. 113–128. Less is known about the extent of China's support for North Korea, and North Korea's role in assisting Iran and Syria. For references to the former, see "North Korea's Nuclear Program, 2005," *Bulletin of the Atomic Scientists* vol. 61, no. 3 (May/June 2005), p. 64; and Leon V. Sigal, *Disarming Strangers: Nuclear Diplomacy with North Korea* (Princeton: Princeton University Press, 1998), p. 20. Regarding the latter, see Mark Fitzpatrick, "Iran and North Korea: The Proliferation Nexus," *Survival* vol. 48, no. 1 (2006), pp. 61–80; and Office of the Director of National Intelligence, "Background Briefing with Senior U.S. Officials on Syria's Covert Nuclear Reactor and North Korea's Involvement," April 24, 2008, http://www.dni.gov/interviews/20080424_interview.pdf.

20. The evolution of Chinese policy, and American reactions to it, are described in Evan S. Medeiros, *Reluctant Restraint: The Evolution of China's Nonproliferation Policies and Practices, 1980–2004* (Stanford: Stanford University Press, 2007).

21. *2007 Report to Congress of the U.S.-China Economic and Security Review Commission, One Hundred Tenth Congress, First Session, June 1, 2007* (Washington, D.C.: GPO, 2007), p. 118.

22. *2006 Report to Congress of the U.S.-China Economic and Security Review Commission, One Hundred Ninth Congress, Second Session, November 2006* (Washington, D.C.: U.S. Government Printing Office, 2006), p. 84.

23. One careful assessment concludes that while China has great potential economic, diplomatic, and military influence, "it lacks the resolve to assert its influence due

to the complexity of the political and security situation in Northeast Asia." Jaeho Hwang, "Measuring China's Influence over North Korea," *Issues and Studies* vol. 42, no. 2 (June 2006), pp. 205–232. Quote from p. 227.

24. For an analysis detailing the benefits to Beijing of a "continued non-violent crisis," see John Michael Ives, "Four Kilograms to Tip the Scale: China's Exploitation of the North Korean Nuclear Crisis," master's thesis, Naval Postgraduate School, Monterey, Calif., December 2007. Quote from p. 9.

25. David Shambaugh, "China and the Korean Peninsula: Playing for the Long Term," *Washington Quarterly* vol. 26, no. 2 (Spring 2003), p. 53. See also Aaron L. Friedberg, "U.S. Strategy in Northeast Asia: Short and Long-Term Challenges," in Wilson Lee, Robert M. Hathaway, and William M. Wise, eds., *U.S. Strategy in the Asia-Pacific Region* (Washington, D.C.: Woodrow Wilson International Center for Scholars, 2003), pp. 18–30.

26. See International Crisis Group, "The Iran Nuclear Issue: The View from Beijing," Asia Briefing Number 100, Beijing/Brussels, February 17, 2010, http://www .crisisgroup.org/en/regions/middle-east-north-africa/iran-gulf/iran/B100-the-iran-nuclear-issue-the-view-from-beijing-.aspx.

27. Mark Leonard, *What Does China Think?* (London: Fourth Estate, 2008), p. 128.

28. Alastair Iain Johnston, "Is China a Status Quo Power?" *International Security* vol. 27, no. 4 (Spring 2003), pp. 5–56.

29. For a detailed accounting of its participation, and the argument that engagement has, in fact, "socialized" China, see Ann Kent, *Beyond Compliance: China, International Organizations, and Global Security* (Stanford: Stanford University Press, 2007).

30. See Allen Carlson, *Unifying China, Integrating with the World: Securing Chinese Sovereignty in the Reform Era* (Stanford: Stanford University Press, 2005).

31. Johnston, "Is China a Status Quo Power?" p. 39.

32. Iain Johnston, one of the leading proponents of "socialization theory," concludes his study of China's participation in arms control regimes by noting cautiously that Beijing's behavior may have shifted in "non-realpolitik directions" on some issues. But he points out that depending in large part on what the United States does next, "these changes can be reversible." Alastair Iain Johnston, *Social States: China in International Institutions 1980–2000* (Princeton: Princeton University Press, 2008), p. 212.

33. This point is highlighted in James Mann's excellent study, *About Face: A History of America's Curious Relationship with China, From Nixon to Clinton* (New York: Alfred A. Knopf, 1999).

34. David Finkelstein, *Commentary on China's External Grand Strategy*, Center for Naval Analyses, CNA China Studies, CIM D0023641.A1/Final, September 2010, p. 7, http://www.cna.org/sites/default/files/research/D0023641_A1.pdf.

35. For a discussion of the "peaceful rise" slogan and the means by which the regime seeks both to benefit from and to control a more diffuse foreign policy–making process, see Bonnie S. Glaser and Evan S. Medeiros, "The Changing Ecology of Foreign Policy–Making in China: The Ascension and Demise of the Theory of 'Peaceful Rise,'" *The China Quarterly* vol. 190 (June 2007), pp. 291–310. In part because Americans do not tend to take them very seriously, the techniques by which the regime seeks to shape the perceptions of foreigners have not been given

the attention they deserve. For an analysis of the ways in which China's official media tries to "spin" coverage of events like the 2001 incident in which a U.S. Navy surveillance plane collided with a Chinese fighter jet, see Peter Callamari and Derek Reveron, "China's Use of Perception Management," *International Journal of Intelligence and Counterintelligence* vol. 16, no. 1 (2003), pp. 1–15.

36. See "Prepared Statement of Dr. Jacqueline Newmyer," in *China's Propaganda and Influence Operations, Its Intelligence Activities That Target the United States, and the Resulting Impacts on U.S. National Security, Hearing before the U.S.-China Economic and Security Review Commission, One Hundred Eleventh Congress, First session, April 30, 2009* (Washington, D.C.: United States–China Economic and Security Review Commission, June 2009), pp. 88–91. Quotes from a February 2009 article in *Reference News,* an internal publication of the Xinhua news agency, p. 89.

37. See American Chamber of Commerce in China, *2010 White Paper on the State of American Business in China,* May 2010, p. 22, http:www.amchamchina.org/article/6309.

38. Regarding the growing interest of the American business community in China during the early 1990s and its critical role in countering pressure from labor unions and human rights groups in the 1994 debate over most favored nation status, see Warren I. Cohen, *America's Response to China: A History of Sino-American Relations* (New York: Columbia University Press, 2000), pp. 229–232. Also Mann's *About Face,* pp. 292–314. By 2000 the coalition supporting permanent normal trading status with China included four U.S.-China trade associations, the American Insurance Association, National Retail Foundation, Electronic Industries Alliance Auto Trade Policy Council, Grocery Manufacturers Association, American Farm Bureau, and the National Association of Manufacturers; large corporations like General Electric, ExxonMobil, Aetna and New York Life Insurance, and America Online; and, for the first time, dozens of smaller high-technology firms. See Ian Urbina, "The Corporate PNTR Lobby: How Big Business Is Paying Millions to Gain Billions in China," *Multinational Monitor* (May 2000), pp. 7–11; and Lizette Alvarez, "High-Tech Companies Making Their First Big Push in Congress on a Trade Bill," *New York Times,* May 18, 2000, p. A15. In addition to the efforts of American companies, the Chinese government has become more sophisticated in lobbying directly on its own behalf. See Marina Walker Guevara and Bob Williams, "China Steps Up Its Lobbying Game," *LobbyWatch,* September 15, 2005, http://projects.publicintegrity.org/lobby/report.aspx?aid=734.

39. See "Statement of Dr. Ross Terrill," in *China's Propaganda and Influence Operations,* pp. 65–68. Quote from p. 67. For example, in late 2010, New York University announced the launch of a new center on U.S.-China relations funded with an initial grant from Rilin Enterprises, "a global construction and logistics firm based in Dandong, China." "NYU Launches Center in U.S.-China Relations," October 25, 2010, http://www.nyu.edu/about/news-publications/news/2010/10/25/nyu-launches-center-on-us-china-relations.html.

40. Mark P. Lagon, "The 'Shanghai Coalition': The Chattering Classes and China," *Perspectives on Political Science* vol. 29, no. 1 (Winter 2000), pp. 7–16.

41. Mann, *China Fantasy,* p. 59.

42. Ibid.

43. The 2010 decision by search engine company Google to withdraw from China was

the first major deviation from this pattern. Regarding the alleged cooperation of American companies with Beijing in its efforts to control and monitor communications over the Internet, see *2008 Report to Congress of the U.S.-China Economic and Security Review Commission, One Hundred Tenth Congress, Second Session, November 2008* (Washington, D.C.: GPO, 2008), pp. 291–301. Regarding Google's decision to shut down its site in China, see Miguel Helft and David Barboza, "Google Shuts China Site in Dispute over Censorship," *New York Times*, March 22, 2010, http://www.nytimes.com/2010/03/23/technology/23google.html?ref=google_inc.

44. Quoted in Ken Silverstein, "The Mandrins: American Foreign Policy, Brought to You by China," *Harper's Magazine*, August 2008, p. 55.

45. Perry Link, "Turned Back at China's Door," *Princeton Alumni Weekly*, February 9, 2005, http://www.princeton.edu/~paw/archive_new/PAW04-05/08-0209/perspective.html.

46. Carsten A. Holz, "Have China Scholars All Been Bought?" *Far East Economic Review* vol. 170, no. 3 (April 2007), p. 36.

47. See Joshua Kurlantzick, *Charm Offensive: How China's Soft Power Is Transforming the World* (New Haven: Yale University Press, 2007).

48. Samuel P. Huntington, *The Clash of Civilizations and the Remaking of World Order* (New York: Simon and Schuster, 1996), p. 234.

49. Ibid.

50. For an elaboration of these arguments, see David C. Kang, *China Rising: Peace, Power, and Order in East Asia* (New York: Columbia University Press, 2007).

51. Washington has recently taken steps to revitalize military-to-military ties with Indonesia, and it has engaged the Communist government of Vietnam in sporadic discussions about joint maneuvers and possible access by the U.S. Navy to the massive facilities it built in the 1960s at Cam Ranh Bay. As a maritime democracy, Indonesia would be a natural addition to the existing coalition. Because of its regime and its contiguity with China, Vietnam would not, but its long history of resistance to Chinese domination will probably push it closer to the United States.

52. For an analysis of the sources and likely limits of Sino-Russian cooperation, see Richard Weitz, "Why Russia and China Have Not Formed an Anti-American Alliance," *Naval War College Review* vol. 54, no. 4 (Autumn 2003), pp. 39–59; Bobo Lo, *Axis of Convenience: Moscow, Beijing and the New Geopolitics* (London: Royal Institute of International Affairs, 2008).

53. See, for example, G. Parthasarathy, "The Axis of Grudging Cooperation," *Wall Street Journal*, May 4, 2010, http://online.wsj.com/article/SB10001424052748704608104575221303790430846.html?mod=wsj_india_main; Daniel Twining, "Diplomatic Negligence," *Weekly Standard*, May 10, 2010, http://www.weeklystandard.com/articles/diplomatic-negligence.

54. Edward Wong, "China and India Dispute Enclave on Edge of Tibet," *New York Times*, September 3, 2009, http://www.nytimes.com/2009/09/04/world/asia/04chinaindia.html.

55. This shift in attitudes was made clear during President Obama's trip to Asia in November 2010, when, among other gestures, he endorsed India's bid to become a permanent member of the UN Security Council. See Ben Feller, "Obama Boosts

India for 'Rightful Place in World,'" Associated Press, November 8, 2010, http://news.yahoo.com/s/ap/20101108/ap_on_re_us/obama_asia.

56. Denny Roy, "Southeast Asia and China: Balancing or Bandwagoning?" *Contemporary Southeast Asia* vol. 27, no. 2 (2005), p. 314.

57. For an excellent overview of most of the cases discussed here, see Evan S. Medeiros, Keith Crane, Eric Heiginbotham, et al., *Pacific Currents: The Responses of U.S. Allies and Security Partners in East Asia to China's Rise* (Santa Monica, Calif.: RAND, 2008). Regarding the Philippines, see pp. 97–123.

58. For a highly bullish assessment, see Busakorn Chantasasawat, "Burgeoning Sino-Thai Relations: Heightening Cooperation, Sustaining Economic Security," *China: An International Journal* vol. 4, no. 1 (March 2006), pp. 86–112. For a more measured evaluation that emphasizes the sources of continued vitality in the U.S.-Thai relationship, see Medeiros et al., *Pacific Currents*, pp. 125–157.

59. Shawn W. Crispin, "When Allies Drift Apart," *Asia Times*, February 14, 2009, http://www.atimes.com/atimes/Southeast_Asia/KB14Ae01.html.

60. For a pessimistic appraisal, see "Unrest in Thailand Indicates Deeper Problems," *Strategic Comments* vol. 16 (May 2010), http://www.iiss.org/publications/strategic-comments/past-issues/volume-16-2010/may/unrest-in-thailand-indicates-deeper-problems/.

61. Rory Medcalf, "Strategic Roles beyond the Paramount Areas: Strategic Roles Northeast and West," *Security Challenges* vol. 3, no. 3 (August 2007), pp. 33–34.

62. Rory Medcalf, "Mysterious Quad More Phantom than Menace," *ABC News*, April 9, 2008, http://www.abc.net.au/news/stories/2008/04/09/22116000.htm.

63. Mohan Malik, "Australia and the United States 2004–2005: All the Way with the U.S.A.?" Asia Pacific Center for Security Studies: Special Assessment, February 2005, p. 7, http://www.apcss.org/Publications/SAS/APandtheUS/MalikAustralia1.pdf.

64. Michael Wines, "Australia, Nourishing China's Economic Engine, Questions Ties," *New York Times*, June 2, 2009, p. A1.

65. Australian Government, Department of Defence, *Defence White Paper 2009: Defending Australia in the Asia Pacific Century: Force 2030* (Canberra: Commonwealth of Australia, 2009), p. 34.

66. Ibid., p. 33.

67. The debate over how Australia should position itself between China and the United States is by no means over. See Hugh White, "As China Rises Australia Must Look beyond U.S. Alliance," *Australian*, September 15, 2010, http://www.theaustralian.com.au/national-affairs/commentary/as-china-rises-we-must-look-beyond-the-us-alliance/story-e6frgdox-1225919850496.

68. Seong-ho Sheen, "Strategic Thought toward Asia in the Roh Moo-hyun Era," in Gilbert Rozman, In-Taek Hyun, and Shin-wha Lee, eds., *South Korean Strategic Thought toward Asia* (New York: Palgrave Macmillan, 2008), pp. 101–128; Sheila Miyoshi Jager, "Politics of Anti-Americanism in South Korea," *Asia Times*, August 5, 2005, http://www.atimes.com/atimes/Korea/GH05Dg03.html.

69. See Ruediger Frank, "A New Foreign Policy Paradigm: Perspectives on the Role of South Korea as a Balancer," *Nautilus Institute: Policy Forum Online*, April 25, 2005, http://www.nautilus.org/fora/security/0535AFrank.html.

70. Mederios et al., *Pacific Currents*, p. 88.
71. See the following article in one of Korea's major English-language newspapers, Sunny Lee, "Post-Cheonan Dilemma: How to Deal with China," *Korea Times*, July 29, 2010, http://www.koreatimes.co.kr/www/news/nation/2010/08/116_70422 .html.
72. Chicago Council on Global Affairs, *Soft Power in Asia: Results of a 2008 Multinational Survey of Public Opinion* (Chicago: Chicago Council on Global Affairs, 2009).
73. See "Fred Hiatt Interviews President Lee Myung-bak," *Washington Post*, April 12, 2010, http://www.washingtonpost.com/wp-dyn/content/article/2010/04/11/ AR2010041103045.html.
74. Peter Lee, "The *Cheonan* Sinking . . . and Korea Rising," *Asia Times*, June 3, 2010, http://www.atimes.com/atimes/Korea/LF03Dg01.html.
75. This shift is described in Sukhee Han, "From Engagement to Hedging: South Korea's New China Policy," *Korean Journal of Defense Analysis* vol. 20, no. 4 (December 2008), pp. 335–351.
76. Gideon Rachman, "Japan Edges from America towards China," *Financial Times*, March 8, 2010, http://www.ft.com/cms/s/0/4a7c23a2-2aef-11df-886b-00144feabdc0 .html#axzz18fotJcaG.
77. John Feffer, "Japan's Three Elections," *Foreign Policy Focus*, September 14, 2010, http://www.fpig.org/blog/japans_three_elections.
78. Ian Johnson, "Arrest in Disputed Seas Riles China and Japan," *New York Times*, September 19, 2010, http://www.nytimes.com/2010/09/20/world/asia/20chinajapan .html?scp=68&sq=&st=nyt.

CHAPTER 9: THE BALANCE OF POWER

1. For details of the so-called maritime strategy, see John B. Hattendorf and Peter M. Swartz, eds., *U.S. Naval Strategy in the 1980s: Selected Documents* (Newport, R.I.: Naval War College Press, 2008).
2. See discussion in chapter 5. Chinese defense spending jumped in 1989 and has continued to increase at double-digit rates since. See table in David Shambaugh, *Modernizing China's Military Progress, Problems, and Prospects* (Berkeley: University of California Press, 2002), p.189.
3. Among the first to grasp this was an air force officer who served during the early 1990s as an assistant air attaché in Beijing. See Mark A. Stokes, *China's Strategic Modernization: Implications for the United States* (Carlisle, Penn.: U.S. Army War College, Strategic Studies Institute, 1999).
4. China's progress in acquiring over-the-horizon radars, satellites, and unmanned aerial vehicles is described in Office of the Secretary of Defense, *Annual Report to Congress, Military and Security Developments Involving the People's Republic of China*, 2010, pp. 2, 7, and 33, http://www.defense.gov/pubs/pdfs/2010_CMPR_ Final.pdf. Regarding the possible development of a Chinese undersea surveillance system see Bill Gertz, "Inside the Ring," *Washington Times*, May 9, 2008, p. 6. The Gertz piece is cited in Ronald O'Rourke, *China Naval Modernization: Implications*

for U.S. Navy Capabilities—Background and Issues for Congress (Washington, D.C.: Congressional Research Service, 2008), pp. 30–31.

5. The potential consequences of such an attack are analyzed in David A. Shlapak, David T. Orletsky, Toy I. Reid, Murray Scot Tanner, and Barry Wilson, *A Question of Balance: Political Context and Military Aspects of the China-Taiwan Dispute* (Santa Monica, Calif.: RAND, 2009), pp. 31–51. The authors conclude that China could temporarily close all of Taiwan's fighter bases using 60–200 short-range ballistic missiles. The result of such a strike would be "a Taiwan with a profoundly reduced ability to defend itself, left open to a range of follow-on actions intended to coerce or conquer it and its people." Ibid., p. 51.

6. The possible dimensions and implications of such an attack, which would likely involve repeated strikes with conventionally armed ballistic and cruise missiles against all U.S. bases in the Western Pacific, including those in Japan and on Guam, are described in Jan Van Tol, *AirSea Battle: A Point-of-Departure Operational Concept* (Washington, D.C.: Center for Strategic and Budgetary Assessments, 2010), pp. 17–41. For insights into Chinese thinking, see Toshi Yoshihara, "Chinese Military Strategy and the U.S. Naval Presence in Japan: The Operational View from Beijing," *Naval War College Review* vol. 63, no. 3 (Summer 2010), pp. 39–62.

7. For details regarding these vessels, see James C. Bussert, "Catamarans Glide through Chinese Waters," *Signal* (December 2007), http://www.afcea.org/signal/articles/templates/Signal_Article_Template.asp?articleid=1433&zoneid=222.

8. See Andrew S. Erickson and David D. Yang, "On the Verge of a Game-Changer," *U.S. Naval Institute Proceedings* vol. 135/5/1275 (May 2009), pp. 26–32. For an overview of recent Chinese writings on the subject of how to "kill" an aircraft carrier, see Roger Cliff, Mark Burles, Michael S. Chase, Derek Eaton, and Kevin L. Pollpeter, *Entering the Dragon's Lair: Chinese Antiaccess Strategies and Their Implications for the United States* (Santa Monica, Calif.: RAND, 2007), pp. 71–76. The best publicly available analysis of the antiship ballistic missile threat is Mark Stokes, *China's Evolving Conventional Strategic Strike Capability* (Washington, D.C.: Project 2049 Institute, September 14, 2009), http://project2049.net/documents/chinese_anti_ship_ballistic_missile_asbm.pdf.

9. After the 1999 NATO air war against Serbia, the PLA promulgated a new doctrine for air defense known as "Three Attacks/Three Defenses" (attack stealth aircraft, cruise missiles, and helicopters; defend against precision strikes, electronic warfare, and enemy reconnaissance). Department of Defense, *Annual Report to Congress: Military Power of the People's Republic of China, 2005* (Washington, D.C.: Department of Defense, 2005), p. 18.

10. The Chinese have been working since at least the turn of the century to develop "technologies, systems, and procedures to detect, track and engage stealth aircraft and cruise missiles." See Wayne Ulman (China Issue Manager, National Air and Space Intelligence Center), in United States–China Economic and Security Review Commission, *China's Emergent Military Aerospace and Commercial Aviation Capabilities*, 111th Congress, 2nd session (Washington, D.C.: United States–China Economic and Security Review Commission, 2010), p. 56.

11. Regarding hardening and the shift to fiber-optic cable, see Office of the Secretary of Defense, *Annual Report to Congress: Military Power of the People's Republic*

of China, 2009 (Washington D.C.: Department of Defense, 2009), p. viii, www .defense.gov/oubs/pdfs/China_Military_Power_Report_2009.pdf.

12. For an overview, see Ashley J. Tellis, "China's Military Space Strategy," *Survival* vol. 49, no. 3 (Autumn 2007), pp. 41–72.

13. "U.S. Navy Boosts Cyber Focus," *DefenseNews* (May 4, 2009), http://www.defense news.com/story.php?i=4070485&c=FEA&s=CVS.

14. For an overview of Chinese thinking on the utility of computer network attacks, see Cliff et al., *Entering the Dragon's Lair*, pp. 51–57. For a summary of publicly available evidence of recent Chinese cyberattacks and probes, see Timothy L. Thomas, "Google Confronts the 'Three Warfares,'" *Parameters* (Summer 2010), pp. 101–113.

15. Shlapak et al., *Question of Balance*, p. xvi.

16. See the description of a RAND study titled "Air Combat Past, Present and Future," in Wendell Minnick, "Rand Study Suggests U.S. Loses War with China," *Defense-News* (October 16, 2008), http://www.defensenews.com/story.php?i=3774348 &c=ASI&s=AIR.

17. Richard Halloran, "PACAF's 'Vision' Thing," *Air Force Magazine* (January 2009), pp. 54–56.

18. Andrew F. Krepinevich Jr., "The Pentagon's Wasting Assets," *Foreign Affairs* vol. 88, no. 4 (July/August 2009), pp. 18–33.

19. For details, see Stockholm International Peace Research Institute, *SIPRI Yearbook 2008* (New York: Oxford University Press, 2008), pp. 364–367.

20. See Keir A. Lieber and Daryl G. Press, "The Rise of U.S. Nuclear Primacy," *Foreign Affairs* vol. 85, no. 2 (March/April 2006), pp. 42–54.

21. In the early 1990s China was thought to have only twenty ballistic missiles with true intercontinental range, but over one hundred shorter-range missiles and bombers capable of striking targets throughout Eastern Eurasia. *SIPRI Yearbook 2008*, p. 366.

22. It is not known how many of these new weapons China will ultimately build. Some sources suggest that the People's Liberation Army Navy (PLAN) will eventually deploy four or five Type 094 submarines, each carrying sixteen JL-2s, with between three and six warheads per missile. (Other sources suggest a more modest twelve JL-2s per submarine, with three or four warheads each.) Added to perhaps several dozen land-mobile ICBMs, some of which could also carry multiple warheads, this would give Beijing a second-strike capability against the United States much larger, and considerably more secure, than what it had only a few years ago. The possible dimensions of the undersea component of China's nuclear deterrent force are dis-cussed in Christopher McConnaughy, "China's Undersea Nuclear Deterrent," in Andrew S. Erickson, Lyle J. Goldstein, William S. Murray, and Andrew R. Wilson, eds., *China's Future Submarine Force* (Newport, R.I.: Naval Institute Press, 2007), pp. 77–113.

23. Regarding the possible dimensions and significance of a greatly expanded force of nuclear attack submarines, see the discussion in Andrew S. Erickson and Lyle J. Goldstein, "China's Future Nuclear Submarine Force," in Erickson et al., *China's Future Nuclear Submarine Force*, pp. 182–211.

24. For an analysis of the likely difficulties and limitations of a possible naval blockade,

see Gabriel B. Collins and William S. Murray, "No Oil for the Lamps of China?" *Naval War College Review* vol. 61, no. 2 (Spring 2008), pp. 79–95.

25. Zhang Wenmu, professor at the Center for Strategic Studies at the Beijing University of Aeronautics and Astronautics, quoted in Andrew S. Erickson and Lyle J. Goldstein, "Introduction: Chinese Perspectives on Maritime Transformation," in Andrew S. Erickson, Lyle J. Goldstein, and Carnes Lord, eds., *China Goes to Sea: Maritime Transformation in Comparative Historical Perspective* (Annapolis: Naval Institute Press, 2009), p. xxi.

26. Andrew Erickson and Lyle Goldstein, "Gunboats for China's New 'Grand Canals'?" *Naval War College Review* vol. 62, no. 2 (Spring 2009), p. 59.

27. The phrase "string of pearls" was apparently first used in a report on energy security prepared by the consulting firm Booz Allen Hamilton for the Office of Net Assessment in the Office of the Secretary of Defense. See Bill Gertz, "China Builds Up Strategic Sea Lanes," *Washington Times*, January 17, 2005, http://www.washington times.com/news/2005/jan/17/20050117-115550-1929r/?page=1. For a discussion, see Christopher J. Pehrson, *String of Pearls: Meeting the Challenge of China's Rising Power across the Asian Littoral* (Carlisle, Penn.: Strategic Studies Institute, 2006).

28. These are the words of Rear Admiral Yin Zhou, discussing a possible base in the Gulf of Aden, where the PLAN has been involved in antipiracy operations. "Chinese Admiral Floats Idea of Overseas Naval Bases," Reuters.com, December 30, 2009, http://www.reuters.com/article/idUSTRE5BT0P020091230.

29. Chinese naval strategists have mentioned this possibility to visiting Western analysts. See Erickson and Goldstein, "Gunboats for China's New 'Grand Canals'?" p. 57.

30. Thomas Christensen, "Posing Problems without Catching Up: China's Rise and Challenges for U.S. Security Policy," *International Security* vol. 24, no. 4 (2001), pp. 5–40.

31. See the discussion of the 863 and 973 Programs, and the 2006 fifteen-year science and technology plan, in *2007 Report to Congress of the U.S.-China Economic and Security Review Commission, One Hundred Tenth Congress, First Session, June 1, 2007* (Washington, D.C.: GPO, 2007), pp. 126–129.

32. See Cong Cao, Richard P. Suttmeier, and Denis Fred Simon, "China's 15-Year Science and Technology Plan," *Physics Today* (December 2006), pp. 38–40. R&D spending grew at around 19% annually between 1995 and 2005. Peggy Christoff, *China's Technology Sector*, a report prepared by the Federal Research Division, Library of Congress under an interagency agreement with the Director of Defense Research and Engineering, Office of the Secretary of Defense, December 2008, p. 1. An increasing fraction of total R&D spending is coming from business enterprises, a fact that should bode well for future innovation. Ibid., p. 130. See also James Wilsdon, "China: The Next Science Superpower?" *Engineering and Technology* (March 2007), pp. 28–31.

33. See Ernest H. Preeg, *The Emerging Chinese Advanced Technology Superstate* (Washington, D.C.: Hudson Institute, 2005), pp. 26–30.

34. For a comparison of several measures, see Alan S. Porter, Nils C. Newman, et al., "International High Tech Competitiveness: Does China Rank #1?" *Technology Analysis and Strategic Management* vol. 21, no. 2 (2009), pp. 173–193.

35. For a detailed discussion of these reforms, many of which began in 1998, see Evan S. Medeiros, Roger Cliff, Keith Crane, and James C. Mulvenon, *A New Direction for China's Defense Industry* (Santa Monica, Calif.: RAND, 2005).

36. See Aaron L. Friedberg, *In the Shadow of the Garrison State: America's Anti-Statism and Its Cold War Grand Strategy* (Princeton: Princeton University Press, 2000), pp. 296–339.

37. The slogan was unveiled in 2003 at the Sixteenth Party Congress. See James Mulvenon and Rebecca Samm Tyroler-Cooper, "China's Defense Industry on the Path of Reform," prepared for the U.S.-China Economic and Security Review Commission, October 2009, p. 5, http://www.uscc.gov/researchpapers/2009/ DGI%20Report%20on%PRC%20Defense%20Industry%20--%20Final%20 Version%20_with%20uscc%20seal_%2002Nov2009%20_2_pdf.

38. Medeiros et al., *A New Direction for China's Defense Industry*, pp. xxi–xxiii.

39. *Military Power of the People's Republic of China, 2009*, p. 35.

40. Ibid., p. 37.

41. Preeg, *Emerging Chinese Advanced Technology Superstate*, p. 33.

42. James Kynge, *China Shakes the World* (New York: Houghton Mifflin, 2006), p. 114.

43. Among the "major special items" for which it seeks indigenous capabilities are high-end integrated circuits, operating system software, next-generation broadband wireless mobile communications equipment, and high-grade numerically controlled machine tools. *Military Power of the People's Republic of China, 2009*, p. 38.

44. Some analysts believe that despite the rapid growth of its economy, China faces deeply rooted obstacles to major innovations of the sort that will be needed to sustain its forward progress in the decades to come. Among these are weak protections of intellectual property rights and a financial system that favors those with political pull rather than new ideas. See Jacqueline Newmyer and Jennifer Glazer, "The Real Great Wall: Barriers to Radical Innovation in China," Long-Term Strategy Project, Cambridge, Mass., DASW01-02-D-0014-0068, September 2006.

45. This was a fact few understood at the time. See Henry S. Rowen and Charles Wolf, *The Future of the Soviet Empire* (New York: St. Martin's Press, 1988).

46. See table 17 in Ashley J. Tellis and Michael Wills, eds., *Strategic Asia 2006–07: Trade, Interdependence, and Security* (Seattle: National Bureau of Asian Research, 2006), p. 409.

47. Robert Gates, "A Balanced Strategy: Reprogramming the Pentagon for a New Age," *Foreign Affairs* vol. 88, no. 1 (January/February 2009), p. 28.

48. Mark Gunzinger and Jim Thomas, "The 2010 Quadrennial Defense Review: An Initial Assessment," Center for Strategic and Budgetary Assessments Backgrounder, February 2010, p. 1, http://www.csbaonline.org/4Publications/PubLibrary/B.20100201 .The_2010_QDR_An_In/B.20100201.The_2010_QDR_An_In.pdf.

49. Pew Center for the People and the Press, in association with the Council on Foreign Relations, *America's Place in the World 2009*, December 2009, p. 12, http:// people-press.org/reports/pdf/569.pdf.

50. Recent polling suggests that more than half of the country now believes that China's emergence may pose a major threat to the United States. Ibid., p. 5.

51. Congressional Budget Office, "The Budget and Economic Outlook: Fiscal Years 2010 to 2020," January 2010, pp. 1–2, http://www.cbo.gov/ftpdocs/108xx/doc10871/Chapter1.shtml#1045449.

52. Ibid. Thanks to an influx of money from worried overseas investors, and deliberate efforts by Washington to stimulate the economy, during the depths of the recent crisis interest rates were unusually low. As they increase, so too will the costs to the federal government. As one observer put it, "The government is on teaser rates. We're taking out a huge mortgage right now, but we won't feel the pain until later." Edmund L. Andrews, "Wave of Debt Payments Facing U.S. Government," New York Times, November 23, 2009, http://www.nytimes.com/2009/11/23/business/23rates.html.

53. Center for Geoeconomic Studies, "U.S. Interest vs. Defense Spending," Council on Foreign Relations, October 26, 2009, http://blogs.cfr.org/geographics/2009/10/26/interest-expense/.

54. Donald B. Marron, "America in the Red," National Affairs no. 3 (Spring 2010), pp. 3–19.

55. The historical average growth for the period since 1875 is 3.4 percent. See David J. Lynch, "U.S. May Face Years of Sluggish Economic Growth," USATODAY.com May 7, 2009. For a relatively optimistic prediction of 2.6 percent growth for the period 2010–20, see Martin S. Feldstein, "U.S. Growth in the Decade Ahead," National Bureau of Economic Research, Working Paper 15685, January 2010, http://www.nber.org/papers/w15685. For reasons having nothing directly to do with the financial crisis (primarily an anticipated drop in productivity), Robert Gordon predicts a 2.4 percent growth rate over the coming two decades. See Robert Gordon, "Revisiting U.S. Productivity Growth over the Past Century with a View of the Future," National Bureau of Economic Research, Working Paper 15834, March 2010, http://www.nber.org/papers/w15834.

56. For a debunking of many of the more pessimistic appraisals of China's performance and prospects, see BoBo Lo, "China and the Global Financial Crisis," Centre for European Reform, April 2010, http://www.cer.org.uk/pdf/essay_974.pdf.

57. Pieter Bottelier, "China and the International Financial Crisis," in Ashley J. Tellis, Andrew Marble, and Travis Tanner, eds., Strategic Asia 2009–10: Economic Meltdown and Geopolitical Stability (Seattle: National Bureau of Asian Research, 2009), pp. 72–76.

58. See "OECD Sees Strong Growth, Low Inflation in China," Reuters.com, November 19, 2009, http://www.reuters.com/article/idUSSGR00205520091119; and Qing Wang, "China: Upgrading 2010 Forecasts on Improved External Outlook," Morgan Stanley.com, February 5, 2010, http://www.morganstanley.com/views/gef/.

59. For a useful overview, see William E. Odom and Robert Dujarric, America's Inadvertent Empire (New Haven: Yale University Press, 2004).

60. See "A Slow-Burning Fuse: A Special Report on Aging," Economist, June 11, 2009. Also Richard Jackson and Neil Howe, The Graying of the Great Powers: Demography and Geopolitics in the 21st Century (Washington, D.C.: Center for Strategic and International Studies, 2008), http://csis.org/files/media/csis/pubs/080630_gai_majorfindings.pdf.

61. See Nicholas Eberstadt, "Born in the USA," American Interest no. 5 (May/June 2007), http://www.the-american-interest.com/article.cfm?piece=272.

62. Many of the most dramatic changes will occur over the next twenty years. According to one recent study, between 2005 and 2015 the working-age population will grow by only 33 million (versus 163 million, 124 million, and 107 million in the preceding ten-year periods). Between 2015 and 2025 it will shrink by 29 million, and over the subsequent ten years, by 77 million. Beginning in around 2030, compared to the U.S. population a larger portion of China's population will be over the age of sixty. Between 2010 and 2030 the number of working-age adults available to support each elderly person in China will fall from over five to just over three. See Richard Jackson and Neil Howe, *The Graying of the Middle Kingdom: The Demographics and Economics of Retirement Policy in China* (Washington, D.C.: Center for Strategic and International Studies, 2004). Figures from pp. 10, 3, and 6, respectively. See also Nicholas Eberstadt, "China's Family Planning Goes Awry," *Far Eastern Economic Review* (December 2009), pp. 24–29.

63. For varying views, see Kevin C. Cheng, "Economic Implications of China's Demographics in the 21st Century," International Monetary Fund, *Working Paper* WP/03/29, February 2003, http://www.imf.org/external/pubs/ft/wp/2003/wp0329.pdf; Wang Feng and Andrew Mason, "Demographic Dividend and Prospects for Economic Development in China," paper prepared for UN Expert Group Meeting on Social and Economic Implications of Changing Population Age Structures, Mexico City, August 31–September 2, 2005; Cliff Waldman, "China's Demographic Destiny and Its Economic Implications," *Business Economics* (October 2005), pp. 32–45.

CHAPTER 10: ALTERNATIVE STRATEGIES

1. For one account of how this could happen, see Gordon G. Chang, *The Coming Collapse of China* (New York: Random House, 2001).

2. M. Taylor Fravel, "Regime Insecurity and International Cooperation: Explaining China's Compromises in Territorial Disputes," *International Security* vol. 30, no. 2 (Fall 2005), pp. 46–83.

3. Minxin Pei, *China's Trapped Transition: The Limits of Developmental Autocracy* (Cambridge: Harvard University Press, 206), pp. 312–313.

4. For a sobering discussion, see Steven R. David, *Catastrophic Consequences: Civil Wars and American Interests* (Baltimore: Johns Hopkins University Press, 2008), pp. 115–146.

5. Susan L. Shirk, *China: Fragile Superpower* (New York: Oxford University Press, 2007), p. 255.

6. See Allen Carlson, "Be Careful What You Wish For: Partial Liberalization (Not Democratization) and Beijing's Approach to China's Periphery," in I Yuan, ed., *Cross-Strait at the Turning Point: Institution, Identity and Democracy*, Institute of International Relations English Series (Taipei, Taiwan: National Chengchi University, No. 54, 2008), p. 132.

7. For example, if rising social unrest happened to coincide with a resurgence of Taiwanese separatism, Beijing might blame Taiwan and, standing behind it, the United States.

8. Jacqueline Newmyer, "Regimes, Surprise Attacks and War Initiation," Long-Term Strategy Project, Cambridge, Mass., October 2005, p. 13.

9. Mark Burles and Abram N. Shulsky, *Patterns in China's Use of Force: Evidence from History and Doctrinal Writings* (Santa Monica, Calif.: RAND, 2000).

10. John J. Mearsheimer, *The Tragedy of Great Power Politics* (New York: W. W. Norton, 2003), pp. 360–402.

11. David D. Hale, *In the Balance: China's Unprecedented Growth and Implications for the Asia-Pacific* (Canberra: Australian Strategic Policy Institute, 2006), p. 5.

12. Fei-Ling Wang, "Self-Image and Strategic Intentions: National Confidence and Political Insecurity," in Yong Deng and Fei-Ling Wang, eds., *In the Eyes of the Dragon: China Views the World* (New York: Rowman and Littlefield, 1999), p. 35.

13. Bruce Gilley, *China's Democratic Future: How It Will Happen and Where It Will Lead* (New York: Columbia University Press, 2004), pp. 232–234.

14. Liu Junning, a Chinese academic who has been dismissed several times from government think tanks, is quoted in Ross Terrill, *The New Chinese Empire: What It Means for the United States* (New York: Basic Books, 2003), p. 336.

15. Ibid., p. 238.

16. Mearsheimer, *Tragedy of Great Power Politics*, pp. 399–402.

17. Elizabeth Economy, "Don't Break the Engagement," *Foreign Affairs* vol. 83, no. 3 (May–June 2004), pp. 96–109.

18. Carla A. Hills and Dennis C. Blair, *U.S.-China Relations: An Affirmative Agenda, a Responsible Course, Report of an Independent Task Force* (New York: Council on Foreign Relations, 2007), p. 5.

19. William S. Cohen and Maurice R. Greenberg, *Smart Power in U.S.-China Relations: A Report to the CSIS Commission on China* (Washington, D.C.: Center for Strategic and International Studies, 2009), p. vi.

20. Ibid., p. 2.

21. Orville Schell and Eileen Claussen, *Common Challenge, Collaborative Response: A Roadmap for U.S.-China Cooperation on Energy and Climate Change* (New York: Asia Society, January 2009). The group that produced this report included many people who subsequently joined the Obama administration, including Asia Society chairman Robert Holbrooke and future secretary of energy Steven Chu. Other studies on this topic published at around the same time include William Chandler, *Breaking the Suicide Pact: U.S.-China Cooperation on Climate Change* (Washington, D.C.: Carnegie Endowment for International Peace, May 2008); and Kenneth Lieberthal and David Sandalow, *Overcoming Obstacles to U.S.-China Cooperation on Climate Change* (Washington, D.C.: Brookings Institution, January 2009).

22. Hills and Blair, *U.S.–China Relations*, p. 83. Similar suggestions for enhanced strategic dialogue are offered in other reports, including Nina Hachigian, Michael Schiffer, and Winny Chen, *A Global Imperative: A Progressive Approach to U.S.-China Relations in the 21st Century* (Washington, D.C.: Center for American Progress, August 2008), p. 10.

23. C. Fred Bergsten, "The United States–China Economic Relationship and the Strategic and Economic Dialogue," prepared statement, in *U.S.-China Relations: Maximizing the Effectiveness of the Strategic and Economic Dialogue*, Hearing before the Subcommittee on Asia, the Pacific, and the Global Environment, Committee

on Foreign Affairs, U.S. House of Representatives, 111th Congress, 1st Session, September 10, 2009, p. 52, http://foreignaffairs.house.gov/111/52146.pdf. Also Bergsten, "A Partnership of Equals: How Washington Should Respond to China's Economic Challenge," *Foreign Affairs* vol. 87, no. 4 (July/August 2008), pp. 57–69.

24. Cohen and Greenberg, *Smart Power in U.S.-China Relations*, p. 6.

25. Hachigian, Schiffer, and Chen, *Global Imperative*, p. 69.

26. Hills and Blair, *U.S.-China Relations*, p. 91; Hachigian, Schiffer, and Chen, *Global Imperative*, p. 70.

27. In her first visit to China as secretary of state in February 2009, Hillary Clinton appeared to lean toward this approach when she declared publicly that the United States would not allow differences over human rights to "interfere" with cooperation on economic, environmental, and security issues. See "Clinton: Chinese Human Rights Can't Interfere with Other Crises," CNN Politics.com, February 22, 2009, http://www.cnn.com/2009/POLITICS/02/21/clinton.china.asia/.

28. Cohen and Greenberg, *Smart Power in U.S.–China Relations*, p. 5.

29. Greenberg, in Hills and Blair, *U.S.–China Relations*, p. 101.

30. Ibid., p. 54.

31. Robert S. Ross, "Here Be Dragons: Myth," *National Interest* (September/October 2009), pp. 19–34.

32. For a sophisticated treatment of the dangers of "mutual hedging," see Evan Medeiros, "Strategic Hedging and the Future of Asia-Pacific Stability," *Washington Quarterly* vol 29, no. 1 (Winter 2005/2006), pp. 145–167.

33. James B. Steinberg, "Administration's Vision of the U.S.-China Relationship," keynote address at the Center for a New American Security, Washington, D.C., September 24, 2009, http://www.state.gov/s/d/2009/129686.htm.

34. John D. Podesta, "The Strategic and Economic Dialogue: Setting the Agenda, Achieving Results," prepared statement, in *U.S.-China Relations*, p. 3.

35. Ambassador Chas W. Freeman Jr., "A China Policy for the Twenty-First Century," *Strategic Studies Quarterly* vol. 2, no. 3 (Fall 2008), pp. 18–29. Quotes from pp. 24, 22.

36. Paul Heer, "A House United," *Foreign Affairs* vol. 79, no. 4 (July/August 2000), pp. 18–24.

37. Washington's seeming indifference to Korea in 1950 and its failure to send strong enough signals to Saddam Hussein in 1990 are two notable examples.

CHAPTER 11: CAN AMERICA KEEP ITS BALANCE?

1. U.S. allies can, and have, posed similar questions. One of the reasons why the Bush administration's 2004–5 effort to dissuade the European Union from lifting its arms embargo on China came as such an unpleasant surprise is that it followed a period in which high-ranking U.S. officials had routinely described Sino-American relations as "the best they have ever been."

2. The "Charter 08" document, originally signed by over three hundred intellectuals, dissidents, rural leaders, and some midlevel government officials, advocates an end to the current system and the prompt adoption of liberal democracy. See the translation by Perry Link, "China's Charter 08," *New York Review of Books* vol. 56, no. 1

(January 15, 2009), http://www.opendemocracy.net/article/chinas-charter-08. In 2009 the Chinese government sentenced Lu Xiaobo, one of the main authors of Charter 08, to eleven years in prison for "inciting subversion of state power." In 2010 Lu was awarded the Nobel Prize for Peace. Austin Ramzy, "In China, News about Nobel Winner Lu Xiaobo Is Scarce," *Time*, October 11, 2010, http://www.time.com/time/world/article/O,8599,2024755.html.

3. Albeit at a very low level of funding, the U.S. government has helped pay for the development and distribution of at least one tool (known as Tor) that helps users get around firewalls and maintain anonymity. Jim Finkle, "Web Tools Help Protect Human Rights Activists," Reuters, August 19, 2009, http://www.reuters.com/article/internetNews/idUSTRE57I4IE20090819. Beijing has reportedly found a way to counter this particular technique, necessitating the prompt development of new ones. See this statement by the software developer, "Tor Partially Blocked in China," *Tor* (blog), September 27, 2009, https://blog.torproject.org/blog/tor-partially-blocked-china. According to Secretary of State Hillary Clinton, the United States is now "supporting the development of new tools that enable citizens to exercise their rights of free expression by circumventing politically motivated censorship." See Hillary Rodham Clinton, "Remarks on Internet Freedom," Newseum, Washington, D.C., January 21, 2010, http://www.state.gov/secretary/rm/2010/01/135519.htm.

4. See Danny O'Brien, "A Code of Conduct for Internet Companies in Authoritarian Regimes," *Electronic Frontier Foundation Deeplinks* (blog), September 14, 2006, http://www.eff.org/deeplinks/2006/02/code-conduct-internet-companies-authoritarian-regimes.

5. See Richard Stone and Hao Xin, "Google Plots Exit Strategy as China Shores Up 'Great Firewall,'" *Science* vol. 327, no. 9964 (January 22, 2010), pp. 402–403.

6. See James Mann, *The China Fantasy: How Our Leaders Explain Away Chinese Repression* (New York: Viking, 2007), pp. 39–47.

7. See Ben Smith, "Behind the 'Chinese Professor,'" *Politico*, October 22, 2010, http://www.politico.com/blogs/bensmith/1010/Behind_the_Chinese_Professor.html.

8. See Pew Research Center for the People and the Press, in association with the Council on Foreign Relations, *America's Place in the World 2009*, December 2009, pp. 17, 33–35. http://people-press.org/reports/pdf/569.pdf.

9. In recent years, the Defense Department has begun to cultivate a number of sources of alternative opinion on China, including the Long-Term Strategy Group, a nongovernment think tank, and the China Maritime Studies Institute at the U.S. Naval War College. (Full disclosure: I have done consulting work for LTSG and a number of my former PhD students were instrumental in setting up CMSI.)

10. For a balanced assessment of what this may mean, see Daniel W. Drezner, "Bad Debts: Assessing China's Financial Influence in Great Power Politics," *International Security* vol. 34, no. 2 (Fall 2009), pp. 7–45.

11. See Brad W. Setser, *Sovereign Wealth and Sovereign Power: The Strategic Consequences of American Indebtedness* (New York: Council on Foreign Relations, 2008), pp. 40–41.

12. Simon Tilford, "Rebalancing the Chinese Economy," Centre for European Reform, London, Policy Brief, 2009, p. 1, http://www.cer.org.uk/pdf/pb_rebalancing_china_nov09.pdf.

13. For a recent statement of many of these arguments, see National Research Council, *Beyond "Fortress America": National Security Controls on Science and Technology in a Globalized World* (Washington, D.C.: National Academies Press, 2009).

14. Mitchel B. Wallerstein, "Losing Controls: How U.S. Export Restrictions Jeopardize National Security and Harm Competitiveness," *Foreign Affairs* vol. 88, no. 6 (November/December 2009), p. 18.

15. "IBM, Maytag Unocal . . . Who's Next in China's Sights?" *Knowledge@Wharton*, November 21, 2005, http://knowledge.wharton.upenn.edu/article.cfm?articleid =1262.

16. John Pomfret, "Between U.S. and China, a Trust Gap," *Washington Post*, October 8, 2010, http://www.washingtonpost.com/wp-dyn/content/article/2010/10/07/AR.

17. See John Markoff, "Old Trick Threatens Newest Weapons," *New York Times*, October 27, 2009, http://www.nytimes.com/2009/10/27/science/27trojan.html.

18. While in government in the period 2003–5 I witnessed two such campaigns: an ultimately unsuccessful attempt to dissuade the United States from enhanced security cooperation with Japan and a more successful effort to discourage arms sales and closer strategic engagement with Taiwan. In both cases a key part of the Chinese message, delivered with concern rather than anger, was that Washington might unintentionally embolden dangerous extremists in Tokyo and Taipei whose reckless actions could drag the United States and China into an unnecessary conflict.

19. This was the phrase Secretary of Defense Harold Brown used to describe the terrifying prospect that should face Soviet decision makers if they were ever to contemplate a nuclear first-strike on the United States. Harold Brown, *Department of Defense Annual Report, Fiscal Year 1979* (Washington, D.C.: GPO, 1978), p. 63.

20. For a variety of proposals along these lines, see Roger Cliff, Mark Burles, Michael Chase, Derek Eaton, and Kevin L. Pollpeter, *Entering the Dragon's Lair: Chinese Antiaccess Strategies and Their Implications for the United States* (Santa Monica, Calif.: RAND, 2007), pp. 95–104.

21. See Barry D. Watts, *The Case for Long-Range Strike: 21st Century Scenarios* (Washington, D.C.: Center for Strategic and Budgetary Assessments, 2008). Soon after taking office, the Obama administration announced its intention to delay development of a follow-on to the B-2 manned long-range bomber. It subsequently expressed interest in acquiring intercontinental-range conventional ballistic missiles, while at the same time indicating concern that these might upset other powers. See Jeremiah Gertler, *Air Force Next-Generation Bomber: Background and Issues for Congress*, Report RL34406 (Washington, D.C.: Congressional Research Service, 2009); David E. Sanger and Thom Shanker, "U.S. Faces Choice on New Weapons for Fast Strikes," *New York Times*, April 23, 2010, p. A1. Among other hurdles, deploying ground-based intermediate-range conventional ballistic missiles similar to China's will require the United States to modify or withdraw from its 1987 Intermediate-Range Nuclear Force Treaty with Russia.

22. Although the process is not yet far advanced, defense planners are now considering how to knit together new and existing capabilities to support a concept for countering China's anti-access strategy known as AirSea Battle. For the best public treatment of what this may entail, see Jan Van Tol, with Mark Gunzinger, Andrew Krepinevich, and Jim Thomas, *AirSea Battle: A Point-of-Departure Operational*

Concept (Washington, D.C.: Center for Strategic and Budgetary Assessments, 2010).

23. Regarding the likely inadequacy of overland energy supplies, see Andrew S. Erickson and Gabriel B. Collins, "China's Oil Security Pipe Dream: The Reality, and Strategic Consequences of Seaborne Imports," *Naval War College Review* vol. 63, no. 2 (Spring 2010), pp. 89–111.

24. For indications that this may be changing, see Robert Ross, "China's Naval Nationalism: Sources, Prospects, and the U.S. Response," *International Security* vol. 34, no. 2 (Fall 2009), pp. 46–81.

25. Beijing's ability to constrict commerce will be further strengthened if it can enforce its claims of sovereignty over much of the South China Sea.

26. For two assessments from different perspectives that reach broadly similar conclusions about the potential strategic costs of unification, see Nancy Bernkopf Tucker, "If Taiwan Chooses Unification, Should the United States Care?" *Washington Quarterly* vol. 25, no. 3 (Summer 2002), pp. 15–28; and Hisahiko Okazaki, "The Strategic Value of Taiwan," prepared for the U.S.-Japan-Taiwan Trilateral Strategic Dialogue, Tokyo Round, March 2, 2003, http://www.okazaki-inst.jp/stratvaluetaiwan-eng.html.

27. The discussion that follows is drawn from Aaron L. Friedberg, "Asia Rising," *American Interest* vol. 4, no. 3 (January/February 2009), pp. 60–61.

APPENDIX: SOURCES AND METHODS

1. I originally read some of these items on the Open Source Center, a U.S. government website that distributes translated materials to various federal agencies and government contractors. Because government regulations forbid public dissemination of these materials, in those cases where I first learned of an article from this source I had a research assistant locate the original and prepare a translation.

2. Of those listed here, Cui Liru, Qin Yaqing, and Wang Jisi have been identified by Western scholars as members of an "informal executive committee" of the Foreign Policy Advisory Council, a "new institution that brings together officials and leading scholars." Linda Jakobson and Dean Knox, *New Foreign Policy Actors in China* (Stockholm: Stockholm International Peace Research Institute, 2010), pp. 35–36.

Index

Page numbers in *italics* refer to figures and maps.